Out of Place

Out of Place

ENGLISHNESS, EMPIRE, AND THE
LOCATIONS OF IDENTITY

Ian Baucom

PRINCETON UNIVERSITY PRESS

PRINCETON, NEW JERSEY

Library of Congress Cataloging-in-Publication Data

Baucom, Ian, 1967–
Out of place : Englishness, empire, and the locations
of identity / Ian Baucom.
p. cm.
Includes bibliographical references and index.
ISBN 0-691-01666-6 (alk. paper).
ISBN 0-691-00403-X (pbk. : alk. paper)
1. English literature—20th century—History and criticism.
2. National characteristics, English, in literature.
3. Commonwealth literature (English)—History and
criticism. 4. English literature—19th century—History and
criticism. 5. Great Britain—Colonies—History. 6. Group
identity in literature. 7. Decolonization in literature.
8. Imperialsim in literature. 9. Colonies in literature.
10. England—Civilization. 11. Race in literature. I. Title.
PR478.N37B38   1999
820.9′358—dc21   98-25219
                                                   CIP

This book has been composed in Berkeley Modified

Princeton University Press books are printed on acid-free paper and meet the
guidelines for permanence and durability of the Committee on Production
Guidelines for Book Longevity of the Council on Library Resources

Printed in the United States of America
by Princeton Academic Press

1 3 5 7 9 10 8 6 4 2
1 3 5 7 9 10 8 6 4 2
(Pbk.)

In memory of Donald Owen Schoonmaker

Mentre che la speranza ha fior di verde

Dante, *The Divine Comedy*

CONTENTS

ACKNOWLEDGMENTS

THERE ARE some genres that attempt the possible, others that address the impossible. This, of course, is one of the latter. But while I cannot adequately acknowledge all the debts I have incurred while writing this book, there are some that I am glad to begin paying, if only on installment. I have had many teachers at Wake Forest and Yale University who have guided my thinking and reading. Foremost among them are Sara Suleri Goodyear, without whom there would have been no book, just a muddle of ideas; Vera Kutzinski, whose patient and critical reading of the text has lent it whatever felicities of form it might possess; and Dillon Johnston, who has not only been an invaluable teacher but who as both a person and a scholar has provided me with a gracious example of how to belong to this profession. Numerous colleagues at Yale and elsewhere have aided my thinking about this book while encouraging me to think about other things as well; I am particularly grateful to Chris Miller, Paul Fry, Sarah Winter, Tom Otten, Maurice Wallace, Lee Oser, Chris Yu, James Najarian, Jeff Shoulson, and Jed Esty.

Patrick Brantlinger and Mark Wollaeger read an earlier version of this text for Princeton University Press, and both provided cogent and helpful criticisms for which I would like to thank them; I thank Mark, also, for his encouragement and support of this and other projects over the past several years. I am grateful also to Mary Murrell and Lauren Lepow for their support and editorial assistance.

My new colleagues at Duke have been extremely welcoming. I would particularly like to thank Jane Tompkins, Michael Moses, Sarah Beckwith, Melissa Malouf, Tom Ferraro, Laurie Shannon, David Aers, Nahum Chandler, and Irene Tucker for helping me, and my family, feel immediately at home in Durham.

Without the love of my wife and children, who have traveled with me and various portions of the manuscript between New Haven, Hekpoort, and Durham, there could have been none of the reading, writing, or reflection that have made this book possible. Wendy, in particular, has been for me what energy was to Blake: eternal delight. Only she knows how eternal, how delightful, how every sentence of this book is a sentence her energy allowed me to write.

In completing this book, I have had occasion to reflect on not only the people who have encouraged and guided me, but the texts that have enabled this piece of writing. They are, of course, too numerous to list here, but there is one that, though it is undiscussed in the pages which follow, I cannot leave unmentioned. The Bible is the first book I learned to read with any care and the first book to teach me to care about reading—for that gift, and countless others, I thank my parents, and the loving God whose Son continues to teach me what it means to be not only a reader but a person in the world.

An earlier version of chapter 5 appeared as "Mournful Histories: Narratives of Postimperial Melancholy," in *Modern Fiction Studies* 42, no. 2 (Summer 1996): 259–88.

Out of Place

LOCATING ENGLISH IDENTITY

It is not—the whole of Anglo-Saxondom—a matter of race
but one, quite simply, of place—of place and of spirit, the
spirit being born of the environment.
—Ford Madox Ford, *The Spirit of the People*

The West Indian or Asian does not, by being born in
England, become an Englishman. In law he becomes a
United Kingdom citizen by birth; in fact he is a
West Indian or an Asian still.
—Enoch Powell, *Reflections of a Statesman*

LOCATION, LOCATION, LOCATION

"The trouble with the Engenglish," a character in Salman Rushdie's *The Satanic Verses* stutters, "is that their hiss hiss history happened overseas, so they dodo don't know what it means."[1] Charmed by this observation, Rushdie devotes much of his energy in the surrounding pages of his text to decoding the sly wisdom of this lesson in English bewilderment. The "overseas" in question is, of course, the vast imperial abroad that, over the course of three centuries, England colonized and that, in the past fifty years, it has been forced to abandon. The above comment implies, however, that we should read imperialism not simply as the history of England's expansion and contraction but as the history of a cultivated confusion. The empire, Rushdie suggests through his sardonic mouthpiece, is less a place where England exerts control than the place where England loses command of its own narrative of identity. It is the place onto which the island kingdom arrogantly displaces itself and from which a puzzled England returns as a stranger to itself.

In recent years, readings of the colonial and postcolonial "conditions" have identified a central deliriousness in the workings of imperial history. Edward Said, Gayatri Spivak, and Homi Bhabha, among others, have complicated a hermeneutics that attends to the stark violences and Manichaean oppositions of imperialism by teasing out the hesitancies and uncertainties that colonialism seemed so adept at producing.[2] Bhabha, in particular, has attended to the discursive ambivalences of imperialism, returning to the writings of Frantz Fanon to discover the geography of imperialism as, above all else, a "zone of occult instability."[3] In describing the territories of British imperialism as spaces of bewilderment and loss which continue to trouble and confound England's subjects, Rushdie indicates that such imperial estrangements of English identity survive the formal end of imperialism, that a postimperial England is itself resident to lingering zones of imperial confusion. This book plots the construction of these spaces of instability in the geographies of Englishness. In the chapters that follow, I examine not one but six spaces— Gothic architecture, the Victoria Terminus in Bombay, the Anglo-Indian Mutiny pilgrimage, the cricket field, the country house, and the zone of urban riot—each of which has housed the disciplinary projects of imperialism *and* the imperial destabilizations and re-formations of English identity.

In reading the narrative of England's imperial confusion as a history of these simultaneously disciplinary and antidisciplinary locales, I have responded to the tutelage of Rushdie's spokesman by offering a slight translation of his epigram. The trouble with the English, in my account of the imperial transformations of English identity, is not that their history "happened" overseas, but that it "took place" abroad. Over the past century and a half, as I indicate in readings of John Ruskin, Rudyard Kipling, E. M. Forster, C.L.R. James, Jean Rhys, V. S. Naipaul, and Salman Rushdie, Englishness has consistently been defined through appeals to the identity-endowing properties of place. During these years, I argue, Englishness has been variously, though not exclusively, defined *as* a Gothic cathedral, the Victoria Terminus, the Residency at Lucknow, a cricket field, a ruined country house, and a zone of riot. By this I mean both that these and other places have served as apt metaphors for writers struggling to define what it means to be English, and that such metaphoric understandings have been literalized, sometimes subtly, sometimes crudely, so that these material places have been understood to literally shape the identities of the subjects inhabiting or passing through them. During this period, this book thus suggests, whatever *specific* "ways-of-being" Englishness has been understood to entail, Englishness has been *generally* understood to reside within some type of imaginary, abstract, or actual locale, and to mark itself upon that locale's familiars. Over the past 150 years the struggles to define, defend, or reform Englishness have, consequently, been understood as struggles to control, possess, order, and dis-order the nation's and the empire's spaces.

Because those simultaneously literal and metaphorical spaces have been understood as synecdoches of the nation's space (even when they are physically present in imperial territory), and because nationalist discourse, as Benedict Anderson suggests, expresses a will to synchronic *and* diachronic coincidences of identity, a will to homogenize the present by submitting it to the sovereignty of the past, these spatial struggles, I further argue, have also been apprehended as temporal contests, primarily as struggles to determine the meaning and the authority of the "English" past and to define the function of collective memory in a discourse of collective identity.[4] The locale, I indicate, serves a disciplinary and nostalgic discourse on English national identity by making the past visible, by rendering it present, by acting as what Pierre Nora calls a *lieu de memoire* that purports to testify to the nation's essential continuity across time.[5] But because even the hardiest *lieu de memoire* is mutable, because it not only occupies space but is occupied by living subjects who, as they visit, inhabit, or pass through it, leave their estranging marks upon it, the locale also serves as the site in which the present re-creates the past, as a "contact zone" in which succeeding generations serially destabilize the nation's acts of collective remembrance, and in so doing reveal England as continuously discontinuous with itself, as that which may repeat itself but always repeats with a difference.[6]

The primacy of the spatial is by no means absolute. During the period examined in this book, other standards—primarily racial and linguistic standards—have been identified as the first principles of Englishness. Indeed, as I shall discuss at some length later in this introduction, in the past few decades a racial narrative of what it means to be English has begun to displace, or has attempted to displace, the localist narrative that is my primary subject. This turn from place to race (which is a marked feature of New Right discourse in England over the past thirty years) must, however, be understood both as the "triumph" of a species of racial nationalism long present in the discourses on Englishness and empire, and as a response to the prior triumphs of localist discourse *and* to the confusions attendant on those triumphs. For the identifications of Englishness with the locale—and with the local knowledges, local dialects, local traditions, and local memories that are held to emerge from the locale—would have forced the many self-appointed defenders of an authentic, pure, and settled way of being English to address a sufficiently complex set of problems (of canon formation and preservation, of determining which of England's many localities were most English, of defining their perfect moment, of definitively differentiating them from their corrupting neighbors, of guarding them against the vicissitudes of history), if England, during the same years in which it was discovering itself in Wordsworth's ruined cottages, Ruskin's memory houses, or the grassy fields of Lord's, had not simultaneously decided to globalize its address, to encounter itself in every corner of the world, and thus to multiply and render subject to an imperial re-formation its locations of identity.

For what did England see when it studied the territories it had colonized? If, as Homi Bhabha argues, every nation defines itself by simultaneously gazing inward, to regard the "*heimlich* pleasures of the hearth," and outward, to confront and repudiate the "*unheimlich* terror of the space or race of the Other" (*Nation and Narration*, 2), what did the English nation see when it regarded a global beyond that was also an imperial within? If Englishness, as I will be arguing, has been understood less as a natural condition than as a sort of second nature, as something communicated to the subject by certain auratic, identity-reforming places, as something, therefore, that can be both acquired and lost, could the global reaches of empire contain spaces in which one could be English? Or was the empire truly beyond the boundaries of Englishness, a radically alien outside within which the colonist would inevitably confront the Kurtzean spectacle of himself or herself "going native"? Was the empire the domain of England's mastery of the globe or the territory of the loss of English-ness? Or, most ominously for figures such as Enoch Powell and his predeces-sors, was it neither of these but the place where Englishness would be re-formed, a place crowded with "other spaces," other cultural locales, other local knowledges and local memories that must begin, sooner or later, to enter the canon, to expand the catalog of Englishness, *and* a place filled with "other races" who, having been forced to enter England's expanded "within," must begin to alter its locations of belonging? If that were so, then Englishness, as Powell conceives it, could survive intact only by refusing to admit that the imperial beyond was, in fact, party to the national within. Its conservators could save Englishness by insisting that the empire had little or nothing to do with England, by defining imperial space as something subordinate to but quite different from English space, and by identifying the empire's subjects as persons subordinate to but quite different from England's subjects—by identi-fying these as *British* spaces and *British* subjects: a solution that manages the neat trick of allowing England to simultaneously avow and disavow its empire. *Or* Englishness could be saved if the nation could be convinced to abandon the spatial model altogether and to enshrine another first principle of English-ness, a racial principle.

But this is allegory, not argument, and an allegory, moreover, that assumes the validity of its organizing, spatial, trope. In the remainder of this introduc-tion, I want to indicate why that trope is not only valid but unavoidable. The rhetorics of spatiality and the subrhetorics of locatedness that are so common a feature of contemporary critical practice and that, as Frantz Fanon, Edward Said, Homi Bhabha, and Adrienne Rich have taught us, are so central to impe-rial culture and to anti-imperial critique, are reexamined in this book not simply because these and other writers have demonstrated their generic power, influence, and urgency (though I do frequently explore precisely their generic logic and significance), but because local inflections of this increas-ingly global vocabulary are central, in specific and historically identifiable ways, to the ideologies of English nationalism, the cult of English memory, the discourses of Englishness and Britishness, and, above all, the imperial and postimperial reformations of English identity.

There is no single moment that neatly defines the point at which ideologies of the local and the locale assert their sovereignty over the discourses of En-glish identity, no originary moment which has led me, in consequence of its sudden appearance, to suggest that the Gothic cathedral, the cricket field, the riot zone, and the other spaces I examine function as contestatory locations of English identity; but there is an identifiable moment in which the nation's elected representatives voted to turn their back on this model of collective identity. And because some things become most readily visible in the moment they are repudiated, I want now to turn to that moment, both for the light it casts on the localist ideology that, for almost two centuries, held together the discourses of Englishness and empire, and for the way it illumines the mediating role that "Britishness" has played in allowing England at once to claim and disclaim the spaces and subjects of its empire.

Britishness

In the summer of 1981, the British Parliament passed Margaret Thatcher's British Nationality Act. In doing so, Parliament wrote into law a bill designed to divorce England from its "overseas" history, a law designed to defend the "island kingdom" against its erstwhile empire. This may sound like an odd claim, particularly as the Thatcher years are frequently identified as years in which the English exhibited a marked nostalgia for imperialism, and not as a time in which the official guardians of the British state were trying desperately, and legally, to forget about Britain's lost empire. It is a paradox of a fairly minor sort that these two accounts of the Thatcher decade are not mutually exclusive. Remembrance, especially nostalgic remembrance, is regularly intimate with forgetting. And it is perhaps quite unsurprising that many contemporary Britons can imaginatively recollect the Raj only by assiduously forgetting about India, and those Indian and other ex-colonial subjects who managed to survive the lowering of the Union Jack, or that the imperial past can be recovered only through a disavowal of the aftereffects of imperialism on the present. In fact, as I will be arguing throughout this book, there is nothing at all unusual or new about this structure of feeling in which many English women and men simultaneously avow and disavow the British Empire, and in which Englishness, consequently, emerges as at once an embrace and a repudiation of the imperial beyond.[7]

If Englishness, as a form of meditation on imperialism, has regularly exhibited a double logic of affirmation and denial, Britishness, in Linda Colley's account, has consistently constituted itself through a rhetoric of disaffirmation. Summarizing the arguments of her influential study *Britons: Forging the Nation, 1707–1837*, Colley concludes, "This is how it was with the British after 1707. They came to define themselves as a single people not because of any political or cultural consensus at home, but rather in reaction to the Other beyond their shores."[8] If there was, thus, nothing particularly new in Parliament's 1981 decision to define the nation negatively by identifying the imperial subjects who were *not* British (the primary object of the Nationality Act), there was nevertheless something radically new in the act's *affirmative* codification of British identity. For as much as Britishness has been repeatedly defined *against* a changing series of opposites, it has also, as a legal category at least, consistently been defined *as* something. The 1981 act rejected that traditional definition. Discarding nine hundred years of legal precedent that recognized a territorial principle as the sole absolute determinant of British identity, the act determined that Britain was, henceforth, a genealogical community. Or, to put matters a little differently and to align them with the primary concerns of this book, whereas through the entire preceding history of the British Empire, Britishness had been affirmatively grounded in a law of place, the 1981 Nationality Act codified a theory of identity that sought to defend the "native" inhabitants of the island against the claims of their former subjects by defining Britishness as an inheritance of race.

Prior to the enactment of the 1981 act, the British law on nationality and subjecthood had been anything but systematic, but it was, nevertheless, characterized by two consistent principles, both of which the Nationality Act repudiated. Before the 1707 Act of Union with Scotland (which created the United Kingdom of Great Britain) there were, before the eye of the law, no "British" subjects to speak of, but there were "subjects," who owed their allegiance to the monarch. The concept of allegiance is derived from the medieval notion that any individual born on a lord's land, or "ligeance," owed that lord loyalty, and this concept, in turn, secured the first principle of what was to become the British law of subjecthood: the *ius soli*.[9] Literally the "law of the soil," the *ius soli* survived unaltered for the better part of nine centuries and provided, at first glance, a remarkably simple rule for the determination of who was and who was not the monarch's—and later a "British"—subject. As Pollock and Maitland declare in their canonical 1895 *History of English Law*, "The main rule is very simple. The place of birth is all-important."[10] If British history were the history of a stably bordered nation, then the rule would indeed be that simple. But Britain's borders, to put it mildly, have been far from stable, and the "rule," consequently, far from simple to apply. As England conquered Ireland, crowned a Scottish king, united with Scotland, and established colonies in North America, the Caribbean, the Pacific, the Indian subcontinent, and Africa, the recourse to a territorial definition of collective identity meant that Britishness, at least as a legal concept, was to become as elastic as the nation's imperial boundaries. The challenge that the *ius soli* forced English jurists and legislators to address century after century was quite clear. Were all the individuals born in the diverse places over which England claimed sovereignty to be considered identically and interchangeably British?

The answer that the jurists gave, to the frequent discomfort of many self-appointed guardians of Britishness and Englishness alike, was a cautious and equivocal yes. The question could be answered in the affirmative in part because while British subjectivity conferred obligations on the subject (primarily the obligation of loyalty), it did not confer any intrinsic rights. Parliament—particularly after the Glorious Revolution—could bestow or withdraw these at will, as selectively as it chose. But the major reason for this answer's being, until 1981, essentially always the same has to do with the nature of English law itself. English law, famously, is not constitutional in the American sense but prescriptive, sternly devoted to custom and tradition. It is based largely on an unwritten common law that, precisely because it is unwritten, has suggested to its defenders that their task is to preserve the law, not to interpret it. Edmund Burke, one of the most ardent celebrants of England's custom of relying on custom, advanced as succinct an explanation of prescriptive law as one could wish in his 1782 *Speech on the Representation of the Commons in Parliament*: "Our Constitution is a prescriptive constitution; it is a constitution whose sole authority is, that it has existed time out of mind. . . . Prescription is the most solid of all titles, not only to property, but, which is to secure that property, to government. They harmonize with each other, and give mutual aid to one another. It is accompanied with another ground of authority in the constitution of the human mind, presumption. It is a presumption in favor of any settled scheme of government against any untried project, that a nation has long existed and flourished under it."[11] Of the laws that have existed in England "time out of mind," few, if any, have held the prescriptive authority of the *ius soli*. And it was the repeated willingness of jurists to adopt the "settled scheme" of identifying as British most, if never quite all, the individuals born on British sovereign territory that was, until 1981, the second consistent principle of the law on British subjecthood.

While the 1608 decision in *Calvin's Case* proved the single most important affirmation of the two fundamental doctrines of nationality law (the decision upheld the transnational validity of the *ius soli* by confirming the nonalien status of a child born in Scotland after the accession of King James I, thus recognizing the common identity of an individual born in a non-English territory over which an English monarch exerted sovereignty),[12] numerous other court findings and parliamentary acts over the years confirmed the twin identification of Britishness with territory and with the custom of maintaining the *ius soli* even as the nation's sovereign territory expanded. Indeed, as important as the *ius soli* was in providing a stable referent for nationality law, the traditionalist practice of invariably honoring that unwritten referent, or, more precisely, of honoring the custom of honoring that referent (whatever practical difficulties such a practice might produce), may have been the most definitively *English* aspect of the legal history Thatcher's party discarded in adopting the 1981 act.[13]

The full implications of adhering to both these principles, regardless of the course of imperial history, are evident in the 1948 British Nationality Bill, the last major piece of legislation that sought to assert the global dimensions of Britishness. In that year, the governments of India, Australia, New Zealand, and South Africa were threatening to follow the lead of Canada, which in 1946 had established an independent category of citizenship; in response to this pressure the British government passed a bill which stipulated that while India and each of the dominion states could confer citizenship on its own subjects, all such citizens, together with the inhabitants of the as-yet-uncolonized imperial territories, who were grouped together with the inhabitants of the United Kingdom as United Kingdom-and-Colonies citizens, would remain British subjects. A frankly fantastic piece of legislation (in the less than laudatory sense of the word), the 1948 bill served to maintain the illusion of sovereignty over the Commonwealth, the dictates of the *ius soli*, the need to oblige tradition, and the, by then, age-old sundering of subjecthood and citizen rights, while at the same time partially acknowledging the political realities of a decolonized and decolonizing world. The consequence of these attempts to balance competing obligations and realities was the invention of a new class of citizens (United Kingdom and Commonwealth) who had no intrinsic rights but who were to claim equivalent subjectivity with a body of other citizens (South Africans, Indians, Australians, Canadians, and New Zealanders) who had whatever rights their governments afforded them.

However confusing these results—among which were that some individuals who failed to qualify for citizenship under the particular rules laid down by individual commonwealth countries discovered themselves to be subjects of Britain but citizens of nowhere, and that the vast number of "British" subjects scattered throughout the world found themselves holding entirely different citizenship rights, or none at all, while nevertheless being assured of their fundamental, or at least rhetorical, likeness—they reflected an entirely predictable application of customary understandings of the *ius soli* as a law dictating that territory conferred identity but not rights. More important, the 1948 bill reinforced the legal conception of Britishness that had emerged over the long centuries of imperial rule. Britishness, the bill announced, coincided with the territory of the nation *and* the empire. It was a global system that could incorporate local differences but would not define itself by local difference. "British" space was thus read as homogeneous, interchangeable, everywhere alike, while "English" space remained unique, local, differentiated: a formula which permitted the empire to be that which was simultaneously *within* the boundaries of Britishness and *outside* the territory of Englishness, that which, relative to the sovereign nation, was at once identical and different. Largely void of any particular meaning, Britishness was a product of its forms of reproduction. Preserved by custom, Britishness announced itself *as* the preservation of custom. Born of the soil, it indulged the claims of genealogy only by substituting territory for ancestry (to the French "Notre Ancestres, Les Gauls," the 1948 act effectively offered the yet more mystic, if hidebound, response, "Our Ancestor, The Soil"). In Benedict Anderson's terms, the model of collective identity enshrined in the 1948 Nationality Act identified Britishness as a mandatory but "unbound" seriality. To be a British subject was to belong to a potentially unlimited collectivity. Wherever there was British territory, one could be British, as one may be a Christian, a Marxist, or a typist wherever the gospel is preached, *Das Kapital* is read, or typewriters are distributed.[14] The difference, of course, is that the typist has a choice.

The individual's inability to choose British subjectivity is only one of the many deleterious features of the 1948 bill and the tradition it represents. I have already mentioned the immediate difficulties the bill created for individuals who found themselves to be subjects of a global system but citizens of no country. Forced to confront the political realities of empire, the bill's strict interpretation of the *ius soli* created further dilemmas. For while all the inhabitants of Britain's sovereign territories were putatively equal, sovereignty was not exerted equally over all the empire's territories. In Nigeria, for example, Britain administered both a colony and a protectorate. Inhabitants of the colony were, hence, both United Kingdom-and-Colonies citizens and British subjects. Those living in the protectorate were neither citizens nor British subjects. Instead, they were identified as British Protected Persons. Individuals born in Uganda, Tanganyika, and Tanzania were also British Protected Persons. In the late 1960s thousands of these "protected" persons, particularly East African Asians, were to discover how little protection the British government was willing to offer them when they were effectively barred from emigrating to the United Kingdom. If the crisis into which these would-be immigrants were thrown can be traced, in part, to a brutally exact reading of the *ius soli* (though it was also attributable to a reconceptualization of subjectivity introduced in a series of 1960s and 1970s acts that I shall discuss below), then there is also a history of equivocation in the application of the law of the soil. While subject law, prior to the 1960s, was regularly applied across perceived racial lines, the administrators of that law nevertheless frequently found ways to deny British subjectivity to individuals who were not "white." In Australia and New Zealand, the Dominion governments regularly, but selectively, administered language tests to exclude Asian and African immigrants from naturalization, and hence commonwealth citizenship and hence British subjectivity. Between 1903 and 1956 no Asians or Africans were naturalized in Australia.[15] In earlier years, the British government had determined that slaves born in the American colonies were not covered by the *ius soli*, thus excluding most of the preemancipation black inhabitants of the New World from British subjecthood.

If the *ius soli* could thus produce discriminatory effects both when it was and when it was not consistently applied, and if the racial exclusions which are an important element of this history of British subject law reveal that a territorial theory of collective identity never truly blinded the law to perceived differences of race, these forms of discrimination nevertheless remain problems of the law. And however important the law is, and has been, for determining who is British, if only in name, the battles over the definition of Britishness have never been simply legal affairs. To be identified by the courts or government ministers as British is not at all the same thing as to identify

oneself with Britishness. Nor, to understate matters entirely, do legal pronouncements that virtually everyone born within British territory is British
guarantee that all those who have thus been identified as Britons will accept
the Britishness of one another. A sense of collective identity rarely, if ever,
proceeds from stipulation. It is, instead, an affective condition, which may
seek to subordinate the law to its purposes but exhibits little interest in conforming itself to the law.

Arjun Appadurai has recently discussed the differences that exist between
such affective and juridical collectivities. He suggests that the tendency of
nations to wander beyond their discernible borders, by distributing their pop-
ulations, laws, civil authority, markets, and images across the globe, produces
disjunctions between ideologies of the soil "as the ground of loyalty and national affect" and discourses of territory "as the site of sovereignty and state
control of civil society."[16] As sovereign territory expands (in Appadurai's sense
as a domain over which a nation exerts some degree of economic, regulatory,
or cultural control), either the territory of affect contracts—to become isomor-
phic with either the "original" boundaries of the nation or with certain revered
and ultra-auratic locations within the nation—or more commonly "other discourses of loyalty" emerge, "sometimes linguistic, sometimes racial, sometimes
religious, but *very rarely territorial*" (48). In the context of the discourses on
imperialism, Appadurai's arguments suggest exactly what I will be arguing
throughout this book: that Englishness has been identified *with* Britishness,
which in its turn has been identified as coterminous with and proceeding from
the sovereign territory of the empire, and that Englishness has also defined
itself *against* the British Empire, first by retaining a spatial theory of collective
identity but privileging the *English* soil of the "sceptered isle" or, more regularly, certain quintessentially English locales, as its authentic identity-determining locations; and then, intermittently over the decades of imperial rule
but programatically from the 1960s onward, by largely abandoning spatial
and territorial ideologies for a racial "discourse of loyalty" and coidentity.

The shift to a racialized conception of collective identity was codified in the
1981 British Nationality Act. Legally, the act's most crucial features were the
abandonment of the *ius soli* and, by virtue of that abandoment, the disavowal
of the prescriptive authority which had stood, for so many centuries, at the
heart of English law. For would-be immigrants to the United Kingdom,
against whom most of the act's provisions were directed, the central aspect of
the law was the substitution of the principle of "patriality" for the law of the
soil in the determination of nationality. The concept of patriality had actually
been introduced in Edward Heath's 1971 Immigration Bill, under which act
patriality conferred a "right of abode" in the United Kingdom. Heath's government invented patriality to allow itself to discriminate among various United
Kingdom-and-Colonies citizens by reserving a right of abode in the United

Kingdom only for those who had actually been born in the United Kingdom or one of whose parents or grandparents had been born there. This provision for the first time marked a clear distinction between the settlement privileges granted those individuals born—or immediately descended from one born—in England, Scotland, and Wales, and the privileges accorded all other United Kingdom-and-Colonies citizens. It indicated, therefore, that the territory of the United Kingdom and the territory of the colonies were not interchangeable, that the "home" soil had greater right-endowing properties than the soil beyond the sea. Perhaps more important than this implicit admission of the foreignness of the United Kingdom's overseas territories was the bill's embrace of genealogical and racial principles of shared identity and rights. For, as the bill's framers clearly understood, by adding the question "who were your ancestors?" to the question "where were you born?" (indeed, in many cases, by making the former question the more important), the act effectively guaranteed that most of those who would qualify as patrials would be the children or grandchildren of whites who had moved abroad rather than the children of Indians, Pakistanis, or Nigerians whose parents or grandparents had been born in the colonies.

Where the 1971 act limited the application of the *ius soli* by identifying certain territories as more authentically British than others, and then added genealogical considerations to the calculus of Britishness, the 1981 act fully subordinated space to time by banishing the *ius soli*'s relevance to the past and then replacing it, in the present, with a purely genealogical principle of British identity. Specifically, the law confirmed the 1971 decision that individuals born in the colonies were not patrials (and hence had no right of abode), but further decreed that neither were persons born in the United Kingdom. Only those whose *parents* had been born in the United Kingdom, or had been legally "settled" there, would henceforth qualify for the newly created "British citizenship." Henceforth, the question that would establish one's Britishness was not, ever, "where were you born?" but always, only, "who were your parents?" The racist implications of the law have been clear to almost everyone who has commented on it (for once again virtually everyone who could give the "right" answer proved to be white),[17] but fewer scholars, at least in the fields of cultural and postcolonial criticism, have recognized the act's revolutionary repudiation of the idea that Britain is, above all else, a place—and a place which honors the idea that it is a place. Some legal historians, to be sure, have addressed this foundational implication of the law. As Ann Dummett and Andrew Nicol note, "It [the revocation of the *ius soli*] was significant far beyond . . . practical consequences: it marked the formal abandonment of a tradition encompassing English and British history and identity, the tradition of the land" (244). The act, in fact, abandoned more than the tradition of the land. It discarded the peculiarly English tradition of tradition. In the cause of defending white Britons against that imminent racial "swamping" which Margaret Thatcher had notoriously decried in a 1978 television interview,[18] the British Nationality Act effectively disavowed two of the doctrines that for centuries had safeguarded the Englishness of Britishness.

BRITISHNESS AND ENGLISHNESS

"Empire," as Gayatri Spivak has pithily observed, "messes with identity," a comment which is usually taken to mean that colonialism disrupts, distorts, and deforms the identities of the colonized.[19] The logic of the 1981 Nationality Act suggests, however, that we should attend to the full rhetorical ambiguity of Spivak's proverb. For the fact that this *British* nationality bill could eviscerate a traditional, Burkean conception of what it means to be *English* indicates that empire can equally disrupt the cultural identity of a colonizing nation. The bill further indicates that Englishness and Britishness are not necessarily coterminous, particularly as each, in turn, negotiates its relation to imperialism. The nonidentity of Englishness and Britishness has, of course, long been apparent to many Scots and Welsh inhabitants of the United Kingdom. But while intra-island protests against the coincidence of Britishness with Englishness tend to suggest that Anglocentric constructions of Britishness erase the cultural identity of those Britons who are not English, the 1981 bill indicates that Britishness can also menace Englishness—at least in its Burkean manifestations.[20]

Parliament's willingness to abandon the English traditions of the *ius soli* and prescriptive law was rendered even more ironic by the fact that the Nationality Act codified the aspirations of a collection of conservative thinkers and parliamentarians explicitly committed to defending the distinctiveness of English culture against an imperial history that affirmed the equivalence of all the empire's subjects and spaces. Primary among these individuals was Enoch Powell, who, in a series of speeches and newspaper articles from the mid-1960s onward, had repeatedly asserted the need to distinguish between English and British imperial culture, and who had insisted that there was no enchanting magic in the nation's soil which would mysteriously transform immigrants, or even the island-born children of immigrants, into Englishmen. Englishness, he argued, did not emanate from British space but was, instead, an inheritance of race. All of these features of Powellite discourse are evident in the "Rivers of Blood" speech, which he delivered in Birmingham on April 20, 1968, and in a follow-up address he gave in London seven months later. The centerpiece of the "Rivers of Blood" address was a letter Powell claimed to have received from a constituent outlining the fate of an elderly woman who, finding her neighborhood increasingly occupied by black immigrants, nevertheless refused to rent rooms in her home to "negroes" and consequently became the "victim" of abuse: "She is becoming afraid to go out. Windows are broken. She finds excreta pushed through her letterbox. When she goes to the shops she is followed by children, charming, wide-grinning piccaninnies. They cannot speak English, but one word they know. 'Racialist', they chant. When the new Race Relations Bill is passed, this woman is convinced she will go to prison. And is she so wrong? I begin to wonder."[21] In these frequently cited sentences, the challenge that a collapsed empire puts to Powell's England is evident, as is, by negative definition, the essence of Powell's conception of Englishness. Threatened by racial pollution (the "excreta," the "wide-grinning piccaninnies"), the disappearance of the English language (the children speak only one word of English), and a territorial invasion ("Windows are broken," the woman is "followed," and, as claimed in an earlier portion of the letter, the once "respectable street" on which the woman lives has become "a place of noise and confusion"), Englishness is here revealed, in the moment of its vanishing, as whiteness, a command of the English language, and a certain kind of domestic space.[22] Most crucially, Powell represents Englishness as something that exists apart from, and utterly fails to coincide with, the lost empire—uncannily figured here as an invading black body.[23]

Despite his propensity for parading himself as a lonely Jeremiah, bravely, and uniquely, crying out in the wilderness, Powell's strategy of disavowing blackness in order to negatively invoke a racially pure English identity draws on a long history of the reading of Englishness as primarily a racial category. In the nineteenth century, in particular, numerous English historians organized their histories of England as race histories of the Anglo-Saxons.[24] Sharon Turner's three-volume *History of the Anglo-Saxons*, published between 1799 and 1805, is, as Paul Peppis argues, emblematic of this historiographic tendency to interpret the English past as a narrative of racial continuity.[25] Writing in this tradition, and deploying a rhetoric that largely anticipates Powell's, Edward Freeman, in his 1876 *History of the English Constitution*, explicitly linked the genius of the English to their ability to maintain a racial essence, "an unbroken national being," even in the face of foreign invasion and conquest. "[What] is Teutonic in us," Freeman insisted, "is . . . the very life and essence of our national being. . . . [Whatever] else we may have in us, whatever we have drawn from those whom we conquered or from those who conquered us, is no co-ordinate element, but a mere infusion into our Teutonic essence."[26] The defensiveness of Freeman's formulation, his grudging admission that the pure blood of the English has been mixed with the blood of England's conquerors and with the blood of those England in its turn has subdued, indicates, however, that, like Powell, Freeman is aware of an alternative reading of English identity that he wishes to replace with his theory of race purity.

That alternative, and preceding, understanding, which emphasized the racial hybridity of the English, is perhaps best summarized in Daniel Defoe's popular 1700 poem *The True-Born Englishman*, a work in which Defoe roundly mocks as willed amnesia any attempt to insist on the nation's racial purity:

> Thus from a mixture of all kinds began,
> That Het'rogeneous Thing, *An Englishman*:
> In eager Rapes, and furious Lust begot,
> Betwixt a Painted *Britton* and a *Scot*:
> Whose gend'ring Offspring quickly learn to bow,
> And yoke their Heifers to the *Roman* Plough:
> From whence a Mongrel Half-Bred Race there came,
> With neither Name nor Nation, Speech or Fame.
> In whose hot Veins new Mixtures quickly ran,
> Infus'd betwixt a *Saxon* and a *Dane*.
> While their Rank Daughters, to their Parents just,
> Receiv'd all Nations with Promiscuous Lust.
> This Nauseous Brood directly did contain
> The well-extracted blood of *Englishmen*
>
> .   .   .   .
>
> The Wonder that remains is at our Pride,
> To value that which all Wise Men deride,
> For *Englishmen* to boast of generation
> Cancels their Knowledge and lampoons the Nation.
> A true-born *Englishman's* a Contradiction,
> In Speech an Irony, in Fact a Fiction. . . .[27]

It is precisely such mocking celebrations of the English as a "Mongrel Half-Bred Race" that Freeman and other nineteenth-century race theorists sought to silence. That they were not entirely successful in this attempt is partially evidenced by Enoch Powell's determination to reawaken the nation to their arguments a century later. In doing so, however, Powell had to combat not only the sardonic logic of Defoe's lyrics but the lasting influence of what David Simpson has called a cult of "localism," which emerged in the late eighteenth and nineteenth centuries, and which "came to be identified with an ideology of nationalism."[28] In direct opposition to the racial hermeneutics of Freeman and Turner, localist discourse identified English place, rather than English blood, as the one thing that could preserve the nation's memory and, in preserving its memory, secure England's continuous national identity. Nourished by Edmund Burke's anti-Jacobin writings, the Burkean cast of much of William Wordsworth's later poetry, and John Ruskin's social criticism, English localists also suggested that England possessed an essential and continuous identity, and maintained that the nation's task was to recover and preserve that identity. But where the race theorists argued that this meant defending

England's bloodlines, in the localists' view it was English place that must be secured—not only in England but in the colonies, where, if England's authentic and auratic architectures of belonging could be reconstructed, these identity-determining sites could secure the cultural identity of the colonists and Anglicize, reform, and civilize the colonized.

While localist ideology, in both its domestic and imperial idioms, was most fully worked out in the nineteenth-century texts I will be discussing in the first two chapters of this book, some measure of its sustained influence, and a fair synopsis of its major doctrines, may be gleaned from an early-twentieth-century work that explicitly sought to elucidate what it was that made the English English, Ford Madox Ford's *The Spirit of the People: An Analysis of the English Mind*. Ford begins his examination of what it is, precisely, that guarantees the Englishness of the English, by picking up where Daniel Defoe left off, by clarifying, that is, what is not essential to Englishness. As he unambiguously states, "In the case of a people descended from Romans, from Britons, from Anglo-Saxons, from Danes, from Normans, from Poitevins, from Scotch, from Huguenots, from Irish, from Gaels, from modern Germans, and from Jews, a people so mixed that there is in it hardly a man who can point to seven generations of purely English blood, it is almost absurd to use the almost obsolescent word 'race.' These fellows are all ourselves. . . ."[29]

But if, on this account, Englishness is not racial, then what is it? Ford is unequivocal. "It is not—the whole of Anglo-Saxondom—a matter of race but one, quite simply, of place—of place and of spirit, the spirit being born of the environment" (43). As anecdotal proof of this conviction, Ford advances the case of William the Conqueror, an undisputed foreigner at first glance, but one whom every schoolboy's history text, and every schoolboy Ford talks with on a train trip he has taken, identifies not only as English but as the first figure of English history.[30] Recalling his own school days, and an excellent young West African cricketer whose cricketing excellence secured, in the minds of his teammates, his Englishness, Ford summarizes his argument by commenting on the common Englishness of his schoolmates, this black youth, and the Norman king.

> We felt intensely English. There was our sunshine, our [cricketing] "whites," our golden wickets, our green turf. And we *felt*, too, that Stuart, the pure-blooded Dahomeyan, with the dark tan shining upon his massive and muscular chest, was as English as our pink-and-white or sun-browned cheeks could make us. It may have been this feeling only. A spirit of loyalty to one of our team. But I think it was deeper than this. It was a part of the history engendered in us by the teachings of the history of the British Islands: it was a part of the very spirit of the people. We could not put it more articulately into words than, "He's been to *our* school." But I am almost certain that we felt that that training, that contact with our traditions, was sufficient to turn any child of the sun into a very excellent Englishman. In our

> history, as we had confronted its spirit, a touch of English soil was sufficient to do
> as much for William the Norman, who, though we call him a Conqueror, seems
> to most English boys eminently more English than the Anglo-Saxon who was
> weak enough to get shot in the eye. (34)

However idealistic this may be, however mistaken Ford might be regarding his various teammates' estimate of Stuart's Englishness, and however disinterested he is in whether Stuart considered himself English or not, this is revealing, not only because it so clearly refuses to believe what Freeman and Powell believe—that Englishness has a racial essence—but because it borrows from the legal discourse on Britishness the preordinate value given to place and situates this at the heart of Englishness also.

But the operation of place, here, is in fact quite different from its function in the juridical definitions of Britishness. For Ford the place of birth is not important. William and Stuart are English not by virtue of having been *born* in England but by virtue of having come into *contact* with "English soil" and, in Stuart's case, English traditions, English schools, and an English cricket field. Place here is not a mere expanse but something that contains and communicates a certain type of tradition. Whereas space in the legal discourses on Britishness serves as the basis for a system of categorization, in this meditation on Englishness place grounds a system of education. Where British space bestows only a common name on all the empire's subjects, English place, Ford believes, reforms the identities not of all Britons but of all those, whatever their ancestry or place of birth, who are exposed to it. English places are not, therefore, necessarily the same as British spaces, either in their affect or in their geographies. There might be contagiously English places scattered throughout the British Empire—cricket fields, for example, or educational institutions that could perform the work of his English school—but there might equally be places within a global empire that possess no identity-estranging magic.

The power that Ford recognizes in place, the power claimed by scores of English writers throughout the nineteenth and twentieth centuries, the power of certain tradition-soaked places to secure and bestow English identity, is one that Pierre Nora has discussed in his work on what he calls *lieux de memoire*. In his essay "Between Memory and History: *Les Lieux de Memoire*," Nora distinguishes between "History" and what he calls "places" and "environments" of memory. The distinction Nora draws between *milieux* and *lieux de memoire*, between environments and places of memory, rests on his conviction that history and memory are fundamentally opposed to one another, and that we inhabit a moment in which history has so nearly triumphed over memory that remembrance can survive only as a sort of beaureaucratic imperative or as a species of fetishism. By History, Nora intends something closer to historiography, something like what Hans Georg Gadamer called "historicism"—the systematic, deauraticized knowledge of the past that succeeds a "traditionalist"

recuperation of the past which has succeeded, in its turn, Enlightenment di-
remptions of traditional myths and superstitions. History, for the Gadamerite
Nora, is ironic, skeptical. It disenchants the past. It preserves the past as one
or another representation of itself. It regards the past as an object of labor, as
a complex fiction susceptible to endless reinterpretations, as something we
rework but, crucially, something incapable of working any meaningful demands on us. Traditional memory, by contrast, is effortless but demanding. It
defines who we are. It delineates an environment in which we live, and move,
and have our being. Environments of memory are not, therefore, static. They
alter and shift like the air that surrounds us, but like that air they are as
necessary to our survival as the breaths that we take, forgetting all the while
that we are breathing. Curiously then, it is precisely at the moment that we
become aware of our environments of memory, precisely at the moment that
we pause to contemplate the breath of the past expanding the lungs of the
present, that that oxygen becomes an alien presence to us, an object to be
studied, filtered, purified, conditioned. In that traditionalist moment, as the
past ceases to be an environment and becomes an object or, more properly, an
invitation to a methodology, memory almost immediately reappears as History. And this, Nora suggests, is our moment. Or nearly so. For, he also argues,
History has not yet utterly banished memory from the world. Instead, largely
owing to our nostalgia for the vanishing environments of memory, memory
survives the traditionalist moment and pervades the historicist moment as a
trace of itself, as a precious residue, a lingering scent haunting certain, prized,
lieux de memoire. In these places, which can be either textual, monumental, or
topographic, the past survives as a fetish of itself. *Lieux de memoire* are therefore cultic phenomena, objects of pilgrimage and veneration, the jealously
guarded ruins of cultural ensembles possessed by a need to stop time or, better
yet, to launch a voyage of return to the past.

Ford's English "places," his cricket fields and schools, are clearly, in this
sense, "*lieux de memoire*," as are virtually all the locations of identity I will be
examining in this book. They are places where an identity-preserving, iden-
tity-enchanting, and identity-transforming aura lingers, or is made to appear.
They are, for Ford and his precursors, the places in which England can locate
and secure its identity. For Ford these *lieux de memoire* may be either natural
or man-made, either meadows or cricket fields. For John Ruskin, who avowed
the identity-influencing powers of place as forcefully as any other postromantic English writer, industrial modernity had largely deprived nature of its ability to guard and shape England's collective self, leaving "ancient Architecture"
as "the only influence which can in any wise . . . take the place of that of
woods and fields."[31] But in the nation's ancient architectures, in those structures which "belong partly to those who built them, and partly to all the
generations of mankind who are to follow us" (*Works*, 8:245), Ruskin insisted
that England could still find that which "connects forgotten and following

ages with each other, and half constitutes the identity, as it concentrates the sympathy, of nations" (*Works*, 8:234).

As these passages indicate, the cult of English localism was not therefore antigenealogical. If anything, particularly in Ruskin and Wordsworth's hands, it evinced an obsessive interest in discovering the principles that not only would connect England's unborn, its living, and its dead but would guarantee that the nation's past, present, and future would be fundamentally alike. To this will to diachronic conformity over time, the imperial project added a synchronic imperative, dictating that English men and women distant from one another in space would be similarly alike. From the mid–nineteenth century the theorists of imperial rule further stipulated that the empire should create a body of colonial subjects who were, in the words of Thomas Babington Macaulay's *Minute on Indian Education*, "English in taste, in opinions, in morals, and in intellect."[32] As Macaulay's directive explicitly acknowledged, this third demand depended on the discovery of a principle of Englishness that was not racial. The genius of the cult of the locale was that it could meet all three of these demands at once—particularly after Ruskin had attributed an identity-forming and reforming power to architecture. For, unlike England's fields and meadows, England's architectures could be exported to the colonies, there to continue their work of maintaining the Englishness of the English *and* to realize the extra benefit of Anglicizing the empire's sometimes unruly subjects. (The belief that actual works of architecture could function so, depends, of course, on a literalizing logic so extreme that it approaches a form of fundamentalism. That the empire's administrators, in their literalist and utilitarian translation of localist ideology, were often fundamentalist or naively materialist in their thinking is only one of the many ironies of England's imperial history.)

Like the theory of Britishness grounded in the *ius soli*, localist conceptions of English identity, in both their subtler and more utilitarian forms, thus envisioned Englishness as an unbound seriality, as something that was not immanent in the blood but was a sort of "second nature," as something that could be acquired, or lost. Englishness was not therefore something to which everyone in Britain could necessarily lay claim—not even everyone born in England, on Ruskin's account, was truly English. Together with many Victorian critics of the metropolis, he believed that vast numbers of the nation's urban inhabitants, exposed to the baleful influence of "crowded tenements," had become more like "Arab[s]" or "Gypsy[s]" than Englishmen (*Works*, 8:227). But they, together with all the empire's subjects, were not, in theory, beyond redemption. Like Ford's African cricketer, they could become English, if only they were exposed to England's authentic and auratic spaces.

And this is precisely the belief that Enoch Powell insisted England had to abandon. As he unambiguously stated in the November 1968 speech he delivered as a follow-up to the "Rivers of Blood" address, "The West Indian or Asian does not, by being born in England, become an Englishman. In law he becomes a United Kingdom citizen by birth; in fact he is a West Indian or an Asian still" (*Reflections of a Statesman*, 393). Neither English by virtue of birth in England, nor even potentially English by virtue of sustained exposure to English scenes, institutions, traditions, or places, the West Indian or Asian cannot ever be, for Powell, what Stuart was for Ford, the urban slum-dweller might be for Ruskin, and William the Conqueror has been for countless generations of schoolchildren: English, by virtue of contact with the locations of Englishness. This refusal to believe that nonwhite immigrants and their children could ever become English amounts, of course, to race prejudice, but it also implies a historic repudiation of the aura of English place.[33] And because that repudiation is so categorical and, in a sense, so heretical, it must be accounted for.

Powell's understanding of the failures of place—one might even say his conviction that the *lieu de memoire* has betrayed its historic mission—exists in an odd tension with the nostalgic celebrations of place that have also been a regular feature of New Right discourse in England over the past quarter century. Patrick Wright and David Cannadine have both analyzed the development in Britain of "a distinctive public mood. . . . withdrawn, nostalgic and escapist, disenchanted with the contemporary scene, preferring conservation to development, the country to the town, and the past to the present"[34] that emerged at virtually the same time as, and was nourished by, the ascendancy of New Right orthodoxies. As both Cannadine and Wright stress, this "traditionalist" turn in British public culture—the paradoxical, if not inexplicable, counterpart to the development-oriented and global-economic fiscal policies of Margaret Thatcher—operated in large part by fetishizing the "quintessential" architectures of Englishness, particularly the architectures of those stately country houses so often built on the profits extracted from the British Empire.[35] When situated alongside what Salman Rushdie calls the "Raj Revivalism" of the 1980s—the nostalgic celebration of the imperial past evident in the television and filmic productions of *The Far Pavilions, The Jewel in the Crown,* and *A Passage to India*—this reauraticization of those English locales which manage to metonymically invoke both a "better" and more "authentic" English past and the rewards of imperial rule seems antithetical to the rejection of the magic of place, the abandonment of the association of Englishness with empire, and the antitraditionalism that I have been suggesting characterize Powell's and Thatcher's sometimes divergent but frequently convergent policies.

We can explain this tension by noting that English conservatives, like most politicians, are not above having it both ways, that valorizations of the local, the traditional, and the imperial have a distinct political value when they can supplement a government's commitments to the transnational (in economic policy) and the anti-imperial (in immigration and citizenship law). On this reading, the coappearance of country-house fetishism, Raj-revivalism, and the policies that culminated in the 1981 Nationality Act reveal, once again, the English state's propensity to simultaneously avow and disavow the imperial determinations of English identity. But there is another way of making sense of these contradictions, particularly as they relate to the problem of place in a discourse on English identity. If, as Cannadine and Wright suggest, the subtext of the nostalgic recovery of England's *lieux de memoire* is a crisis within Englishness, a perception that some essential form of English identity is vanishing from the earth, then the very investment in the therapeutic qualities of distinctively and auratically English places betrays both a sense that it is in these places that Englishness can be recovered and the awareness that, as monuments to the identity which has been lost, these places serve only to monumentalize that loss. As fetish objects, these *lieux de memoire* are thus at once objects of desire and the objects which manifest the lack that feeds that desire. The more fervently they are embraced, the more fully will they disappoint the embracer as they gesture beyond themselves to the Englishness they can at best represent, and by representing never quite manage to be. In Gadamer and Nora's terms, the very traditionalist turn to these *lieux de memoire* is both that which flickeringly invests them with an identity-reforming magic, and that which eventually guarantees their disenchantment, their reappearance as historical artifacts that testify to the disappearance of tradition and memory.

If England's resonant spaces are thus susceptible to an inevitable historicization, to a waning of affect, then, for a thinker such as Powell—for whom Englishness, whatever its particular significances, has always exhibited an unbroken "continuity"—something other than English place must be discovered to secure the unaltered essence of Englishness. As they discover that "their" soil has lost the power to make an Englishman of an Asian or a West Indian, and by implication—and, after 1981, by law—that that soil has lost the power to make them English, Powell's Englishmen must find something other than the auratic locale to guarantee that they will be able to speak to the ghosts of the past the words that Ernest Renan avowed were the "hymn" of every nation, "We are what you were; we will be what you are."[36] For Powell that other thing is, of course, race.

But if the primary thrust of Powell's discourse is that race must be substituted for place as the guarantor of English identity because place has proven too weak to play the role that Ford, Ruskin, and others demanded of it, then Powell also manages to reveal the exact opposite opinion: that race must stand in for place because place too effectively determines identity. In the letter he read in the "Rivers of Blood" speech, Powell's villains are clearly the black immigrants and their children who torment the "once quiet" street's white landlady, but they are not the only villains. The street is also culpable, as, in a sense, it has to be. For if Powell's reconceptualization of Englishness were motivated simply by his belief that England's places could no longer safeguard the nation's identity, then the final failure of place would not necessarily coincide with the arrival of black immigrants in England: the aura of place would have failed as surely and as inevitably as traditionalism breeds historicism. But clearly, for Powell, that is not the case. Throughout his speeches and writings the growth of Britain's black population coincides with the need to abandon a spatial theory of identity. And this is because for Powell what is finally threatened by the growth of a black population in England is less the white body than the metropolitan landscape—which the immigrants remake, as they have remade the "once quiet" street.[37] And in remaking that street, in transforming it into a place of "noise and confusion," the island's immigrants, he bitterly admits, remake England and Englishness.

If that were not the case, then Powell could view the nation's black immigrants only as a curiosity, as a nearer manifestation of that imperial ensemble "built around" an England which had always managed to preserve an "unaltered" existence fundamentally "uninvolved" with the "strange, fantastic structure" of the British Empire.[38] But the entire tenor of Powell's polemic is that England can no longer take its essence for granted, that a black population is promising to fundamentally alter England and what it means to be English. And, crucially, he indexes the black immigrants' capacity to transform English culture by their ability to transform the nation's architectures of belonging. It is no accident that the allegory of the old lady is also an allegory of a home and a street, that what Powell is offering to defend is a "neighborhood" and a house. In his November speech Powell offered three further examples of black malfeasance; in each case the "immigrants" have incurred his wrath by vandalizing a home. The implicit argument of each of these anecdotes is that place does determine identity, that England's places are being occupied and despoiled, and that as the nation's houses and streets are remade, Englishness itself is deleteriously transformed. Ultimately, it is because of this, because place, in these allegories of trespass, exerts *too great* an influence over the shape of English identity, and because England's places, from the 1950s onward, have been increasingly occupied and shaped by black immigrants and their children, that Powell insists that the nation must invent some other grounding principle of Englishness.

Powell's implicit acknowledgment that place might determine identity, and his insistence that it not be allowed to, can be read as manifestations of a border anxiety intrinsic to the discourses of Englishness and empire. In essence, so long as the imperial frontier is distant, so long as it does not correspond with England's national, shoreline boundaries, Englishness, for Powell and those of like minds, can safely be identified as the gift of place. But once the "fantastic structure" of empire collapses in on itself, once the postimperial frontier is drawn in Bristol or London, once white Britons can no longer ignore the fact that they share their streets with the "strange races" of the empire, the "once quiet" street is found, or made, to lose its identity-determining magic, the rules of the game are rapidly scrapped, and a new principle of identity is discovered, or invented.[39] In law the name of that new principle is "patriality"; in practice it is race.

ENGLISHNESS AND EMPIRE

Powell's theories, and the 1981 act that put those theories into law, rendered hegemonic a racial narrative of English identity which, it must again be stressed, had circulated long before the 1960s, and which has contributed to a sustained, virulent, and operative history of racism in Britain, but which, until the 1980s, was not the official narrative of England's corporate and continuous selfhood. Collectively, then, his theories and the act constituted a sort of Foucauldian event in the discourses of Englishness and empire. But the fundamental sentiment that inspired Powell and Thatcher, the conviction that Englishness was in some or other fashion threatened by empire, was not at all new. As Richard Helgerson has shown, Englishness has been understood as something that must ward off an imperial invasion since at least the end of the sixteenth century.

Samuel Daniel's 1599 poem *Musopholis*, Helgerson suggests, typifies a strain of anti-imperial anxiety and resentment foundational to the establishment of an early modern English nationalism. In a crucial passage of the poem—which is primarily a defense of learning but, more important, a defense of the vitality and promise of the English language—a scholar who has just boasted that the English language may someday conquer the world is challenged for his pretension:

> Is this the walke of all your wide renowne,
> This little Point, this scarce discerned Ile,
> Thrust from the world, with whom our speech unknowne
> Made never any traffike of our Stile?
> And in this All, where all this care is showne,
> To inchant the fame to last so long a while?
> And for that happier tongues have wonne so much,
> Think you to make your language such?
> Poore narrow limits for so mightie paines,
> That cannot promise any forraine vent.[40]

The sneering condescension of these lines is reminiscent, for twentieth-century readers, of the mocking tones of V. S. Naipaul, chastising "third world" writers and intellectuals for their nativist sentiments. And that, more or less, is the point Helgerson makes in his reading of the passage. Daniel, Helgerson argues, is forced at this moment to regard England, as Naipaul regards the "third world," from the perspective of someone whose "happier tongue" *has* "wonne so much," someone whose language has found ample "forraine vent"—someone very much like Virgil, "whose *Eclogues*," Helgerson notes, "spoke of 'the British wholly divided from the world.'"[41] Viewed from this Virgilian perspective, England looks very much like a nation still in thrall to the departed Roman Empire, whose language was still the language of education in England at the time of Daniel's writing. For Daniel, Helgerson concludes, "the civilized center was elsewhere; the uncivilized periphery at home. . . . Far from being in a position to 'refine' the 'unformed Occident,' English itself was in need of refining."

Daniel's fundamental message to his readers was, thus, quite clear. If English was, in time, to become an imperial language, a language that could distribute itself across uncounted "strange shores. . . . T'enrich unknowing Nations" (255), it must first purify itself of foreign contaminations and exert an internal mastery over the nation's educational institutions, its world of letters, its court life, its legal system, and its religious practice. In order to embrace its imperial destiny, England must first repudiate the lingering linguistic dominance of the Roman Empire and cast off the French tassles of the "Norman yoke." Daniel was not alone in this belief. Over the course of the late sixteenth and early seventeenth centuries, English lawmakers, educators, and writers initiated numerous efforts to cleanse the English language of foreign influences, to regularize its grammar, to substitute English for French in court proceedings, and to institute English as the language of religion.[42]

Almost all of these endeavors betrayed the workings of the double logic at the heart of Daniel's poem. Positioned against imperialism when England was read as an invaded and contaminated territory, the English language was reequipped for imperial conquest when England was celebrated as a nation about to subdue "strange shores." If Englishness, as Helgerson stresses, was thus construed in the sixteenth and seventeenth centuries as possessing a linguistic essence, this conception of English identity also implied a structuring doubleness in the temporal and spatial narratives of Englishness. Temporally, for Daniel and his contemporaries, England existed both after empire—as a once invaded nation—and before it—as a nation about to conquer the world.[43] Spatially, Daniel tropes Englishness as discrete, local, and self-quarantining *and* as expansive, global, and self-replicating. Thus, as Daniel and others defined the English language as a language refusing and pursuing imperial sovereignty, English history as the history of a nation rejecting and embracing imperial conquest, and English space as a space withdrawing from and coinciding with imperial territory, Englishness—even in the decades in which England possessed little more than a hypothetical empire—emerges as something that can be spoken of only in relation to imperialism, as something entirely, but schizophrenically, "involved" with questions of empire. Schizophrenia may, however, be too harsh a word for the pattern of avowal and disavowal that structures the writings of Daniel and his fellows. For, unlike many of their later countrymen, the empire they were defining Englishness against was not the same as the empire they were defining Englishness as and for (though, to be sure, in instructing England that the success of an English empire depended on the nation's ability to simultaneously localize and globalize its cultural vernacular, they were seeding the germs of that delirious epistemology which Rushdie suggests has, for centuries, defined an English way of knowing, or not knowing, what it means to be English).

The apparent ease with which Daniel could resolve paradox by damning Roman while extolling English imperialism was no longer available to Samuel Johnson when, in 1747, he picked up the work of regularizing an English language that had by then, as Daniel imagined, spread to numerous "strange shores." In the *Plan* to the dictionary he was to complete in 1755, Johnson, like Daniel, puts on a Roman persona, assuming a position relative to the language he is about to "settle" that is apparently identical to the rhetorical position Daniel had adopted in his poem: "When I survey the plan which I have laid before you, I cannot, my Lord, but confess that I am frightened at its extent, and, like the soldiers of caesar, look on Britain as a new world, which it is almost madness to invade. But I hope, though I should not complete the conquest, I shall at least discover the coast, civilize part of the inhabitants, and make it easier for some other adventurer to proceed farther, to reduce them wholly to subjection, and settle them under laws."[44] While Johnson's rhetorical ploy seems to privilege a Roman vision of England, it betrays less the continuing mastery of Rome over England than the dogged persistence of an imperial trope that, in the centuries after Daniel's writing, has been almost ritualistically deployed by writers trying to define one or another feature of the nation's cultural identity.[45] Once again, Johnson reveals the indebtedness of the rhetoric of Englishness to the rhetoric of imperial conquest, and, once again, he does so by troping England not as the agent but as the object of an imperial invasion. What distinguishes Johnson's rhetorical maneuver from Daniel's, however, is that in the *Plan* the invading imperialist (who is also, paradoxically, the servant of Englishness, the one who will give the nation a coherent linguistic identity), while imaginatively foreign, is, in fact, English. The double—and contradictory—relationship of Englishness to empire that in Daniel's poem was held this side of the delirious through the distinction between an English and a Roman empire here crosses the meridian of schizophrenia as Johnson identifies his English dictionary as the agent and the object of an English imperialist's conquest.

What in the *Plan* is largely a metaphor for the writing process becomes in the "Preface" of the completed dictionary a historical truth as Johnson maintains that the English empire has literally invaded the English language. Like much of the *Plan* in sentiment, and in its regular recourse to colonial rhetoric, the "Preface" is a morbidly self-pitying piece of writing in which Johnson explains what a wretchedly difficult task it has been to "settle" the English language "under law." In one typical passage that sounds more like the dispirited complaint of a colonial administrator than the grumblings of a lexicographer, Johnson laments, "I found our speech copious without order, and energetic without rules: wherever I turned my view, there was perplexity to be disentangled, and confusion to be regulated; choice was to be made out of boundless variety, without any established principle of selection; adulterations were to be detected, without a settled rule of purity; and modes of expression to be rejected or received without the suffrages of any writers of classical reputation or acknowledged authority."[46] One of his greatest difficulties, Johnson indicates, is in dealing with the "spots of barbarism impressed . . . deep in the English language" (ii). While he admits that he cannot account for the origin of all these barbaric words, he does identify one particularly deleterious influence on the purity of the English language, international and imperial commerce: "Commerce, however necessary, however lucrative, as it depraves the manners, corrupts the language; they that have frequent intercourse with strangers, to whom they endeavour to accommodate themselves, must in time learn a mingled dialect, like the jargon which serves traffickers on the *Mediterranean* and *Indian* coasts. This will not always be confined to the exchange, the warehouse, or the port, but will be communicated by degrees to other ranks of the people, and be at last incorporated with the common speech" (xiii). Of the words that have crept into the English language in this way, surreptitiously spreading beyond the quarantine zones of the empire's ports, Johnson indicates that he has "registered [them] as they occurred, though commonly only to censure them, and warn others against the folly of naturalizing useless foreigners to the injury of the natives" (v). The scaremongering rhetoric of such passages enables Johnson to dramatize the historical truth he seems to have stumbled on in the course of compiling his dictionary. Imperialism, he warns his countrymen, is neither containable nor unidirectional: it has a reversible economy of flow. The linguistic minglings necessary to sustain the empire's business on the shores of the Indian coast cannot be confined to that distant horizon: they return to England along with the empire's fleets. Empire, Johnson indicates, corrupts. It corrupts the language and contaminates the language's native speakers. It imprints "spots of barbarism" in the tongue; it smuggles "useless foreigners" into the linguistic heart of Englishness.

But if English imperial endeavors threaten the purity of the English language, if England is, for Johnson, the ultimate victim of its own imperial ambitions and practices, the injury that the English empire does to England is consequent not simply on the hybridizing propensities of imperial commerce but on the measures which must be taken to combat those hybridizations of the English language. Ironically, for Johnson, the damage done to England by its empire is compounded by the violence directed against England by the nation's immigration officers, by individuals such as Johnson himself, the linguistic policeman who, in being compelled to guard the language against the intrusion of "useless foreigners," finds himself submitting the language to a disciplinary regime that is inimical not only to the general nature of all signifying systems but to the peculiar heterogeneity of the English tongue. Discovering himself laboring at this odious and vain task, Johnson pauses to pour contempt upon himself and his nativist allies:

> Those who have been persuaded to think well of my design, require that it should fix our language, and put a stop to those alterations which time and chance have hitherto been suffered to make in it without opposition. With this consequence I will confess that I flattered myself for a while; but now begin to fear that I have indulged expectation which neither reason nor experience can justify. . . . With equal justice may the lexicographer be derided, who being able to produce no example of a nation that has preserved their words and phrases from mutability, shall imagine that it is in his power to embalm his language, and secure it from corruption and decay. . . . With this hope, however, Acadamies have been instituted, to guard the avenues of their languages, to retain fugitives, and repulse intruders; but their vigilance and activity have hitherto been vain; sounds are too volatile and subtile for legal restraints; to enchain syllable, and to lash the wind, are equally the undertakings of pride, unwilling to measure its desires by its strength. (xiii)

Johnson's mockery of himself and of those committed to the domesticating epistemologies of empire does not mean that in the course of writing his dictionary he has wholly abandoned his desire to "fix" the language, "retain fugitives," and "repel intruders." These remain his ambitions even as he laments their necessity and documents the impossibility of their accomplishment. Rather, what characterizes the "Preface" is the self-accusing and self-congratulating voice of a regretful but loyal imperialist. Committed to the civilizing mission of empire, Johnson is also devoted to debunking its disciplinary pretensions. Willing to repel the foreigners the English empire has introduced into England, he is aware that this means he must also subject the "natives" to a totalizing system of policing. Horrified by the mutability and hybridity of the English language, he yet manages to indicate that "if an Academy should be established for the cultivation of our [pure] style . . . I, who can never wish to see dependence multiplied, hope the spirit of *English* liberty will hinder or destroy [it]" (xiv).

With this last admission, Johnson betrays the full ambivalence of this meditation on Englishness: issuing from, and menaced by, imperial adventuring and imperial policing, the volatile, unruly, and colonized English language emerges as both the hero and the villain of his piece. Condemned for its vagrant variousness, its resistance to Johnson's project of imperial reform, the language is simultaneously congratulated for its refusal to bow to systematic disciplinary procedures. Which of course means that Johnson, in his imperial guise, is also the hero and the villain of the "Preface." Gazing at a language that names an imperial culture wounded by its own imperialism, Johnson finds himself celebrating that language when it resists totalization and damning himself for presuming to discipline it, while at the same time damning the language for its unruliness and celebrating himself for colonizing it. Deeply unsure whether English is at its best when subject to an autoimperial reform that will rid it of its "spots of barbarism," or when the language indulges those hybridizing energies which are, paradoxically, the sign of England's anti-imperial "spirit of liberty," Johnson finally, and reluctantly, acknowledges that Englishness can be spoken of only, indeed can exist only, in a perilously intimate relationship with the empire that ravages and defines it.

By the middle of the nineteenth century, as the British Empire continued to expand and consolidate itself and as England became more closely entwined with the cultures, peoples, languages, and products of the British Empire, the paradoxes with which Johnson was wrestling became ever more intense. As we have seen, from the seventeenth century onward standard interpretations of the *ius soli* dictated that virtually all the empire's subjects be legally identified as British. By the turn of the nineteenth century, in the opinion of some commentators, this globalized conception of Britishness had become more than a legal fiction. Linda Colley suggests that for the early Victorians Britishness had come to symbolize an affective form of coidentity to which the various peoples of the empire could lay claim in order to overlook their perceived national and racial differences.[47] But whether nineteenth-century Britons believed that the empire should be understood as English, and that Englishness, by implication, should be considered subject to some form of imperial determination, was another question altogether.

As Michael North has demonstrated, Johnson's desire to distinguish the English language from the language of the British Empire, a concern animated by his belief that the empire was corrupting the native tongue, found numerous adherents in the nineteenth and twentieth centuries. This conviction was bitterly summarized by Robert Bridges in a tract written for the Society for Pure English: "wherever our countrymen are settled abroad there are alongside of them communities of other-speaking races, who, maintaining among themselves their native speech, learn yet enough of ours to mutilate it, and establishing among themselves all kinds of blundering corruptions, through habitual recourse infect therewith the neighbouring English."[48] But while such nativist defenses of the Englishness of the English language flourished throughout the Victorian and Edwardian eras, from the end of the eighteenth century the protectionist rhetoric that had been at the center of English disavowals of imperialism since at least Samuel Daniel's day began to concentrate less on guarding the English language against the deleterious influences of empire than on securing the integrity of England's authentic places.

A STRANGE DISCIPLINE

Like the linguistic theories of Englishness, localist rhetoric emerged from a negative dialectic. But the opposite against which the English locale, and hence the English nation, was defined in the late eighteenth and early nineteenth centuries was not, initially, an imperial opposite. Rather, during the years of the Jacobin ascendancy in France, and immediately thereafter, English place was defined, primarily by Burke and Wordsworth, in opposition to French theory. Thereafter, drawing on lessons learned from Burke's antirevolutionary writings (particularly his lessons regarding the value of local knowledges, customs, and traditions), Wordsworth, and social critics such as Ruskin who were deeply influenced by Wordsworth, defined England's signature *lieux de memoire* in opposition to the metropolis and the British Empire (corrupt regions of culture that, quite frequently, were made to signify one another).

That Burke's anti-Jacobinism amounted, in large part, to a celebration of the subject as "he" is found cloaked in the traditions that have become a "second nature" to him; a consonant condemnation of the "natural" self, stripped naked of the covering cloth of tradition by the abstract speculations of the ideologues of reason; a valorization of custom over theory; and an election of commonsense Englishness over totalizing Frenchness—these are critical commonplaces that require little rehearsal.[49] Of greater pertinence, here, are the ways in which the English romantics, Wordsworth chief among them, spatialized Burke's appeals to custom and thus awarded the resonant English locale the power to preserve Englishness against Enlightenment modernity, England—with only the slightest hyperbole—against France, and, in time, Englishness against the British Empire.

Alan Liu and David Simpson have both recently analyzed the localist prejudices of English romanticism. Simpson, in particular, has associated Wordsworth's popularity among his countrymen with an antirevolutionary sentiment that "after 1789" discovered in the rural locales Wordsworth mythologizes in his poems, and even in Wordsworth's Dove Cottage, "everything that seemed most admirably and solidly British (and, in another historical sleight of hand, most *English*)."[50] David Bromwich, in his turn, has explicitly linked this romantic localism to Burke's social and political theory, suggesting that "what may have first drawn Wordsworth to explore Burkean habits of feeling is that they give an unexampled moral authority to an idea of place" (*A Choice of Inheritance*, 56). But the fullest account of the Burkean cast of Wordsworth's thought, the anti-Jacobin work of his poetry, and his success in localizing Burke's traditionalist philosophy of English culture, is undoubtedly James Chandler's *Wordsworth's Second Nature: A Study of the Poetry and Politics*.[51] Chandler's study provides a convincing account of the poet's reflections on his youthful flirtation with Jacobinism and his eventual rejection of abstract reason, a rejection that entails Wordsworth's election of Englishness over Frenchness as dramatized, and enabled, by his discovery of the famous "spots of time"—those redemptive locales which, Chandler suggests, are also Burkean "spots of tradition," or, one might say, the poet's anticipatory version of Nora's *lieux de memoire*.

On Chandler's reading, the Jacobin narrative of the ninth and tenth books of the 1805 *Prelude*, is, in effect, an extended allegory on Christ's parable of the prodigal son (which Wordsworth was to recoup in the later poem "Michael"). Wordsworth begins by recalling how, on departing England for France, he exposed himself to the temptations of abstract speculation:

> This was the time when, all things tending fast
> To depravation, the philosophy
> That promised to abstract the hopes of man
> Out of his feeling, to be fixed thenceforth
> For ever in purer element,
> Found ready welcome. . . .
>
> . . . .
> . . . the dream
> Was flattering to the young ingenuous mind
> Pleased with extremes, and not the least with that
> Which makes the human reason's naked self
> The object of its fervour. What delight!—
> How glorious!—in self-knowledge and self-rule
> To look through all the frailties of the world,
> And, with a resolute mastery shaking off
> The accidents of nature, time, and place,
> That make up the weak being of the past. . . .
>
> (10:805–23)[52]

Following this dalliance with a French philosophy that, in its repudiation of the "accidents" of "time, and place," and its ready dismissal of "Ancient prejudice, and chartered rights, / Allegiance, faith, and laws by time matured, / Custom and habit" (9:331–33) is undoubtedly Wordsworth's poetic miniature of Burke's caricature of Jacobinism, the poet falls gradually into despair, eventually sickening before the sight of the "naked self" of reason (another Burkean borrowing):

> Thus I fared,
> Dragging all the passions, notions, shapes, of faith,
> Like culprits to the bar, suspiciously
> Calling the mind to establish in plain day
> Her titles and her honours, now believing,
> Now disbelieving, endlessly perplexed . . .

> . . . till, demanding proof,
> And seeking it in everything, I lost
> All feeling of conviction, and, in fine,
> Sick, wearied out with contrarieties,
> Yielded up moral questions in despair. . . .
>
>   (10:888–900)

Like the prodigal of the gospels, Wordsworth eventually abandons this "tempting region" (10:811) and returns home, where he discovers not a forgiving father but that father's localized analogue, the redeeming "spots of time," which, proleptically encountered while he is still on the road back to England, "revived the feeling of my earlier life / Gave me that strength and knowledge full of peace, / Enlarged and never more to be disturbed, / Which through all the steps of our degeneracy, / All degradation of this age, has still / Upheld me, and upholds me at this day" (10:924–29).

The use of the words "our" (in "our degeneracy") and "this age" (rather than "my age") indicate that while Wordsworth is recalling a time of personal crisis and recovery, he is also generalizing from his experience, depersonalizing it, and offering to his readers a lesson in how they might collectively survive the "degeneracy" of "this age." The spots of time that are Wordsworth's personal prophylactic against French contamination are also, in other words, England's. And this is because the "former life" they revive is not only the poet's but the nation's. The "strength and knowlege" they communicate are precisely the strength and knowledge of those English "Custom[s] and habit[s]" which, in Burke's words, bind together "those who are living, those who are dead, and those who are to be born."[53] These are the customs that Wordsworth, in France, was tempted to abandon, but which he eventually reclaims and exhorts his countrymen to reclaim. As Chandler succinctly puts it, "powerful evidence linking the spots of time to English nationalism can be found in Wordsworth's claim that being turned against his country was the very heart of his moral crisis. . . . The healing spots of time mark his reunion. It is a reunion not only with the English countryside but also with the English mind and character, with a way of feeling" (200–201).

Wordsworth's redemptive localism, and his understanding of Englishness as a species of mnemonic localism, are evident in texts other than The Prelude. In the "Preface" to Lyrical Ballads, as Simpson argues, Wordsworth's insistence that he will not provide a "systematic defense of the theory upon which these poems are written," coupled with his endorsement of "powerful feelings" that have been "long and deeply" felt and contemplated, positions him "with Burke" in a stand "for custom and tradition, for the habitual conventions of a relatively immobile and quite unrevolutionary subculture."[54] But Wordsworth most thoroughly "localizes" Burke's "prescriptive" philosophy—he most fully indicates that the customs, the memories, the traditions, and hence the identity of England are immanent within the nation's auratic locales—in "The Ruined Cottage" and "Michael." The two poems, as Chandler indicates, exhibit a common narrative form and a common didactic purpose. In each, Wordsworth draws the attention of the reader, whom he figures in both poems as someone wandering across the English countryside, to an apparently inconsequential "spot" (Margaret's dilapidated cottage and the collapsed sheepfold Michael built for his wayward son), whose melancholy narrative he then delivers. And in both poems the poet's purpose is not only to rehearse these particular stories but, more important, to teach his readers a "strange discipline,"[55] which is, precisely, the discipline of reading—and in reading being bettered by—the locale.

This formal skill, which the poems seek to inculcate in their readers, is not, however, finally distinct from the particular stories the poems convey. In an attempt to summarize those stories without doing too great a violence to Wordsworth's verse, one might say that the lesson they convey is that metropolitan culture, rather than revolutionary France, is now the enemy of Englishness, primarily because the city induces a forgetfulness of precisely the skill the poems teach—the skill of reading and valuing England's memorial places. This moral is particularly evident in "Michael," another prodigal son narrative (though one that requires the reader to return home in the son's place), in which the shepherd's child, vanishing into the "dissolute city," and eventually losing himself in "a hiding place beyond the seas," forgets the obligation of loyalty he owes to his father by failing to remember the sheepfold his father has built for him. Prior to Luke's departure for London, Michael takes him out to the half-built fold, where he attempts to teach his son the lesson Wordsworth desires to teach his readers:

> . . .Lay now the corner-stone,
> As I requested; and hereafter, Luke,
> When thou art gone away, should evil men
> Be thy companions, think of me, my Son,
> And of this moment; hither turn thy thoughts
> And God will strengthen thee: amid all fear
> And all temptation, Luke, I pray that thou
> May'st bear in mind the life thy Fathers lived. . . .
> . . .a covenant
> 'Twill be between us. . .

(403–15)

Michael's tragedy is that Luke does not learn this reading lesson. He does not learn to hold in memory the image of the covenantal place that holds within itself the memory of his ancestors and their way of life. He seems, at first, to understand. But, departed from the presence of the place, he forgets. Which is what Wordsworth will not allow his readers to do, and what he suggests England's spots of time will not permit the English to do if only the nation can be taught, once more, to visit and read its *lieux de memoire*.

And this is the lesson that Ruskin, who was not above expressing his occasional displeasure with Wordsworth, learned from the poet, and that many of the empire's administrators learned as they attempted to preserve the Englishness of all those English men and women whom the Crown dispatched "beyond the seas." Ruskin explicitly acknowledged his debts to Wordsworth on several occasions. In *Fiction Fair and Foul*, he attests that he has "used Wordsworth as a daily text-book from youth to age, and have lived, moreover, in all essential points according to the tenor of his teaching" (*Works*, 34:349), a sentiment he echoes in a letter to the Reverend W. L. Brown: "Wordsworth may be trusted as a guide in everything, he feels nothing but what we all ought to feel—what every mind in pure moral health *must* feel, he says nothing but what we all ought to believe—what all strong intellects *must* believe" (*Works*, 4:392, emphasis original).

Some measure of the ways in which Ruskin, in fact, used Wordsworth as his guide and textbook, and in so doing consolidated the association of nationalist and localist discourses, may be taken from the comments with which Ruskin concluded his appraisal of J.M.W. Turner's painting *The Fighting Temeraire, Tugged to Her Last Berth to Be Broken Up* in a letter he wrote to the London *Times*. The *Temeraire* was, in the early nineteenth century, one of England's most famous ships. It had been captured from the French navy and had fought with Nelson at Trafalgar (thus doubly symbolizing the triumphs of England over France). But in 1838 it was retired from service, demolished by a London ship-breaker, and its parts resold—an ignomious end to the life of a nationalist treasure, and one from which Turner, in his painting, and Ruskin, in his comments on the canvas, belatedly sought to rescue the venerated ship—an endeavor in which, it should be noted, they were not alone. The demolition of the *Temeraire* and Turner's painting of its last voyage inspired a rash of patriotic scribblings devoted to the memorialization of this vessel that, for many Victorians, seemed to embody "the wooden walls of old England." Henry Newbolt wrote a poem on the ship, as did Gerald Massey. J. Duff composed an aria lamenting her demolition. Richard Monckton Miles composed a sonnet on Turner's canvas, and Thackeray suggested that, with the ship destroyed, the painting should be preserved, at all costs, as "a magnificent national ode."[56] Ruskin was, then, not alone when in his letter he effectively instructed the nation to include the *Temeraire* among England's *lieux de memoire*. What is unique in his correspondence is the skill with which he linked this nautical covenant between England's past and the nation's present with Wordsworth's rural "spots of tradition," thus simultaneously underscoring the

Englishness of the ship and emphasizing the nationalist significances of Wordsworth's poetic project.

> The utmost pensiveness which can ordinarily be given to a landscape depends on the adjuncts of ruin; but no ruin was ever so affecting as this gliding of the vessel to her grave. . . . And this particular ship, crowned in the Trafalgar hour of trial with chief victory—prevailing over the fatal vessel that had given Nelson death—surely if ever anything without a soul deserved honour or affection we owed it here. Those sails that strained so full bent into the battle . . . those sides that were wet with long rivulets of English life-blood . . . surely, for these some sacred care might have been left in our thoughts—some quiet space amid the lapse of English waters?
>
> Nay, not so. We have stern keepers to trust her glory to: fire and the worm. Never more shall sunset lay golden robe on her, nor starlight tremble on the waves that part at her gliding. Perhaps, where the low gate opens to some cottage-garden, the tired traveller may ask, idly, why the moss grows so green on its rugged wood; and even the sailor's child may not answer, nor know, that the night-dew lies deep in the war-rents of the wood of the old *Temeraire*. (*Works*, 13:171–72)

On the hypothesis that one of the beams of the sacred vessel has become the gate of a Wordsworthian cottage, Ruskin exactly duplicates the pedagogic imperative of Wordsworth's "The Ruined Cottage" and "Michael" while reversing the narrative sequence of the poems. For whereas Wordsworth's poems work by dispelling the traveler's initial ignorance of the tale mortared in the ruins and correcting the reader's original inability to read the ennobling locale, Ruskin's letter begins by providing the narrative of national triumph that he, at least, knows how to read in the timbers of the ship, and ends by lamenting his countrymen's ignorance and illiteracy. The lesson, however, is the same, and crucially so. For the readers who have read Ruskin's letter and Wordsworth's poems now know that in their country travels they will encounter, and be bettered by, memory-haunted locales which house not only family traditions but the nation's past, and glorious, and true identity.

Ruskin's epistle on the *Temeraire* is symptomatic of a theory of corporate identity that he developed in a number of his major prose works, most notably *The Seven Lamps of Architecture* and *The Stones of Venice*. In these works, Ruskin outlined a philosophy of culture that identified the arrangement and inspection of public spaces as crucial activities in the construction of national identity. Architecture in particular, he argued, exists as more than a felicitous, or unfortunate, ornamenting of the landscape. It also manifests itself as a visible expression of a people's cultural identity and, even more important, as the curator of national memory. This last suggestion meant that for Ruskin, as for Wordsworth and Burke, the need to define English culture entailed a struggle to define the national past, to secure the obedience of the present and the future to that past, and to defend that privileged past from the depredations of a metropolitan and imperial modernity. It also meant that these struggles would hinge on the nation's ability to preserve, inhabit, and read those public spaces which physically located England's past—and with that past its true identity. The great virtue of architecture, Ruskin insisted, was that it at once disclosed an image of authentic Englishness to the viewing public—so long, that is, as it was Gothic architecture—and reconstituted the identity of its audience, remaking England's subjects into that which they had once been and have now, once again, seen.

Rhetorically deployed in the 1790s as a proof against Jacobin contaminations, England's *lieux de memoire* were increasingly positioned by Ruskin and other nineteenth- and early-twentieth-century writers (Thomas Carlyle and A. W. Pugin among them) against the metropolis, which, in its turn, was regularly troped as a province of forgetfulness where the Lukes of this world abandon the England of their fathers and, in its slum quarters, as a zone of cultural primitivism and racial alterity. (George Sims, in one of the nineteenth-century urban treatises I discuss in the following chapter, characteristically referred to London's working-class neighborhoods as "a dark continent" inhabited by "wild races.")[57] From the midcentury onward, particularly after the 1857 "Mutiny" in India and the 1865 Morant Bay "rebellion" in Jamaica, the participants in the "Condition of England" debates increasingly identified the British Empire as yet another threat to Englishness and, in an extension of localist ideology that is the primary subject of this book, the resonant and memory-enshrining English locale as the one thing that could guard England against an imperial contamination.

Locating Identity

The story of how localist discourse was taken up by Victorian social critics as a defense of Englishness against the cultural corruption of empire, adapted by imperial officials as a means of administering the cultural imperatives of empire, and refashioned by colonial and postcolonial writers as they enlarged and collapsed the boundaries of Englishness—a story that begins, for the purposes of this study, with Ruskin's and Carlyle's reaction to the Morant Bay uprising and ends with Salman Rushdie's response to the racial hermeneutics of Enoch Powell's speeches and the 1981 Nationality Act—is taken up in the several chapters that constitute the remainder of this book. It is a complicated story, and because it is one that, like all complex narratives, abhors the précis, I will not repeat in advance contracted versions of arguments that need to be, and I trust have been, carefully developed in those chapters. Instead, let me conclude this introduction by noting some of the things that the writers I examine understood to be at issue as they confronted the globalization of England's theater of address, and that I understand to be at stake in examining their work.

The globalizing imperatives of empire, coupled with the localist discourse of Englishness that imperialism in part helped to produce (in much the same fashion as the globalizing logic of the postmodern helps to *produce* the local knowledges it is often held to simply oppose), forced the question of Englishness into the epistemological crisis celebrated in that epigram of Rushdie's with which I began ("The trouble with the English is that their history happened overseas, so they don't know what it means"). While Rushdie's Victorian and Edwardian predecessors did not phrase the problem exactly as he does, they also understood that the nation's uneasy commitment to its empire had massively complicated the task of defining what it meant to be English in large part by making it so difficult simply to determine what kind of place England was. By this I do not mean that the imperial project made it any harder for Ruskin, Carlyle, Ford, and others to decide which particular sites qualified as those *lieux de memoire* which could preserve England's essential identity; but that, for the subjects of both a nation and an empire, the task of "locating" English identity became ever more complex as England struggled to define the relationship between the national "here" and the imperial "there."

Even when Englishness was understood to be properly resident "here," somewhere safely "inside" the nation, even when it was conceived as something spatially local, or near at hand, Englishness defied its suitors by greeting them across a temporal chasm. Only ever confidently present in the past, it manifested itself in the auratic locale only at the cost of displacing itself in time, rendering itself recollectable but, finally, ungraspable. Ford, like Ruskin and Carlyle, frequently understood Englishness so, as a sort of genius loci rustling in the nation's meadows or tripping across its cricket fields, but always directing its petitioner to the past, to an authentic, English, "then." But Ford was also willing to equivocate, to acknowledge that the empire had multiplied England's spaces of belonging, to admit that England's signature locales were both "here" and "there," within the island and out along the imperial frontier:

> Thus nowhere in the world, so much as in England, do you find the spirit of the home of ancient peace; nowhere in the occidental world will you find turf that so invites you to lie down and muse, sunshine so mellow and innocuous, shade so deep or rooks so tranquil in their voices. You will find nowhere a *mise-en-scène* so suggestive of the ancient and the enduring as in an English rose-garden, walled in and stone pathed, if it be not in an English cathedral close. Yet these very permanent manifestations of restfulness were founded by the restless units of European races, and these English rose gardens and cathedral closes breed a race whose mission is, after all, to be the eternal frontiersman of the world. (51)

Forged by the conquest of others and forging itself for foreign conquest, England, Ford avers, is both resident in the backward-looking "here" and emerging from the imperial "there"; it is both a rose garden and a frontier. But if

England, on this reading, is always coming into being along its distant frontiers, then it again proves ungraspable, though now not because Englishness
necessarily precedes any given English subject's life, but because, like the imperial frontier with which it is coincident, it is an eternally shifting, eternally
contested space of struggle.

As Johnson in the "Preface" to his dictionary unwillingly admitted, however, the "here/there" dichotomy is itself false. Even in the years prior to the
empire's collapse, as he knew, the languages, peoples, products, and images
of the empire's "frontiers" were eternally, daily, returning to England, bringing the "there" back "here." And however desperately Enoch Powell and the
authors of the 1981 Nationality Bill have wished to ignore or to deny this
simple fact, their efforts have come too late to achieve their desired effect.
Centuries of imperial history cannot be wished, or legislated, away. If postromantic English localism can be read, at least in part, as a defensive response
to the global project of the British Empire (that is, as one of those reaction-
formations which Appadurai suggests typify nationalist responses to the nation's enlargement of its civic, economic, and juridical territory), then one
can also say that by creating for English localist rhetoric a global theater of
address, the British Empire ensured that England would lose sovereign command of its "own" spaces of identity. For in creating an empire whose com-
mercial, political, demographic, and cultural economies depended on a continuous traffic between the English here and the imperial there, England
rendered its spaces of belonging susceptible to a virtually infinite, and global,
series of renegotiations. As Nigerian, Indian, and West Indian women and
men took residence in England, entered England's public schools, and performed on England's cricket fields, *and* as women and men in Lagos, Delhi,
and Port-of-Spain entered, or were ushered into, the empire's court chambers, schoolhouses, and playing fields, their identities *were* transformed. But
as these subjects took their places within the locations of Englishness, they
also took partial possession of those places, estranging them, and, in the process, transforming the narratives of English identity that these spaces promised to locate.

The localist discourse that I have outlined in this introduction offered to
resolve a series of crises in English identity by inviting the nation to recollect,
enter, and defend England's redemptive locales. In making this invitation,
Wordsworth, Ruskin, Ford, and their intellectual fellows suggested that identity *is*, finally, locale; that we are the product of the spaces we inhabit. I have
spent some time outlining this localist ideology because the colonial and postcolonial writers whose work I examine in this book have largely proceeded on
the conviction that this theory of identity is true. This does not mean that
Rudyard Kipling, E. M. Forster, C.L.R. James, Jean Rhys, V. S. Naipaul, or
Salman Rushdie pays Ruskin or Wordsworth homage or even acknowledges
their existence—though Forster and Naipaul do—but that all of these writers

have lived in worlds over which the shadow of a localist ideology has fallen. As each, in turn, has addressed the imperial transformations of English identity, they, like Ruskin, have represented the struggle for Englishness as the struggle to preserve, possess, or hybridize a certain sort of space. This is perhaps most obviously true for Salman Rushdie, who maps the urban riot as a contemporary space of English belonging, and for C.L.R. James, who plots the colonial cricket field as one of those terrains in which the imperial reinventions of English identity become most evident.

As James indicates in *Beyond a Boundary*, the imperial officers who made it their business to lay cricket pitches on every available sward of colonial green did so not merely to divert themselves but to preserve their own identities and reform the identities of their subjects. The colonists, he maintains, hoped that the cricket field might function as Ruskin had indicated the Gothic edifice could function, as a disciplinary metonym of Englishness. In James's reading, the pitch exists as an imperial translation of English space and English time. It promises to make the imperial "now" coincident with an English "then"; to reveal the unchanged presence of the English past in the imperial present; and, in Ruskin's words, to "connect forgotten and following ages." In creating this radical simultaneity across time, the field again reveals the struggle for Englishness as a struggle to *relocate* the past. As they laid cricket pitches from Bombay to Trinidad, the English, James suggests, attempted to do more than simply open a field of play. They invoked an absent England and expressed their belief that, in re-presenting that England, both they and their subjects would be remade in the image of the relocated past.

But as James's text further reveals, in laying those pitches, the landscapers of empire also made the English past available to a colonial act of reinvention, a disobedient labor of remembrance. James will not allow the reader to forget that the pedagogical field can be made into a performative space, or that remembrance frequently discloses itself as a shifting process that can remake the image of the thing remembered. His text, like so many of those considered here, understands the act of recollection as a work of reading and dares to admit that, in reading, we do not faithfully reproduce what we have seen but partially constitute our object. This understanding of the powers of the subject to refashion the inhabited space or the inspected thing provides an essential supplement to Ruskin's understanding of the powers of the locale to reform the subject. The colonial cricket field, and the other "English" spaces that I examine, emerge then as increasingly complex sites in the imperial dialectic of Englishness. They are, as Wordsworth and Ruskin insisted, crucial to the construction of English identity. But they exist not only as determining but as determined cultural locations, as spaces of memory that alter the identities of the persons inhabiting, viewing, or passing through them, and that simultaneously suffer a sea change as wave after wave of the empire's subjects wash over them.

The various parliamentary acts, court findings, poems, speeches, and prose treatises I have discussed in this introduction indicate that from the time that the British Empire was little more than a hypothesis, the concepts of Britishness and Englishness have existed only in some or other relation to imperialism, generally in a dual relation of affirmation and denial. More important, these documents, and the texts I examine in the following chapters, suggest that the relationship has hinged on the resolution, or the irresolvability, of a spatial paradox that insinuates itself into our very attempts to express that relationship in language. The trouble with the English *is* that "their" history happened overseas; but it is also the problem of the possessive pronoun which at once separates and links the "English" and the "overseas history" that may or may not be "theirs." To say it is not "theirs" is to affirm that the histories of India, Nigeria, and Jamaica are autonomous histories, independent histories, local histories, in which England played a part but that England never managed to possess. But to say this is also to permit "the English" to say that "theirs" is not a global but a local history, to deny that the imperial beyond was ever a living part of the English within, to suggest, as Enoch Powell suggested, that England was uninvolved, untroubled, unaffected by "its" empire, and that the history of Englishness, consequently, is an entirely local affair. To suggest the opposite is not, therefore, to deny that local histories exist, but to deny that they are ever perfectly self-enclosed, to insist that history is no respecter of the nation or the locale. It is to affirm that the beyond is also the within, that Englishness, like Britishness, has been, and continues to be, subject to a global reformation, to affirm that writers such as Rushdie, James, and Naipaul, together with all the subjects of the British Empire and *all* the inhabitants of Powell's "once quiet" street, can confidently assert that England's history is also "theirs."

Chapter One

THE HOUSE OF MEMORY: JOHN RUSKIN AND THE ARCHITECTURE OF ENGLISHNESS

Has the English nation changed, then, altogether?
—Thomas Carlyle, Letter to Hamilton Hume

Therefore, when we build, let us think that we build forever.
—John Ruskin, *The Seven Lamps of Architecture*

Two Riots

On the evening of August 21, 1866, a dinner in the city of Southampton, on the southern coast of England, sparked a riot. In the Philharmonic Hall, the mayor, a smattering of earls, and some one hundred of Southampton's finer citizens had gathered to welcome the arrival of Edward John Eyre, the recently dismissed governor of Jamaica. Eyre, who had returned to England just nine days previously, entered the hall as something between a hero and a disgrace. One year earlier, while still governor, he had responded to a disturbance outside the Court of Petty Sessions in the Jamaican town of Morant Bay by imposing martial law over large portions of the island.[1] On the Thursday evening on which he declared martial law, Eyre knew only that on Tuesday, October 10, three court officers had been killed in a clash with a body of black Jamaicans. By Friday the 13th, when Eyre arrived in Morant Bay with an escort of troops, he had received additional intelligence, including a terse report announcing that "the blacks have risen," and a number of statements attributing atrocious acts to the "rebels." What the governor did not discover on his arrival in Morant Bay was a continuing rebellion, or even a collection of rebels. The town and its surrounding environs were quiet. Undeterred by this strange calm, Eyre ordered his troops into the countryside. In the succeeding weeks, as a parliamentary committee was to report to an astonished England, Eyre's forces executed over four hundred black Jamaican men, women, and children, flogged another six hundred, and burned at least a thousand houses. The English troops suffered not a single casualty. When news of these events reached England, the government, unsure whether to congratulate Eyre for saving the colony or to censure him as a mass murderer, opted to relieve him of his post, initiate an inquiry, and recall him to England. By the time that Eyre arrived in Southampton's Philharmonic Hall he was a national celebrity— alternately vilified and extolled, cursed as a monster and hymned as the man who had prevented a Jamaican rendition of the Indian Mutiny of 1857. The well-shod citizens of Southampton who had gathered to toast Eyre were no doubt motivated in part by the simple desire to catch a glimpse of this suddenly, if gruesomely, famous man. But if their interests were undoubtedly prurient, they had nevertheless assembled for reasons other than curiosity. They had rallied to announce their adulatory verdict on the governor's conduct. In the words of Lord Shrewsbury, who raised the last glass of thanks to the amply feted guest, "In the face of a rebellion which might extend over the whole of the island and end in the extermination of the entire white population . . . Mr Eyre by his exertions has saved the colony to Her Majesty."[2]

Outside the hall, things were less friendly. In one of those strange alliances with which history seems delighted to surprise us, a significant portion of the English working class had risen to the defense of the wounded black Jamaicans they were otherwise content to colonize. Prompted by the perorations of emancipationist organizations and the outraged rhetoric of John Bright, John Stuart Mill, and other leaders of the Reform movement, many members of the working class had come to identify their plight with the sufferings of Jamaica's black citizens. For years following the events at Morant Bay, vast crowds assembled throughout England to demonstrate in favor of Reform roared their approval for speakers who rose to denounce Governor Eyre's villainies.[3] On the evening of August 21, the men and women of Southampton proved themselves no strangers to this passion. As Eyre and his admirers drank one another's health, thousands of workers gathered outside the Philharmonic Hall, armed with placards denouncing this "Banquet of Death" and the "Wholesale Murderer" inside. At the conclusion of the feast, as Eyre and his new friends left the hall, the crowd grew even more incensed. In the rather horrified words of the *Times* correspondent reporting these happenings to an amazed London reading public, "By the time the dinner party was about to break up a divided mob blocked up the street in front of the hall. A large majority groaned and hooted everyone who came out and demanded that the 'bloodthirsty tyrant' should be handed over to them. . . . A violent rush was made to surround each carriage as it drove off, such was the anxiety of the bulk of the mob to insult Mr. Eyre personally."[4]

Eyre escaped the Southampton crowd, but he was not able so easily to slip his accusers nor, henceforth, to elude his admirers. The bitter August splitting of the city of Southampton was only the first sign that Eyre's return to England augured a broad cultural rupturing that would divide the country for some time to come. In the months and years that followed, the "Governor Eyre Controversy" grew no less rancorous. By the end of the decade, the person of Edward John Eyre had come to occupy the attention of virtually every important figure of Victorian life. Though Governor Eyre's most vocal critics were the crowds of working-class radicals who gathered from time to time in England's parks, squares, and streets to demand their pound of ex-gubernatorial flesh, his most prominent accusers were the members of the Jamaica Committee, a body of nineteen M.P.'s convened in December 1865 to seek a judicial reckoning for Eyre's Jamaican activities. The first chairman of the Jamaica Committee was Charles Buxton, who, in July of 1866, resigned in favor of John Stuart Mill. Aligned in direct opposition to the Jamaica Committee was the Governor Eyre Defense Committee, chaired first by Thomas Carlyle and then by John Ruskin. Before the Eyre scandal finally drifted into silence in 1872—seven years after the first spilling of blood in Morant Bay—the two committees were to enlist the aid of legions of Britons. The Jamaica Committee recruited not only Buxton and Mill but Charles Darwin, Thomas Henry Huxley, Charles Lyell, and some eight hundred other prominent Victorians, including a very large body of Oxford and Cambridge dons. Ruskin and Carlyle were joined in the governor's defense by Charles Dickens, Alfred Tennyson, Charles Kingsley, and an assortment of seventy-one peers of the realm, six bishops, twenty members of parliament, forty generals, twenty-six admirals, four hundred clergymen, and thirty thousand other contributors to the governor's legal defense fund.[5] To say that the nation had declared an intellectual civil war on itself over fifteen October days in the distant island of Jamaica may constitute an exaggeration, but if so, it is the mildest of hyperboles. For what even the banal mathematics of these lists suggests is that that struggle fought outside of a Jamaica courthouse had spilled, rhetorically at least, into Victoria's England.

Though that conflict rumbled on through countless public demonstrations, dinner rooms, gentlemen's clubs, and, in time, court chambers, it received its fullest articulation in the pronouncements of that handful of men unwaveringly committed to either the vilification or the redemption of Governor Eyre. As John Stuart Mill, Charles Buxton, Thomas Carlyle, and John Ruskin devoted themselves to the resolution of this scandal, Governor Eyre began to disappear from the center of debate. The discussion of Morant Bay became less an inquiry into the actions of one man than an examination of how the pursuit of empire was redefining what it meant to be English. On this issue—the imperial determination of English identity—there was, despite all the differences regarding Edward Eyre's conduct, remarkably little disagreement, even if the involved parties could never have admitted this to one another. For what both Eyre's detractors and his defenders ultimately realized was that to speak of England was to speak no longer simply of the green and pleasant isle but also of that vast imperial abroad that, over the course of the eighteenth and nineteenth centuries, England had colonized.

Both the most vehement denunciations and the most ardent celebrations of Eyre's conduct served to collapse any conception of England as a discrete, ocean-bounded space. Neither party represented the happenings in Morant Bay as distant and primarily Jamaican events. Nor, as we might alternatively predict, were they partially distanced by being spoken of as "British" happenings. The uprising, and its suppression, were figured with an almost casual unanimity as English occurrences. This may seem obvious, or even insignificant, but it is not. For the marking of Morant Bay as an event *within* English history signals a crucial Victorian reimagination of the relations that obtained between England and its empire. That reconceptualization demanded, among other things, that those black West Indians whipped, tortured, and executed by the governor's men be spoken of as English.[6] This discursive opening of Englishness to blackness—which was, to be sure, little more than discursive—reflects a broader movement in which, over the course of the nineteenth century, the cognitive map of England was increasingly understood to have become almost homologous with the achieved map of the empire. No one event prompted this massive elaboration of the imaginary community of Englishness; nor should this primarily symbolic expansion of England's borders to the boundaries of the empire in any way be taken as uncontested or final. John Stuart Mill's discussion of the nature of colonial space in *Principles of Political Economy* may be taken as voicing allegiances to both perspectives while finally expressing the firm conviction that to look on the empire is to look on England.

> These [outlying properties of ours] are hardly to be looked upon as countries, carrying on an exchange of commodities with other countries, but more properly as outlying agricultural or manufacturing estates belonging to a larger community. Our West Indian colonies, for example, cannot be regarded as countries with a productive capital of their own . . . [but are rather] the place where England finds it convenient to carry on the production of sugar, coffee and a few other tropical commodities. All the capital employed is English capital; almost all the industry is carried on for English uses; there is little production of anything except for staple commodities, and these are sent to England, not to be exchanged for things exported to the colony and its inhabitants, but to be sold in England for the benefit of its proprietors there. The trade with the West Indies is hardly to be considered an external trade, but more resembles the traffic between town and country.[7]

After the Indian Mutiny of 1857 this transition from an essentially mercantilist theory of imperialism, in which England's colonies were represented as little more than factories or shopfronts, to an epistemology of empire in which the colonies were troped as England's outlying counties, was firmly underway. Parliament's 1859 decision to relieve the East India Company of responsibility for the government of India is less symbolic of this transformation than its post-Mutiny determination to award Queen Victoria an "Oriental" title, and in so doing to reinvent the monarch as the place where England and India became one.[8]

For the contestants in the Eyre controversy, this translation of imperial into English space meant that there could be no quarantine against the contaminations of Morant Bay, no curtain dividing the audience and the actors of this tragedy. In gazing, however belatedly and however distantly, upon this violent scene, England's metropolitan elite found itself not merely implicated but infected. Again and again, the outraged voices raised on either side of the embattled governor settled on the complaint that through his actions, or the actions of the men and women he had punished, England itself had become polluted. Of the multitudes of pronouncements on Morant Bay, two discourses, one in condemnation of the governor, the other in his defense, may serve to illustrate this convergence of otherwise opposed views on the shock of England's corruption.

On July 31, 1866, Parliament met to debate a resolution from the Jamaica Committee demanding that Eyre be censured. Though John Stuart Mill chaired the committee, the task of carrying the resolution fell to Charles Buxton, the previous chairman of the committee and a man whom Eyre's supporters viewed as infinitely more moderate than Mill even though he was the son of Thomas Fowell Buxton, the famous abolitionist and former leader of the Anti-Slavery Society. Buxton began his address by listing the violent acts performed by Eyre's forces and then brought his attention to bear on the conduct of the military officers who had manned the courts-martial that sentenced so many Jamaicans to death:

> I would a thousand times rather have followed a son of mine to the grave than have had him sit as a member of that court martial, and have shown himself so lost to every feeling not only of humanity but of personal honour—so dead to every generous youthful impulse—as to have stooped to the utter degradation of being merely the executioner, the hangman, the base instrument used by the authorities to consign these 400 trembling wretches to the whipping post and the gallows. . . . The whole country, and the whole of Christendom, which has looked on with more interest at this matter than is perhaps generally known, will fully understand the question on which we shall divide is simply as to whether England will sanction these butcheries. I await that decision with the deepest anxiety. It would, indeed, be a blow to the cause of humanity, it would indeed be a dark stain on the character of the British people, should the House bestow its sanctions upon such doings.[9]

As Buxton's emphasis shifts from a discussion of what forms of public behavior "England" will sanction to the discovery of a "stain" cast on the "British people," his discourse manages to name not only the horror that the Morant Bay uprising occasions and the fundamental anxiety subtending that horror but one of the central teleological plots of empire. Speaking as an Englishman, and in the name of England, Buxton can preserve the integrity of his and his fellows' Englishness only by simultaneously avowing and disavowing the actions of the governor and his officers, by acknowledging that their handling of the uprising implicates England and by insisting that that implicatedness can be redeemed only if England acts to repudiate the soldiers' actions. So long as that delicate double structure is in place, Buxton can speak as a representative of Englishness. But once he entertains the possibility that "these butcheries" might be doubly avowed, once he admits that the nation might admit *and* "sanction" its involvement, he speaks no longer in the name of Englishness but in that of Britishness. While Buxton might simply be loosely substituting Britishness for Englishness in his closing sentence, it is in many respects that substitution that breeds his anxiety, an anxiety that the imperial project at once affects and threatens to annul a distinctive form of English identity, that the plot of empire is a plot of the re-formation and the vanishing of Englishness. Buxton's speech thus signals his awareness that the Morant Bay Courthouse occupies the uneasy, shifting boundary between Englishness and Britishness, that this imperial locale threatens to disrupt the nation's ability to distinguish a "healthy" English past and a corrupted British and imperial future which promises to remake a now-menaced England in its degraded image.

To say that that better, purer, lost England in whose name Buxton implicitly protests exists only as the product of a nostalgic imagination is, if not entirely irrelevant, largely beside the point. For while the past is always some form of fiction, Buxton's agony before the apprehended loss of a past England is undeniably real. If, as Raymond Williams has shown, the mourning of an abandoned, true England—which can be named only as that past from which the present falls away—emerges as the most common gesture in the modern history of English social criticism, then Buxton's agony marks a shifting within that history.[10] Unlike the Burke of the *Reflections* or the Wordsworth of the "Michael" fragment and *The Excursion*, Buxton's mourning identifies imperialism—again not in itself, but in its Morant Bay idioms—rather than Enlightenment theory or metropolitanism as the plague devouring an organic Englishness.[11] But while Buxton dreads the unclean stain of that corrupt and corrupting imperialism, he continues to believe that some other form of imperialism might yet be possible, that England might finally hold to its empire without suffering any lasting deformation.

Thomas Carlyle would have ridiculed that fantasy, so long, that is, as it was attached to the notion that the whipping post and the gallows were signs of England's deformity. For, to Carlyle's mind, these stern medicines, far from being the germ of England's corruption, were the one thing that promised to vaccinate England against the contaminations of empire. Though he early surrendered his chairmanship of the Governor Eyre Defense Fund to John Ruskin, Carlyle maintained an intense interest in Eyre's case. In a letter to Hamilton Hume, written on August 23, 1866, he unburdened himself of his convictions: "The English nation never loved anarchy, nor was wont to spend its sympathy on miserable mad seditions, especially of this inhuman and half-brutish type; but always loved order and the prompt suppression of seditions, and reserved its tears for something worthier than promoters of delirious and fatal enterprises who had got their wages from their sad industry. Has the English nation changed, then, altogether?"[12] Much of Carlyle's language is unsurprising. We could expect little else from a writer who a year later, in his essay "Shooting Niagara," proposed that the black Jamaican was happier enslaved than emancipated. In that essay, however, Carlyle's horror before the vision of a liberated black "swarmery" devoted to "dirt, disorder, nomadism, disobedience, folly, and confusion" once again transforms itself into that vision of *England's* dying hinted at in the letter to Hume. "National death," he warns his countrymen, "well deserved annihilation, and dismissal from God's universe, that and nothing else lies ahead for our once heroic England."[13] In both the letter and the essay, England's death results from the essential replicability of the black Jamaican's "fatal enterprise." Riot, Carlyle fears, will become endemic to England as the English working classes acquire the habit of black "anarchy." As emancipationists such as Buxton turned their attention to the politics of Reform, the island's working classes, Carlyle suggests, would adopt the will to "swarmery" he detects in Jamaica's black citizens, and in so doing would usher England into "a millennium, such as never was before. . . . [a millennium] of buzzing, humming, swarming" (*Miscellaneous Essays*, 9). Looking about himself, Carlyle notes the reform-minded crowds gathered to insist on English and Jamaican liberties and sees a cultural deliriousness first cultivated in the colonies now affecting England's "ballot-boxing, Nigger-emancipating, empty, dirt-eclipsed days" (*Miscellaneous Essays*, 30). In the riotous, if symbolic, coupling of the English and Jamaican laboring classes, Carlyle discerns a bestialization of England, a descent into half-brutishness that will make Morant Bay not a space of disturbance within the British Empire but the breeding ground of a deformed Englishness. Gazing again on those fifteen October days, Carlyle abandons the problem of Governor Eyre's conduct and poses one of the central questions that I have attempted to answer in this work. In pursuing the businesses of empire, Carlyle wonders, "Has the English nation changed, then, altogether?"

SHADOWS ON THE WALL

The Governor Eyre controversy, which has continued to haunt English and imperial historiography, was eventually resolved as a practical matter by Eyre's acquittal, in June 1868, on all charges and by Parliament's 1872 decision to defray the cost of the governor's legal expenses. My interest in this affair, however, is less in the resolution of the debate that Eyre's conduct occasioned than in the uneasiness that this debate announced. This discomfort can perhaps best be summarized by the nervous query that Thomas Carlyle put to Hamilton Hume. Had imperialism, the great sage demanded, fundamentally altered what it meant to be English? Had England, in hoisting its flag across the globe, not simply "done" half the world "into English" but commissioned its own translation? This is the question, the uneasiness, that resides at the heart of the Eyre affair.

While the answer that I offer to Carlyle's query is finally an unambiguous "Yes," some measure of this question's complexity can be gauged if we consider that Carlyle and Buxton, in attempting for very different reasons to ensure that England not change, seem to offer profoundly opposed versions of the threatened national past. Whereas Carlyle's vanishing England is an England of whipping posts, gallows, and discipline, Buxton's England is imperiled by exactly these things. But Buxton and Carlyle, and the Jamaica and Eyre Committees, are alike in one crucial respect: their Englands are confidently present only in the past. Both camps apprehend the labor of securing or redeeming Englishness, whatever that might be, by assuring the obedience of the present to an imaginary past, and both associate the contemporary unsettling of Englishness with imperialism. The struggle for English identity becomes, then, the dual struggle of defining the national past and of preserving this invented past from the contaminations of empire.

That struggle does not end with the dissolution of the Jamaica or the Eyre Committee. Nor, until the recent consolidations of a racial theory of Englishness, has this tussle over English identity significantly departed from the terms adopted in 1866. From the middle of the nineteenth century to the last quarter of the twentieth, Englishness has been repeatedly defined as a certain moment that must be either recovered or forgotten. Most crucially, however, the nation's authentic moment, and hence England itself, has consistently been identified with some particular arrangement of cultural space. The disturbance outside the Morant Bay courthouse proved so troubling to Carlyle, Buxton, and their fellows because it suggested that imperialism was converting England's space into the space of the riot. And it was to contest this possibility that John Ruskin added his voice to the chorus of voices which, through the middle decade of Queen Victoria's reign, identified the Morant Bay uprising as one of the keys to unlocking the intersecting riddles of Englishness and empire.

When, on September 7, 1866, John Ruskin appeared before the members of the Governor Eyre Defense Committee to offer his first spoken words on the controversy swirling around the ex-governor's handling of the uprising in Morant Bay, he began his remarks by insisting, as so many of his contemporaries were subsequently to argue, that "the question now to be brought home to the English people was not whether Mr. Eyre had erred in this act or the other" (*Works* 18:553), but a question concerning the very nature of what it meant to be English: "Whether this cry [surrounding Governor Eyre] and the feeling it represented, were indeed the voice and thought of the English people it was now," he argued, "to be determined" (*Works*, 18:554). To illustrate this argument, Ruskin referred his auditors to a story he had read in the newspaper.

Some months previously a drunken man had wandered, late at night, into the garden of a London house. The owner of the house, seeing the man, had fetched a gun and shot the trespasser, killing him. At his trial, the owner was acquitted on all charges. "The jury," Ruskin happily announced, "did not even bring him in guilty of manslaughter." From this anecdote, the great critic constructed his lesson on Morant Bay. If, he asserted, "for the protection of your person, and of a few feet of your own property, it is lawful for you to take life, on so much suspicion as may arise from a shadow cast on the wrong side of your wall," then surely it must be legal to take life in defense not only of "sixteen thousand men, women, and children . . . [but] of a province involving in its safety that of all English possessions in the West Indies" (*Works* 18:553). To argue otherwise, Ruskin insisted, was to deny the English people the right to defend themselves against trespass, a denial that he could view as nothing short of "suicidal."

In representing the uprising as an allegory of trespass, Ruskin contributed his voice to a debate that, as I have noted, was increasingly coded less as an inquiry into the legality of one man's actions than as an examination of the imperial deformations of English identity. In a letter to the *Daily Telegraph* published a year prior to this speech, Ruskin had represented his labors on Eyre's behalf in precisely these terms. Contrasting himself to Mill and Eyre's other critics, whom he disdainfully identified as "Mob's men," Ruskin announced that he was "a Re-former, not a De-former." In choosing to insult his opponents in this way, Ruskin chose his words exactly. For in the actions of Mill and the other "deformers"—his sneering name for the utilitarians and the radical leaders of the Reform movement—Ruskin discovered not simply a fondness for mob protest but a programmatic devotion to England's reinvention. The utilitarian's willingness to turn "a white family out of their home that you might drive a shorter road over their hearth" (*Works* 18:551), and the radical's desire to champion the black Jamaican crowd, struck Ruskin not as disjunct policies but as interchangeable commitments to England's wholesale dissolution. In either case, he depicted his opponents as advocates of trespass and himself as the unembarrassed defender of the English home. In his reading, the October happenings in Morant Bay revealed themselves not simply as challenges to the authority of imperial rule but, more important, as very real threats to England's architectures of belonging.

The language that Ruskin uses in calling his audience's attention to England's peril is revealing. For what he finds to be most endangered, most threatened with a lasting imperial deformation, are not the nation's people but England's houses (a rhetorical ploy almost exactly echoed a century later by Enoch Powell in his "Rivers of Blood" address). As he recollects the uprising, the images of terrified English women and gibbeted black bodies that had so fascinated the metropolitan press disappear from view and another, more subtly troubling vision emerges to haunt him and his countrymen: the vision of "a shadow cast on the wrong side of your wall." That shadow, which Ruskin invokes not once but twice in his very brief speech, locates the sublime terror of Morant Bay. It intrudes, phantomlike, into the licit quarters of English habitation. It trespasses and stains, carrying the imperial "without" into the national "within," blackening not the body of the English subject but the surface of England's walls. In decrying that violating mark and representing his defense of Governor Eyre as a defense of England's spaces of belonging, Ruskin was catering, in part, to a personal obsession. But if this willingness to represent the defense of Englishness as the guarding of England's architectures was for Ruskin a private religion, in the following years a preoccupation with the violability, or inviolability, of "English" space was to become central to the narratives of England's imperial translation. In elaborating his defense of England's authentic and identity-fashioning spaces, Ruskin took over, refined, and helped to preserve a romantic ideology that identified Englishness with certain symbolic *and* literal spaces of belonging, and in so doing he passed on to many of his contemporaries and successors a conviction that the unsettlings of English identity were located where he found England's deformation lurking: in riot, trespass, and the imperial shadows falling on the nation's walls.

PAST AND PRESENT

By naming himself a "Re-former" in his letter to the *Daily Telegraph*, Ruskin signaled to his readers his understanding of himself not simply as a conservative but as a nostalgic. His devotion to the past can be read in the care that he took in pausing to hyphenate this word. One need not, however, trouble over a hyphen to discover Ruskin's lifelong commitment to the redemptive possibilities of return. From his earliest writings Ruskin had privileged England's past over the nation's present. In a travel diary written in 1835, the year before he entered Oxford, Ruskin made a note to himself that anticipated much of his most mature thinking regarding the imbricated narratives of culture, memory, and place. "It is very provoking," he mused, "the charms of a place always increase in geometrical ratio as you get farther from it, and therefore 'tis a rich pleasure to look back on anything, though it be with a dash of regret. It is singular that almost all pleasure is past, or coming."[14] At first glance there is nothing particularly revelatory in this well-phrased but apparently modest little insight. It seems to express no more than the all-too-familiar sentiment of the tourist approaching or departing a beloved place, or to signal the insistent emplacement of a rhetoric of nostalgia in the tourist's consumption of culture and place. It is, however, precisely in its elaboration of a complex rhetoric of nostalgia that this passing comment demands our attention, both because it sets echoing a series of ideas that will resound again and again in Ruskin's later work, and because it allows us to begin to examine the place of culture and the function of memory in Ruskin's discourse of national belonging.

For the moment, however, let us return to the rhetorics of nostalgia. Ruskin's nostalgia, a type of regretful pleasure, includes a moment in which the memory of a place becomes a painfully pleasurable yearning for that absent place and so encompasses a familiarly elegiac order of temporality in which the present mourns and celebrates its past. But there is another order of temporality at work here. In addition to the recollective nostalgia of the departed traveler, Ruskin imagines also an anticipatory or proleptic nostalgia.[15] That which is "far off" may be distant not only in the past but also in the future, and by throwing the nets of nostalgia over the distances of the future Ruskin has hauled in a bountiful catch. For the pleasures of the future include both the pleasure of that which is yet to come and the anticipated pleasure of looking back on the present from afar, from a distance at which the present becomes an absent past that may be nostalgically recuperated. This proleptic nostalgia, in which the traveler anticipates the bitter pleasure of occupying the present only in memory and thus begins the work of forgetting or evacuating the present in order that it might later be remembered or imaginatively reoccupied, finds its most common moments in the practices of tourism, in the buying of the souvenir or the taking of the photograph, moments in which the present begins to annul itself by anticipating its re-presentation as an artifact or memory. In Ruskin's writing this proleptic nostalgia, which values the present primarily for its capacity to become the celebrated and mourned memory of some displaced futurity, collaborates with a recollective nostalgia, which identifies the present solely as a receptacle for the memories of the past, to evacuate the present as a valued space of cultural habitation. As the young Ruskin quite elegantly noted, "all pleasure is past, or coming."

The essay on the "Lamp of Memory" in *The Seven Lamps of Architecture*, a text that Ruskin interrupted his work on *Modern Painters* to write, and which constitutes a work less of architectural than of social and cultural criticism, includes a passage that echoes the comments of the young tourist. It is a lengthy passage but is worth citing in full:

> Every human action gains in honour, in grace, in all true magnificence, by its regard to things that are to come. It is the far sight, the quiet and confident patience, that, above all other attributes, separate man from man, and near him to his Maker; and there is no action nor art, whose majesty we may not measure by this test. Therefore, when we build, let us think that we build forever. Let it not be for present delight, nor for present use alone; let it be such works as our descendants will thank us for, and let us think, as we lay stone on stone, that a time is to come when those stones will be held sacred because our hands have touched them, and that men will say as they look upon the labour and wrought substance of them, "See! this our fathers did for us." For indeed the greatest glory

of a building is not in its stones, nor in its gold. Its glory is in its Age, and in that deep sense of voicefulness, of stern watching, of mysterious sympathy, nay, even of approval or condemnation, which we feel in walls that have long been washed by the passing waves of humanity. It is in their lasting witness against men, in their quiet contrast with the transitional character of all things, in the strength which, through the lapse of seasons and times, and the decline and birth of dynasties, and the changing of the face of the earth, and of the limits of the sea, maintains its sculptured shapeliness for a time insuperable, *connects forgotten and following ages with each other, and half constitutes the identity, as it concentrates the sympathy, of nations.* (*Works*, 8:233–34, emphasis added)

Ruskin returns in this passage to his youthful attempt to dislocate himself from the present and to identify as the exclusive sources of his pleasure that which is past, or coming. But if he returns to a habit of contemplation that erases the present, he does so now not in the name of pleasure alone, although he expresses a very sensual delight in touching the sacred stones of memory, but in the name of national identity. Ruskin's erasure of the present and his yoking of the acts of remembrance to the domains of the past and the future, to forgotten and following ages, involves far more than the stabilization or disposition of that archive of personal memories which constitutes individual subjectivity. It involves, rather, the construction of a national library, of a memory house that will collect and preserve the nation's cultural identity.[16]

The constitution of national identity resolves itself in many ways, as Ruskin's French contemporary Ernest Renan recognized, as a contest over memory and forgetfulness. In the lecture "Qu'est-ce qu'une nation?" that he delivered at the Sorbonne in 1882, Renan asserted, "[T]he essence of a nation is that all individuals have many things in common, and also that they have forgotten many things."[17] The forgetfulness of which Renan spoke, the forgetfulness essential to the construction of a narrative of national identity, is not absolute nor utterly detached from the acts of remembrance. It manifests itself instead as an act of compulsory forgetting that precedes and enables an act of determinate and authorized remembrance, as a provisional erasure of history which clears the space for a reinscription of the event within the legitimate narrative of national belonging. Forgetfulness here becomes that mandatory amnesia which permits the construction of what Raymond Williams has called a selective tradition. What Renan specifically indicated his countrymen should forget were those marks of internal differentiation or rupturing, such as the St. Bartholomew's Day Massacre, whose illegitimate memorialization would fragment the national community. What he wished them to hold in common, as Benedict Anderson has suggested, was partially this compulsion to forget, a shared memory of the obligatory forgetting of difference. But Renan also wanted his fellows to collectively remember a selective tradition of national glory, and to communally anticipate the future repetition of this glorious tradition. As Renan notes, "The Spartan song—'We are what you were; we will be what you are'—is, in its simplicity, the abridged hymn of every patrie" (19).

By identifying this hymn as the song of the nation, Renan returns to the operations of a recollective and a proleptic nostalgia and, like Ruskin, identifies the nation as an exclusive alliance with the temporalities of the past and the future. In the nation's contest over the remembered and the forgotten, he argues, no space remains for the present other than a site in which the past is recollected and the future is anticipated. In the comments that immediately follow his citing of the Spartan song, Renan makes this quite clear: "More valuable by far than common customs posts and frontiers conforming to strategic ideas is the fact of sharing, *in the past*, a glorious heritage and regrets, and of having, *in the future*, a shared programme to put into effect" (19). Renan does, however, allow that the present completes this equation in one crucial respect. It is in the present, he insists, that the people remember, anticipate, and forget. It is in the present that "consent" must be given to what the nation will remember, to what it will be nostalgic for, to what it will determine repetitively to be. Renan does not, however, indicate how this consent will be given, or constrained, or what space of articulation the present affords this crucial principle. On this point Ruskin proves himself far more explicit. It is, he insists, architecture, that "distinctively political art," which "connects forgotten and following ages with each other," defines the space in the present where the past and the future meet, and delimits a space of belonging in which the nation determines what it will remember, what it will forget, and, so, what it will be. "We may," Ruskin asserts, "live without her, and worship without her, but we cannot remember without her" (*Works*, 8:224).

But the concept of memory may be deceptively simple, and in order to understand what Ruskin believed architecture achieves in allowing the nation to remember itself, that concept must be attended to. Benedict Anderson, in his elegant and influential study, *Imagined Communities: Reflections on the Origin and Spread of Nationalism*, returns to the writings of Walter Benjamin to discuss the structures of temporality under which the national community operates. Anderson finds, primarily in Benjamin's "Theses on the Philosophy of History," two orders of temporality that govern our conceptions of being in history. These are what Benjamin calls Messianic time and homogeneous, empty time. The time of the nation, Anderson suggests, may best be understood in terms of this latter, homogeneous, empty time. The logic of the nation, in his reading, is a logic of simultaneity, a logic that invokes coincidence, a logic that situates the subject in a synchronic relation to an anonymous body of peers who together define the unity of the imagined community. In the simultaneous temporality of nationhood, a "transverse, cross-time, marked not by prefiguring and fulfillment, but by temporal coincidence, and measured by clock and calendar" (*Imagined Communities*, 24), expands across the bounded space of the nation, uniting an otherwise dissociated body of subjects in a symbolic commonality of simultaneity. This idea of the collection of the nation in a homogeneous and empty time erases, however, the concept of memory and even of the past. The nation recognizes itself in an absolute and continuous present, rather than remembering its connection to a recollected anteriority. In Anderson's account, an amnesiac present, in which the act of recognition has replaced the acts of memory, utterly absorbs the imaginary community of the nation.

Benjamin's Messianic time, however, is a time of insistent and inescapable remembrance. In the chapters appended to the second edition of *Imagined Communities*, Anderson, who seems to have recognized that an account of nationalism which occludes the problems of memory and forgetfulness must necessarily be inadequate, returns to this figure to consider its embedding in the discourses of national belonging. Messianic time, in Benjamin's account, discloses itself as an order of temporality that represents an essentially typological relationship, a relationship of prefiguration and fulfillment, between present time and the time of the past. The typological moment of Messianic time, however, represents a moment not simply of achieved prophecy, but of redemption. In this sense, Messianic time inscribes a relationship to the past that, as Benjamin has it, "carries with it a temporal index which is referred to redemption. There is a secret agreement between past generations and the present one. Our coming was expected on the earth."[18] Messianic time collapses onto "the time of the now" a past time in which the now was already present, and which the now redeems. In Benjamin's conception, Messianic time marks the present as a time that at once anticipates the future and recollects the past, and a time in which both anticipation and recollection are manifest in and one with a redemptive now.

A profound similarity links Benjamin's Messianic time, Ruskin's orders of recollective and proleptic nostalgia, and Renan's Spartan song. "We are what you were; we will be what you are" might be not only the hymn of the patrie but also the redemptive avowal of a Messianic temporality and the promise that Ruskin's memory houses make to the nation. Ruskin's architectural spaces of belonging offer to guarantee the nation precisely that sense of agreement between past and present generations which Benjamin identifies as central to the redemptive unfolding of Messianic time, and which Renan hears chanted in the Spartan song.[19] As Ruskin urged in the passage cited above, "Therefore, when we build, let us think that we build for ever. Let it not be for present delight, nor for present use alone; let it be such works as our descendants will thank us for, and let us think, as we lay stone on stone, that a time is to come when those stones will be held sacred because our hands have touched them, and that men will say as they look upon the labour and wrought substance of them, 'See! this our fathers did for us'" (*Works*, 8:233–34). If this comment indicates that the nation survives in the auratic touchstones of a mnemonic architecture, it also suggests that that memory, which the nation's architecture locates and guarantees, must be apprehended not as a simple act of remembrance but as an allegory of redemption in which the past redeems the nation's present, and in which the present will be redeemed as some future's past. In either case, Ruskin codes memory as a form of saving nostalgia that resolves the identity of the nation by connecting forgotten and following ages and erasing the present.[20]

IN DARKEST LONDON

In beginning this reading of Ruskin's representations of memory, architecture, and national culture, I have been speaking only in general terms of the past, the present, and the future. In order fully to understand what these figures signify in Ruskin's work, however, we must lend these abstractions a local habitation and a name. If, as I have suggested, Ruskin exhibits a pronounced compulsion to forget the present, then what was he struggling so anxiously to forget? On the day he addressed the Governor Eyre Defense Committee, Ruskin suggested that the nation should dismiss from consideration an imperial event that was transforming what it meant to be English as swiftly as a London jury dismisses a charge of manslaughter brought against a man defending his house against an act of trespass. But this by no means implies that Ruskin was an anti-imperialist. Indeed, as is evident from his Slade Lectures on Art, Ruskin was a firm believer in England's imperial mission, largely because he was generally convinced that England would stamp its character onto its colonial subjects rather than being transformed by them: "[England should] found colonies as fast and as far as she is able, formed of her most energetic and worthiest men—seizing every piece of fruitful waste ground she can set her foot on . . . [in order that the colonized should be] transformed from savageness to manhood, and redeemed from despairing into peace" (*Works*, 20:42–43). Indeed, rather than advocating the abandonment of England's overseas empire, what Ruskin most commonly suggested his countrymen should forget was London. But Ruskin argued so, at least in part, because in gazing on London, he, like many of his contemporaries, discovered a city that seemed to have become the "savage" waste ground its citizens were supposed to discover, and civilize, abroad; because in looking at the metropolis he saw a city that seemed, uncannily, to situate the imperial "without" inside the national "within." Ruskin was, however, far too complex a thinker to argue by simple analogies. And if we are to see how he read the city as an imperial threat to England's authentic places of belonging, we will need first to examine how he understood it to embody a threat to English memory.

In a relatively late series of essays entitled *Fiction, Fair and Foul*, Ruskin begins a discussion of the works of Walter Scott with an account of a walk he had recently taken through his childhood neighborhood on the outskirts of

London. Much to his horror, he finds the once pastoral neighborhood savagely scarred by "the peculiar forces of devastation induced by modern city life," and, after a brief protestation of his inability to describe what he has seen, he proceeds to do just that:

> The fields on each side of it [the neighborhood's central lane] are now mostly dug up for building, or cut through into gaunt corners and nooks of blind ground by the wild crossings and concurrencies of three railroads. Half a dozen handfuls of new cottages, with Doric doors, are dropped about here and there among the gashed ground; the lane itself, now entirely grassless, is a deep-rutted, heavy-hillocked cart-road, diverging gatelessly into various brickfields or pieces of waste: and bordered on each side by heaps of—Hades only knows what!—mixed dust of every unclean thing that can crumble in drought, and mildew of everything that can rot or rust in damp; ashes and rags, beer-bottles and old shoes, battered pans, smashed crockery, shreds of nameless clothes, door-sweepings, floor-sweepings, kitchen garbage, back-garden sewage, old-iron, rotten timber jagged with out-torn nails, cigar ends, pipe-bowls, cinders, bones and ordure, indescribable; and variously kneaded into, sticking to, or fluttering foully here and there over all of these, remnants, broadcast, of every manner of newspaper, advertisement or big lettered bill, festering and flaunting out their last publicity in the pits of stinking dust and mortal slime. (*Works*, 34:266–67)

Ruskin dedicates the ensuing pages of the essay to an attempt to find some way, in the reading of Scott's novels, to forget this awful and apocalyptic vision of the ruinous sprawl of metropolitan modernity. Indeed, in his claims in the sentences prior to this paragraph, as in his insistences in the paragraph itself, that what he describes is in fact "indescribable," Ruskin seems to be trying to convince himself that he has already forgotten what he has seen, or at least that he has forgotten the words that might name what has appeared to him. But of course he cannot forget—if only because the city, as he involuntarily discovers, continues to write its own text of discard—and the essay becomes in many ways less a discussion of Scott's work than a wrestling with the uncannily persistent return of this scabrous city into the spaces of the nation's cultural imaginary.

Ruskin's attempt to find some resistance in Scott's work to the depredations of modernity becomes in this essay an extremely personal effort to rescue his own past, associated symptomatically with the country, from the violations of a present, associated, with equal predictability, with the city. Ruskin's repeated inability to forget that wounding city or to erase its imprint from his own writing renders his effort peculiarly poignant. His inability to forget manifests itself in a displacement of Scott's writings and in a protracted examination of those contemporary urban literatures which he typifies as fictions of "decomposition." These fictions of decomposition, which he also calls the literatures of the "prison house" or the "railroad," and which he tends to associate with the writings of Charles Dickens, represent, and to Ruskin's mind celebrate, a city threateningly coded as a site of translation.

The city that Ruskin discovers in these texts, and the city that he discovers overwhelming the England of his childhood, reveals itself, in fact, as a triply coded site of translation. London, he learns, had translated itself onto the countryside and thus carried itself violently over onto the geography of the past; it had become the site into which the English citizenry was being translated, the ruinous space into which vast numbers of English women and men were being borne; and it had become the space in which, as many of these English migrants descended into poverty, they transformed themselves into local allegories of the empire's distant "savages."

The image of a city incessantly translating itself, the image of a migratory city carrying itself over onto its adjacent spaces, is of course not unique to Ruskin's work. By the middle of the nineteenth century the city of London, in many of its inhabitants' eyes, had grown with unbridled energy into something sublime, terrifying, and strange. Two anonymous contributors to the *Working Man's Friend* and *Household Words*, weekly London journals, marked this note of bafflement and anxiety in the presence of the unsettled city. "London," one averred, "has not grown in any natural, reasonable, understandable way . . . it has swollen with frightful rapidity. It has taken you unawares, it has dropped upon you without warning; it has started up without notice; it has grown with stealthy rapidity, from a mouse to a mastodon."[21] "In the presence of London," exclaimed the other, "it is just as it would be if you should meet a man fifty feet high . . . you would be in a state of perpetual astonishment."[22] In 1857 Matthew Arnold, in his inaugural lecture as professor of poetry at Oxford, would represent such metropolitan delirium as the tyrannic spirit of the times: "The present age," he nervously insisted, "exhibits to the individual man who contemplates it the spectacle of a vast multitude of facts awaiting and inviting his comprehension . . . an immense, moving, confused spectacle which, while it perpetually excites our curiosity, perpetually baffles our comprehension."[23]

These readings of the metropolis, coded distinctly in terms of the spectacular and terrifying Burkean sublime, tend to represent the city itself as migrant, as some strange, unexpected, and uninvited wanderer creeping up on an unregarding nation. As such, they are responses both to the incredible growth of London, which in the ten years from 1841 to 1851 alone increased its population by some 30 percent, and to the nature of that growth. Not only was London the point of arrival for the great majority of those men and women who, over the course of the century, were being displaced from the English countryside; it had also become the center of a great national and imperial economy of circulation that had written the social cartography of Victorian England as a chart for the distributive and redistributive flow of the nation's and the empire's commodities, texts, and human bodies. In these senses, London was indeed a "moving spectacle." Open to the great influx of bodies moving from the country to the city, and to the immense system of bodies and objects moving into and out of its spaces in a vast circular migration across the surfaces of the island and the empire, it was multiply written as a migrant and migrating space.

Both the growth of the city's population and the ever-expanding distributive institutions of its national and imperial economy marked the metropolis's architecture. On an average day in the midcentury, the *Times* shipping intelligence reported passages in transit between London and Bombay, Madras, Calcutta, Algoa Bay, Mauritius, Ceylon, Sydney, Port Philip, Aberdeen, Dundee, Belfast, Glasgow, and divers other ports. Over the course of the century, London's merchants had constructed an immense system of dockyards and warehouses to accommodate these ships with their flood of tourists and colonial subjects and their innumerable pounds of goods. As these docks and warehouses were built, the railway system sprawled across the city and the countryside. The decade of the 1840s marked the height of the mania for railway construction. Between 1845 and 1846, Parliament passed 465 acts authorizing the expenditure of over 200 million pounds for the laying of 9,497 miles of new railway tracks.[24] As these new lines, carrying 330 million passengers a year by 1870 and over a billion passengers a year by the turn of the century, cut their way across the English countryside, they cut also into the architectural fabric of the cities, demolishing great swaths of the metropolitan terrain that had to be cleared for the laying of lines and the construction of stations and termini.

This swarming of the economy's distributive institutions had a profound impact on the architecture of the metropolis. Nicholas Taylor has suggested that the great expanses of the dockyards, the vast gloomy interiors of the warehouses, the immense barreled vaults of the great railway stations, and the dark retreating vacancies of the railway tunnels introduced an architecture of awful sublimity to the city.[25] If this is so, it is not only because of the awful and vast Burkean darkness of these newly erected public spaces, but also because they articulated in built space the increasing dominance of a cultural aesthetics of movement and speed. The sublimity of these sites is marked not only in their mortar and bricks but in the capacities they represent to distribute with great rapidity an ever-increasing quantity of bodies and goods, and to redistribute the very spaces of the city itself: to imperialize the city, and to urbanize the countryside.

Ruskin repeatedly associates the image of a migrant city ruinously translating itself onto the countryside with this emergently dominant aesthetics and with the great engines of modern movement—the railroads. In the passage that I have cited from *Fiction, Fair and Foul*, the fields in the old country neighborhood have been savagely cut "by the wild crossings and concurrencies of three railroads," and it is along the lines of these rails that the city has sprawled outward and written its apocalyptic text onto the countryside. In *The Seven Lamps of Architecture*, Ruskin represents the threat that the present poses to the past and the future directly in terms of the threat which the city and its railroads pose to the countryside:

> The place both of the past and the future is too much usurped in our minds by the restless and discontented present. The very quietness of nature is gradually with-drawn from us; thousands who once in their necessarily prolonged travel were subjected to an influence, from the silent sky and slumbering fields, more effec-tual than known or confessed, now bear with them even there the ceaseless fever of their life; and along the iron veins that traverse the frame of our country, beat and flow the fiery pulses of its exertion, hotter and faster every hour. All vitality is concentrated through these throbbing arteries into the central cities; the coun-try is passed over like a green sea by narrow bridges and we are thrown back in continually closer crowds upon the city gates. (*Works*, 8:246)

The railroads threaten here to open ever more of England's spaces to the trans-lative inscriptions of the metropolis and to write, in iron letters, the signatures of the city and the machine onto the quietness of nature. What is perhaps more significant, however, is that Ruskin sees the railroads as threatening to enshrine the metropolitan principle of movement as *the* cultural aesthetics of modernity.

Raymond Williams has suggested that the genius of Charles Dickens lay partially in his ability to recognize and to represent the centrality of this new aesthetics. Dickens, he argues, was able to perceive "the altered, the critically altered relationship between men and things, of which the city was the most social and visual embodiment. In seeing the city, as he sees the railways, as at once the exciting and the threatening consequence of a new mobility, as not only an alien and indifferent system but as the unknown, perhaps unknow-able, sum of so many lives, jostling, colliding, disrupting, adjusting, recog-nising, settling, moving again to new spaces, Dickens went to the centre, the dynamic centre, of this transforming social experience."[26] If this is so, it is little wonder that Dickens emerges as the prime target of Ruskin's *Fiction, Fair and Foul*. For if Dickens was able to see the metropolis as an embodied principle of movement and to force his readers to view the people of the city—the dislocated, displaced, and migrant people who inhabited this astonishing and unsettled metropolitan space—Ruskin, in turning his eye on this city and on Dickens's writing, could perceive only a metropolitan principle of decomposi-tion capable of fracturing the nation's spaces of belonging and of erasing the nation's memories of the past and its anticipations of the future. Above all, at the dynamic center of Dickens's moving city, Ruskin saw an image of death. His criticisms of *Bleak House* are invariably criticisms of the manner of the characters' dying and of the sheer number of deaths in the text. There seems to be some hidden dread lurking behind this dissatisfaction with the tawdriness and the ubiquity of death in Dickens's novel, a dread that has less to do with the passing of Dickens's metropolitan characters than with the apparent ability of the city to reap a harvest of death. Within the line of Ruskin's thought this dread is quite justified. For if, as his language suggests, the enemy of memory is forgetfulness, and the god of forgetfulness is death, then London, Ruskin feared, had become the temple of that god.[27] If there was any one thing that Ruskin avidly wished to forget, it was this cancerous and devouring city, this mortal and de-composing wound festering in the nation's spaces of memory.

But of course Ruskin could not forget it, not only because he could never fully dismiss Dickens and the other novelists of the "railroad station," or because he could not avoid seeing the very literal sprawl of an imperial metropolis perpetually decomposing and recomposing itself, but because, with Dickens, he could not fail to see the people of the city, the ever greater numbers of English women and men, pouring into the sublime and destroying metropolis. Ruskin repeatedly notes the presence of these English migrants alongside disgusted representations of the migratory city in *Fiction, Fair and Foul* and *The Seven Lamps of Architecture*. In the former work, he pauses at one point to lament "the hot fermentation and unwholesome secrecy of the population crowded into large cities, each mote in its misery lighter, as an individual soul, than a dead leaf, but becoming oppressive and infectious each to its neighbour, in the smoking mass of decay" (*Works* 34:268). In the latter, he interrupts himself late in the text to decry "the crowded tenements of a struggling and restless population [that] differ only from the tents of the Arab or the Gipsy by their less healthy openness to the air of heaven, and less happy choice of their spot of earth; by their sacrifice of liberty without the gain of rest" (*Works*, 8:227). Ruskin's Orientalist language and his passing allusions to the regions of Dante's and Milton's hell seem, in these passages, to consign this "struggling and restless population" to some space of hopeless alterity, to the "crowded tenements" of some pandemonium startlingly erected in the heart of the city. In reading the urban presence of the poor and the laboring classes in this fashion, Ruskin was, of course, by no means alone.

In the preface to *London Labour and the London Poor*—a text in which the figure of the hidden, or of a shadowy people who will emerge from hiddenness in the light of the writer's illuminating investigation, acquires what was rapidly to become a conventional centrality—Henry Mayhew finds secreted in London essentially what Ruskin was to find lurking there: "It [the text, in Mayhew's own appraisal of its character] is curious, moreover, as supplying information concerning a large body of persons, of whom the public has less knowledge than of the most distant tribes of the earth . . . and as adducing facts so extraordinary, that the traveler in the undiscovered country of the poor must, like Bruce [an English explorer in West Africa], until his stories are corroborated by after investigators, be under the imputation of telling tales, as travelers are generally supposed to delight in."[28] Writing some thirty years later, George Sims, in his despairing volume *How the Poor Live and Horrible London*, struck the same note:

> I commence with the first of these chapters a book of travel. An author and an artist have gone hand in hand into many a far-off region of the earth, and the result has been a volume eagerly studied by the stay at home public, anxious to know something of the world in which they live. In these pages I propose to record the result of a journey into a region which lies at our own doors—into a dark continent that is within easy walking distance of the General Post Office. This continent will, I hope, be found as interesting as any of these newly explored lands which engage the attention of the Royal Geographical Society—the wild races who inhabit it will, I trust, gain public sympathy as easily as those savage tribes for whose benefit the Missionary Societies never cease to appeal.[29]

These allusions, by both Mayhew and Sims, to the exotic and alien spaces of England's unfolding empire are of critical significance. The laborers and the poor constituted, these texts suggest, an interruptive presence in the metropolitan center of the nation, an interruption so profound that, in order to be approached, it had first to be displaced. For these middle-class emissaries to penetrate the darkness of the working classes' spaces of inhabitation, the nature of that darkness had first to be classified as a zone of exotic dislocation. In an essentially autocolonizing gesture, Sims and Mayhew rewrite the map of the city as a map of English *and* imperial space. In choosing to represent the laboring class's conditions of habitation and belonging, they, and countless other writers, chose first to insist that they were entering an unexplored, uncivilized, and colonial space, a space of cultural and racial alterity disturbingly present in the heart of the great metropolis.[30]

In thus reading the English working classes and the English poor less in terms of class than in terms of race, in suggesting that in crossing into the country of the poor, the traveler crosses not simply a territorial but a racial divide, Mayhew and Sims join Ruskin in exaggerating the alterity of these Britons in order to insist with the greatest vehemence that their readers recognize the presence of an alien nation in the center of the great city. They also, with Ruskin, reproduce Carlyle's willingness to read the working-class and slum quarters of England's cities as spaces in which a metropolitan crisis in the imagined community of Englishness is at once imitative and prophetic of an imperial crisis. As the urban ghetto and the imperial frontier are troped as descriptively interchangeable, the borders of the empire begin to collapse inward, spilling into the nation's cities what Mayhew will identify as "hordes of vagabonds and outcasts" (1–2), and Ruskin will mournfully refer to as an encampment of "Arabs" and "Gipsys."

While such representations of the English working classes and the English poor clearly exploit a racial hermeneutic of otherness explicit within the "worker/slave metaphor" that Catherine Gallagher suggests had been at the heart of the Condition of England debates throughout the nineteenth century, they do so by establishing a metaphoric equivalence between the black and white subjects of the British Empire that stresses neither the economic nor the political questions which are Gallagher's concern but problems of mobility.[31] For Mayhew and Ruskin the racial alterity of the working classes and the poor is expressive primarily of a cultural primitivism that manifests itself in a predisposition to wandering, to unsettlement, to intentional homelessness. The threat they articulate is the threat of nomadism, a point on which Mayhew, in the introductory essay of his text, is particularly clear:

> Of the thousand millions of human beings that are said to constitute the population of the entire globe, there are—socially, morally, and perhaps even physically considered—but two distinct and broadly marked races, viz., the wanderers and the settlers—the vagabond and the citizen . . . it would appear that not only are all races divisible into wanderers and settlers, but that each civilized or settled tribe has some wandering horde intermingled with, and in a measure preying upon it. . . . According to Dr Andrew Smith, who has recently made extensive observations in South Africa, almost every tribe of people who have submitted themselves to social laws, recognizing the rights of property and the reciprocal social duties, and thus acquiring wealth and forming themselves into a respectable caste, are surrounded by hordes of vagabonds and outcasts from their own community. . . . It is curious that no one has at yet applied the above facts to certain anomalies in the present state of society among ourselves. That we, like the Kafirs[,] . . . are surrounded by wandering hordes . . . possessing nothing but what they acquire by depredation from the provident, industrious, and civilized portion of the community. (1–2)

It is in their vagabondage, their gypsyism, their unwillingness, in the terms Carlyle uses to speak of both black Jamaicans and working-class Englishmen, to "convert nomadic contract into permanent" (*Miscellaneous Essays*, 31), that the English working classes and the island's poor are, here, most like their imperial doubles, and most threatening to England. And it is precisely Carlyle's bleak vision of an age of "swarmery" in which the English poor will complete the nation- and identity-deforming work of their colonial doubles, in which, indeed, the one group will prove indistinguishable from the other and both will be found roaming about England's cities, that, these texts suggest, England had already begun to witness.

English Identity in an Age of Mechanical Reproduction

If, in regarding the nation's cities as emblems of England's present, Ruskin, like many of his contemporaries, saw not a space of belonging and collection but a space of decomposition, not a comforting image of home but a troubling vision of the imperial beyond, not monuments to the domestic English past but intimations of its future identity as home to the lapsed empire's migrants, there was, to his mind, one last and equally pernicious threat that the restless metropolitan present posed to the nation's remembrance of the past and to its future ability to secure in memory a composed and composing image of itself. If, in the twentieth century, Walter Benjamin was able, albeit with some ambivalence, to celebrate the capacity of mechanical reproduction to shatter the aura of the reified cultural artifact, Ruskin, in his century, could only condemn the savage power of mechanical reproduction and the machine. Ruskin frequently associates the threat that the machine poses to the cultural integrity of England with the mechanist metropolis's capacity to displace itself beyond its boundaries, but he associates this threat more closely with the plight of the laboring classes. For if any variety of factors had displaced vast numbers of working-class women and men from the country and deposited them as an alien nation in the island's cities, mechanical reproduction threatened to alienate them from the one thing that promised to connect them to the national community—their labor. Over the last half of his life, this insight became somewhat of an obsession with Ruskin, and his essay "The Nature of Gothic," in *The Stones of Venice*, resolves itself as nothing less than an extended analysis of the perils of mechanical reproduction and labor alienation.

"The Nature of Gothic" celebrates irregularity, fluctuance, and the work of the hand. The great virtue of Gothic architecture, Ruskin thought, was its imperfection. That imperfection, which announced itself in the irregular lines of embrasures, vaults, and buttresses, represented in cut stone the imperfect nature of a fallen humanity and, perhaps more important, the liberation of the worker from the stultifying perfection of mechanical reproduction. The machine, Ruskin argued, was capable of producing again and again flawless imitations of some original object, structure, or artifact. The laborer, he further suggested, could be forced to act as some similar though sinewed machine dedicated to the production of one perfect object after another. However, to value or require such mechanical perfection, as Ruskin insisted the industrial culture of nineteenth-century England did, was at once to submit to the worship of the simulacrum and the machine, rather than to a deity that met humanity at the point of its flaws and imperfections, and to sacrifice the humanity of the laborer. "Men," Ruskin avowed,

> were not intended to work with the accuracy of tools, to be precise and perfect in their actions. If you will have that precision out of them, and make their fingers measure degrees like cog-wheels, and their arms strike curves like compasses, you must unhumanize them. All the energy of their spirits must be given to make cogs and compasses of themselves. All their attention and strength must go to the accomplishment of the mean act. The eye of the soul must be bent upon the

finger-point, and the soul's force must fill all the invisible nerves that guide it, ten hours a day, that it may not err from its steely precision, and so soul and sight be worn away, and the whole human being be lost at last. (*Works*, 10:192)

The outrage and dread that animate this remarkable passage mark a return to the apocalyptic visions of *Fiction, Fair and Foul*. Here, however, Ruskin fears not merely that the restless and unsettled present will write its iron- and steam-driven signature over the surfaces of the English countryside, but that bands of steel will sinew the human itself.

Ruskin saw this rendering of the laborer into some strange mechanical Frankenstein as resulting not only in an unrelenting individual drudgery but in the revolutionary alienation of an entire class. In a series of passages that seem remarkably to anticipate the writings of Marx, Ruskin warns his readers of the dire consequences that threaten to follow the present course of events:

> Let me not be thought to speak wildly or extravagantly. It is verily the degradation of the operative into a machine, which, more than any other evil of the times, is leading the mass of nations everywhere into a vain, incoherent, destructive struggling for a freedom of which they cannot explain the nature to themselves. . . . To feel their souls withering within them, unthanked, to find their whole being sunk into an unrecognized abyss, to be counted off into a heap of mechanism numbered with its wheels, and weighed with its hammer strokes—this, nature bade not,—this, God blesses not,—this, humanity for no long time is able to endure. (*Works*, 10:194–95)

Whereas Marx, however, predicted that revolution must follow such degradation, Ruskin sought some way to rescue the laborer from the tyranny of the machine by returning to the past. Specifically, he sought a return to that culture of labor and production which had produced, as its great emblem, the Gothic cathedral.[32] This attempt to erase the present and to rewrite in Victorian England the text of a medieval culture of labor had a dual rationale. Ruskin endeavored to save the working classes from the dark satanic mills by displacing the centrality of mechanical reproduction and by returning to a cultural moment that valued the labor of the hand, and he sought to save culture from the hegemony of the copyshop by elaborating an aesthetic philosophy that insisted on the essential imperfection, incompleteness, and irreproducibility of the cultural artifact.[33]

These two purposes come together in Ruskin's celebration of the flaw. Stephen Greenblatt, drawing on the work of Thomas Greene, has discussed what he calls the resonance of the cultural object.[34] Greenblatt associates this resonance with the essential vulnerability of the artifact and with its emplacement in history. Any object, Greenblatt notes, is subject to wounding, defacement, tearing, or partial erasure. Despite the attempts of museum curators and the other guardians of culture to hide these fracturings of the artifact, much of the work of reading the object, Greenblatt insists, resides in the reading of these resonant flaws with which time has marked the object. The attempt to erase these marks represents, he further suggests, an attempt to dislocate the artifact from its position, or positionings, in history. In *The Seven Lamps of Architecture*, Ruskin considers such resonant scorings of the architectural pages of culture in his discussion of what he calls "the parasitical sublime," and suggests that it is precisely these woundings of the structure or object which draw the historical lines interconnecting the past, the present, and the future. In "The Nature of Gothic," he suggests more radically that such resonant flaws not only are added to the cultural object across the course of time but must be regarded as present in and essential to the object in the very moment of its production.

The mechanically reproduced object, he allows, does not seem to be marked by such flaws or imperfections. But this, he insists, is precisely the problem with machine-produced work. It pretends to an immaculate flawlessness that belies the imperfection and incompleteness of humanity and of culture. "Accurately speaking, no good work whatever can be perfect, and *the demand for perfection is always a sign of a misunderstanding of the ends of art. . . .* Imperfection is in some sort essential to all that we know of life. It is the sign of life in a mortal body, that is to say of a state of progress and change. Nothing that lives is, or can be, rigidly perfect; part of it is decaying, part nascent. . . . Accept this then for a universal law, that neither architecture nor any other noble work of man can be good unless it be imperfect" (*Works*, 10:204). Ruskin values Gothic architecture exactly because it admits such imperfection in its fluctuating lines and makes no attempt to conceal the marks of the trembling human hands that cut its irregular stones. In thus celebrating its own imperfection, the Gothic frees the laborer from the servile compulsion to imitate and rewards the flowerings of imagination, even those which are blasted in the bloom. Through this reading of Gothic, Ruskin recognizes culture as the eternally incomplete, as something that can never be photographed and obediently reproduced. He identifies culture as always in the midst of its own invention, as nascent, budding, and decaying. Ruskin's organic metaphors enforce his insistence that the logic of culture implacably opposes the logic of the machine. In insisting, however, that culture be always apprehended in the midst of its eternally changeful flowering, Ruskin profoundly complicates the act of cultural remembrance. For if national culture is eternally nascent, budding, and decaying, which moment of its flourishing is the nation to record on the pages of memory?

It is possible, of course, to suggest that Ruskin wishes no one moment to be remembered but desires that a full succession of moments or images be committed to memory. In this case, however, the past becomes less a still that the present and the future nostalgically recuperate than an unfolding series of images that compose a sort of filmic archive. The re-presentation of the past then begins to look suspiciously like Benjamin's essentially filmic reproduction of the work of art. Then again, this should strike us as not so very strange, for both Ruskin and Benjamin are apparently committed to resisting cultural reification. Both are devoted to a hermeneutics of decay that embraces, on the one hand, the dilapidation of the artifact and, on the other, the decay of the artifact's aura. Benjamin codes this resistance as an act of absentminded and distracted perception that, in the essay on mechanical reproduction, he associates with the contemplation of two phenomena: film and architecture. In his reading, the subject viewing a film or contemplating a piece of architecture perceives a text of sufficient thickness that the act of perception becomes less a reproduction of the image than a reproduction of a fluctuating series of images. This act of consumer reproduction allows Benjamin's audience to resist the tyranny of the work of art, permits Ruskin's artisan to resist the dictates of a slavish code of imitation, and enables both writers to introduce a moment of fluctuance and changefulness to the work of cultural production.

As I shall discuss below, however, this repudiation of mechanical reproduction—which amounts, under the signs of a celebration of the resonantly imperfect work of the human hand, to an embrace of a principle of cultural uncertainty—creates grave problems for Ruskin. To save England's spaces of cultural habitation from the primitive restlessness of the working classes and the wounding sprawl of the metropolis is no minor task. To do so through a recourse to Gothic indeterminacy represents, perhaps, not only a hint of desperation but a measure of confusion. For in seeking to return to a culture of production that reified imperfection and the broken line, Ruskin risks monumentalizing in the labor of the hand that very thing which, when manifest in the wanderings of the city or the savagery of the laboring classes, he wishes to forget—a principle of migrant uncertainty. There are moments in which Ruskin shows himself aware of this contradiction in his thinking; moments in which, in order to preserve the integrity of an authentic space of English belonging, he abandons his suspicions of a mechanical code of cultural reproduction and turns to celebrate the obedient re-presentation of an auratic and fixed cultural original. Indeed, he does more than merely celebrate such acts of mimetic obedience. In the concluding chapter of *The Seven Lamps of Architecture*, he insists upon them. Deeply distrustful of the rhetoric of decomposition that had begun to infect his thinking, he insists on the need for an exact and perfect reproduction of a cultural original and on the necessity of establishing a grammar or law of cultural production dedicated to the flawless representation of a threatened architecture of Englishness.

Before turning to a reading of Ruskin's grammars of obedience and remembrance, I would like, however, to pause to conclude this rather extended anatomization of what I have been suggesting Ruskin struggled most of his adult life to "forget," by considering an image that he decidedly would have preferred not to remember. On December 26, 1866, Ruskin paid a visit to the

Crystal Palace, a structure that he thoroughly loathed and to which he despairingly referred as the "Metropolitan cathedral" of the century. Ruskin had visited the Crystal Palace before and, in 1851, had written a pamphlet on its opening. In the pamphlet, Ruskin discusses many of those subjects that I have been examining. He saw the Crystal Palace as posing a particular challenge to the composition of the nation's cultural memory: it represented the possibility of England's surrender to mechanical and metropolitan excess and, by its very excess, called the nation to return to its ancient architecture. The nation, he suggested, could enshrine the Crystal Palace as its memory house and dedicate itself to the worship of the present, or it could refuse this shrine to the contemporary, remember its glorious past, and dedicate itself to preserving for future generations the nation's many palaces of memory. It is obvious which course Ruskin advocates, and the bulk of the essay is less a discussion of the Crystal Palace than a return to the rhetoric of nostalgia and a call to connect forgotten and following ages in a redemptive act of national remembrance. But in much the same fashion in which he could not quite forget that childhood neighborhood savaged by the restlessly migratory metropolis, Ruskin could not quite forget the Crystal Palace. On the day after Christmas in 1866, he found himself paying the hated site a visit.[35]

On entering the structure he discovered, in the space in the palace that would have been an apse had it actually been a cathedral, a rather frightful object that might be read as an emblem of much that Ruskin sought to forget: "Do you recollect what occupied . . . the apse of the Crystal Palace? The head of a Pantomime Clown, some twelve feet broad, with a mouth opening from ear to ear, opening and shutting by machinery, its eyes squinting alternately, and collapsing by machinery, its humour in general provided for by machinery, with the recognised utterance of English Wisdom inscribed above—'Here we are again'" (*Works*, 19:217). Here, in the metropolitan cathedral, in what might be viewed as the sanctum sanctorum of that present age which Ruskin perceived to be threatening the nation's memory, its past, its future, and its authentic spaces of national habitation and belonging, he found himself being mocked by some bizarre, mechanical god, being winked at, leered at, and above all challenged by the calm assurance of the clown's motto to try to forget what he was seeing.

THE GOLDEN STAINS OF TIME

I have been arguing that Ruskin's attempts to define a national culture resolved themselves as a contest over the nation's memory and the architectural spaces that he identified as the nation's memory houses; that Ruskin coded the act of remembrance as a recollective and proleptic act of saving nostalgia which, in order redemptively to connect the past and the future, dedicates itself to a forgetting of the present; and that what Ruskin was trying ardently to forget were the moving spectacles of the imperial metropolis and the machine. The question that remains to be answered is in some respects obvious, but it is perhaps also the most difficult of all questions that can be asked about Ruskin. If this is what Ruskin was trying to forget, then what was he struggling to remember and to compel his readers to remember? In answering that question, we must understand not only what Ruskin hoped to recollect but how he apprehended the act of remembrance, and how he understood the relations among memory, place, and a discourse of national belonging. We may grasp some measure of the complexity of this issue when we consider that, while Ruskin saw the act of remembrance as essentially an act of reading, in his writings reading emerges as a highly determinate and intricate activity.

As Ruskin, revealing his debts to Wordsworth, makes clear in the concluding paragraphs of "The Nature of Gothic," architecture becomes less a structure of built space than a figure of intellection when the subject renders its surfaces textual and comprehends it as embodying a narrative that must be interpreted and remembered.[36] It is in this form that the work of architecture inscribes the spaces of cultural memory and can be seen to compose a library of national remembrance. But, as Ruskin recognizes, the works of architecture are not fixed texts. They are imperfect and incomplete in their composition. They are vulnerable to wounding, to tearing, to decay. They are flawed and flawing, eternally decomposing and recomposing themselves. How then are they to be not only remembered but redeemed, recuperated in an act of present and future reading? Which text is the viewer to save in an act of essentially allegorical reading? Which incarnation of the work should the nation remember in the present and preserve for future acts of memorialization, and which fragmentations of the library of remembrance are the present and the future to forget?

Ruskin addressed many of these questions in the final chapters of *The Seven Lamps of Architecture*. But, and crucially so, he addressed them twice. In the essays "The Lamp of Memory" and "The Lamp of Obedience," Ruskin offers responses to these problems of remembrance which are so markedly distinct from one another that they locate a virtually insuperable fracturing in his thought, a fracturing that defines, along the lines of memory, two radically opposed ways of conceiving of culture and national identity. Precisely at this point, at which he had to compose a discourse of national belonging through a manipulation of the acts of forgetting *and* the acts of remembrance, his rhetoric splits. Ruskin recognizes that he cannot save England simply by compelling it to forget the uncertainties of the present, reckless age; he must also constrain the nation's memory. He now recognizes that he has to define what Renan calls a shared past and to offer "in the future, a shared programme to put into effect."[37] He has to compose the hymn of the patrie, to name that which England was and that which—in a redemptive unfolding of Messianic time—England will be. What does he decide England was, England must remember, England must again be?

Gothic.

But, and this is the point of fracture, which Gothic? The Gothic of medieval deference, authority, and obedience? Or the Gothic of broken lines, flawed artifacts, imperfect architectures? Ruskin venerated both. He honored both the fixity of the acts of Gothic obedience and the uncertainty of the works of Gothic production. Which, then, should the nation remember? Which would redeem England's spaces of collection and belonging? Uncertainty or fixedness? Imperfection or obedience? The wandering rocks or the prison houses of memory? In the final two chapters of *The Seven Lamps of Architecture*, Ruskin chooses both. In doing so, he attempts, disastrously but fascinatingly, to define national culture as both an architecture and a dismantling. He identifies England as that which is always already given, and to which the subject owes obedience, and as that which is always only happening, and which the subject helps to fabricate.

Ruskin begins the final chapter, "The Lamp of Obedience," by clarifying the intent of the previous two hundred pages. "It has been my endeavour," he instructs us, "to show in the preceding pages how every form of noble architecture is in some sort the embodiment of the Polity, Life, History, and Religious Faith of nations" (*Works*, 8:248). Each of the lamps of architecture he has named—the lamps of sacrifice, beauty, truth, power, life, and memory—represents, he suggests, one of the principles upon which the nation must found itself. But there is one final and more basic principle, Ruskin continues, upon which the nation rests: "that principle, I mean, to which Polity owes its stability, Life its happiness, Faith its acceptance, Creation its continuance,—Obedience" (*Works*, 8:248). As the remainder of the essay examines that to which the nation owes its obedience, it swiftly becomes apparent that England and its people must obey a law of strict imitation.

Ruskin wishes to suggest that culture, like language, must have a grammar and a law "as strict and as minutely authoritative as the laws that regulate religion, policy, and social relations" (*Works*, 8:251), and that that grammar and that law must be learned and submissively obeyed. He invokes, on several occasions, the pedagogical analogy in calling for "an architecture whose laws might be taught at our schools from Cornwall to Northumberland, as we teach English spelling and English grammar" (*Works*, 8:253). He then pauses to remind his readers of the significance of his discussion: "All the truth which there is in our English nature, all the power of our English will, and the life of our English intellect, will in this matter be as useless as efforts and emotions in a dream, unless we are contented to submit architecture and all art, like other things, to English law" (*Works*, 8:255). This act of submission amounts to nothing less than the enshrinement of a disciplinary and pedagogical principle of cultural reproduction that bears profound implications for the concept of cultural remembrance. Ruskin's framing of the principle of cultural obedience as a principle of "strict copyism" depends on the existence of an authentic and authoritative cultural original that the nation will recognize, remember, imitate, and submit to. In this conception, culture remains fixed, the space of national belonging determined and unchanging, the act of reproduction a faithful translation of a stable text, and remembrance an uncomplicated gesture of re-presentation. In this essay, Ruskin seems to have abandoned his hatred of the dehumanizing act of slavish imitation and his suspicions of the reified, flawless, and auratic cultural artifact in order to cleanse culture of the infections of decomposition, and to demand the collection of the nation in an authentic, fixed, and infinitely reproducible space of belonging. He intends not only to establish a fixed and reproducible space of national belonging but also to establish this space as a sort of reformatory that might discipline the identities of England's subjects.

Homi Bhabha has discussed the ways in which the Victorian and Edwardian administrators of empire attempted to secure the boundaries of their own identities and to discipline the identities of the subjects of empire. These efforts resolved themselves, he argues, as attempts to submit the identity of the colonizer and the colonized to a reified image of Englishness by disposing in the colonies allegories of the home culture in the presence of which the identities of the English would be stabilized and the identities of the African or Indian subjects of empire would be re-formed.[38] Although Bhabha does not discuss the architectural inscriptions of these disciplinary allegories of Englishness, the architecture of empire, as the comments of the Anglo-Indian architect T. Roger Smith indicate, frequently articulated a conformity to this dream of disposing across the field of the imperial terrain the touchstones of an essential and authentic Englishness that might magically translate, or render into English, the identity of the colonial subject. Addressing the Royal Society of Arts on the subject of imperial architecture, Smith insisted that "as our administration exhibits European justice, order, law, energy, and honour—and that in no hesitating or feeble way—so our buildings ought to hold up a high standard of European art. They ought to be European both as a rallying point for ourselves, and as raising a distinctive symbol of our presence to be beheld with respect and even admiration by the natives of the country."[39] Smith's formulation of the reasons for erecting in built space the emblems of a European aesthetic ideal constitutes a virtual caricature of Bhabha's arguments. The European architectures disposed across the imperial terrain would, he suggests, define both the rallying point for the autodisciplining of the European colonist's identity and the auratic site before which the native would submit with admiration and respect to the re-formation of his or her identity.

Through his interventions in the Victorian war of architectural styles, Ruskin helped to ensure that much of this Euro-imperial architecture would be Gothic in style, and so contributed to the construction of a vast network of Gothic cathedrals, post offices, and railway stations across the surfaces of the empire. Nevertheless, he was himself less concerned with the ways in which these architectural structures could act as touchstones to discipline and re-form the identities of the empire's subjects than with the ways in which an auratic architectural space could help to discipline the identities of these colonial subjects' island cousins—the English laboring classes. In the *Seven Lamps of Architecture*, the laboring classes appear most frequently in the guise of a wandering tribe of "Gipsys" or "Arabs" crowding into the reeking tenements of the nation's cities. But in the essay on the lamp of obedience these English migrants stage a more threatening return in the figure of the "railway navvy." The navvies, a class of men whom Ruskin found "especially reckless, unmanageable, and dangerous" (*Works*, 8:263), were the wandering laborers employed to build the railroads that Ruskin beheld despoiling the English countryside and tearing the pages of the nation's memory. Conventionally stereotyped as Irish migrant workers, the navvies symbolized not only the dangers of vagabond labor but, as the Irish in much nineteenth-century English discourse were figured as black, racial alterity.[40] In this unholy alliance of a reckless, migratory body of race-strangers and a wounding, devouring machine, Ruskin identified the apotheosis of that culture of movement and the now which he understood to be disfiguring the texts of the nation's memory and decomposing its spaces of belonging. It is in the name of saving the nation, of saving memory, of saving the past and the future from these satanic men and their dark machines that Ruskin proposes the construction of a disciplinary and reformative architecture of Englishness.

In the halls of this utopic cultural habitus, whose form would reproduce with strict exactitude the form of a medieval original, the nation could pause and compose both itself and the identities of its subjects. "How many and how bright would be the results in every direction of interest," Ruskin almost hysterically raved, "not to the arts merely, but to national happiness and virtue, it would be as difficult to preconceive as it would seem extravagant to state: but the first, perhaps the least of them would be an increased sense of fellowship among ourselves, a cementing of every patriotic bond of union, a proud and happy recognition of our affection for and mutual sympathy with each other, and our willingness in all things to submit ourselves to every law that could advance the interest of the community" (*Works*, 8:259–60). In the reformatory spaces of this architecture of obedience, Ruskin believed he had discovered that common space of engaged belonging which he saw disappearing over the course of the century as the commons were enclosed, the rural laboring classes were forced gradually to abandon the countryside, and the island's cities began to write their moldering and iron signatures ever more largely over the surface of the country. Perhaps more significant, he also believed that in the spaces of this imitative architecture the nation could recollect itself in an act of faithful and legislated remembrance and could define a stable and fixed house of memory in which it could connect its not-yet-forgotten and successive ages.[41]

But Ruskin's language and his use of metaphors betray him. In asking the nation to bind itself in an act of strict imitative obedience to a fixed body of cultural law, Ruskin calls for the submission of culture "like other things, to *English* law." In making that call, he exhibits a convenient forgetfulness of the nature of that law, for English law is not fixed, nor even fully collected. It is, as I discussed earlier, a law devoted to prescriptive, customary intepretations, a law that grounds itself in the worship of tradition. But it is also, because it is not grounded in a fixed constitutional dispensation, a miscellany of parliamentary acts, regal declarations, court rulings, and common practices. It is an ad hoc, scaffolded and rescaffolded body of law; a law, like the Gothic structure, subject to the fracturings and accretions of history; a law that cannot be simply remembered or reproduced because, like culture, it exists always in the midst of its own composition and dismemberment. The volatility of English law tends to unsettle Ruskin's call for cultural codification, and to trouble his supplementary call for the submission of culture to a grammar.

As Ruskin himself admits, grammar, like the law, possesses a signal uncertainty. "When," he notes,

> we begin to teach children writing, we force them to absolute copyism, and re-quire absolute accuracy in the formation of the letters; as they obtain command of the received modes of literal expression, we cannot prevent their falling into such variations as are consistent with their feelings, their circumstances, or their characters. So, when a boy is first taught to write Latin, an authority is required of him for every expression he uses; as he becomes master of the language he may take a license, and feel his right to do so without any authority, and yet write better Latin than when he borrowed every expression. In the same way our architects would have to be taught to write the accepted style. (*Works*, 8:257)

Despite the return of the notion of the "accepted style" at the close of this passage, Ruskin has been forced to make a crucial admission. He has been forced to acknowledge that, though language, like the law, may have its dominant modes and authorities, it cannot utterly displace variation and fluctuance from the spaces of its articulation. Later, he will try to contain this performative principle, to introduce a rule of "license" that will limit the admissability of such acts of decompositive invention. But he will be unable fully to repress the marginal and deconstructive returns of a performative uncertainty into his essentially structuralist conception of language and culture.

If both English law and grammar are finally unfixed, then that architecture which Ruskin imagined as defining a national space of cultural belonging and which he wished to submit to a grammar and a law must be seen as similarly incomplete and indeterminate. More significant, the nation's readings and remembrances of this vulnerable stone-and-marble text must be seen as composing a resonantly uncertain narrative of the space of national habitation and belonging. And it is with Ruskin's recognitions of the inescapably shifting and fluctuating natures of memory, culture, and the nation that I wish to conclude this chapter.

In the penultimate chapter of *The Seven Lamps of Architecture*, "The Lamp of Memory," Ruskin makes his most straightforward statements regarding the place of architecture in the constitution of national identity. In this essay, he insists that the nation collects itself in memory, that memory must be understood as both the recuperation of the past in the present and the redemption of the present in the future, and that the nation's memory resides in its architecture. It is also here that he considers and celebrates the vulnerability of architecture and, by implication, the instability of memory, culture, and the nation. The essay on obedience that follows this subtle exploration of the "Lamp of Memory" indicates that Ruskin was not entirely comfortable with the implications of his own arguments, that he was unwilling, finally, to recognize the embedding of a decomposing cornerstone in the nation's house of memory.

Whatever the reason for Ruskin's rapid disavowals of his own arguments, those arguments remain as resonant flaws in his own thinking, and appropriately so. For Ruskin approaches the problem of uncertainty in a discourse of national identity through his reading of the place of the flaw in the stony text of memory. Toward the end of "The Lamp of Memory," he considers the marks that history cuts into the architectural structure, and discusses the ways in which a reading of architecture can encompass a reading of history. He has already indicated that the greatest glory of a building lies in its age because in aging, the architectural edifice becomes an enduring page onto which the nation writes its history. In a crucial passage, he suggests that "it is in *that golden stain of time*, that we are to look for the real light, and colour, and preciousness of architecture" (*Works*, 8:234). In identifying the centrality and the legibility of this golden stain, Ruskin admits that architecture must be read not as a single but as a dual, or multiple, text. He recognizes that the nation must read the work of architecture's structure—its form, its walled, ceilinged, and ornamented space—but also that the nation must read the *writings* on the walls—the stains, fractures, and graffiti that time and history have superimposed on the original text. Architecture, and hence memory, emerge, then, as eternally incomplete and insistently multiple pieces of writing.

Ruskin spends some time thinking through these signs of the multiplicity and uncertainty of architecture and memory, and, as an irresistibly systematic thinker, he eventually lends a name to the phenomena he describes. The rents, stains, fractures, and flaws that mark the surface of the architectural page of memory are, he says, signs of a "parasitical . . . sublimity" (*Works*, 8:238). "Engrafted" onto an originally unmarked surface, this is a sublime that rends or tears the vulnerable text. It is a mark of encroaching ruin. But it is also, to hold with the organic metaphor of "engrafting," a mark of fecundity, of hybrid reproduction. By coding architecture as a site of multiple writings, the parasitical sublime hybridizes the cultural artifact. To the extent that this hybridizing reinscription perpetually marks and remarks the architectural structure as a site of fluent and fluctuating textuality, it determines that the readings and remembrances of this site will be equally fluent and fluctuating, and that the space of cultural habitation and belonging which this architecture locates will be radically uncertain, effluent, multiple.

In situating architecture at that point at which the past and the future are joined and at which the nation composes itself in the collection and recollection of forgotten and following ages, Ruskin sought to define for the nation a common space of cultural belonging that might resist the fatally wounding decompositions of a restless and discontented age. But in choosing architecture as the figure for the nation's cultural habitus, Ruskin identified a cultural artifact far less stable than he at first imagined or than he was finally able to admit. In the course of his reading of the role that architecture plays in defining the nation's spaces of belonging and in securing the nation's memories of itself, he was forced to recognize even in this apparently stable structure a principle of decomposition that had less to do with the reckless course of his century than with the irremediable uncertainty and instability of all the spaces and artifacts of culture. He discovered (and then endeavored immediately to forget) that the imbricated narratives of culture, memory, and place are insistently fluctuating and eternally multiple, and that the nation, like architecture, dwells perpetually in the midst of its own invention. Echoing the tones of that pantomime clown, those golden stains of time which are the signs of the nation's continuous dismemberment, decomposition, and reinvention might be heard saying to him, "Here we are again."

Chapter Two

"BRITISH TO THE BACKBONE":
ON IMPERIAL SUBJECT-FASHIONING

I have done the state some service.
—William Shakespeare, *Othello*

He considered his own identity, a thing he had never
done before, till his head swam.
—Rudyard Kipling, *Kim*

ART AND THE INDIAN MIND

In January of 1858, John Ruskin delivered an address at the Kensington Museum in London. Though his topic was ostensibly aesthetic—he had come, he said, to discuss "the effect of art on the human mind"—he began by calling his audience's attention to the political events that had been taking place in India over the course of the previous year. Beginning in May of 1857, regiment after regiment of Indian soldiery had risen against their British officers. By the end of the year much of the subcontinent was in revolt. English troops sent out by Parliament to aid the India Company's forces were, at the time of Ruskin's speaking, still involved in quelling the insurrection and in exacting a gruesomely comprehensive revenge for this act of "mutiny." For months the London papers, when not filled with accounts of English gallantry, had inked their pages with descriptions of native atrocity.

It was to the inspection of these Indian cruelties that Ruskin directed his audience's eye, not, however, before first requesting his fellows to gaze upon an apparently more pleasant manifestation of Indian "personality." "Among the models set before you in this institution, and in the others established throughout the kingdom for the teaching of design," Ruskin benevolently noted, "there are, I suppose, none in their kind more admirable than the decorated works of India. They are, indeed, in all materials capable of colour, wool, marble, or metal, almost inimitable in their delicate application of divided hue, and fine arrangement of fantastic line. Nor is this power of theirs exerted by the people rarely, or without enjoyment; the love of subtle design seems universal in the race" (*Works*, 16:261). With this nod in the direction of Indian "racial" capacity complete, Ruskin returned to the stated theme of his lecture and revealed to the curious patrons of the Kensington Museum the "effect" of such "fantastic" and "subtle" work on the Indian's "moral character":

> We have had our answer. Since the race of man began its course of sin on this earth, nothing has ever been done by it so significant of the bestial, and lower than bestial degradation, as the acts of the Indian race in the year that has passed by. Cruelty as fierce may indeed have been wreaked, and brutality as abominable been practiced before, but never under like circumstances . . . cruelty stretched to its fiercest against the gentle and unoffending, and corruption festering to its loathsomest in the midst of the witnessing presence of a disciplined civilization— these we could not have known to be within the practicable compass of human guilt, but for the acts of the Indian mutineer. (*Works*, 16:262–63)[1]

The outrage that animates this passage is startling; as is Ruskin's ability to read the English presence in India as "gentle and unoffending." But while Ruskin indulges himself in a notably hyperbolic burst of rhetoric, nothing of particular interest emerges from this hysterical reading of imperial history. In this condemnation of the "mutineer," Ruskin risks being what he so rarely allows himself to be: a wholly conventional and unoriginal thinker. What is of interest is not the description Ruskin offers, but the cause he discovers for Indian cruelty, and the connection he draws between the fantastic lines of native design and the acts of the Indian mutineer. The Indian, Ruskin suggests, is bestial, degraded, abominable, and corrupt not despite his subtle art, but, at least in part, because of it.

For while Ruskin admits that Indian art is "refined," it is not, he insists, "natural." It teaches the natives of the subcontinent a contempt for the sanctity of the human body and the dictates of nature. "[Indian art] either forms its compositions out of meaningless fragments of colour and flowings of line; or, if it represents any living creature, it represents that creature under some distorted and monstrous form. To all the facts and forms of nature it willfully and resolutely opposes itself; it will not draw a man, but an eight-armed monster" (*Works*, 16:265). In the presence of such images it is no wonder, Ruskin suggests, that the Indian would become the "bestial," "degraded," "loathsome," mutineer; unsurprising that worshiping at the shrines of Kali, the Hindu goddess of war who is the "original" of Ruskin's eight-armed monster, the Indian would become the monstrosity he has gazed upon. Contrasting the abominable mutineers with the rustic Scottish soldiers who proved so vital in quelling the insurrection, Ruskin concludes his argument so: "Out of the peat cottage come faith, courage, self-sacrifice, purity, and piety, and whatever else is fruitful in the work of Heaven; out of the ivory palace come treachery, cruelty, cowardice, idolatry, bestiality,—whatever else is fruitful in the work of Hell" (*Works*, 16:263). If Ruskin's audience had imagined that in discussing the Mutiny he was abandoning his aesthetic discourse in favor of a discussion of the affairs of the moment, they would have been quite mistaken. What Ruskin was offering instead was a lesson in the complex influence of the aesthetic on history and identity.

Turning, in this chapter, from a general consideration of Ruskin's theories of culture, memory, and place to an examination of the imperial articulations of those theories, I wish to dwell on this lesson a little, to consider the ways in which Ruskin's suggestion that cultural artifacts and architectures shape identity informed an imperial project dedicated to the fabrication and safeguarding of Englishness, to examine how imperial adaptations of such theories eventuated in the construction of a vast network of imperial reformatories that promised to secure the Englishness of the colonist and to ensure the Anglicization of the colonized. Of these multitudes of disciplinary artifacts I have chosen to consider two: the Victoria Terminus in Bombay and Rudyard Kipling's *Kim*. But if we are to understand how the train station and the novel function as allegories of one another, and how both, in turn, express their devotion to a theory of the normalized subject derived in large part from Ruskin, we must spend a little more time with him.

ARCHITECTURE AND IMPERIALISM

Ruskin's frequently perverse genius disclosed itself in any number of insights. Few, however, have been as influential as his suggestion that the artifacts of culture help to produce our identities, that the objects we handle and the structures we inhabit significantly affect our individual subjectivities and our collective histories. This is the message that resides at the heart of Ruskin's Kensington lecture, *The Stones of Venice*, and *The Seven Lamps of Architecture*. Each of these texts, however, encodes an ancillary lesson. Of all those structures in which women and men worship, labor, and learn, Gothic architecture, they suggest, is the finest. For Gothic is not only, Ruskin argues, an architecture produced by the free hand of the devoted laborer rather than one fashioned by the cold precision of the machine; it is also the architecture of that medieval *Gemeinschaft* which the English nation, to its peril, had abandoned.

As Victorian England confronted the coming of a new century, Ruskin was by no means alone in mourning this abandoned, recollectively utopian world. Thomas Carlyle, in *Past and Present*, had projected a chastening image of the ordered and idyllic medieval community at Bury St. Edmunds into the parlors of the nation's reading public. William Morris, in his way, proved equally nostalgic for this imagined England. A. W. Pugin, the only man to equal Ruskin's influence as a nineteenth-century critic of architecture, was, if anything, a more ardent apostle of the cloistered past. And as he attended to the hooting, smashing anarchies of the working classes in the final pages of *Culture and Anarchy*, Matthew Arnold was to come perilously close to defining "culture" as synonymous with "the strong *feudal* habits of subordination and deference."[2] Ruskin's contribution to the social criticism of his time was, then, less to turn England's eye to the saving Camelot of this medieval past than, with Pugin, to suggest that this auratic past could perhaps be reclaimed if its architecture could be recovered. If, as Ruskin had suggested to the audience gathered at the Kensington Museum, identity is in many ways a function of those cultural objects by which we are surrounded, then, he repeatedly argued, the nation could perhaps be saved by the reconstruction of its cultural landscape. To redeem England from the wild course of modernity, it was necessary, Ruskin insisted, to return the nation to its Gothic past, to re-form the island's subjects by ushering them into the vaulted corridors of a Gothic habitus.[3]

Ruskin's dream of return is, of course, at once metaphoric and literal. While it remains difficult to determine how thoroughly Ruskin believed in the efficacy of saving England through the actual erection of Gothic cathedrals, post offices, banks, and mechanics' institutes, it is clear that his belief in the power of architecture to shape individual and collective identity was unwavering, and that his contemporaries chose to read him quite literally. In the final decades of the nineteenth century, the English government and the nation's universities, corporations, and city councils, bowing their heads in Ruskin and Pugin's direction, embarked on a vast program of architectural construction. Not all the public buildings that were erected in the latter half of the nineteenth century were Gothic, but most of the major edifices constructed in England during these years were vaulted tributes to those lost Middle Ages that Ruskin and Pugin spent so much of their adult lives conjuring back into existence. Alfred Waterhouse's Manchester Town Hall (1868–77), Thomas Worthington's Albert Memorial (1862–67), Thomas Deane and Benjamin Woodward's University Museum in Oxford (1855–60), and G. E. Street's London Law Courts (1874–82) are only the most celebrated of these structures.[4] Across the surface of the nation, as the century drew to a close, the island's architects and governors were devoting England's public spaces to the redemptive return of the medieval past.

The late-Victorian triumph of Gothic was, however, most complete not in England but in India, in the cities, cantonments, and stations of the British Raj. The architects and engineers of the colony's Public Works Department had at their disposal not only the writings of Ruskin and Pugin but also such journals as the Camden's Society's *Ecclesiologist*, a periodical devoted to disseminating Pugin's Gothic principles, and the *Builder*, the leading architectural publication of the period, whose pages were filled with plans for Gothic cathedrals, Gothic post offices, Gothic law courts, and Gothic train stations. With the Gothic blueprint everywhere at hand it was perhaps inevitable that fragments of the subcontinent would be reconstructed as displaced and belated thirteenth-century Englands. When, in 1862, the energetic Sir Bartle Frere was appointed governor of Bombay and initiated an ambitious building program, this is precisely what happened. By 1880, a medievalist shadow had fallen over the Indian metropolis. Frere had given Bombay a Gothic law court, post office, public works building, secretariat, university library, university convention hall, market, police court, school of art, customs house, and yet more buildings. In the faintly bemused words of one historian of imperial architecture: "As a result, paradoxically, Britain's finest heritage of High Victorian Gothic architecture lies in Bombay."[5]

The reinvention of Bombay as a medieval English city clearly owed something to the ability of journals such as the *Ecclesiologist* and the *Builder* to define a regulated grammar of architectural style. But the boundless enthusiasm with which Frere and other English administrators embraced Gothic testifies to something more than a sensitivity to fashion. Charged with the difficult task of governing India in the uneasy years following the 1857 revolt, Frere and his fellows chose to expend vast sums on building projects because they believed what Ruskin had been telling his Kensington audience: that the identity of the empire's subjects was to a significant degree a product of the objects and structures which they beheld and inhabited. Ruskin had spent years informing England that there was a direct relationship between the arrangements of space and the contours of the personality. Frere and his brother officers understood that this implied, or more than implied, an analogous relationship between architecture and the arts of imperial rule. They identified architecture, as Ruskin had construed it, not merely as a symbol of empire but as an implement of imperial governance, and chose to believe that they could advance the work of disciplining their subordinates by re-forming the spaces of the colonial habitus. To a rank of men charged by Lord Macaulay with the task of producing a body of subjects "English in taste, in opinions, in morals, and in intellect" (*Selected Writings*, 249), it seemed that Ruskin and Pugin had provided a means of fulfilling that responsibility. In addition to following Macaulay's advice and teaching the natives of India a canon of English letters, the administrators of the empire would adhere to the Gothicists' directive and expose the subcontinent's inhabitants to England's "national" architecture.[6] Transported across the oceans, the Gothic cathedral would become what Macaulay had suggested the empire itself should be: a factory for the production of English identity.

This understanding of the subject-producing capacities of architecture received perhaps its fullest explication in a lecture titled "Architectural Art in India" delivered by the imperial architect T. Roger Smith to the Royal Society of Arts in February of 1878. In that address, as noted in the previous chapter, Smith argues that "the right thing in designing and executing our buildings is that they should be English."[7] In pursuing this theme, he lends to the "English" edifice an almost miraculous affect. Somehow, he suggests, the laying of stone in a particular way, the sloping of an arch along a specific line, the bounding of space according to a given design, will not only cow the Indian and cause him to behold the colonist "with respect and even with admiration," but will ensure that "the English collector remains British to the backbone in the heart of India" (281). As this final comment indicates, Smith was himself less concerned that the auratic spaces of imperial architecture would Anglicize the Indian than that they would preserve the colonist's essential identity.

That that identity shifts, in the course of Smith's sentence, from being English to being British is not insignificant. In lazily assuming an equivalence between the two terms, Smith's comments may represent little more than the common English practice of reducing Britishness to Englishness. But as I shall be suggesting in this chapter, his substitution of British for English reveals more than he may intend, for it allegorizes a process in which, as the administrators of the empire fought to defend *English* identity, they found themselves constructing a model of personhood that was as various as the terrains of the *British* Empire. In securing the Englishness of the colonists by ensuring that they remain British to the backbone, Smith and his fellows risked making Englishness analogous with Britishness (rather than the other way around), and in the process, as both the Victoria Terminus and Kipling's novel reveal, they thus recoded Englishness as a global and variegated way of being in the world. For the moment, however, let us honor Smith's apparent intention and allow him to assume that Britishness is little more than Englishness writ large. For even on that understanding an anxiety regarding the cultural identity of the paradigmatic colonist clearly pervades Smith's talk. "In the heart of India," his paper constantly implies, the English will cease to be English, and his address increasingly becomes a lecture on how to prevent this from happening.

Smith's prescription is evident. The English edifice, his talk asserts, will act as a sort of visual therapy to guard the colonist against the threat of identity loss. One becomes, or remains, English, Smith maintains, by observing, handling, entering, and brushing against English objects. Smith advises his auditors to remember that in occupying India,

> We have not sought to divest ourselves of our national habits, or manners, dress, or laws, even when convenience would have been consulted by so doing. The broadcloth of the civilian, and the gold lace and epaulettes of the soldier, are eminently unsuited to tropical climates, where the natives, when they dress at all, wear cotton or cambric. But it is because they are infinitely associated with Englishmen, as such, that custom has decreed the retention of these things. . . . Now, why should our architecture be an exception to this rule? We go to India, Europeans with pale faces, a strange tongue, and unfamiliar customs; and our position as the foreign governing race, and as a race which does not settle in the country, and intermarry with the natives, but which has its home far away over the seas and retains all its personal relations with that home, makes such a course of conduct reasonable—in fact, inevitable. (280)

The broadcloth and the epaulette emerge in this reminder as more than fabric. They are reproduced as objects invested, to borrow a phrase from Conrad, with "something unmistakably real."[8] They gesture beyond themselves to a chain of "infinite associations" with everyday life in England. Less sartorial than mnemonic artifacts, the broadcloth and the epaulette offer to render that "far away" England immanent, to return their wearers to the island across the seas, to communicate to the displaced colonists wearing them a "personal" and stabilizing "relation" with home. It is as such a fetish—or, in his preferred idiom, as such a "rallying point"—that Smith recommends English architecture to the servants of empire.

If, in following Smith's rhetoric, we have entered the provinces of commodity fetishism, we have not, however, left the courts of Ruskinism. For Ruskin and Smith read the cultural artifact as possessing a similar power. To view or to come into contact with an English object is not only to be made aware, or reminded, of England; it is, both men assert, to become at least provisionally or momentarily English. Gothic architecture, or the epaulette, is in this sense not merely a mnemonic device or an auratic cultural allegory, but a touchstone. Like the alchemist's rock such objects promise to transform the toucher into the touched. In less mystic terms—though, to be sure, something essentially mystic animates both Ruskin's and Smith's thinking—the architect's lecture does no more than confirm Ruskin's suggestion that we are to a large extent what we inhabit and view, and he makes of this insight a lesson in imperial rule. India, he announces, can be disciplined, Anglicized, and made safe for the English psyche through the disposition about the subcontinent of England's touchstone architecture.

Thirty years following Smith's lecture to the Society of Arts and half a century after Ruskin's Kensington address, this understanding of the disciplinary function of architecture had become one of the fundamental hypotheses of England's imperial epistemology. In a lead article of the September 1912 issue of the *Builder*, an anonymous author offered the following observations under the rubric "Imperialism and Architecture":

> Colonies and dependencies may be acquired by conquest, but their retention demands a higher cultivation as well as a superior military strength. Power without the civilizing influence of culture is ignorance ruling knowledge with a rod. . . . If knowledge and culture have been the necessary accompaniments of successful imperialism in the past, they are its essentials today. . . . The expression of imperial character through the medium of architecture is a policy which the Mother Country should encourage. Divergence from a course set by the parent which is unattributable to the inherent demands of climate and location means imperial disintegration. . . . If our imperialism is to be completely effective throughout the length and breadth of the Empire the Mother Country must see to it that her national character is expressed not only in the architecture of the cities she founds, but also in the public buildings of the cities she rules.[9]

This is largely, and recognizably, cant. But the status of such rhetoric as cant is remarkable. What, in Ruskin, had been novel reworkings of romantic thought have become, within fifty years, the stuff of cliché. The "strange discipline" that Ruskin learned from Wordsworth, the discipline of reading the auratic locale in order to be redeemed by it, is here represented as the basic common sense of imperial rule.

The great virtue of architecture, the writer implies, lies in its spectacular character. Like the uniform, it imprints a signature of Englishness onto the body of its inhabitant and the retina of its observer. The viewer, gazing on this massive articulation of English "style," is visually touched by what she or he sees, and in being so intimately touched begins the process of surrendering to the authority of the seen. The existence "of such an empire-pervading style throughout colonies, dependencies, and protectorates," the author insists, "will tend to annihilate distance and conduce to an imperial liberty, equality, and fraternity. Out of political it will create personal ties, and into closer relation will bring the ambitions of those whose destiny it is to excel" (346). If the ideologues of the French Revolution had claimed that their actions had the power to create a new order of man, the author of this essay attributes no less reformative a capacity to the spectacular works of imperial architecture. Gazing upon these stylized allegories of Englishness, the native, he believes, will inevitably begin to be restyled.

In the First Epistle of Saint John, the evangelist suggests that merely by looking upon the person of Christ, the observer will become like him.[10] The notion that architecture will at once pacify, charm, and Anglicize the colonial subject operates on an identical mimetic principle and in so doing refines the business of cultural policing—so that the labor of securing imperial hegemony becomes less a matter of winning the natives' hearts and minds than one of governing their eyes. As Bernard S. Cohn has illustrated, the sheer demographics of the imperial enterprise dictated that English colonial authorities, who were frequently outnumbered by a ratio of more than a thousand or even ten thousand to one, had to rely on more than the threat of direct force for the maintenance of their rule. This meant, as the author of "Imperialism and Architecture" suggests, that the English were regularly forced to rely on almost purely visual displays of their power to secure their hegemony.[11] The author of the essay emphasizes the importance of this contest for the control of colonial vision through a series of negative arguments when he comes to consider the cases of Canada and Australia where, in the one case, America is an excessively visible presence, and, in the other, photographic technology threatens to tempt the imperial subject to an act of cultural infidelity: "In Canada today there are but too evident tendencies to an appropriation of American ideals and methods of expression. . . . England as the hereditary exemplar is fast losing ground. . . . In Australia the remoteness of any such civilizing neighbours removes the danger of such an unnatural alliance; but even here we must remember that the eyes of the Australian are, by the spread of literature and the illuminations of the photographer, open to the architecture of the world" (346). Turning back, at last, to the city of Bombay, we can begin to see what motivated Governor Frere to expend such vast quantities of Her Majesty's coin on the construction of an armada of Gothic edifices. Confronted at virtually every corner by these immense and auratic allegories of Englishness, colonizer and colonized alike could experience the pleasures, or discomforts, of gazing upon a displaced England and, in so gazing, of being "done into English."[12]

This certainly is what Ruskin's arguments imply, and what T. Roger Smith, Governor Frere, and our anonymous author desired. According to our author, however, this is not at all the effect these buildings would have produced. Of Frere's prodigious labors the writer has only this sneering comment to make: "The recent erection of public buildings in Bombay in a pseudo-Indian-cum-English style is a distinctly retrograde step" (346). If we are to believe the *Builder's* editorialist, despite Frere's best intentions, something had clearly gone wrong. In order to understand what went wrong and to grasp what this implied for the imperial labors of cultural subject-fashioning, we must follow the writer's lead and determine what the colonial observer would actually have seen when looking upon these edifices.

WELCOME TO THE VICTORIA TERMINUS

Imperial discourse, like all discourses, refuses univocality. While Gothic was the idiom in which Governor Frere and the majority of India's colonial administrators chose to express the Englishness of imperial architecture, it was not the only style available to them. In 1912, when he was commissioned to design the imperial capital in New Delhi, Edwin Luytens fashioned a resolutely neoclassical city. Forty years ealier, when T. Roger Smith concluded his address to the Society of Arts, William Emerson, a fellow Anglo-Indian architect, rose to suggest that Smith's lecture was deeply misguided, that it was, in fact, imperative that the empire's architects build not English but Indian structures.[13] The Gothic palaces of Bombay, while largely representing a triumph for Smith and Ruskin in an Anglo-Indian battle of the styles, also represent a minor victory for Emerson and his followers. For upon close examination, Frere's buildings disclose themselves as at once resolutely English and occasionally, but recognizably, Indian. They reveal themselves, in a word, as hybrids.[14]

The most famous of the Gothic edifices in Bombay, indeed the most celebrated Gothic structure in India, is the Victoria Terminus Train Station. Closely modeled on Sir Gilbert Scott's St. Pancras Station in London, it appears at first glance to be the closest that the imperial traveler can come to encountering England in India. It is an immense building. Sweeping wings flank a domed central chamber crowned by intricately decorated rooflines. The groined vaults, the arches, the stonework, and the marble are perfectly

Gothic. Standing within the station's central hall, the visitor gazes up at a wooden heaven, rising above elaborately carved stone arches, and sparkling with gold stars. To enter the Victoria Terminus is, apparently, to come home to Ruskin's England. But if Victoria Terminus is England in India, and a space in which the Indian is made to be English, then this is an England that has been tropicalized. For staring down at the traveler from the ribs of the central vault, peering across from the grillworks of the windows, or resting negligently on the dome above, are the beasts and foliages of the subcontinent. Victoria Terminus is English Gothic, but it is an English Gothic that has been subjected to a creeping tropicalization. As an English work of art, the terminus announces that from now on to be "English" is also, however marginally, to be Indian. If, as its patrons had suggested, we are what we inhabit, handle, and gaze upon, then the colonial subject, observing this work of architecture, would acquire an Englishness that has been subtly estranged; an Englishness which, relative to that which Ruskin had in mind, is "almost the same, but not quite."[15] Smith, in beginning his address to the fellows of the Society of Arts, had announced that the prime object of English architecture in India must be to distinguish itself from an indigenous architecture which when "closely examined" indicates that "many different races have worked upon it. . . . [and exhibits] the traces of migrations, conquests, changes of style and other marks of difference" (278). Closely examined, the Victoria Terminus reveals that it has become what it was built to erase, that that imperial commitment to the production of the Same which it so massively symbolizes has been superinscribed by the "marks of difference."

It may be tempting to complete a reading of the Victoria Terminus at this moment, to conclude that in building his Gothic network, Governor Frere had erected a series of cultural reformatories which produced not English but hybrid identities. But a lingering question remains. If the details of the Victoria Terminus mark this as a hybrid and a hybridizing structure, how did those details come to decorate the station? Where did those trespassing plants and animals come from?

They came from the workshop of Mr. Lockwood Kipling, father of a more famous son.

Lockwood Kipling was one of the primary sponsors of an Indian Arts and Crafts movement that promoted Indian handiwork and design.[16] As professor of architectural sculpture at the Bombay School of Art, he had directed preparations for the "Oriental" details added to Victoria Terminus and the city's other Gothic edifices. It is, however, precisely the status of these objects as "details" that renders incomplete a reading of the terminus devoted to the celebration of tropicalization and hybridization. As Thomas Metcalf has discussed, catalogs of Indian design motifs had been available to Anglo-Indian architects and art scholars since Owen Jones had published his *Grammar of Ornament* in 1868, a work that was succeeded in 1890 by Swinton Jacob's six-volume *Jeypore Portfolio of Architectural Details*. Metcalf argues that these encyclopedias of detail catered to an English investment in the exotic picturesque. They exist, his argument suggests, as a paper bottle into which the Anglo-Indian could dip when the desire arose to splash an Oriental perfume onto the marble ligatures of the Raj. But as Sara Suleri has indicated, the English deployed the picturesque as something other than a cultural cologne. Instead, Suleri holds, the picturesque "becomes synonymous with a desire to transfix a dynamic cultural confrontation into a still life, converting a pictorial imperative into a gesture of self-protection that allows the colonial gaze a license to convert its ability not to see into studiously visual representations."[17] If the picturesque exists as such an idiom of bracketing and containment, then the detail announces itself as a means of exoticizing the empire's architectures and of freezing the subcontinent's most "foreign" acts of self-articulation in place. The *Portfolio* of Indian design emerges, then, as a textual museum, and the detail as little more than a collectible. Crouching beneath or above the Victoria Terminus's Gothic heaven, Kipling's tropical plants and animals appear now to have been brushed with the empire's embalming ointments. They are, the reader of this imperial artifact realizes, not simply the hybridizing symbols of imperial failure, but the casual displays of a power negligently confident of its ability to capture and tame.

It is less important that the reader privilege one of these interpretations of the detail over the other than that we allow ourselves to incline to both interpretations. For in their manifestation as disciplinary *and* antidisciplinary objects, the tropical details that ornament the Victoria Terminus code the Gothic railway station as a deeply schizophrenic artifact and define a space of interpretive ambivalence in the hermeneutics of imperialism. On final inspection, the terminus seems to be at once the factory of Englishness that John Ruskin, T. Roger Smith, and Governor Frere intended it to be, *and* to be a monument to the imperial production of hybrid identities, *and* to be a space in which the colonial state reveals its capacity to collect and exhibit alterity. The same object produces all of these readings—not in sequence, but simultaneously. Our dilemma, as readers, lies in attending to that simultaneity. For in acknowledging this concert of interpretations, we do more than admit to a critical indecisiveness. Like the colonial subject, we hazard becoming what we have seen. Confronted by the bewildering facade of the Victoria Terminus, the postimperial readers of this edifice run the risk of surrendering to its baleful affect, and of assuming the schizophrenia that we had thought we only gazed upon.

The temptation to resist this derangement is strong. It seems better to assert mastery over this artifact, to identify it either as an apparatus of state discipline or as a hybridized and subverted architecture. But this temptation should be resisted. For it is, ultimately, the character of such overdetermined artifacts as the Victoria Terminus to produce not stable meanings but crises of reading. The confusions that such objects both locate and produce are their most salient feature. That confusion is, finally, the one thing that typifies the narratives of empire and Englishness. If this confusion has no absolute moment of origin, then it can at least be identified in a turn-of-the-century imperialism increasingly devoted to the labor of fabricating English identity. But if we wish to understand the confusions that haunt this imperial project of subject-fashioning, then we would be well served by turning from the Victoria Terminus to a text that brings together the discourses of cultural discipline, identity production, hybridity, and entrapment.

Sahibization

To enter Kipling's *Kim* is, in some ways, not to depart but to reenter the Victoria Terminus. Here, once again, the reader discovers a mass of exquisite Oriental detail, a virtual museum of exotic set pieces. Behind this wealth of ornament squats a vast and intricately designed imperial architecture, a sprawling structure devoted less to commerce than to discipline, a cultural reformatory disguising itself as a wonder house. Written over the whole is a brooding nervousness regarding identity, a yearning for the accomplishment of Englishness, and, at the same time, a perverse delight in the virtuoso display of alterity. Above all, in traveling with Kim through Kipling's India, we reencounter a colonial fascination with control advertising itself as a fondness for waywardness.

Kipling's recognition of the tendency of the imperial state to mask its disciplinary intentions allows him to produce a work that, like the Bombay railway station, plays on the advantages and pleasures which the police derive from going "under cover." But while the pure delights of subterfuge may account for much of the popular success of the novel, those readers who have struggled to identify *Kim's* place in the discursive history of English imperialism have frequently found themselves perplexed by the appearance of Kipling's police in the costumes of the picaresque. Edmund Wilson, in his reading of *Kim* in *The Wound and the Bow*, chooses to acknowledge and then to shrug off this interpretive dilemma: "What the reader tends to expect is that Kim will come eventually to realize that he is delivering into bondage to the British invaders those whom he has always considered his own people, and that a struggle between allegiances will result. . . . We have been shown two entirely different worlds existing side by side, with neither really understanding the other, and we have watched the oscillations of Kim, as he passes to and fro between them. But the parallel lines never meet; the alternating attractions felt by Kim never give rise to a true struggle."[18] This analysis, which manages to recognize Kim's dual loyalties to an unpoliced, nomadic exoticism and to a regulatory institution of colonial rule, while blithely suggesting that these multiple fidelities occasion no narrative distress, has raised no small number of critical eyebrows. Noel Annan responds to Wilson by arguing that Kipling represents no conflict of loyalties, because no such conflict could exist. Kim's burgeoning career as a surveillance officer of the colonial state does not mock his on-the-road life, Annan insists, precisely because the colonial police, far from threatening Indian waywardness, exist to preserve the meanderings of subcontinental culture.[19]

While Annan seems overwilling to endorse this apology for imperialism—which is, in effect, the museological argument of empire, the argument that England serves India as the curator serves the collection—this pastoralist interpretation of the Raj certainly emerges as *one* of Kipling's founding attitudes in the writing of *Kim*. From the very first page of the novel, when we discover Kim playing outside the Lahore Wonder House (an institution that Lockwood Kipling at one time curated), Kipling exposes the reader to a vision of the colonial state benevolently inventing itself as India's cultural guardian. Several pages later, as Kim exits the imperial museum with the lama he has just met, the little friend of all the world reveals that he has learned the Wonder House's lesson. Like the curator who has guided him through the museum's magical space, he will fulfill his imperial responsibility to catalog and collect: "This man [the lama] was entirely new to all his experience, and he meant to investigate further, precisely as he would have investigated a new building or a strange festival in the Lahore city. The lama was his trove, and he purposed to take possession."[20]

Edward Said, responding to such moments and others in which Kipling has the natives of India explicitly endorse the pastoral care of the colonial state, has joined in the criticism of Wilson's reading: "So far is Kipling from showing two worlds in conflict, as Edmund Wilson would have it, that he has studiously given us only one, and eliminated any chance of conflict altogether."[21] Said's impatience with Wilson, which is also a frustration with Kipling, is emblematic of a recent critical tendency to resolve the difficulties of reading *Kim* by discovering it to be devoted solely to the strategies of imperial control. Wilson's parallel lines, in these readings, not only fail to come together; they simply fail to exist—and Kipling's India is anatomized as a bleak Foucauldian world in which surveillance and discipline are everywhere, and always triumphing. As Thomas Richards has it, in one of the most brilliant and also one of the grimmest of such analyses, "In this novel it always turns out that, so far as the state is concerned, there is no such thing as a nonconducting medium; everyone, and everything, consciously or unconsciously, forms part of the state's internal lines of communication."[22]

While Richards's reading is frequently superb, it is also deeply problematic. In privileging the disciplinary to the exclusion of all else, Richards operates on a fairly impoverished theory of imperial intentionality. To read *Kim* as a novel that represents no conflict between the police and the partisans of the picaresque—or, according to the idiom that Richards borrows from Deleuze and Guattari, which depicts the nomad as always already in the service of the state—is to read the plot of imperial desire as a plot of eternal accomplishment. Richards tends to assume no slippage between what the colonial state wishes and what it achieves, and thus represents imperialism as a sort of an-entropic desiring machine. Ironically, this puts him in the position of offering the Raj homage—not as an admirer, but as a reluctant witness to an omniscient, infallible, godlike power.

But the Raj was not a perfectly dispersed system of disciplines. However brutal, however powerful, the colonial state was frequently bewildered. Even its supermen, like that master of spies Colonel Creighton, nodded. To argue otherwise is to refuse the difficulty of the narratives and artifacts of empire, to choose critical mastery over critical bewilderment. If the Victoria Terminus has taught us that at times we must incline to bewilderment, then *Kim* contains the same lesson. For the novel, like the Bombay railway station, defines a delirious space where the lines of the disciplinary and the insubordinate meet—a space occupied, once again, by the subject of an imperial project of identity formation—a space occupied by Kim. The difficulty of *Kim*, and the reason, perhaps, that critics such as Richards fail to see anything in it but the triumphs of imperial discipline, attaches to Kipling's decision to show us the state smugly victorious and sublimely confused in reference to the same thing: the reformed, Anglicized, sahibized identity of Kim. "Who is Kim? Who is Kim?" the narrative continues to wonder for ages after Kim has become, quite literally, the child of the colonial state. This ceaselessly repeated query invokes the barely hidden anxiety of that vast project of imperial adoption dramatized in Kipling's narrative. What, Kipling wonders on behalf of his sleepless nation, has England done in ushering this wild child into the house? "Who is Kim?" the text relentlessly worries, and with that question breathes life into a more banal iteration of colonial and parental dread: "And can he be controlled?" The problem with Kim, of course, is that the more Creighton and his cohorts attempt to reform his identity, the more confused it becomes; and the more schizophrenic Kim grows, the more he threatens that disciplinary apparatus whose perfect agent he is made to be. If *Kim*, like the Victoria Terminus, frequently appears to be little more than an exhibition of the great work of imperial subject-fashioning, then the lesson of this exhibition seems rather clear: the trouble with imperialism, as Gayatri Spivak has observed, is that it "messes with identity."[23]

Kipling commences his meditation on the instabilities of imperial identity in the opening two paragraphs of the novel, which, though lengthy, are worth citing almost in full:

> He sat in defiance of municipal orders, astride the gun Zam-Zammah on her brick platform opposite the old Ajain-Gher—the Wonder House, as the natives call the Lahore Museum. Who hold Zam-Zammah, that "fire-breathing dragon," hold the Punjab, for the great green-bronze piece is always first of the conqueror's loot.

There was some justification for Kim—he had kicked Lala Dinanath's boy off the trunnions—since the English held the Punjab and Kim was English. Though he was burned black as any native; though he spoke the vernacular by preference, and his mother-tongue in a clipped uncertain sing-song; though he consorted on terms of perfect equality with the small boys of the bazaar; Kim was white—a poor white of the very poorest. The half-caste woman who looked after him (she smoked opium, and pretended to keep a second-hand furniture shop by the square where the cheap cabs wait) told the missionaries that she was Kim's mother's sister; but his mother had been nursemaid in a colonel's family and had married Kimball O'Hara, a young colour sergeant of of the Mavericks, an Irish regiment. He afterward took a post on the Sind, Punjab, and Delhi Railway, and his Regiment went home without him. . . . His estate at death consisted of three papers—one he called his "ne varietur" because those words were written below his signature thereon, and another his "clearance certificate". The third was Kim's birth-certificate. Those things, he was used to say, in his glorious opium hours, would yet make little Kimball a man. (49–50)

These paragraphs, which launch Kim on his course of adventure by tacking ever further back into his prehistory, can be read as a tortuously qualified gloss on the solitary opening word: "He." In so agonistically approaching that "he," the text exposes the reader to the ardors of imperial introduction. The novel suffers the indignity of not knowing how to introduce its subject, not because Kipling has regarded Kim offhandedly, but because, however closely he is studied, Kim evades classification. "He" cannot be readily introduced because, as Kipling discovers in the very act of presenting Kim to us, "he" is yet unknown. For the remainder of the text, Kipling will struggle simply to provide Kim with a name. "Little friend of all the world," "Beloved," "R17" are all offered as adequate names for a character who, with each passing moment, grows more pseudonymous. But none of these locutions will answer the question that the narrative, from its opening moments, never ceases to ask: "Who is Kim?"

Confronted, for the first time, with the uncertainty of Kim, Kipling offers the reader not a name but a genealogy and a list. The logic of the list, which begins by asserting Kim's Englishness, is curious. It works first by telling us that to be English is to exercise imperial dominion, and that Kim is English. Then it informs us of the ways in which Kim—by virtue of his blackness, his selection of languages, and his choice of companions—fails to be English. Finally it reaffirms that Kim is, nevertheless, what he has first been known to be. But along the way, that first thing has disappeared. Kipling now affirms Kim to be not English but white. Englishness, the first casualty of Kim's absentminded war on identity, has momentarily vanished as a category of being. If, as I have suggested, Kipling's text can be read as a dramatization of the labors of imperial subject formation, then it can also be read as an extended response to the shock of this loss. The business of reforming Kim, Kipling belatedly discovers, has become the labor not simply of rendering this child serviceable to the state, but of recovering Englishness for imperialism, of confirming T. Roger Smith's dream that the empire be a place where one can be simultaneously English and British "to the backbone." As Smith's loose syntax and Kipling's text ultimately indicate, however, that may not be possible. Kipling discovers that in desiring Englishness, the imperial state effectively exiles its object of desire from its grammars of rule as it surrenders itself to a logic of substitution that replaces Englishness with Britishness and Britishness with a question mark. "Who is Kim?"

In the opening paragraphs of the novel, Kim is, finally, little more than a body, a racial essence around which Kipling can begin the work of reconstructing Kim's English identity. To assure the reader that that body is, in fact, white, the narrator obsessively traces Kim's genealogy. That plotting of genetic inheritances must, unfortunately, detour through the complicating presence of a half-caste mother and a wastrel Irish father. Kipling, however, hastily dismisses the woman's claim over Kim and, after pausing over the corpse of the Irishman, delivers us at last to the presence of a birth certificate, a document that promises to erase any lingering willingness we might have to read India not as a place in which the English cease to be, but as a place in which the English cease to be white. From this moment, the birth certificate, which Kim hangs as a fetish around his neck, will act less as a register of his existence than as the parent of his being. Its paper, inks, and official imprints will make a man of him and, by providing Kim with a fixed, archival genealogy, will apparently allow Kipling to redeem Englishness from the confusions of empire. The birth certificate, as its eventual reader Mr. Bennett indicates, confirms that Kim "is certainly white" (134). This, finally, is the only thing that Kipling can affirm in his extended, nervous introduction of Kim. Yet, apparently, it is enough. For from the fact of his whiteness, Kipling will attempt to argue backward through the strange logic of his initial list to reassert not precisely that Kim is English but, almost as valuably, that Kim is, or can be made into, a sahib. Sahibness emerges, then, as the middle step in the passage from whiteness back to Englishness. If Kim is white, Kipling's argument goes, then he can be turned into a sahib; and if he is turned into a sahib, then he can be made into an Englishman; and if he is done into English, then the text can at last answer the question with which it has been tormenting itself. "Who is Kim?" Kipling may ask one last time. "English," he will now be allowed to respond, "to the backbone."

The invention of Kim as a sahib begins at that moment in which Mr. Bennett and Father Victor read his birth certificate and deduce that this piece of writing, and not Kim's blackened skin or his vernacular discourse, encodes the true text of his identity. As the two divines discuss their queer find, the lama, who is present at this fateful meeting, asks his young disciple what the chaplains intend to do with him. "Make me a Sahib," Kim responds, and then slyly adds, "so they think. The day after tomorrow I return" (141). The latter comment escapes the clerics' notice—if not Kipling's—and they resolve to claim Kim for his father's regiment and begin his reeducation. Father Victor arranges for Kim to be sent to St. Xavier's, a boarding school in Lucknow, and here his sahibization begins in earnest.

Kipling quite openly represents the Gothic walls of St. Xavier's as a pedagogical prison house (the colonial school on which St. Xavier's is based was, predictably, Gothic in design). As Kim enters the school, Kipling curtly, though a little mournfully, notes, "The Gates of Learning shut with a clang" (171). The ambiguity of this formulation is decidedly odd, for it seems to indicate that Kipling at least partially regrets the fate to which he has assigned his character. One might think that Kipling, having chosen not to shirk his duty to the colonial state, now contemplates the imminent lobotomization of Kim with something like sorrow. In allowing himself that sorrow, however, Kipling forgets Kim's word of reassurance to the lama. Like the two clerics, he has now convinced himself that Kim can be reformed. Looking on the imposing Gothic walls of St. Xavier's, he sees only an inexorable disciplinary power and tacitly urges the reader both to note his compassion and to confirm that his decision to incarcerate Kim represents grim necessity. Utterly forgotten are Kim's whispered words of mockery: "Remember, I can change swiftly. It will all be as it was" (139).

In the chapters that follow the clanging of St. Xavier's gates, Kim, while apparently submitting for months at a time to the pedagogic reconstruction of his personality, again and again escapes the school. As he notes this serial delinquency, Kipling hunts, a trifle desperately, for some better regimen of reform than a mere exposure to Gothic architecture and the rote drilling of the classics. Kipling now recognizes that to prevent Kim from making sahibness— or, more ominously, Englishness—just another costume which he can slip into and out of, Kim must somehow be persuaded to consent to his reinvention. It is here, of course, that Kipling turns to cartography, a science of spatial policing whose imperial inflection as a program of surreptitious wandering seems designed to appeal to Kim's fondness for intrigue and his innate surveying eye. But before Kipling captures Kim for, and by, cartography, he contrives to convince the little friend of all the world of the merits of orderliness by inverting a venerable parental stratagem. He enlists Lurgan Sahib, one of Colonel Creighton's many subordinates, to teach Kim the fear of the dark.

In one of the most ponderously plotted sections of the text, capped by one of its weirdest scenes, Kipling emblematizes St. Xavier's failure to sahibize Kim as the school's failure to convince him of the value of arithmetic. Having escaped yet again from the school, Kim dons one of his many disguises and joins the camp of Mahbub Ali, a Muslim horse trader and espionage operative. Lying at night among Mahbub's followers, Kim surrenders to the ironizing pleasures of an antimathematical bliss: "Kim was happy. Change of scene, service, and surroundings were the breath of his little nostrils, and thinking of the neat white cots of St. Xavier's all arow under the punkah gave him joy as keen as the repetition of the multiplication table in English" (185). By the middle of the following chapter, Kim has completely revised his estimate of systematized mathematics.

Between the initial and the revised opinion, he has been handed over to Lurgan Sahib—an Orientalized Englishman redolent of "a whiff of musk, a puff of sandal wood, and a breath of sickly jessamine-oil"—to have his memory trained. Before Lurgan begins Kim's mnemotechnic instruction, he submits his young guest to an ordeal. Lurgan smashes a jar on the floor of his house and has Kim inspect its fragments:

> Lurgan Sahib laid one hand gently on the nape of his neck, stroked it twice or thrice, and whispered: "Look! It shall come to life again, piece by piece". . . . To save his life, Kim could not have turned his head. The light touch held him as in a vice, and his blood tingled pleasantly through him. There was one large piece of the jar where there had been three, and above them the shadowy outline of the entire vessel. He could see the veranda through it, but it was thickening and darkening with each beat of his pulse. . . . So far Kim had been thinking in Hindi, but a tremor came on him, and with an effort like that of a swimmer before sharks, who hurls himself out of the water, his mind leaped up from a darkness that was swallowing it and took refuge in—the multiplication table in English! (201–2)

There is about this resolution, which comes so soon after the sole earlier mention of the multiplication table, a clumsiness atypical of Kipling, a clumsiness that reveals something of the author's desperation. The novel descends at the close of this overtly bizarre moment into the embarrassments of the didactic. Kipling holds out Lurgan, exotically clad in the fabrics and mysteries of the East, as an ominous symbol of Kim's unrepentant future—much as Conrad holds out Kurtz to Marlow. In case Lurgan's cloying perfumes are not warning enough, Kipling spices the air with the musky hints of pederasty—the waiflike Hindu boy who lives with Lurgan deports himself as something beween a son and lover—and proceeds to inform the wayward Kim that he risks becoming, like Lurgan, a pedlar in exoticism, a "monstrous hybridism" (288), a cultural transvestite. Kim responds unambiguously to this portrait of Englishness deformed, which owes as much to the pornographic as to the idioms of going native. Confronted with a now terrifying Orientalism, a swallowing darkness, he abandons Hindi and rescues himself with the multiplication table in English. St. Xavier's, apparently, has triumphed at last. Kipling has cultivated in Kim a dread of alterity. Henceforth, wherever Kim goes, he will carry the multiplication table with him as an allegory of St. Xavier's and a saving talisman of sahibness.

But if Kipling is to have Kim truly submit to the regulation of his identity, then he must have Kim learn a reason other than fear to devote himself to the imperial virtues of order, system, and number. And here, as the plot of Kim's sahibization becomes a plot of his mathematization, the narrative of Kim's life joins the narrative of imperial cartography. Kim, who must be not only numbered but rendered self-enumerating, can be redeemed for orderliness, Kipling discovers, by his enlistment in the mathematization of the subcontinent. Kim becomes an imperial cartographer, and his taste for wandering can thus be both indulged and rendered serviceable. For wherever he goes, he will at once extend the quadrant of colonial control and accelerate his own transformation into an imperial adding and measuring machine.

The Survey of India

The mapping of the subcontinent, officially known as the Survey of India and colloquially referred to as the "Great Game," was an immense, protracted, and varied task. The survey began in 1767, when Lord Clive appointed James Rennell surveyor general of Bengal, and continued without interruption until India's independence in 1947. In the earliest years of the survey, English cartographers concentrated on plotting serviceable roads, productive land, hill forts, and remarkable natural features. In 1806, William Lambton, armed with a theodolite, began the work of triangulating the entire subcontinent and reducing the surface of India to a comprehensive and rigorously accurate chart. In 1865, Thomas Montgomerie addressed the survey's most intractable problem: that of getting mapmakers into the forbidden territory of Tibet. Montgomerie alighted on the solution of training Indians in the use of the compass and sextant, disguising them as pilgrims, equipping them with an array of hidden instruments—including 100- rather than 108-bead rosaries with which they could count off their paces—and sending them across the border to advance the work of the survey.[24] It is among this group of costumed cartographers that Kipling places Kim.

In joining Kim to this band of wandering mapmakers, Kipling identifies the problem of refashioning Kim's identity with the dilemma of India's Montgomerie-era cartographers. The mapping of India, as Thomas Richards has demonstrated in the most intriguing sections of his essay on *Kim*, was a vital element in the English attempt to control the empire less by occupying it than by knowing it, classifying it, and rendering it visible. Faced with possession of imperial territories too vast to be directly and continuously controlled, the English state had little choice but to exercise its power in the production of knowledge. That that knowledge could not always be retranslated into power was, if not irrelevant, frequently ignored. The accumulation of information in what Richards terms an "imperial archive" created the illusion of control for an imperial state incessantly dreaming the nervous dream of its own demise. Within that archive, the map occupies a position of privilege. Its fiction remains the one most seductive to the imperial state: the fiction of fixity, of ordered, visible, and bounded space. Kipling depicts Colonel Creighton, the Montgomerie-inspired figure of his novel, as a devotee of that fable. At once the director of the survey and the chief of Indian intelligence, Creighton understands that the security of the colonial state depends on his ability to render visible and to map the territory England purports to possess.

Creighton must, however, confront a vexing imperial dilemma. In order to chart—and so imaginatively discipline—the biggest blank on the subcontinental map, the cross-border territory of Tibet, he has to rely on a small band of costumed wanderers, a tribe of nomads whose activities seem to subvert the interests of imperial cartography. The object of the survey, as Creighton cannot fail to understand, was not the production of knowledge in a pure, disinterested state but the production of an ordered, demarcated, and fixed terrain. That object encompasses the policing of movement. It implies, in fact, the absence of movement. Maps represent roads, but not travelers; railways, but not passengers. More significant, maps adore boundaries, and the argument of the boundary is the argument of territorial fixity. Indeed, the promise of the survey is to fix India not only as a governed territory in space but as a permanent possession in time. The wanderings, displacements, and spatial uncertainties of nomadism seem, then, to articulate a direct threat to the spatial and temporal permanencies of cartography, to be the surplus that the map not only cannot represent but must repress. As Richards suggests, Creighton's genius lies in his recognition that the opposition between the nomad and the cartographer can be dissolved, that cartography depends in the moment of its production, if not in the moment of its consumption, on the wandering, exploratory movement of the surveyor. If the nomad could be induced to produce a record of his wanderings, then the colonial state, Creighton recognizes, could harness the nomad to the policing of movement and the ordering of space.

Creighton's value to Kipling resides in the neatness with which, in solving this problem of imperial cartography, he simultaneously solves the author's problem with Kim. In discovering a vocation in which waywardness ceaselessly converts itself into an act of policing, and in which the wanderer continuously exchanges identity with the theodolite, he introduces Kim's anxious parent and biographer to a career in which this most nettlesome of children can do the state some service. Recognizing this, Kipling hands Kim over to Creighton with almost unseemly—but understandable—haste. But the value of this gift is ambiguous. For while Kim appears to be the perfect child for the marriage Creighton has fashioned between cartography and nomadism, he also represents a constant danger to Creighton's system. So culturally fluent that he can slip with ease into the unmapped spaces of Tibet disguised as a lama's acolyte, yet so nomadically fluid that he perpetually threatens to slip loose from Creighton's control, Kim constantly promises to embrace wandering as an end in itself, to become the very embodiment of a principle of uncertain movement that the colonial state exists to exterminate.

The importance of this imperial urge to extinguish the nomadic cannot be overestimated. Kipling's text hinges on it. If we follow Edward Said and Thomas Richards and read the novel as a minor specimen of the tragic, then we have no choice but to conclude that in tutoring Kim, and in teaching him to embrace the disciplinary imperatives of the Great Game, Creighton erases the little friend of all the world—until at last he exists as nothing other than a code name. Kipling, in directing the reader to construe the text as a rewriting of *Othello*, offers his support for this interpretation. According to the author, we are to identify Kim, like the Moor, as a character who has "done the state some service," and who completes that service by acceding to his self-annihilation. For this reading to succeed, we must regret Kim's fate; we must join Kipling in mourning what becomes of the little friend. This is why Kipling labors so diligently to elicit our sympathy for Kim. For that sympathy, or outrage, emerges as the condition of the state's triumph over Kim. As we curse Kim's disappearance, and his resurrection as the zombielike R17, we affirm that Kim, like India, has indeed been enumerated, and that the colonial state has at long last succeeded in its deadly work of subject-fashioning.

By identifying such a mournful reading of the novel as the only available reading of the text, however, we ignore the profound fragility of Colonel Creighton's system, deny the indebtedness of his police to the trespassive, and abandon those textual moments in which the subcontinent refuses to be mapped and Kim declines to be a sahib. A less partial reading of the text demands our recognition that, like the Victoria Terminus, Kim's sahibized identity resists closure, persistently indicates that "many different races have worked upon it. . . . [and exhibits] the traces of migrations, conquests, changes of style and other marks of difference" (T. Roger Smith, "Architectural Art in India," 278), and our admission that Colonel Creighton's map of India suffers a similar scoring. When closely examined, the artifacts of imperial cartography that Creighton's agents have produced disclose themselves as allegories of imperial Gothic.[25] Pretending to imprint onto paper, rather than marble, the signature of a confidently panoptic colonial state, these maps again write the text of the Raj's hybridization. They are the products of a system of rule that can sustain its fantasies of ubiquitous surveillance only by enlisting, or even inventing, a body of wandering, nativized, fifth columnists. To produce its disciplinary maps of the subcontinent, and so ensure that India remains English, the colonial state finds that it must not only consent to but cultivate its own tropicalization. In contributing to the Anglicization of India, Colonel Creighton finds himself in the odd position of Orientalizing England.

Creighton's embarrassment is not limited to the scandal of the Raj's tropicalization. Not only are his maps contaminated by the marks of difference; they are, at crucial points, blank. The cartographic model of imperial rule establishes a simple equivalence between power and knowledge. To govern India, Creighton suggests, is to know the subcontinent, a formula justifying that perilous dabbling in ethnography which threatens always to become the act of going native. Creighton holds to the conceit that he and his white subordinates can costume themselves in the fabrics of India while remaining resolutely English—an act that Ruskin would have told him was impossible. His gambit depends not only on his, and Kim's, ability to remain unpolluted by that India they are so constantly touching, but, more obviously, on the perpetual production of knowledge. To fail to know is to have risked the loss of Englishness and to have nothing to show for this gamble, to surrender both identity and rule. As Kipling admits, Creighton and his cohorts occasionally fail in this fundamental responsibility.

In the opening chapter of the text, as the curator of the Lahore Museum concludes his tour of the Wonder House, he opens "a mighty map" and shows it to the lama. For all the courtesy that the curator has heretofore shown the holy man, this primal scene of imperial instruction unfolds itself as an act of complacent arrogance, as less a sharing of information than an unveiling of England's ability to know the subcontinent, to order India's spaces, and to render them visible to its own inhabitants. Gesturing with his pencil, the curator draws the lama's eye "from point to point": "Here was Kapilavastu, here the Middle Kingdom, and here Mahabodhi, the Mecca of Bhuddhism; and here was Kusinagara, sad place of the Holy One's death." Gazing at this awesome artifact of imperial power, the humbled lama responds as his pedagogue might have expected: "The old man bowed his head over the sheets in silence for a while, and the Curator lit another pipe" (57). If Kipling's text was solely an anatomy of imperial discipline, the scene would end here; but it is not, and the scene does not. Moments later, after explaining his quest for the River of the Arrow, the lama returns the curator's attention to the map:

> The lama drew a long breath. "Where is that River? Fountain of Wisdom, where fell the arrow?"
>
> "Alas, my brother, I do not know," said the Curator.
>
> "Nay, if it please thee to forget—the one thing only that thou hast not told me. Surely thou must know? See, I am an old man! I ask with my head between my feet, O Fountain of Wisdom. We *know* He drew the bow! We *know* the arrow fell! We *know* the stream gushed! Where, then, is the River? My dream told me to find it. So I came. I am here. But where is the River?"
>
> "If I knew think you not I would cry it aloud?"
>
> "By it one attains freedom from the Wheel of Things," the lama went on, unheeding. "The River of the Arrow! Think again! Some little stream, maybe—dried in the heats? But the Holy One would never so cheat an old man."

"I do not know. I do not know."

The lama brought his thousand-wrinkled face once more a handsbreadth from the Englishman's. "I see thou dost not know. Not being of the Law, the matter is hid from thee." (57–58)

The enduring, almost uncanny, humility of the lama makes this an exchange that can be easily misread; for in it the lama, however briefly, translates the rhetoric of humility into an idiom of civil insubordination and sly mockery. Bending his head to his feet, addressing the curator as that fountain of wisdom which he has represented himself to be, investing his discourse with a tone of urgent supplication, the lama plays the child to this mighty representative of the Raj, repeating his "Where, where?" until he drives the curator to confess his own inadequacy. The curator, in fact, admits to more than ignorance. He acknowledges that the empire has founded itself on a bordered epistemology and confronts the limit of colonial knowledge. In so doing, he, along with the reader, becomes aware of the existence of the unmapped and the unmappable within the cartography of imperialism. At the close of this brief exchange, the curator is a shattered man, trapped within the agony of mouthing over and again those words that the English in India could not afford to utter: "I do not know. I do not know."

The curator is not the only figure so mocked in Kipling's narrative, nor the only individual whose faith in the power of the colonial state breaks. Kipling, who has labored so diligently to convince the reader that he can redeem the tragedy of Kim's annihilation through the victories of Englishness and the state, finds himself similarly mocked and disappointed. At the last he discovers that Colonel Creighton will sacrifice Kim's Englishness to the imperatives of imperial rule, and that India, governed as Creighton and his allies see fit to govern it, simply is not a place in which one can remain unalterably English to the backbone. His narrative emerges, then, as no less tragic; but what it finally represents as tragic is not the ransom paid for the recovery of Kim's Englishness but the betrayal of Englishness by the officers of the Raj.

Throughout the greater part of the text, we have been led to believe that Creighton, like Father Victor, Mr. Bennett, and Kipling himself, remains committed to Kim's sahibization, that, indeed, Kim's sahibization not only is consistent with Creighton's disciplining of India but will emerge as an offshoot of the colonel's policing labors. It is therefore something of a surprise to discover, fairly late in the novel, that Creighton has little interest in either Kim's sahibness or his Englishness. On yet another of those occasions on which he has made his break from St. Xavier's, Kim falls into the hands of Hurree Babu, another of Creighton's operatives. Hurree, rather than returning Kim to school, equips the boy with an array of passwords, undercover gimmicks, and disguises and sets Kim loose to wander, concluding his instructions to the astonished orphan with these rather startling words: "This half year . . . is to make you de-Englishized, you see" (232). In the paragraphs that immediately

follow this pronouncement, Kim, instead of reveling in this unexpected liberation, contemplates the implication of Hurree's words with something like
horror:

> "Now I am alone—all alone," he thought. "In all India is no-one so alone as I . . .
> I, Kim."
> A very few white people, but many Asiatics, can throw themselves into amaze-
> ment as it were by repeating their own name over and over again to themselves,
> letting the minds go free upon a speculation as to what is called personal identity.
> When one grows older, the power usually departs, but while it lasts it may de-
> scend upon a man at any moment.
> "Who is Kim—Kim—Kim?"
> He squatted in a corner of the clanging waiting-room, rapt from all other
> thoughts; hands folded in lap, and pupils contracted to pin-points. In a minute—
> in another half second—he felt he would arrive at the solution of the tremendous
> puzzle; but here, as always happens, his mind dropped away from those heights
> with a rush of a wounded bird, and passing his hand before his eyes, he shook his
> head. (233–34)

Kim's bewildered shock before the sudden sublimity of his identity should not
entirely surprise us. He has, once again, been abandoned—not by another
adoptive parent but by a narrative of belonging. However much Kim has re-
belled against St. Xavier's, he has come to understand the benefits of his reinvention as a white and a sahib. To be "de-Englishized" is, before all else, to be
expelled from a history that he thought he had been invited to join. Kim, a
more subtle reader of the confusions of empire than most of the adults who
surround him, decodes Hurree's words as an invitation to cultural loneliness.
That loneliness, he understands, is the sole reward for the freakishness that
Colonel Creighton, through Hurree, has offered him. Even Kipling, regarding
Kim in this critical moment, cannot avoid identifying him as something of a
monster: a putatively white but performatively Asiatic hybrid, cognitively
trapped in that maze where mythical monsters literally dwell. Kim translates
this loneliness and freakishness back into that question which we—and he,
and Kipling—had thought was already answered in favor of his sahibization.
"Who is Kim?" he demands of himself again, only to discover himself as a
dizzying and unnameable excess.

   That excess, consonant with what Kipling will later call "the monstrous
hybridism of East and West" (288), not only *produces* a profound sense of
cultural bewilderment and estrangement; it is *produced*, and, crucially, it is
produced by the colonial state. As Kim meets himself in this late episode, he
encounters a self that has been manufactured by the officers of the empire as
a multiple personality, a self that has at once been elaborately sahibized and
meticulously de-Englishized. The immediate reason for this is obvious
enough: Creighton cannot afford to have Kim move too far from those worlds

he must eventually infiltrate. Alternatively put, Creighton's decision to re-Orientalize Kim reflects his decision to guarantee English rule in India through the pursuit of knowledge rather than the cultivation of Englishness. If Kim, on Creighton's behalf, is ever to chart that unmapped space which the lama has uncovered in the cartography of empire, then, Creighton recognizes, he must be taught, not precisely to sacrifice his incipient Englishness, but to make it no more than one among a series of cultural costumes. However pragmatic this decision looks to Colonel Creighton, Kipling can view it as nothing but disastrous. For it implies that the empire, advertised as a factory for the production of English identity, can sustain itself only through a commitment to tropicalization, that the immense project of imperial subject-fashioning which Kipling has at once been describing and extolling can succeed only by producing individuals who are stupefied, hybridized, and schizophrenic. If the Raj is a place that must remain British to the backbone, then, Kipling discovers in the shock of this moment, it will remain British only by subjecting the English to a rigorous regimen of de-Englishization.[26]

CRITICAL DELIRIUM

With these scandals, and Kim's collapse before the excess of his Anglo-Indian identity, we have returned to that condition of bewilderment which, I have suggested, haunts the labors, artifacts, and *readings* of imperialism. What, finally, are we to make of Kipling's text? At every turn it seems, perversely, to undo itself, to inscribe itself now as a narrative of the accomplishment of Englishness, now as a document of England's hybridization; here as a plot of entrapment, there as a hymn to escape; first as an ode to the policing of empire, then as an elegy for the picaresque. We might suggest that through the construction and collapsing of these dichotomies, Kipling erases any limit on the colonial state's boundaries, renders discipline everywhere, insinuates the police into every act of waywardness. We might also suggest the exact opposite: in the unmapped spaces written over the imperial map of India, and the de-Anglicization of the sahibized Kim, we could equally discover the subversion of all the works of imperial discipline.

Neither of these responses should strike us as satisfactory, for both depend on the repression of sufficient moments in the text that selecting either *one* of these interpretations amounts to an act more of censorship than of reading. Apparently only bewilderment remains, and the embarrassment of naming Kipling's text as disciplinary and antidisciplinary, as devoted to the imperial fabrication of Englishness, and despairing of that fiction. Our bewilderment is, however, nothing less than appropriate. For in inclining to confusion, we recognize that we have become, as Ruskin predicted, what we have regarded. Like the bemused visitor to the Victoria Terminus, we stand before Kipling's great work, aware that we are gazing upon a deeply ambivalent, almost schizophrenic artifact, a work that commits itself to identifying the empire as a place in which one can remain, or become, English to the backbone, and simultaneously guarantees that henceforth it will be impossible to say what it means to be English. In our own frustration and bafflement we can read the urgent cadence of that question which untiringly animates Kipling's text. In attending to our inability to answer the question "Who is Kim?" we can experience, if only fleetingly, the nervous bewilderments of an empire dedicated to the production of an Englishness it has lost the ability to name.

When John Ruskin rose to address his Kensington audience in January of 1858, he found that he could not discuss a matter as apparently apolitical as Indian decorative technique without first referring his auditors to the Mutiny of 1857. While Ruskin's decision to ally a reading of subcontinental aesthetics with an interpretation of this historic event derived largely from his philosophy of culture, his invocation of the Mutiny also revealed something of the influence which that violent event had over Victorian and post-Victorian understandings of imperialism. The Mutiny—or Insurrection, as it has belatedly come to be known—shocked England. More fully than the uprising at Morant Bay, it revealed to Britons at home and abroad the violence that frequently attends imperial rule, and disclosed the vulnerabilities of the English body and the imperial self to that violence. Governor Frere's Victoria Terminus and Kipling's *Kim* can both be seen as works constructed in response to this sudden sense of vulnerability. Both works pretend to guard England from an imperial wounding by re-forming the identity of the colonial subject. India, they imply, can be made safe for the English only if it is converted into a cultural sanitorium. Yet, even as they promise to submit the colonial subject to a rigorous regimen of cultural normalization, both the novel and the train station seem as capable of producing delirious hybrids as they are of discharging obediently English patients.

Chapter Three

THE PATH FROM WAR TO FRIENDSHIP:
E. M. FORSTER'S MUTINY PILGRIMAGE

There is no commoner word on Indian lips to-day than
atonement. England, they say, has never made atonement;
and she must do it before we can be friends.
—Edward Thompson, *The Other Side of the Medal*

A consideration of Forster's work is, I think,
useful in time of war.
—Lionel Trilling, *E. M. Forster: A Study*

THE UNTOUCHABLES

However bewildering an artifact Governor Frere's Victoria Terminus proves to
be, the train station does manifest an interest in the possibilities of cultural
exchange, a willingness to organize the empire around a series of "contact
zones."[1] That the theory of identity the edifice so massively represents assumed that these contact zones could be efficiently policed, that in these locations of culture Indian identities would always be exchanged for English, is,
Kipling's novel suggests, one of the more costly arrogances the British Empire
permitted itself. That opinion would have been seconded by a great many of
the Raj's officers who, in the years following the 1857 Insurrection, far from
pursuing Frere's policies labored to minimize the possibilities of meaningful
exchange between the colonists and the colonized, who, indeed, saw in the
uprising a bloody object lesson in the immense dangers that attached to any
significant contact between the English and their colonial subjects. At a crucial moment in E. M. Forster's *A Passage to India*, Major Turton, the ranking
colonial officer in the city of Chandrapore, turns to his English subalterns to
offer some advice on colonial relations that exactly captures this sentiment:
"Intercourse, yes," he intones, "Courtesy, by all means. Intimacy, never,
never."[2]

One need not have been party to Major Turton's conversation to have received this message. A simple glance around the town in which he was speaking would have sufficed to demonstrate that his injunction on intimacy was
written into the very architecture of this outpost of the empire. From the
opening lines of the novel, Forster's text meticulously maps an imperial to-

pography whose organizing principle seems to be in accord with the major's dictum.

> Except for the Marabar Caves—and they are twenty miles off—the city of Chandrapore presents nothing extraordinary.... The streets are mean, the temples ineffective, and though a few fine houses exist they are hidden away in gardens or down alleys whose filth deters all but the invited guest.... There is no painting and scarcely any carving in the bazaars. The very wood seems made of mud, the inhabitants of mud moving....
>
> Inland, the prospect alters. There is an oval Maidan, and a long sallow hospital. Houses belonging to Europeans stand on the high ground by the railway station.... On the second rise is laid out the little civil station, and viewed hence Chandrapore appears to be a totally different place. It is a city of gardens.... The toddy palms and neem trees and mangoes and peepul that were hidden behind the bazaars now become visible and in their turn hide the bazaars.... It is sensibly planned, with a red-brick club on its brow, and farther back a grocer's and a cemetery, and the bungalows are disposed along roads that intersect at right angles. It has nothing hideous in it; ... it shares nothing with the city except the overarching sky. (3–5)

Screened off from the native quarters of the city by that row of trees which Homi Bhabha has suggested mark the "anxiety" line of empire, the colonist's civil station appears to be a world apart, a world closed in on itself, a world serenely, or perhaps nervously, refusing to make contact with the India that surrounds it.[3] As such, as Bhabha also notes, Forster's Chandrapore is an almost perfect instance of that devotion to spatial policing which Frantz Fanon, in the opening chapter of *The Wretched of the Earth*, suggests is the first business of empire:

> The colonial world is a world cut in two. The dividing line, the frontiers are shown by barracks and police stations. In the colonies it is the policeman and the soldier who are the official, instituted go-betweens, the spokesman of the settler and his rule of oppression.... It is obvious here that the agents of government speak the language of pure force. The intermediary does not lighten the oppression, nor seek to hide the domination; he shows them up and puts them into practice with the clear conscience of an upholder of the peace; yet he is the bringer of violence into the home and into the mind of the native.
>
> The zone where the natives live is not complementary to the zone inhabited by the settlers. The two zones are opposed, but not in the service of a higher unity. Obedient to the rules of pure Aristotelian logic, they both follow the principle of reciprocal exclusivity. No conciliation is possible, for of the two terms one is superfluous. The settler's town is a strongly built town, all made of stone and steel. It is a brightly lit town, the streets are covered with asphalt, and the garbage cans swallow all the leavings, seen and unseen, unknown and hardly thought

about. . . . The town belonging to the colonized people, or at least the native town, the Negro village, the medina, the reservation, is a place of ill fame, peopled by men of evil repute. They are born there, it matters little where or how; they die there, it matters not where, nor how.[4]

In this anti-Gramscian world, where the "settlers" cannot be bothered to mask the operations of brute force that secure the "dividing line," the very streets and walls and sight lines seem to make utterly redundant Major Turton's blunt prohibition on intimacy. That Turton nevertheless feels obliged to offer his lesson reveals his conviction that such object lessons are not, in fact, enough.

Turton can believe this because, as Forster's novel indicates, he belongs to a community still living with the memory of a time in which, it believes, such lessons were ignored, a time in which intimacy was attempted, and rudely rewarded. Like the majority of the other English residents of Chandrapore, as Jenny Sharpe has convincingly argued, Turton continues to live within the memory of the 1857 uprising, to occupy an India that remains haunted by the ghosts of the Insurrection, an India obsessively anticipating a return to the Mutiny's time of war.[5] And it is to forestall a repetition of the Mutiny that he forbids his fellows to seek that intimacy which is a mutiny's precondition. In doing so, Turton is far from alone. For in the years that followed the 1857 uprising, English India surrounded itself with reminders of the peril through which it had passed, reminders that frequently did, in fact, take architectural form, grisly *lieux de mémoire* scattered about the subcontinent on each of whose walls the discerning colonist could read Turton's message.

If Bhabha and Fanon are right to suggest that all imperial cultures exist in large part to erect and guard those internal frontiers which mark the limits of colonial intimacy, then the forms those "dividing lines" take nevertheless vary from one imperial territory to another. They exist not simply as generic "boundaries" but as dividing lines that articulate particular narratives of prohibition, territorial policing, and spatial identification. Distributed throughout the British Empire, these internal frontiers were defined not simply as abstract limit spaces but as locations of memory, as auratic and identity-informing sites that, like the scattered timbers of the *Temeraire* or the stone walls of Michael's cottage, could teach the colonist what it meant to be English. In India, in the years after 1857, such frontiers were increasingly marked by monuments to the Mutiny, monuments that, for the English colonists, became a series of almost Wordsworthian ruins which they were enjoined to visit and accurately interpret, and which, if they were visited and read, would pronounce an injunction on intimacy that was also a nervous prohibition on contact, on touching and being touched. In turning, in this chapter, from Kipling to Forster, I wish to consider how the labors of imperial subject-fashioning give way to this nervousness, to examine how the Mutiny monuments, by governing English remembrances of the war of 1857, redefined imperial Englishness as a refusal to be touched, and to explore the ways in which Forster violated that law of untouchability written onto the surface of these *lieux de memoire*.

Oh, What a Lovely War

The Mutiny of 1857 survived its happening in myriad forms. For readers in England as well as India, it existed on the pages of history books, newspapers, collections of letters, and memoirs.[6] It survived in anecdotes and on the brightly colored surface of battle maps. For the colonial inhabitants of India, however, it endured most resonantly not as some form of written text but as a series of monuments on a tourist route. But if we are to understand the significances of those monuments and that route, and the path that they track to Forster, we must begin, not by opening our Murray's handbook (though shortly we must do that also), but by returning to 1857, the year of the war. On May 14 of that year, Lieutenant Frederick Roberts of the Bengal Horse Artillery, later Field Marshal Earl Roberts, commander-in-chief of Her Majesty's forces in India, wrote the first of a series of letters that his daughter published nearly seventy years later. "In these letters, some thirty in number," as his daughter relates in her preface to the published text of the young lieutenant's correspondence, "is to be found the story of his personal experiences during the stirring days of 1857–58 as told to his father, mother, and sister."[7] Roberts's letters are the correspondence of a very young man. At the time of the outbreak of the Insurrection (conventionally dated as May 10, 1857, on which day the Third Cavalry in Meerut, enraged by the summary court-martial and imprisonment of eighty-five of their fellows, revolted), Roberts was twenty-four. Over the next twelve months, the young lieutenant was involved in what, from the colonists' perspective, were the three major actions of the war: the siege of Delhi, occupied for four months by the insurrectionists, and eventually reoccupied by the colonists in mid-September; the "relief" of the Residency at Lucknow where for six months Indian troops laid siege to Sir Henry Lawrence, chief commisioner of Oudh; and the recapture of Cawnpore, a place rendered infamous by English propagandists as the site where the "mutineers" killed several hundred English civilians and cast their bodies in a well. Roberts's youthful ethical sensibility is evident in his letters as he decries the slaughter of imperial innocents while blithely reporting the massacre of Indian civilians and the blowing of prisoners from the mouths of cannon— "rather a horrible sight," he admits, but nevertheless, "the death that seems to have the most effect" (12). But his youth is even more vividly displayed by his repetitive reading of the war as a grand opportunity for career advancement.

Roberts occasionally sees the war as a vast exercise in imperial discipline, a violent stamping of England's authority onto the bodies of the colonized and the surface of the colony. Indeed, it is this need to mark England's authority as a visible and awe-inspiring inscription that accounts for the uniquely posi-tive effect of passing cannon shot through the bodies of the imprisoned. More frequently, however, Roberts reads the war as defining an economy of promo-tion in which the piles of shattered bodies lying all about him figure as accu-mulations of personal capital. The young lieutenant dreams of the medals he will win and of his promotion to the rank of major. A few days after proudly informing his sister that "when a prisoner is brought in, I am the first to call out to have him hanged" (140), he writes to inform his father of the inevitable consequence of his resolution: "It would be a great thing for me to get a Major-ity now. . . . Few young fellows have had the luck to see so much hard service as I have, and I can't help thinking the reward will come ere long" (147–48). This ability to read luck in the figure of a corpse dangling from a tree defines the keynote of Roberts's letters. As he invents an economy of violence which translates the corpse into a figure of luck and translates luck into the certainty of reward, Roberts makes clear that access to this system of exchange depends only on the one thing that the corpse did not possess: loyalty.

This, finally, would be the lesson that Roberts's countrymen and readers drew from this and a multitude of other accounts of the "stirring days of 1857–58." Edward Thompson, who in 1924 published an account of the Mu-tiny which expressed a grave dissatisfaction with orthodox readings of that event, insisted upon this English desire to read the Mutiny, and subsequent Indian history, according to the metaphors of loyalty:

> See then what long shadows the Mutiny and, still more, our misrepresentation of the Mutiny have cast through two generations! We would repudiate the sugges-tion that our Empire is a rule of masters over slaves. Yet we judge as slave-drivers would, and assess the virtues of our fellow-citizens as a hunter assesses those of dogs. The great question is, Is an Indian loyal? Is he "true to his salt?" . . . What-ever happens, whatever causes of grievance some incredible stupidity may have forced upon them, still—are they loyal? As a chaplain of the Indian Ecclesiastical Establishment—that exacting service—asked a friend of mine, who was trying to explain to him that Rabindranath Tagore was a considerable literary man, "But is he loyal?" That was the only point of interest.[8]

In this movement toward the imperatives of loyalty, an optics of imperial inspection emerges that sees India as a fragment of the nation rather than as a part of the empire and views the Indian as a citizen rather than as a subject. For only in viewing the Indian as a citizen rather than as a conquered subject may England impress upon him or her the obligations of loyalty rather than the narrower need to submit to an occupying power. This act of re-visioning could have marked a crucial moment in the discourse of empire, a moment that imbues the colonial subject with the cultural and juridical rights attaching to English identity and which demands that the pursuit of empire incorporate a renegotiation of the subjective boundaries of Englishness. This is indeed what the demand for Indian "loyalty" implies. But of course this is not what happened.

The reading of the Insurrection as an epic of betrayal did not promote a movement toward the enfranchisement of the colonial subject. Instead, it secured the inscription of a narrative of empire that identified the Indian as a person of whom England demanded the obligations of citizenship, but from whom the nation withheld the rights of an English subject. As Thompson recognized, the English memorialization of the Mutiny depended on a simultaneously strong and weak reading of betrayal, a reading predicated on a profound misunderstanding of the relations of loyalty and citizenship, and an equally bewildered misreading of the relations of conquest and gratitude. The lesson that the English drew from these confusions was to persist in misreading, enacting a narrative of the subcontinent's past and future that misrecognized a plot of oppression and resistance as a plot of loyalty and betrayal. That lesson, implicitly confirmed by the memorialization of the Insurrection as a "mutiny," was rendered explicit in Queen Victoria's proclamation of November 1, 1858, which, in transferring the government of India from the India Company to the Crown and in laying upon the peoples of India the obligations of "faithfullness," defined the trope of loyalty as the subcontinent's governing metaphor.[9]

For the postwar subjects of English India, loyalty did have its rewards. If it could not purchase an Indian the right, perhaps rather dubious, to be considered and treated as "English," it could guarantee the right to be patronized by the English ruling class. For the English themselves, it secured the imperial right, in Lieutenant Roberts's childish terms, to be "lucky." During the years of 1857 and 1858, Roberts's luck—which was eventually to be translated into an earldom—lay, however, not only in his ability to hang prisoners, win medals, and be promoted but in the opportunity that the war provided for travel, the opportunity to become acquainted with the map of India, the opportunity, in a word, for tourism.

On numerous occasions, Roberts pauses in his recounting of his military exploits to dreamily invoke the exotic places that he is about to visit—if the war will only last long enough. On the 24th of July, he informs his mother that "please God, before I write again, I shall have ridden thro' Delhi, and then I hope to join some Force going either towards Rohilkund, and Oude or Gwalior—all new countries to me, and all of which I am anxious to see" (29). Two weeks later, his appetite for fighting undiminished, he continues in a similar vein: "Ere many months we will have such a force of Europeans in the Country that I hope all these petty Rajahs will rise, so that we may make one sweep, and wind up taking Cashmere! where I shall be very happy to spend every hot weather roaming about the beautiful places there" (40). Five months later, the young lieutenant writes home to inform his family of yet another of the war's travel opportunities: "After the place [Lucknow] is in our possession, a great portion of the troops will, I imagine, go into quarters while the rest must occupy and quiet Bareilly, Moradabad, etc. I should like to be sent with this column, as I have never seen that part of the country, besides I still a hankering for going North again" (130). These pronouncements exhibit an evident element of bravura, but they reveal more than this. For centuries before 1857, India had been a place of travel, habitation, and labor for English men and women. In the years following the Insurrection, and especially after the transportation revolutions of the late nineteenth century, the subcontinent increasingly became a space of tourism. The production of India as a touristic space depended both on the quelling of the native's rebellious sentiments and on the invention of scenic routes of travel through the subcontinent. In the making of these tourist maps of India, the war of 1857–58 proved indispensable.

For Roberts, the war, pursued from one scene of fighting to another, existed as an excuse for a series of rather haphazard travels through the subcontintent. For his successors, the memorialization of the war allowed for the production of a determinate map of the Mutiny. That map embraced the three sites that the colonists viewed as key to the war's unfolding: Delhi, Lucknow, and Cawnpore. This triangular mapping of the Mutiny provided the blueprint for English histories of the events of 1857–58, histories that invented the Mutiny as, primarily, a narrative of these three places. But this map of events proved to be of use not only to English historians; it also became the map by which tourist agents and guidebook publishers plotted a course of travel through the subcontinent. If, for Roberts, war and tourism were often identical events, for his successors a tour of India was to become an act of revisiting the scenes of the Insurrection's violence. As Bernard Cohn has noted, "For the Englishmen in the latter half of the nineteenth century, travelling in India as visitors or in the course of their duties, there was a regular Mutiny pilgrimage to visit the sites of the great events—the Delhi Ridge, the Memorial Well and the Gardens in Kanpur, capped by a large marble statue of the Angel of Resurrection, and the Residency in Lucknow."[10] In these acts of pilgrimage, the map of India was revealed not only as an instrument and product of war but as an artifact which, in wedding the emergent practices of tourism to the discourses of cartography and war, determined that the traveler in India was always the student of an imperial narrative of loyalty and betrayal.

Roberts's letters, written at a time when the marriage of the practices of cartography, war, and tourism was only promised, were published by his daughter in 1924. In that same year, the firm of John Murray published a revised version of their *Handbook for Travellers in India, Burma, and Ceylon*, a text in which the cartographic union of war and tourism is complete. The text of the *Handbook* is arranged simply enough. One hundred pages of introductory material follow a few pages of advertisements for books about India, passages to the subcontinent, and tourist services catering to the needs of the traveler in India. The introductory material includes advice on clothing, servants, railways, and the people of India and concludes with an account and map of the Mutiny. The remainder of the text, six hundred pages, comprises an exhaustive series of descriptions of the cities, towns, villages, temples, mosques, caves, and palaces of the subcontinent.

This encyclopedic account is not, however, truly exhaustive. It cannot be. The subcontinent is simply too vast—as indeed, the smallest locale must be—for it to be comprehensively represented. The *Handbook* may represent the common response of the colonial writer before the sublime immensity of India, the attempt to contain India by transforming it into a catalog or list. But the editor, at least, does not pretend to have captured the subcontinent. In his prefatory notes to the reader, the editor indicates that "No attempt has been made to indicate tours in India, Burma, or Ceylon."[11] With this refusal, he seems to identify this imperial space as simply too vast to reduce to a sequence of routes. He suggests that India's enormity resists the closure of the itinerary; that it can be cataloged but not guided through.

But again, this is not precisely true. For despite his protestations, the editor has, after all, discovered a map capable of lending a sense of order to India's elusiveness. In the description of the Mutiny which concludes the introductory material of the *Handbook*, the editor refers his readers to the pages that describe the Mutiny sites. If the reader, in fact, turns to these pages, he or she will find that the editor has defined not only a tour through the book but a passage through India. As the *Handbook* informs the reader of the history of the Insurrection, it leads the traveler from one Mutiny city or cantonment to another, exhorting the traveler to perform a reverent pilgrimage through those cities and barracks towns, those apses, stairwells, and bedrooms where in the summer of 1857 the presence of the English in India was so profoundly challenged. Confronted with the enormity of India, the impossibility of collecting it, the editor has, after all, reduced it to a route, to what Cohn has called a Mutiny pilgrimage. In thus offering a transactable map of the subcontinent, the *Handbook* functions to constrain the traveler's experience and, more significant, the traveler's memory of India. Despite its pretensions to a hypertextual indeterminacy in its representation of the subcontinent, the *Handbook* has provided a narrative of the colonists' experience of India, a narrative written on the monumentalized, mnemonic spaces of the Mutiny sites, rewritten on the pages of the souvenir text, and obsessively written once more on the spaces of the traveler's memory: a narrative of the impossibility of imperial intimacy.

That narrative begins in Delhi at the foot of the Kashmir Gate, where the traveler arrives, *Handbook* in hand, having just reread an account of the Mutiny. (Although an imperial recounting of the Mutiny closes the introduction to the *Handbook*, the description of each city or town marked as a stop on the Mutiny route is preceded by a retelling of the tale.) In Delhi, the *Handbook* directs the traveler, or reader, or indeed the wanderer who is both at once, to begin a tour of the city at the Kashmir Gate where the signs of native betrayal and imperial martyrdom are amply and multiply traced:

> On the outer face of the Kashmir gate is a memorial tablet of the Explosion Party. . . . On the inside the outlines of the Quarter Guard, in which so many European officers were murdered on the 11th May 1857, are still traceable. . . . In front of the gate is St James Church, built by Colonel Skinner, C.B. whose Delhi residence stood on the opposite side of the clear space here; in the churchyard are the old dome-cross bearing the marks of the bullets fired at it in 1857, and a memorial cross to the victims of the Mutiny. . . . The road now divides into two branches with a long grass plot at the centre. At one end of the latter is the granite memorial of the officers of the Telegraph Department who fell in 1857. (265)

The catalog of betrayal's architecture does not end here. At the foot of the Lahore Gate, the editor informs his countrymen and women, "on the 11th May 1857, was killed the Commissioner of the Division, and in the rooms above were murdered the wounded Collector and Commandant, the Chaplain, and two ladies" (265). The Hall of Public Audience in the palace of Delhi is remembered as the site where the thanksgiving service of the Delhi Field Force was held in September of 1857, the court of the palace as the place "round the edge [of which] were murdered, on 16th June 1857, some fifty Christians who had escaped the massacre of the 11th" (267). And on and on it goes. If the *Handbook* does not direct the traveler's attention to a grave, it gestures to a memorial tablet; if not to a memorial tablet, then to the scars that the mutineers' bullets traced into the wall of a church; if not to the bullet holes, then to the bedroom walls where the blood of an English lady splashed. It seems as if nothing else exists, or if there is something else—a temple or a mosque—it exists only as the awful scenery that framed this tragedy of betrayal. A monument to the Mutiny lies everywhere: a lurid scene to remind the colonial traveler of what occurred, to force him or her to remember, to ensure that in the contemplation of India's abundant alterity he or she not forget the lesson in imperial etiquette intoned by Forster's Collector: "Intimacy, never, never."

An obsessive, almost hysterical quality haunts the construction and reconstruction of this narrative, a need to account for virtually each colonist's death, an Ancient Mariner's need to tell and retell. Confronted with the elusive vastness of India, confronted with what, in another context, Conrad called the "great demoralization" of empire,[12] this seems to be the one narrative to make sense of the whole enterprise, a narrative that, in its predictable and comforting ghastliness, can be depended on, if nothing else can. The centrality of this narrative of betrayal to the discourse of the English empire cannot be overestimated. It is a narrative that will haunt Forster's A *Passage to India*, a narrative of betrayed intimacy for which the English colonists were profoundly nostalgic. Forster's English community in Chandrapore will demand to have the pleasure of rereading this narrative when they insist that it has traced its disfiguring yet reliable and unifying text onto yet another of India's sites of tourism, the Marabar Caves, where the "offense" that Adela suffers provides them a comforting occasion to rally around their Englishness, their distinction, their nobility. Rewritten on the walls of the cave, this narrative of intimacy betrayed pleasurably affronts the English. It encourages them with one another. It is a boon. "Although Miss Quested had not made herself popular with the English, she brought out all that was fine in them. For a few hours an exalted emotion gushed forth, which the women felt even more keenly than the men, if not for so long. 'What can we do for our sister?' was the only thought of Mesdames Callendar and Lesley, as they drove through the pelting heat to enquire. Mrs. Turton was the only visitor admitted to the visiting room. She came out ennobled by an unselfish sorrow" (199). "Each felt that all he loved best in the world was at stake, demanded revenge, and was filled with a not unpleasing glow, in which the chilly and half-known features of Miss Quested vanished, and were replaced by all that is sweetest and warmest . . ." (203).

The *Handbook* most clearly signals this nostalgia for betrayed intimacy in its description of Lucknow, the site on the Mutiny pilgrimage to which it directs the traveler on his or her departure from Delhi. The text instructs the reader to proceed as swiftly as possible from the entrance of the city to the Residency of the Commissioner. "The Residency," the *Handbook's* editor remarks with assurance,

> Is the spot which all Englishmen will wish to visit first in Lucknow. . . . The gardens are beautifully arranged and perfectly kept, and the place is now one full of the peacefulness which properly belongs to sad scenes long since enacted, in the midst of which, one can think, *thankfully and proudly*, of the events and deeds of that summer of 1857:
>
> > Ever the labour of fifty that had to be done by five,
> > Ever the marvel among us that one should be left alive,
> > Ever the day with its traitorous death from its loopholes around,
> > Ever the night with its coffinless corpses to be laid in the ground.
> > Heat like the mouth of a Hell, or a deluge of cataract skies,
> > Stench of old offal decaying, and infinite torment of flies. (399–400)

This is a strange and crucial passage in the *Handbook*, a passage whose weirdest logic attaches to the figure of gratitude. The Residency, the editor believes, has become a site of thanksgiving, a site where the proper response of the English traveler is to give thanks for the memories that the scene metonymically locates. The editor completes this suggestion by defining the nature of those memories, by suggesting that the English should be grateful, among other blessings, for traitorous death, coffinless corpses, the mouth of Hell, offal decaying, and an infinite torment of flies. At first glance, this is astonishing. On further consideration, it is not.

For the firm of John Murray is instructing the English traveler to be grateful not for these grisly consequences of the war but for the war itself, and for the narrative of empire that the war locates. Carl von Clausewitz, in a famous section of his text *On War*, offers a distinction between Absolute and Real War. Absolute War, he maintains, is war in the fullness of its waging. Its time is a time of applied destruction, a time of the continuous disruption of social order, a time in which, relative to the moments of peace, "everything is more mobile, and psychological forces, individual differences, and chance play a more influential part."[13] Real war, by contrast, and somewhat paradoxically, defines the moment of war's suspension, the moment in which war exists solely as a potentiality. It is a time of uneasy calm, a time of "tension between two elements, separate for the time being," a time of confusion in which "the men who habitually act, both in great and minor affairs, on particular dominating impressions or feelings rather than according to strict logic, are hardly aware of the confused, inconsistent, and ambiguous situation in which they find themselves" (*On War*, 579). The confusions and ambiguities of dwelling in such a time produce an experience of "incoherence and incompleteness" (*On War*, 580) familiar to us from our recent experience of the Cold War, and more than familiar to India's post-Mutiny colonists. That experience may indeed always be the experience of an imperial ruling class. The imperial state creates itself through the waging of war, but it maintains itself not by waging but by threatening war against its subjects. For the state to survive, for the empire to exist profitably, war itself, Clausewitz's Absolute War, must be suspended. This, in the language of empire, is politely described as maintaining the peace. But during the times of "peace," the officials of the state, who can never forget that their real relation to their subjects originates and endures in a capacity to inflict violence upon them, must also maintain the threat of war. The product of this dual obligation to maintain the war and maintain the peace is what Paul Virilio refers to as the war of peacetime.[14] This peacetime war produces an experience of uneasiness, of perpetually remembering and awaiting an outbreak of violence, an experience of incoherence and incompleteness.

The English visitor's gratitude for the memories evoked by the Residency in Lucknow follows from this sense of incoherence. There, as at the other sites of the Mutiny pilgrimage, he or she may discover a war that exists in memory as neither incoherent nor incomplete, a war that, in surviving as the monument of itself, may be used for the dual purposes of comforting the colonizers and threatening the colonized. The threat that the Mutiny memorials articulate to the native subjects of empire is evident enough: it is the threat of renewed punishment, the threat of a revisitation of the awful violence that the colonists inflicted upon their "disloyal" subjects. The comfort that the memorials locate is rather more complex. It is partially the comfort of having survived, of having endured, and won. But it is also the comfort of anticipating the renewal of Absolute War, of passing proleptically and in memory from the tense and difficult task of sustaining the empire through the maintenance of discipline to the invigorating labor of renewing the empire through the infliction of violence. Standing in reverent awe before the memorials of the Mutiny, the English traveler is like Rupert Brooke joyously approaching the trenches of France: liberated from the incomplete and frustrating task of maintaining the peace, the pilgrims can plunge, "as swimmers into cleanness leaping," into the obviousnesses of unembarrassed war.[15]

The Mutiny pilgrim is, in fact, more amply rewarded than Brooke. In gazing on the Residency, or the Delhi Ridge, or the well in Cawnpore, the Anglo-Indian may do more than apply the simples of violence to a psyche wounded by the awkward labor of maintaining the colony in the simultaneous conditions of war and peace. He or she can also read these memorials as signs in a narrative of imperial belonging. That narrative grounds itself on the moment which the Mutiny celebrates: the moment of betrayal. It is, strangely but logically, in the act of being betrayed that the colonists understood themselves to belong in India. By reading the Insurrection of 1857–58 as a tragedy of Indian disloyalty and by discovering in it the certainty that any intimacy with their subjects would be rudely violated, the colonists were able to represent themselves not as India's oppressors but as its gallant and benign victims, as a people more sinned against than sinning, and to derive the secondary advantage of a justification for racial separatism.

In thus discovering the Mutiny as the pretext for a narrative of imperial belonging, the colonists rendered a visit to the Mutiny sites an act of Ruskinian remembrance and anticipation in which the present and future are subordinated to a privileged past, and memory emerges as the angel of history and the god of the everyday. As the official history of the Mutiny became for the English the narrative that, in Bernard Cohn's terms, "explained their rule in India to themselves," the memory of the Mutiny increasingly exerted its authority over the colonial community's cultural and political imaginary. In this submission of imagination to memory, the temporality of English India, already hybridized by a dual devotion to the times of war and peace, splits still further. To the state's schizophrenic identification with the multiple temporalities of war is added the individual colonial subject's submission to the allegorical time of the uncanny. Committed, as representatives of the state, to the temporal confusions of the "war of peacetime," the colony's English men and women suffered a further devotion to the return of the repressed, a bewildering commitment to the fond and simplifying nightmare of the Mutiny's repetition. In light of these confusions, it is no surprise to discover Forster's Anglo-Indians rejoicing in the grim hope that Dr. Aziz's "affront" to Adela Quested might signify the beginning of the Mutiny's return and a release from the complexities of their responsibility "to do justice and keep the peace" (*Passage to India*, 51). Confronted with the events that took place in the Marabar Caves, the Anglo-Indian community in Chandrapore can return, like the visitor to the Lucknow Residency, to the visible signs of that plot of betrayal, martyrdom, and violated intimacy which lent the imperial project at least an imaginary unity, coherence, and lucidity.

GHOSTS OF THE INSURRECTION

The English were not, however, wholly unanimous in their readings of the Mutiny. In 1925, Virginia and Leonard Woolf's Hogarth Press published an alternative account of the Insurrection: Edward Thompson's *The Other Side of the Medal*. Thompson's text is partially a work of historiography, partially a piece of cultural criticism. *The Other Side of the Medal* consists of four sections, the longest of which treats misrepresentations of the Mutiny in works of English history and provides evidence of English atrocities excised from such works.[16] It is when Thompson turns from historiography to cultural criticism, however, that he becomes most interesting. Like Ruskin, Thompson is obsessed with the problems of collective memory, and the introductory and concluding sections of his text are written as attempts to understand the ghostly and wounding survivals of the Mutiny in Anglo-Indian memory. The figure of the wounded ghost is, in fact, central to Thompson's reading of the Insurrection. In his account, the Mutiny survives not as architecture or as site but as a forbidding spectral wanderer, which he feels compelled to confront and which he urges his countrymen to meet.

Thompson grapples with that ghost throughout the bulk of his text, both because he finds that he must and because he recognizes that if the English are to rethink the Mutiny, it will not be sufficient for them to read alternative histories. It is also, he maintains, necessary that England be weaned from the *lieux de memoire* pleasures of the Mutiny pilgrimage and given metaphors other than loyalty and betrayal around which to construct its memories. This, borrowed from *Hamlet*, is Thompson's new metaphor: "Right at the back of the mind of many an Indian the Mutiny flits as he talks with an Englishman—an unavenged and unappeased ghost" (30). In the pages that follow this announcement, Thompson proceeds to give that ghost flesh. For page after page, he draws his readers' attention to the violence that the armies and officials of the British Empire inflicted on the peoples of India during and after the Insurrection. As he does so, his ghost moves backward in time, assuming again the aspect of a corpse that is alternately riddled with English bullets, hung from a tree, branded with English irons, drowned in a river, consumed in flame, or blown from the mouth of an English cannon. A universe of death occupies Thompson's pages, and a host of corpses. This he sees when he inspects the Mutiny, this he imagines the people of India to see, and this he demands that the people of England see. More than the mutilated corpse, however, he observes the corpse's ghostly survival in memory. Or, to be more exact, he sees memory surviving as a ghost.

This, finally, is where the value of Thompson's text lies. In troping memory as a work of sacralized architecture, the English custodians of the Mutiny made the act of remembrance a devotional responsibility. They submitted the present and future to the past, worshiped the past, and held themselves redeemed by it. By troping memory as a ghost, Thompson makes the act of remembrance an experience of haunting. He imagines the present and future as vulnerable to the past, regrets the past, and finds the empire terrorized by it. The difference is crucial. In the movement from one term to the other, Thompson asks the English to recognize that the Mutiny cannot redeem India but continues to hold the subcontinent in torment. He does not imply that the Mutiny must pass from the realm of the remembered to the realm of the forgotten, but that the ghost of the Mutiny must be laid to rest through an act of atonement.

Thompson's call for a gesture of atonement derives from his fear that if the ghost of the Mutiny is not laid, it will not merely survive as an embittering memory in the minds of the native subjects of India but will repeat itself in history. Writing shortly after the April 1919 massacre at Amritsar—where General Dyer's troops fired on and killed hundreds of Indian civilians—he detects in that event, as in others, a willingness on the part of the colonial authorities to resolve the increasingly difficult problems of English rule by reenacting the narrative of the Mutiny. More troublingly, as he turns from this event to cast his eye on the seventy years that have passed since 1857, Thompson sees the Mutiny, over and again, exerting its influence on Indian history as a spirit of repetition.

In the penultimate section of his text, Thompson discusses three events in postwar Indian history in which he discovers the English acting under the ghastly influence of their memories of the Mutiny. The first event relates to the actions of a Mr. Cowan, deputy commissioner for Loodhiana, who in 1872 responded to a disturbance in the town of Maler Kotla by imitating the behavior of the English officers of the war of 1857–58: he lashed forty-nine men to the barrels of cannon and blew shot through them. The punishments meted out in Kabul in 1879, following the second Afghan war, define the second event on which Thompson fastens as an "example of the working of the Mutiny-trained or Mutiny obsessed mind" (94). In that year, Frederick Roberts, promoted to the rank of general in the years since 1857, declared martial law and set about continuing the work at which he had proved so adept during the Mutiny. In the concise words of his contemporary, Sir Henry Cotton, "Martial law was established, men were hanged in batches . . . the country was ravaged for supplies, and village-burning was the order of the day."[17] The third event is that which most horrifies Thompson: the massacre at Jallianwalla in Amritsar. Of that event, and General Dyer's role in it, Thompson has this to say: "He [Dyer] was our representative, braver than we are but certainly not more stupid, and it was our inherited thought that drove him on. The ghosts of Cooper and Cowan presided over Jallianwalla" (97).[18] It is to escape the presiding influence of these violently recurrent spirits that Thompson proposes the enactment of a gesture of atonement.

Here, however, Thompson's imagination seems to fail him. While he can point, again and again, to the need to atone for the past, he struggles to suggest what form that gesture might take. Too willing to read Indian history as an enactment of Hamlet's tragedy and dilemma, he finds himself, like Hamlet, unable to decide how to lay to rest the subcontinent's unavenged and unappeased ghosts, and unwilling to adopt the Danish prince's final, violent, solution. Atonement remains in his text a word on the page. The best he can do is attempt to translate the concept into Sanskrit and then to translate the Sanskrit into English again: "There is no commoner word on Indian lips to-day than *atonement*. England, they say, has never made atonement; and she must do it before we can be friends. The word in their minds is the Sanskrit *prayashitta*, usually translated atonement; but its meaning is rather a gesture. It is not larger measures of self-government for which they are longing, it is the magnanimous gesture of a great nation, so great that it can afford to admit mistake and wrong-doing, and is too proud to distort facts" (131–32). While this translative movement from English to Sanskrit to English might be seen as an act of linguistic juggling, as a sort of verbal trickery in which the gesture that Thompson seeks constantly eludes his grasp just as he is making contact with it, Thompson in fact discovers his act of atonement in this very movement of language.

In his final definition, the gesture that, he insists, India awaits becomes little more than an act of admission and an act of record keeping. It is, he implies, in articulation, in the simple act of admitting error and correcting a distorted historical register, that England can make its gesture of atonement. And this, of course, is precisely what Thompson has done in the pages of his text. If, as I have suggested, atonement in this text remains a word on the page, that, for Thompson, is entirely appropriate. The gesture that will bury the ghost of the Mutiny is complete, he suggests, in his act of writing. This is perhaps too easy, even self-serving; but Thompson can manage no more, and this apology affords him the pleasure of closing his text as Hamlet, the secret hero of the work, closed his life—not as a dispenser of violence but as a voice.

One last thing must be said about that voice. Atonement, Thompson insists, must be made in order that the cycle of Mutiny repetition might be broken. But it must be made for two additional reasons: that England might heal itself and that the English and the Indians might be friends. Thompson's reading of the Mutiny, and of collective memories of the Mutiny, depends on his understanding that this mid-nineteenth-century event has implications for the twentieth-century politics of imperial rule *and* for contemporary constructions of English identity. He represents the Mutiny as a wound in England's cultural anatomy and insists that for England to be great, for it to free itself from a festering madness that manifested itself in the worship of violence and degradation, it must cleanse that wound. Finally, though, Thompson expresses a concern less for the condition of the blood-addicted English than for England's continuing relationship with India. His ultimate word on the Mutiny is one not of correction but of desire. The closing sentences in his text are written out of a sense of yearning, out of a desire for friendship. "With such men," he says, speaking of the inhabitants of India, "an understanding is possible, and friendship, and forgiveness" (133). This longing for friendship with which Thompson concludes his text is, in many ways, at the heart of the entire work. It is revealing, however, that he can bring himself to speak of friendship only in his final pages and that, of all the things he describes in his text, it is the nature of this friendship that he is least able to explain. He can do little more than name it. In fact, he can do no more.

The place of friendship lies outside this text, and its time is outside the time of Thompson's writing. He can locate friendship only in postponement, only in anticipation, only in the difficult and perpetually deferred time of desire. In this, Thompson is not alone. E. M. Forster, a far greater writer than Thompson, would also struggle to find the time of friendship in an age of empire, and it is to Forster's struggle to understand and to locate the friendship for which Thompson yearned that I will now turn, though not without pausing to recognize that, in some vital way, Thompson's text can be seen as pointing Forster in the right direction. William Kerrigan has observed that Milton's object in *Samson Agonistes*, a minor epic of imperialism, is to find "the way to strength from weakness."[19] Thompson's text, like Forster's, is animated by a similar negotiation of imperial paradox, an attempt to discover the way to friendship from war.

THE PATH FROM WAR TO FRIENDSHIP

Lionel Trilling was not thinking about the Mutiny when he began his celebrated study of E. M. Forster's novels, but, as is evident from the first words of his text, he was thinking about violence. This, at once intriguing and concise, is Trilling's introductory sentence: "A consideration of Forster's work is, I think, useful in time of war."[20] The movement that Trilling recommends in this sentence, from a consideration of the time of war to a reading of the pages of Forster's texts, depends on the great critic's understanding that there is something in those pages which reveals itself as war's alternative. That something, Trilling goes on to argue, is the working of a liberal imagination that finds solace, and delight, not in the simplicities and ethical reductivenesses of violence but in the difficulties of moral complication. It is useful to read Forster, Trilling suggests, because in his work there are none of those apparent moral absolutes whose pursuit ends so often in the organized infliction of violence. Instead, there is perpetual moral complication and contradiction, an unrelenting revelation of the complicity of "good-and-evil," a "helter-skelter distribution of graces" by an author who is "always shocking us by removing the heroism of his heroes and heroines" (18). This, to Trilling's mind, is all to the good, for it derives from a profoundly ethical attitude of moral uncertainty from which war, with its confident separations of the damned and the graced, cannot proceed.

Trilling may be quite correct in making these arguments. His advocacy of such "moral realism" might also be read, however, as a prescription for quietism, and Theodore Adorno, at least, would have had little patience for this solution to the "problem" of Auschwitz. Whatever our opinion of Trilling, it is quite apparent that much of Forster's work, which may have some or no value as an antidote to war, is written in response to the possibilities of war. If there is that in Forster's writing which exists as war's imaginary alternative, then that alternative is indeed complicated and uncertain, though the word which I would give to it is not liberalism but friendship.

Forster's passage to the difficulties of friendship might be traced in a number of his works. *Howards End* could certainly open itself to such a reading. But my interest here is in an imperial discourse of friendship and war, and I will restrict my attention to Forster's Indian writings. The earliest of those writings (though not the first to be published) seem at first glance to have little to do with these issues. In fact, however, these texts—Forster's letters and journals from his 1912–13 visit to India—locate the writer's initial movements toward the problem that haunted Edward Thompson: the problem of locating, in India, a path from war to friendship.

Forster made the first step along that path in October of 1912 when he, with his friends R. C. Trevelyan and Goldsworthy Lowes Dickinson, embarked on a visit to India. During the seven months of his travels in the subcontinent, Forster kept a journal and wrote numerous letters to family and friends in England. In 1953 he published selections from these writings, together with the letters written during his 1921 residence as the personal secretary of the Rajah of Dewas, in *The Hill of Devi*.[21] The letters of 1912 and 1921, which are accompanied and interrupted by Forster's commentary, amount, in the careful selection and arrangement of their published form, to narratives of Forster's friendship with the Rajah, who is generally referred to as H.H., His Highness. The journal of the 1912–13 visit is, in comparison, a looser, less overtly disciplined text, which touches upon Forster's friendship with H.H. but does not limit itself to the narrative of their intimacy.

The journal is, in fact, precisely what one would expect it to be: a meandering, uneven account of Forster's travels, a tourist's diary. As a tourist, Forster is fairly conventional in his interests and prejudices. He spends much of his time shopping for postcards and souvenirs. Though aware that he is likely to incarcerate in the drawer of a wardrobe any Indian dress that he might purchase for himself, he cannot resist obtaining various items of native clothing. In Delhi, he buys a number of perfumes for his aunt so that he will have "something really Indian" to give her. On one occasion, he even steals two leaves from a peepul tree, sacred, he has been told, to Buddhists, and adds these to his collection. This continuous hunting for collectibles is, of course, a fundamental and apparently innocuous touristic practice. But, as Susan Stewart has suggested in her remarkable study *On Longing*, the tourist's accumulation of souvenirs amounts to more than an innocent pastime.

Adela Quested, whom we first encounter in *A Passage to India* as the most eager of tourists, is a prisoner of the tourist longing for the "authentic." The first words that she speaks in the novel, like the last words that Edward Thompson speaks in *The Other Side of the Medal*, are words of desire. Unlike Thompson, however, Adela yearns for touristic experience, not friends. "I want to see the real India" (22), Adela informs her acquaintances in the English Club at Chandrapore and with these words announces a problem central to all Forster's Indian writings: the problem of how to *see* India. Forster's answer, ultimately, will be that, if nothing else, India must not be seen as the tourist sees it. But this problem of imperial inspection begins, for Adela and for Forster, with the tourist's vision.

The optic of tourism, and particularly of imperial tourism, is an optic of possession, animated by a desire to freeze the inspected object in time, to locate experience as an accessible, fixed, and re-presentable artifact. It is an optic of remembrance in which blindness is troped as forgetfulness and in which present, continuous experience is figured as a threat to the sustained visibility of *the* moment of touristic inspection. The problem of the tourist, as Adela Quested's comment reveals, is to know what to see, how to see, and how to remember what has been seen. The perpetual risk that the tourist runs is not that too little will be seen but that so much will be seen that nothing "real" can be remembered. It is in resolving this twin dilemma of optics and remembrance that the souvenir proves so valuable. As Susan Stewart has it:

> The double function of the souvenir is to authenticate a past or otherwise remote experience and, at the same time, to discredit the present. . . . We might say that this capacity of objects to serve as traces of authentic experience is, in fact, exemplified by the souvenir. . . . We do not need or desire souvenirs of events that are repeatable. Rather we need and desire souvenirs of events that are reportable, events whose materiality has escaped us, events that thereby exist only through the invention of narrative. Through narrative the souvenir substitutes a context of perpetual consumption for its contexts of origin. . . . The souvenir speaks to a context of origin through a language of longing, for it is not an object arising out

of need or use value; it is an object arising out of the necessarily insatiable demands of nostalgia.[22]

Stewart's reading implies an essential lack at the center of the touristic experience, a lack arising not out of a defect of vision but out of an excess. As the tourist moves on from the privileged moment of seeing, vision fails to cease, and the host of sights crowding in on the eye threaten to erase the desired sight from the domains of memory and the "reportable." The souvenir guards against this erasure. It sustains the materiality of a fading vision. It literally locates experience and enables the tourist who clutches and displays it to report a narrative of that experience. The function of the souvenir is to secure memory and to discipline it. Within the exercise of that function, the souvenir, Stewart suggests, reveals a predilection for the past. Because it exists both as memory's guardian and as the curator of the authentic, it tends to identify "the real" as that which is absent, lost, or vanishing. If desire is posited on a temporality of displacement, then the souvenir articulates yearning not as anticipation but as regret; it locates desire's object not in the future but in the past; it announces a refusal of the present and a longing for what has been. This emplacement of the souvenir in a nostalgic economy of desire is evident not only in Adela Quested's assiduous search for visions of the "real India" but in the 1912 journal's record of Forster's own responses to India.

Both in his collection of "really Indian" things and in his response to the Indians he meets, Forster reveals a pronounced preference for the Indian past. He most clearly marks this desire for the coincident appearance of an ancient and an "authentic" India in his appraisals of the costuming of the Indian body. Over and over, he records his revulsion before the image of an Indian clad in European clothes. Forster shudders when his servant Baldeo begins to abandon his native dress in favor of European costume, and refuses to advance Baldeo money to replenish his tattered wardrobe, knowing that he will use the money to buy trousers rather than the dhoti that Forster prefers. Forster is still more appalled by Baldeo's son, who has betrayed his culture in his choice of clothes: "I didn't like the son much," he sniffs in his journal, "a fashionable youth in pumps, and carried a cane."[23] For Forster, however, the most revolting moment comes when he attends a wedding at the home of an "advanced Mohammedan" family in Simla, and he forces himself to endure the dual spectacle of the Indian body and Oriental culture costumed in European dress.

Forster's hosts, much to his displeasure, had decided to "rationalize" the marriage proceedings. The bride appeared unveiled. A poet read a poem on "conscience," which an interpreter translated from Urdu into English. The poet, who spoke English, disliked the translation and insisted on correcting and upbraiding his interpreter. The Muslim guests, mingled in a crowd of Hindus, Christians, and Sikhs, grumbled about the irregularity of the ceremony. The groom, who was apparently less "advanced" than his bride, squirmed noticeably. "It was," Forster averred, "depressing, almost heartrending." Toward the end of the ceremony a paired set of events occurred that cast the hideousness of India's "Europeanization" into relief:

> Before the Moulvi finished a gramophone began, and before that was silent a memorable act took place. The sun was setting, and the orthodox withdrew from us to perform their evening prayer. They gathered on the terrace behind, to the number of twenty, and prostrated themselves towards Mecca. Here was dignity and unity; here was a great tradition untainted by private judgment; they had not retained so much and rejected so much; they had accepted Islam unquestioningly, and the reward of such an acceptance is beauty. . . . Crash into the devotions of the orthodox birred the gramophone—
>
> I'd sooner be busy with my little Lizzie,
>
> and by a diabolic chance reached the end of the song as they ended the prayer. They rejoined us without self-consciousness, but the sun and the snows were theirs, not ours; they had obeyed; we had entered the unlovely chaos that lies between obedience and freedom—and that seems, alas! the immediate future of India.[24]

Between the gramophone and the Europeanized Indians who wind it, and the orthodox Muslims bowed in the obedient postures of prayer, it is clear where Forster's loyalties lie. His eye inclines with longing to the "authentic" beauty of a vanishing India and turns with horror from the present and future manifest before him. In awarding the "orthodox" the laurel of beauty, Forster defines the past, or at least the "residual"—in Raymond Williams's sense of the word—as the realm of the aesthetic.[25] But there is more than a simple question of aesthetic preferences involved here. In collecting the bodies of the men at prayer as visual trinkets, Forster identifies their pious postures as a gesture of refusal. He enlists the vision of their "obedience" to guard his memory against the birring intrusions of the gramophone. In this moment of longing and refusal, Forster transforms the bodies of the orthodox into souvenirs, and if these are not keepsakes that he can purchase and pocket, they are nevertheless souvenirs that he can collect and preserve in the materiality of text.

Forster's 1912 journal is marked through and through with the movement evident in this scene, a movement in which he selectively apprehends India, and produces the landscapes, artifacts and people of the subcontinent as tourism's sites and souvenirs. This fabrication of India as a zone of touristic experience proceeds, as Stewart has suggested, from a discourse of longing and an attitude of refusal. Forster manifests that refusal as an act of censorship, a gesture of selective inspection and remembrance. Out of this partiality of vision, remembrance, and writing, India emerges as the tourist's picturesque object of desire. While Forster can be seen censoring himself and producing a tourist's India throughout the journal, this amendment of vision is most evident in the movement from the private record of experience he keeps in the journal to the more public narratives of his letters, and the still more public narratives of his published travel essays. As Forster expands his audience from himself to his correspondents and to a general reading public, he increasingly censors his narrative, refuses more and more, until India emerges purified and picturesque.[26]

If Forster manufactured the India he encountered in 1912 and 1913 as a space of tourism, then the sort of tourism that he adopts and which his writings enable is, however, not the war-tourism of the Murray's handbook. Forster, in this text, does not perform the Mutiny pilgrimage. Indeed, he scarcely acknowledges the Mutiny in his journal, and when, on his visit to Lucknow, he cannot avoid alluding to it (the second of just two references), he does so only to reject the Mutiny's malignant influence over the place. When one considers what an immense effort it would require for an Englishman traveling in India during these years not to encounter the abundant memorials to the war, the absence of the Mutiny in Forster's journal emerges as perhaps this text's most striking feature. This absence is still more notable when one realizes that Forster used as the guidebook to his travels the 1912 edition of the Murray's handbook, a text that one cannot consult without encountering the Mutiny. Forster's negotiation of this absence should be seen not as accidental but as central to *his* production of a subcontinental space of tourism. If he cannot see, record, or remember India outside of an optics of imperial tourism, then, it is evident, he will at least refuse to see the India upon which the Mutiny tourist is enjoined reverently to gaze.

This refusal of the image of the Mutiny, seems, however, to commit Forster to the picturesque, to the vision of a reified, precious India threatening always to collapse into a souvenir of itself. This India, though it is the India of the greater part of the 1912 journal, is not one that will ultimately satisfy his desires. Adela Quested, whose voice in the earliest pages of *A Passage to India* in many ways echoes the touristic voice of Forster's journal, expresses the writer's dissatisfaction with the India he has fabricated: "'I'm tired of seeing picturesque figures pass before me as a frieze,' the girl explained. 'It was wonderful when we landed, but that superficial glamour soon goes'" (27). By the close of his seven-month tour, Forster, like Adela, senses the picturesque frieze of India—which he has been largely responsible for manufacturing— beginning to lose its appeal. Unwilling to regard India as little more than a museum of the Mutiny, he grows dissatisfied with the alternative, exotically pretty vision of the subcontinent that he has produced for himself.

In the final week of his visit, Forster made a note in his journal that he would spend much of the next ten years of his life amplifying, and that would provide the clue to his discovery of a more desirable way, in Adela's words, of seeing the "real India": "Poor Indians'll do nothing yet: no constructive policy except vague 'education': but it is character not knowledge they need, and they will get this best by building up framework of social intercourse. At present educated class has built up no conventions. . . . *On the other hand a capacity for friendship triumphing over suspicion and forgetfulness. This must bind"* (*Hill of Devi*, 224, emphasis added). The most mysterious word in this passage is "forgetfulness." Neither in the passage itself nor in the surrounding sentences is there any indication of what Forster fears might be forgotten, or even of whom he believes guilty of an excess of forgetfulness. In a text that so often predicates a vision of India on the capacity to forget—to forget the unsightly, the present, the Mutiny, Europeanization—the suggestion that forgetfulness must be resisted is startling. This resistance to forgetfulness implies a rejection of the manner in which Forster has been seeing and remembering India, a rejection of an optics of imperial inspection that defines what it will see and remember by determining what it will forget. There is a further, and more obvious, implication to Forster's comment. Friendship, he now avers, exists in, or derives from, an act of remembrance. In *A Passage to India*, it will become evident that friendship proceeds from a remembrance of precisely the thing which Forster, in his journal, labored most mightily to forget: the Mutiny's moment of crisis. In that text, Forster will realize what is only suggested in this late journal entry. He will discover a capacity for friendship in a moment of crisis articulated as a moment of Mutiny repetition and remembrance. In the intimacy between Fielding and Aziz that derives from this moment, he will labor to triumph over suspicion and forgetfulness in order to bind England to India, not through a monumentalization of the Mutiny or an appreciation of the Indian picturesque but through an act of friendship.

An Imperial Caress

In 1953, Forster published the journal of his 1912–13 tour of India in *The Hill of Devi*. Preceding the text of the journal, which runs to some 120 pages, are Forster's selection of the letters that he wrote during the months of his travel. There are five letters in all, covering a scant nine days of Forster's trip—six days in late December, three in March. All of the letters relate to his acquaintance with the Rajah of Dewas, with whom Forster spent the week from Christmas to New Year and whom he briefly reencountered in Delhi in March. Taken together, these five letters constitute an extremely selective narrative of Forster's travels. The letters are a censored version of the journal, and they are censored to effect. Where earlier, in the public narratives of his letters and published travel essays, we have seen Forster amending the private narrative of his journal to produce India as a space of tourism, here the writer, returning to publish his letters forty years after the event, has edited himself in the interest of producing India as a site of friendship.[27]

Forster's friendship with H.H., the relentless theme of these letters and of the lengthy notes with which Forster accompanies them, began, like the friendship of Fielding and Aziz, in a moment of crisis. In December of 1912, a bomb was thrown at Lord Hardinge, the viceroy of India, as he was proceeding to a durbar in Delhi. Hardinge was only slightly wounded, but the event sent a shiver down the Anglo-Indian spine. On December 23, with the news of the bombing still very current, Forster met the Rajah of Dewas at a club in Indore and was invited by H.H. to spend a week with him in Dewas. Remembering that meeting, Forster, in the note to his letter of December 25 (the date of his arrival in Dewas), commented, "It is appropriate that I should have first seen the Ruler of Dewas at a moment of crisis. When he leapt up to greet me in that Indore club, he was in the midst of composing an enormous telegram of sympathy, congratulation, and indignation to the Viceroy on the subject of the Delhi outrage" (*Hill of Devi*, 6). Though Forster downplays the "outrage" in the remainder of his note, in the letter to which it is appended he indicates an awareness of the violence that might have issued from the assassination attempt: "After the news [of the bombing] came, several Englishmen—officials of high position too—were anxious for the Tommies to be turned to fire at the crowd, and seemed really sorry that the Viceroy had not been killed, because then there would have been a better excuse for doing such a thing" (6). In this desire of the officials of the colonial state to see their viceroy dead that they might take vengeance on a crowd of bystanders, Edward Thompson would surely have seen the workings of the "Mutiny trained or Mutiny obsessed mind" and the malign spirit of the Mutiny working its dreadful and repetitious influence over the narrative of English India. In *The Hill of Devi*, however, Forster's labor is not to trace the Mutiny's eternal return but to derive from this moment of crisis, in which the Mutiny threatens to repeat itself, an alternative plot of empire, to locate in crisis the beginning moment of a narrative of intimacy.

In Forster's journal, H.H. does not emerge as a very likeable figure. After his first full day as H.H.'s guest, Forster commented in the journal, "A land of petty treacheries, of reptiles moving about too cautious to strike each other. No line between the insolent and the servile in social intercourse: so at least it seems to me. In every remark or gesture, does not the Indian prince either decrease his 'omerta' or that of his interlocuter? Is there civility with manliness here?" (*Hill of Devi*, 169–70). A day later the writer shows himself much annoyed by the Rajah's disparagement of homosexuality: "Not good manners to me, I should have thought, but he must know. Sorry he did, as I was ready to like him and shall now dwell on his egoism and tortuousness" (*Hill of Devi*, 170). Forty years later, however, as Forster introduces H.H. to an English reading public, he is more than ready to like H.H. and offers to the world a prince who has been stripped of his reptilian humors and clad in angelic garb, "He was charming," Forster now remembers, in the note that sums up his six-day visit; "he was lovable, it was impossible to resist him or India" (*Hill of Devi*, 12). Forster, working as his own revisionist, is laboring mightily here.

While it is important to note this labor, to recognize that Forster is not simply remembering a friend who has suddenly become identical with India, but is manufacturing a portrait of friendship, it should also be noted that this is not an entirely disingenuous piece of work. Between the writing of the journal in 1912 and the publication of the letters in 1953, Forster spent a great deal of time with H.H, returning to Dewas in 1921 to take up residence for six months as H.H.'s personal secretary. During that time, the writer and the prince became far more intimate than they had been during the six days in 1912. If, returning to his first impressions of H.H. after those intervening experiences, Forster displays an obvious partiality of remembrance, that is perhaps only to be expected. But the refurbishment of H.H. in *The Hill of Devi* is not merely the result of Forster's subsequent affection for his erstwhile employer; it is the consequence of a deliberate attempt to indicate that, contrary to the final words of *A Passage to India*, friendship between an Indian and an Englishman could be accomplished not only in a deferred time of desire but in an experienced time of the now.

There is an obvious problem with this. By substituting the time of remembrance for the time of postponement, as Forster does here, he continues to deny friendship accomplishment in the time of the present. The fiction of *The Hill of Devi* is that this is not so, that imperial friendship can exist in a given present, that the problem is not to discover a time for intimacy but, by returning to and sifting a historical record, to identify friendship's metaphors. In the five letters he offers his readers and in his notes to the letters, Forster constructs a catalog of those tropes. That catalog encompasses not only a negotiation of crisis, a commitment to remembrance, and a struggling with the temporality of intimacy's achievement, figures upon which I have already touched, but also encodings of friendship not yet mentioned. In this micronarrative of intimacy with which Forster begins *The Hill of Devi*, he identifies friendship as intimate with invitation, gift giving, cultural transvestism, embarrassment, and loss.

As much as Forster represents his friendship with H.H. as beginning in a moment of crisis and Mutiny repetition, he shows it also to issue from an act of invitation. On meeting Forster, H.H. simply and courteously invites him to come visit his home in Dewas. It is a slight moment, but one whose mystery Forster will continue to fathom. When, in 1922, Forster returned to England from his second visit with H.H. and set to work completing the manuscript of *A Passage to India*, which he had begun and abandoned after his first trip, he would construct that text around a series of invitations to intimacy.[28] Fielding and Aziz continuously issue invitations to one another: to come to one another's homes, to enter the privacy of the bedroom, to share articles of clothing, to gaze upon the image of the beloved dead. The Collector invites the better class of local Indians to enter into the forbidden spaces of the English club. Aziz invites Adela and Mrs. Moore to his home, swiftly recants, and invites them instead to a picnic at the Marabar Caves; and it is from this gesture of courtesy, the one invitation too many, that disaster ensues, as well as the crisis in which Fielding and Aziz manufacture an abortive friendship. Invitation in this novel acts as the ticket that purchases a passage from a touristic inspection of India to a vision of the one thing that Forster believed could bind England to India, a capacity for friendship.

Ten years before the completion of his novel, Forster was aware of this capacity of the invitation to deliver what he and Adela Quested yearned for but could not discover in the practice of tourism: a vision of and connection to the "real" India. In a November 12 letter to his mother published in *The Hill of Devi*, he comments, "My feeling about India is that if one hadn't introductions one would miss all the best things; it is impossible that the ordinary tourist should do all that I have done, and I do feel lucky and grateful" (*Hill of Devi*, 142). In a letter written six weeks later from the Guest House at Dewas, Forster returns to this theme. "It is odd," he muses in reflecting on the benefits of his invitation to be H.H.'s guest, "that I should have seen so much of the side of life that is hidden from most English people" (*Hill of Devi*, 10). In identifying his privilege as a guest as being a privilege of vision, Forster returns to one of his most constant preoccupations—the problem of how to see, how to discover an optics of imperial inspection that does not invariably present to the English eye an image of war or the picturesque but enables a vision of hidden and outlawed intimacies.

While intimacy in *The Hill of Devi* begins with an invitation, it rapidly proceeds to a moment of cultural transvestism. The greatest success of Forster's first visit to Dewas came during a feast that H.H. threw for him and a number of other guests. Prior to the dinner, Forster was in his room with his servant dressing himself in his best "English evening things," when someone appeared at his door: "There was a cry of 'May I come in?' and enter the Rajah, bearing Indian raiment for me also. A Sirdar (courtier) came with him, a very charming boy, and they two aided Baldeo to undress me and redress me. It was a very funny scene. At first nothing fitted, but the Rajah sent for other garments off people's backs until I was suited" (*Hill of Devi*, 7–8). This, despite its humor and easy grace, is a packed scene. It begins again with an act of invitation (though now it is an invitation that H.H. extends to himself to enter Forster's chamber) followed by the giving of a gift and completes itself in the moment of Forster's cross-dressing. The force of the scene can be located in all three of these moments but is most intense in that moment with which Forster is least comfortable: the moment of his denuding. The movement of princely and servile hands over his body, stripping him of his clothing and dressing him in Indian raiment, is a matter of obvious, if slight, embarrassment for Forster. In the letter to his mother, he covers his embarrassment at this public and mildly erotic unclothing and clothing of his body by suggesting that it was funny and that he could view it as so. But humor is not the prevailing tone of this passage.

It is, instead, a scene of gentleness and generosity in which embarrassment exists but is negotiated as the body is confessed and decorated. The lineaments of this gentle tableau of intimacy's conception were impressed on the page of Forster's letter to his mother, written on the surface of his memory, and inscribed yet once more in *A Passage to India* in those scenes where Fielding and Aziz negotiate the beginnings of their friendship through a similar exchange of invitations and clothing.

In the justly famous moments in the text in which Aziz, invited to Fielding's home, enters the Englishman's bedroom as he is dressing and, discovering that Fielding has broken his collar stud, removes his own and presents it to him, this movement from invitation, through gift giving, to transvestism repeats itself. Here, of course, the Indian is dressed in European clothing, but, again, the body and the dressing of the body with the gift provide the spaces and gestures of friendship's achievement. A hint of embarrassment also intrudes on this scene, a scent of shame that attaches to the nudity of the body. In the novel, Forster does not deflect this through the invocation of humor but covers shame with a veil of invisibility. A door stands between Fielding and Aziz, screening each, in his moment of undress, from the other. Like lovers touching in the dark, the friends are aware of one another's bodies without being able to see one another. For a writer to whom the problem of vision was so crucial, this suspension of visibility is critical.

Fielding and Aziz seem never to suffer the embarrassment or enjoy the pleasure of gazing upon one another's unclad bodies. But this is only apparently so. When Fielding emerges from behind the door into Aziz's view, he is not fully dressed: he lacks the collar stud, which Aziz then provides him. For this brief moment, Aziz can look upon the partially dressed Englishman. Thereafter, Fielding is fully dressed. But Aziz is not. Absent his collar stud, he is now no longer fully clothed, and for the remainder of the day, Fielding, though he does not know it, will gaze upon the symbolically undressed body of his friend. Ironically, it is Ronald Heaslop, Adela's priggish fiancé, who will note the gap in Aziz's costume, comment upon it, and relish it as an item of embarrassment. Fielding and Aziz, however, will be caught within a continuously shifting field of vision in which their connection to one another, which, in its inaugural moments, Forster figures as a visible coincidence of dress, is undermined. The superiority of vision, which Aziz first possesses in seeing Fielding's briefly "unclad" body, will shift to Fielding, though he will not know it.

This early failure by Fielding and Aziz to discover a moment in which their views of one another are balanced, in which they are equal and complicit in their inspections of each other's costuming, is repeated at a late moment of their friendship. On the night following the trial, Fielding, who is now Aziz's guest at a banquet, appears in Indian clothing. Though Aziz is content to think that he has successfully "Orientalized" his friend, Fielding feels only an "excessive awkwardness" (279) in his dress and begins to see himself as a cultural impostor. In a friendship that fails for reasons neither man can name, these disparities in their inspections of one another are crucial. United in their acts of looking upon one another, and particularly in their acts of looking upon one another's cultural transvestism, they have nevertheless suffered a failure of vision, and that failure damns the friendship. Forster and H.H. suffer a similar lack of complicity of vision in the confession and costuming of the body. But at that moment in which H.H. comes to his room to undress him and make him a gift of clothing, Forster feels untroubled by H.H.'s failure to disclose himself, discovering in his own embarrassment, and in the prince's gentle handling of it, an invitation to intimacy. With this revelation and clothing of his body, Forster has found a way to render friendship tangible. He has discovered—in the image of the body of the friend and in the gifts with which that body is clothed—what he has been *looking* for: the objects of an imperial optics no longer willing to bind itself to the inspection of souvenirs and monuments to war.

A decade after H.H. made this gift of clothing to him, the prince offered Forster another gift that was no less instrumental to the establishment of their friendship but which proved, at the very least, rather more embarrassing. During the six months of his residence as H.H.'s personal secretary in 1921–22, Forster determined to take a lover. He made his intentions known to a young servant, who responded, but was indiscreet. Mortified at the thought that H.H., who had made it clear that he found homosexuality repugnant, would find out, Forster dropped the boy and for some days lived in "shame and terror," convinced that H.H., who seemed suddenly distant, had been informed of his flirtation. Unwilling to continue in this fashion, Forster resolved to approach H.H. and "confess":

> I said that I must see him alone, and the conversation then proceeded more or less as follows:
>
> "My mind is clear at last, and I can now speak: I haven't been able to do so before. As I think you know, I am in great trouble."
>
> "Tell me Morgan—I have noticed you were worried."
>
> "I have tried to have carnal intercourse with one of the coolies and it has become known."
>
> "With a coolie-girl?"
>
> "No, with a man. You know about it, and if you agree I think I ought to resign."
>
> "But Morgan—I know nothing about it—this is the first I've heard of it."
>
> His voice was kind, but I wished I was dead. I had made even a greater fool of myself than I thought possible . . . I needn't have confessed.[29]

Though Forster concludes his recollection of this awkward moment by suggesting that his confession has been unnecessary, he is, in fact, not correct. The act of confession is one of intense privacy; its moment is a moment of deliberate vulnerability. The confessing subject can accept, even court, this vulnerability because of the assumption of secrecy. But secrecy is not confession's sole precondition. In rendering a confession, the subject engages in a regulated manipulation of the economies of memory and forgetting. In its moment of articulation, the confession is an act of remembrance, in which the voice transfers an article of shame from an archive of personal remembrance to a space of public inspection. But this space, in which the confessor fleetingly places the shameful memory, is a space of privilege that may be entered only by invitation. To be invited into this space is to be identified as the confessor's intimate and to assume a burden of forgetfulness. For in the moment following the enunciation of the confession, the confessor's silent request is that what has been remembered and confessed be forgotten, or placed in that strange and sealed realm of remembrance we call forgiveness. On either side of the confession lies silence, but the silence that follows confession is a collaborative muteness, a silence that only the confessor and the listener may broach, and then only to remember what they have agreed publicly to forget. In confessing to H.H., Forster appears to court the prince's censure but actually solicits the embrace of his forgiveness and silence; he asks H.H. at once to remember and forget his embarrassment, to participate in it, to assume it as their mutual possession. The word for this is friendship.

Friendship's confessions are not always confessions of embarrassment, but friendship seems often to approach a moment in which we remember a private shame and offer it as a sort of gift, as an invitation to make embarrassment mutual. Certainly this is true for Forster, who will discover in Aziz's embarrassment at the squalor of his dwelling an opportunity for the Indian to secure his intimacy with the Englishman by sharing his rooms with Fielding, and who will locate in his own embarrassments the origins of his friendship with H.H. In summarizing the rather sordid events that proceeded from his confession to the prince, Forster exhibits an uneasy recognition of the importance of his confession and what followed it: "When I look over that year, my verdict is unfavourable on the whole. I caused so much trouble all round, and my intimacy with H.H., the only gain, would have been achieved anyway I think" (*Hill of Devi*, 324). It must be allowed that Forster is correct, that he might have achieved intimacy with H.H. in some other way. But regarding this other path to friendship, Forster can only speculate, and he never in fact suggests an alternative route that he might have taken to intimacy with H.H. The friendship, to argue tautologically, was achieved as it was, through confession and the gift of embarrassment. The friendship would not, however, have been what it was if H.H. had not surprised Forster with his response to this confession, if he had not added to the gift of Forster's embarrassment the gift of a lover.

Much to Forster's surprise, H.H. indicated to him that he saw no real problem with his taking a lover and went so far as to offer to assist him in selecting

a companion. H.H. invited a servant up from the temple, paraded him before
Forster, and asked what he thought. Forster, unattracted to the young man,
demurred. Several days later, however, Forster reopened the subject: "On impulse I said, 'I wish you would get a boy for me.' The subject rose promptly to
the surface of his mind and he said without apparent effort: 'I was waiting for
you to mention it Morgan—not the least difficulty—let Kanaya come and
shave you—no possible suspicion . . . then if you like him, and he's willing, all
right, otherwise we'll find other work for him'" (*Hill of Devi*, 317–18). There
is a return in this moment to the banquet night of 1912, to H.H.'s procure-
ment of Indian clothing for his guest and his willingness to work patiently
with Forster until an appropriate and fitting gift has been found. Here, however, as H.H. labors to discover not a gift of clothing but the gift of a human
being, the prince emerges not as Forster's couturier but as his pimp. Rustom
Bharucha has commented on this role that H.H. plays, with Forster's complicity and assent, as Pandar to his friend. "While the Maharaja appears to us,
quite literally as a character—he is whimsical and delightfully absurd in his
manoeuverings and strategies—one should also keep in mind that he embodies power. As the ruler of the state he *owns* Kanaya's life. . . . And significantly,
as his Highness's friend, Forster also assumes an ownership of Kanaya."[30] Forster, as Bharucha is aware, seemed entirely untroubled by his partnership in
this transfer of human ownership. He met Kanaya, liked him, and took him as
a lover. We never, however, discover whether Kanaya was amenable to the
arrangement. He does not speak; he is spoken for. Sadly, indeed quite horri-
bly, this is unsurprising.

Kanaya, in this arrangement, is treated not as a human being but as a gift,
little different from the gift of clothing that Forster had received from H.H.'s
hands a decade before. Forster does make a perfunctory effort to pretend
otherwise. "The third meeting with Kanaya," he recalls, "was punctual and
gratified my desires. As is usual with me, I at once felt interest and tenderness
towards him and hoped we might become friends" (*Hill of Devi*, 319). Kanaya
and Forster do not, however, ever become friends. By the end of their affair
Forster despises him, mixes intercourse "with the desire to inflict pain," and
has grown to feel that "he was a slave, without rights, and I a despot whom no
one could call to account" (324). Kanaya does, however, assume a role in the
development of a friendship in which, now, both invitation and violence have
preceded intimacy. In growing intimate with, and possessing, Kanaya's body,
Forster does not become friends with this "slave" but deepens his friendship
with the man who provided the slave's compliant body. Sara Suleri has noted
that in *A Passage to India*, Adela Quested "plays the part of a conduit or pas-
sageway for the aborted eroticism between the European Fielding and the
Indian Aziz."[31] Kanaya plays a similar role for Forster and H.H. His body
serves as the scene of a rape that Forster and his host will maintain as their
private secret. The servant's body lies between them as the object for which

Forster confesses a shameful desire, as the gift that H.H. offers his guest in the place of penance, and as the space that H.H. and Forster collaboratively violate in their trespass to intimacy. As Adela is the conduit through which Fielding and Aziz will pass in their movement toward one another, so Kanaya is the ticket that will purchase Forster's passage to friendship in India.

THE ENDS OF INTIMACY

As the final and most famous words of Forster's *A Passage to India* testify, Aziz and Fielding's friendship fails. "Why can't we be friends now?" Fielding demands of Aziz as they are out riding. "It's what I want. It's what you want." To this poignant request, the narrative responds, "But the horses didn't want it—they swerved apart; the earth didn't want it, sending up rocks through which riders must pass single file; the temples, the tank, the jail, the palace, the birds, the carrion, the Guest House, that came into view as they issued from a gap and saw Mau beneath: they didn't want it, they said in their hundred voices, 'no, not yet,' and the sky said, 'No, not there'" (362). A continuum of desire links these closing locutions and the ultimate sentences of Edward Thompson's *The Other Side of the Medal*. That longing for friendship which succeeds the text of Thompson's narrative, and which, I have suggested, precedes the writing of Forster's novel, is not satisfied in the later text, merely echoed. Beginning where Thompson ends, Forster cannot go any further. He does not disavow friendship but does discover it frustrated. Finding no moment of accomplishment in the difficult time of the now, Forster once more condemns friendship to the tantalizing time of postponement.

Though there is general critical recognition of its failure, there is little agreement about why this friendship fails. Lionel Trilling, who delighted in the awkwardnesses, contradictions, doubts, and self-deceits of Forster's characters, might have put it down to the author's penchant for moral complication, to an unwillingness to resolve too easily in an accomplished friendship the problems and brutalities of empire. One of his primary criticisms of the novel, however, is that in this text Forster is too ready to abandon an ethic of uncertainty. He finds Forster, through his plot of friendship, too willing to suggest the banal wisdom that "by reason of the undeveloped heart the English have thrown away the possibility of holding India. For want of a smile an Empire is to be lost."[32] In light of this apparent turn by Forster from moral complication to friendship, Trilling finds himself at a loss to explain why the friendship does, indeed, fail. Trilling's bafflement is in many ways a product of his too glib reading of the novel's anatomy of friendship, of his desire to counterpose friendship to difficulty, and to reduce Forster's catalog of intimacy's tropes to the stupidity of the smile. Friendship in *A Passage to India* is, however, complication, not the easy tug that unties difficulty's knot. If Trilling is correct in suggesting that empire is not to be saved, or redeemed, by the friendships that it precedes with its rude and violent acts of self-invitation, Forster's annulment of Aziz and Fielding's friendship can be read as signaling his awareness of that same difficult knowledge.

Edward Said, in his reading of the novel, offers a more assured interpretation of the friendship's collapse. He attributes Fielding and Aziz's failure to Forster's complicity with an Orientalist discourse intent on manufacturing the East as the West's impossible opposite. "We are left at the end," Said argues, "with a sense of the pathetic distance still separating 'us' from an orient destined to bear its foreignness as a mark of its permanent estrangement from the West."[33] Ironically, through this reading, Said translates this moment of failure into a moment of success. It is, he suggests, the object of that Orientalist discourse in which he locates Forster's text to delimit the East. Orientalist discourse, Said argues, succeeds in that moment when a connection, of the Wordsworthian sort of which Forster was always dreaming, fails to occur. In failure, and failure's announcement of a limit that cannot be crossed, lies the Orientalist's success. To fail to fail would be, Said's argument implies, simply too dangerous. It would render possible too perilous a trespass of Major Turton's injunction on intimacy. That Said's reading so easily aligns Forster's narrative voice with the forbidding cadences of the Collector is a matter of obvious concern. In dwelling on Orientalist intentionality, which selects failure as its ordained trope of accomplishment, Said tends to disregard the complexities and inadequacies of imagination. His reading implies that Fielding and Aziz's failure must express Forster's narrative intention rather than Forster's imaginative collapse. Such a reading seems, at best, inattentive to Forster's troubled labors to render visible and to locate the relationships of intimacy engendered by a trespass of the Orientalist—and Anglo-Indian—limit. Said amplifies this inattentiveness by his rather loose translation of Forster's language. For where Forster wearily refers friendship to a postponed and unnamed future, in a gesture that does not deny friendship but refuses it accomplishment in the time of the now, Said has Forster refusing not only the present but the future also. In the place of a failure *now*, Said has Forster announcing a *permanent* estrangement. Forster's "not yet" cannot, however, simply be translated into a "not ever," for if that "not yet" enacts a displacement of possibility, and desire, it does not announce an absolute refusal.

Rustom Bharucha, in an essay rather too willing to discover a happy ending to Forster's novel, expresses a similar dissatisfaction with Said's reading. "My problem with this interpretation," he notes, "is that it is much too strategic in its focus and situation in the wider spectrum of Orientalist thought. Yes, there is separation in the final moments of *A Passage to India*, but it is so subtly juxtaposed with intimacy that one might say that Aziz and Fielding have acquired a mutual understanding of each other for the first time—perhaps because of the separation. . . . The irony that Forster suggests so seductively is that Aziz and Fielding *are* friends at the moment of parting."[34] Like Said,

however, Bharucha discovers a success in the novel's closing moment of failure. Yet success here is achieved not despite failure but because of failure, or,
oddly, *as* failure. Friendship, in this reading, becomes the moment of separation and of loss. By drawing a connection between the writing of the novel and
an event which immediately preceded it, Bharucha finds evidence to support
this contention that in Forster intimacy is complicit with loss. In 1923, as
Forster was about to begin the work of completing his abandoned manuscript,
his Egyptian friend and lover Mohammed-el-Adl died. On the 25th of March,
Forster entered one of several passages into his diary in which he brooded over
this loss: "You are dead Mohammed, and Morgan is alive and thinks more
about himself and less of you with every word he writes. You called out my
name at Beebitel hagar station after we had seen that ruined temple. . . . It was
dark and I heard an Egyptian shouting who had lost his friend: Margan, Margan—you calling me and I felt we belonged to each other, you had made me
an Egyptian. When I call you on the downs now, I cannot make you alive, nor
can I belong to you. . . ."[35] Bharucha wishes to read this as a moment in which,
through loss, friendship triumphs—not as a mere connection or affirmation,
but as a translation of identity. "There is not otherness in this friendship," he
declares. "The categories of 'you' and 'me' are dissolved; Forster can be Egyptian" (114). From such a conclusion, Bharucha infers that loss is friendship's
condition, that it enacts a calculus of cancellation in which, deprived of his
identity by separation and the dark, the Englishman can assume the identity
of his departed friend and literally become an Egyptian. By implication, Fielding can become an Indian and belong to Aziz in the very moment of their
return to that condition of mutual invisibility with which their friendship
began.

The language of Forster's diary, however, refuses Bharucha's reading. In the
diary, Forster brackets the moment of his Orientalization with a recognition of
the impossibility of sustaining such a state of magical translation. The passage
begins with Forster's acknowledgment of his growing inability to think about,
or remember, Mohammed and concludes with Forster's affirmation that he
cannot belong to his friend. Forster hems in the moment of invisibility in
which he imagines that he does belong to Mohammed—a moment clearly
echoed in the scene of Aziz and Fielding's screened introduction—with more
enduring passages of time in which he cannot render Mohammed visible,
apprehending this failure of vision as the annulment of intimacy rather than
the seal of friendship. In memory Forster can call Mohammed from the deeps,
but only in memory; and remembrance, Forster discovers, cannot survive the
encroachments of the now.

Forster's novel finally and reluctantly returns to this arresting problem of
friendship's temporality. Forster's tropes of friendship—rich, copious, and
difficult—include his attempts to locate intimacy in the divergencies of invitation, gift giving, transvestism, confession, and embarrassment. But his ulti-

mate problem is not to compute friendship's physics but to fix its time. In resolving this problem, which is also the problem of knowing how to render friendship, or the body of the friend, presently visible, Forster finds himself unable to resist a return to the uncanny, repetitive, and typological temporality of the Mutiny. Fielding and Aziz acquaint themselves with one another through the embarrassing exchange of the collar stud, but they become intimate in the crisis of the Marabar Caves. While Adela constructs and then abandons a reading of the caves in which uncertainty and disappointment are construed as signifying rape, her English fellows in Chandrapore are only too willing to locate the caves in an alternative but familiar reading of imperial crisis.

Desperately nostalgic for the violences of the Mutiny, the English community in Chandrapore, like Lord Hardinge's English officers, discover in Adela's sufferings less an outrage than an opportunity to return to the "stirring days" of 1857, to discover in this act of "betrayal" confirmation of their treasured narrative of imperial belonging, to contemplate the pleasurable possibility of turning and firing at the crowd. The police officer charged with investigating Aziz's "crime" swiftly interprets the Indian doctor's disloyalty as a return of this Anglo-Indian repressed. "Read any of the Mutiny records," he advises Fielding in attempting to explain to him what has really happened in the Marabar Caves, "which rather than the Bhagavad Gita should be your bible in this country" (187). Mrs. Turton, the Collector's wife, trumps the inspector. She indicates a precise knowledge of those records and recommends a return to the efficacious punishments meted out in those glorious days: "They ought to crawl from here to the cave on their hands and knees whenever an Englishwoman is in sight," she insists, "they oughtn't to be spoken to, they ought to be spat at, they ought to be ground into the dust" (240). Mrs. Turton's hysteria is not her exclusive property. It is a collective possession of Chandrapore's English community, a possession most visibly on display as the English gather in their club to contemplate strategy and prepare themselves lest the "niggers attacked" (200). Huddled together in that space, the English are able to return in memory to the time of the Mutiny, to lend their banal surroundings the aura of one of the Mutiny pilgrimage's canonical sites: "The club was fuller than usual, and several parents had brought their children into the rooms reserved for adults, which gave the air of the Residency at Lucknow" (200).

Fielding, who is present at this grim but oddly celebratory and rallying occasion, determines that for his purposes, as for Edward Thompson's, friendship must be enacted as a gesture of public articulation, as an act of speaking which will dispute the unique pretextual authority of the Mutiny. Rising before the assembled members of the club, Fielding calmly insists, "I believe Dr. Aziz to be innocent" (210). This is another slight but crucial moment. In offering Fielding this opportunity to play Abdiel before the satanic host, in allowing him to insist that it is not inevitable that a plot of violence and betrayal emerge from the empire's moments of crisis, in permitting him to read the Marabar Caves as something other than yet another Mutiny *lieu de memoire*, Forster identifies his narrative of friendship as the Mutiny's counterplot and implies that Fielding is most Aziz's friend at this difficult moment in which he suggests that this crisis might be the occasion not for violence but for intimacy, not a moment of repetition but one of beginning.

Sara Suleri has argued that the essential sadness of Forster's narrative inheres in the inability, emblematized in the collar stud scene, of Fielding and Aziz to locate the possibilities of "erotic trust" in anything more than the repressed rituals of "dressing with decorum."[36] This may be so. To my mind, however, the greater sadness attaches to Fielding's declaration. For this moment defines the limit of Fielding's friendship with Aziz. Their intimacy, which is so publicly exorbitant in this moment, proves unable to survive his testimony. Thereafter, they will be together, will celebrate together, will feast together, but will be unable to separate one another, or their memories of one another, from this moment in which, though absent from one another, their convictions are so amply mutual. Beyond this moment their discourse will decay: "a pause in the wrong place, an intonation misunderstood, and a whole conversation went awry" (305). From this collapse of intelligibility and the collapse of vision so starkly realized on the feast night when Fielding, in Indian garb, finds himself awkwardly and unperceivedly aping his friend, their divorce issues. Hereafter, friendship survives for Aziz and Fielding solely as an item of memory, as a remembrance of a moment of crisis in which the Mutiny could have been rewritten but in which solidarity was offered instead.

Forster's failure, finally, is due not to his inability to imagine the lineaments of an imperial friendship, or even to his exaggeration of the capacities of friendship to save empire with a smile, but to his incapacity to locate friendship outside of this moment of crisis in which intimacy is offered as war's alternative. Friendship atrophies in this text because it cannot survive the encroachments of the mundane. Resolutely committed to discovering intimacy in a monumental, and antimonumental, moment, Forster finds his characters' friendship crippled not by the return of the repressed but by the banal rearrivals of the everyday. An object of desire whose time is the time of remembrance and anticipation, Fielding and Aziz's intimacy cannot cope with a present that refuses to announce itself as exhilarating and critical. This is the sad knowledge to which Forster returns at the close of his text, and which, unable to speak himself, he has the Indian landscape speak for him. In this moment of closure the only answer that Forster offers to the problem of friendship's failure is the answer of temporal frustration. Ultimately, Forster represents failure as a property of imperial history, as the inability of the English or the Indian subject to find and sustain a workable present in which, divorced from their commitments to memory and anticipation, the inhabitants of empire can achieve and hold their illicit objects of desire.

Chapter Four

PUT A LITTLE ENGLISH ON IT:
C.L.R. JAMES AND ENGLAND'S FIELD OF PLAY

> What interests me, and is, I think, of general interest, is that
> as far back as I can trace my consciousness the original
> found itself and came to maturity within a system that was
> the result of centuries of development in another land,
> was transplanted as a hot-house flower is transplanted
> and bore some strange fruit.
> —C.L.R. James, *Beyond a Boundary*

> [They] *made of* the rituals, representations, and laws
> imposed on them something quite different from what
> their conquerors had in mind. . . .
> —Michel de Certeau, *The Practice of Everyday Life*

Not There, Not Yet

While Forster consistently represents the death of intimacy as consequent on an imperial construction of time, in the closing pages of *A Passage to India* he identifies failure as a temporal *and* a spatial phenomenon. As Fielding and Aziz take their last ride, India's rocks, temples, jails, palaces, and guest houses, indeed all the visible features of the subcontinental landscape, echo the mournful cadences of the text's famous "not yet" with an equally dour "not there." This is not the first time that Forster has had his map of India mouth the rhetoric of disappointment. From the opening pages of the novel, Forster commits himself to a hyperbolically antipicturesque and frustrating cartography of imperialism: "Except for the Marabar Caves—and they are twenty miles off—the city of Chandrapore presents nothing extraordinary. . . . The streets are mean, the temples ineffective, and though a few fine houses exist they are hidden away in gardens or down alleys whose filth deters all but the invited guest" (3–5). Though Forster spends most of his sorrowful energies in constructing a temporal plot of failure and loss, this optics of imperialism, which seems devoted to mapping out a space of imperial inhabitation that exists to disappoint, never vanishes from his text. If we were to extrapolate a general cartography of imperialism from this melancholy survey of India, we would find that England, in raising the Union Jack across the globe, had yoked itself to a geography of disappointment.

While it may be tempting to suggest that England met its empire solely within such a space of frustration, and that England's long imperial adventure succeeded only in incorporating a region of failure into the extended cartography of Englishness, to attend exclusively to such elaborately weary plots of disappointment would once again amount to little more than an act of censorship. For other visions of imperial space exist within the vast archives of empire, visions suggesting that the empire could dispose itself not solely as a map of violation, and of loss, but as a space of accomplishment. It is with one of those other images that I wish to begin this chapter, with a textual snapshot of a strangely beautiful body and a complex space in which imperialism emerges not as that which brands the spoor of failure onto England but as that which re-creates the locations of Englishness.

A Long, Low "Ah"!

The image is of a slovenly and unruly man and of a stroke, a gesture, a unique and delightful movement of the body. It is an image framed by the bedroom window of a small boy living in Trinidad near the turn of this century. Peering through that window, the young C.L.R. James would follow the play on the cricket pitch across the street, and, as often as not, his eyes would fix on the figure of Matthew Bondman. He was not, by the standards of James's mother and aunts, a reputable figure, "He was generally dirty. He would not work. His eyes were fierce, his language was violent and his voice was loud."[1] But when he turned to the playing of cricket, Matthew Bondman was transformed in the eyes of the boy, and in the mind of the man who, writing some fifty years later, chose to begin his subtle and brilliant memoir of a life, a place, and a game with a portrait of Bondman's athletic artistry. "Matthew had one saving grace—Matthew could bat. More than that, Matthew, so crude and vulgar in every aspect of his life, with a bat in his hand was all grace and style. . . . He had one particular stroke that he played by going down on one knee. It may have been a slash through the covers or a sweep to leg. But, whatever it was, whenever Matthew sank down and made it, a long, low 'Ah!' came from many a spectator, and my own little soul thrilled with recognition and delight" (14). Frozen in the moment of that stroke, Matthew Bondman figures the intoxicating and rebellious experience of the sublime. That "slashing" stroke cuts, as the sublime must, through the leaden weight of convention, rupturing the customary arrangement of the visual field. It shocks and delights the spectator and thrills the soul. But it does more than this. For the stroke is an emblem not only of rupture and release but also of discipline. Bondman not only masters the stroke, the stroke masters him. It subordinates him and his body to its own logic and to the logic of the game of which it is a part. It is the stroke that, in the eye of the boy and the mind of the man, tames, if only for a moment, Matthew's unruly fierceness. It gives him "grace and style." It incorporates him into the society from which the disapprobation of James's aunts and mother have excluded him. At play in the fields of the empire, Bondman's violent alterity is disciplined, and he is invested, for a moment, with that fetishistic if shifting quality which British colonialism both worshiped and, in part, invented: Englishness.

That the British colonists paid exorbitant tribute to the idea of Englishness is not the subject of this chapter. Rather, turning from those moments of imperial failure that so trouble and haunt E. M. Forster's writing, I wish to examine the cricket field as a space of imperial accomplishment, a space, once again, of intimacy and apparent discipline, but one in which an imperial writing of English identity frees itself from the tropes of wounding and disappointment to stage Englishness as a collaborative performance. In addition to reading C.L.R. James's *Beyond a Boundary*, this chapter will range across the nineteenth and twentieth centuries, between the spaces of Thomas Arnold's Rugby, Queen Victoria's Diamond Jubilee celebrations, and James's own island "home," between texts that reveal a defining intimacy in the construction of one particular idea of English cultural identity and a profound instability in this idea of Englishness, an instability that is revealed, if only for a moment, in the movement of Matthew Bondman's bat across the subversive and disruptive space of the sublime and the disciplinary fields of colonial power. My intention here is neither to suggest that England transplanted its already formed culture to the colonies, nor that that culture was wholly manufactured abroad, but that Englishness was and is collaboratively written in both these spaces *and* in the space "between" England and its erstwhile empire, in the imaginary space of the boundary, in the fluctuating and uncertain space of translation.

"They taught us nothing. . . . But I Think they taught it very well"

In tracing the influence of cricket on his life and on the life of the community in which he was raised, James ventures back to the middle years of the English nineteenth century to explore the social arrangements that allowed three men to exert a peculiar influence over the Victorian invention of English national culture and, through this invention, over the culture of English colonialism. The three were Thomas Arnold (the revered headmaster of Rugby and the father of Matthew Arnold), Thomas Hughes (the author of *Tom Brown's Schooldays*, an immensely popular chronicle of public school life at Rugby during the years of Arnold's tenure), and W. G. Grace (the preeminent Victorian cricketer). James suggests that an intimate bond enabled these men to establish a model of Englishness that, for fifty years or more, constrained constructions of English cultural identity. The cerebral and moralizing headmaster and the vigorous athlete were not, James allows, natural allies, but they, and the principles they represented, were inextricably linked by the popular, sentimental work of the novelist. Arnold and Grace met in the space occupied by Hughes's intended audience—the middle- and upper-class English boy. That boy, particularly during his public school years, became a synecdoche of the idea of English identity which these three men helped to construct, an idea that became a dominant figure in the Victorian and colonial discourses on English identity. Before turning to this boy, however, we must consider the pedagogical spaces in which Arnold, Hughes, and Grace, in their various ways, invented and disciplined his identity.

Thomas Arnold became headmaster of Rugby in 1827 and held the post for fifteen years, until his death in June of 1842. His tenure as headmaster marks what one might call an event in the discourse of Englishness. It signaled, as Raymond Williams argues in *The Long Revolution*, the arrival of a middle-class dominance in the control of the public schools and precipitated the rapid and massive expansion of those schools and of their ability to discipline a hegemonic representation of English cultural identity.[2] As David Newsome indicates in his study of Victorian education, *Godliness and Good Learning*, Arnold led this middle-class capture of the pedagogical factories of Englishness:

> In the nineteenth century it is especially noticeable that the middle classes, already economically powerful and—as the century progressed—increasing steadily in their political significance, were gradually displacing the aristocracy as the arbiters of taste, the guardians of morality and as the power that dictated contemporary conventions and values. . . . One of the most important manifestations of this rising influence of the middle class was the emergence of the public schools as important national institutions. In the first place, it is clear that the pressure of middle class opinion led to the reforms of the older public schools by Arnold, the Arnoldians and others. In the second place, the popularity of the reformed schools led to the creation of a great many new schools in the 1840's and 1850's, largely fashioned on the Rugby model.[3]

The Arnoldian control of public school life and of the idea of Englishness that the public school came to represent was eventually transformed from within the school system itself, or, to be more precise, from the playing fields that surrounded the school. Until the time of this transformation, however, Arnold, his ideas, and his disciples held sway over Rugby, the public schools, and a Victorian attempt to define the nature of Englishness.

But what precisely did Arnold, and the middle-class idea that he symbolized, represent? What did he wish to inscribe on the body of the schoolboy and, through this inscription, on the nation itself? Morality, or, to be more precise, the moral code of the "Christian gentleman" put to the service of the state. In a lecture that he delivered at Oxford a year before his death, Arnold spelled out his aims: "There are certain principles which the state wishes to inculcate on all its members, certain habits which it wishes to form, a certain kind and degree of knowledge which it wishes to communicate; such, namely, as bear more or less immediately on its great end, its own intellectual and moral perfection, arising out of the perfection of its several members. Now . . . as far as this instruction is applied to the young, it goes under the name of education; as far as it regards persons of all ages, it generally takes the form of religion."[4] But for its celebratory tenor, Arnold's language is remarkably reminiscent of Pierre Bourdieu's critique of the institutions of national pedagogy. In his study *Reproduction in Education, Society and Culture*, Bourdieu suggests that national institutes of pedagogy do not merely reproduce a dominant ideology but erase the visibility of the violences by which a particular ideology assumes a hegemonic position in society. He further contends that the function of national pedagogy is less to communicate the content of any particular ideological figuration than to reproduce, in the pedagogical relation, the relations of power which allow that ideology to exist, while at the same time, by naturalizing the pedagogical relation, to mask the violence that it reproduces and on which it depends.

> In any given social formation, the dominant educational system is able to set up the dominant pedagogical work as the work of schooling without either those who exercise it or those who undergo it ever ceasing to misrecognize its dependence on the power relations making up the power relations in which it is carried on, because (1) by the means proper to the institution, it produces and reproduces the necessary conditions for the exercise of its internal function of inculcating, which are at the same time the sufficient conditions for the external function of reproducing the legitimate culture and for its correlative contribution towards reproducing the power relations; and because (2) by merely existing and persisting as an institution, it implies the institutional conditions for misrecognition of the symbolic violence it exerts.[5]

Later in this chapter, I will return to the issue of pedagogic misrecognition to suggest that the national pedagogy of Victorian Englishness misrecognizes not only the violence that it exerts and by which it is enabled, but also the spaces of uncertainty within its own discursive field, spaces of uncertainty made visible by the performances of the writings of James and others. For the moment, however, let us return to Arnold, an educator for whom, as Bourdieu suggests, the purpose of education was less to instruct or to impart a specific body of information than to construct and discipline the identity of the student. As Arnold noted: "He who educates must take a higher view, and pursue an end accordingly far more complicated. He must adjust the respective claims of bodily and mental exercise, of different kinds of intellectual and physical labour; he must consider every part of his pupil's nature, physical, intellectual, and moral; regarding the cultivation of the last, however, as paramount to that of either of the others" (38).

Arnold pursued these goals by combining in himself the roles of educator and cleric, and by reforming the disciplinary systems of fagging and pre-fecting. He was the first headmaster of the founding nine English public schools to combine in one person the functions of headmaster and pastor. The weekly sermon that he delivered to the assembled mass of schoolboys was the central and regulating moment of the school calendar, one which Thomas Hughes has famously described:

> The oak pulpit standing out by itself above the school seats. The tall gallant form, the kindling eye, the voice, now soft as the low notes of a flute, now clear and stirring as the call of the light infantry bugle, of him who stood there Sunday after Sunday, witnessing and pleading for his Lord, the King of righteousness and love and glory, with whose spirit he was filled, and in whose power he spoke. . . . We listened, as all boys in their better moods will listen (aye, and men too for the matter of that), to a man who we felt to be, with all his heart and soul and strength, striving against whatsoever was mean and unmanly and unrighteous in our little world.[6]

But what did "the Doctor" communicate to his students? An idea of manliness, of moral discipline and purity? Perhaps. Though, as young Tom admits, the boys grasped little of this: "We couldn't enter into half of what we heard; we hadn't the knowledge of our own hearts or the knowledge of one another; and little enough of the faith, hope, and love needed to that end" (*Tom Brown's Schooldays*, 123). What they could perceive was the figure of the man himself, his authority, and the fact of their subordination to him. This is, in fact, the very thing that Arnold was communicating—an order of subordination and obedience, of submission to the authority of the moral code that, though not understood, was nevertheless manifest in his person.

What Arnold was inscribing on the boys was the pedagogical relation itself, its metonymic figuration of the state's relation to the individual, and the de-ity's relation to the human. In a situation in which the information communi-cated to the boys approached a zero point, Arnold wrote the stark discursive arrangements of authority and discipline (represented by the very spatial orga-nization of the chapel and his physical presence) on the boys. As Bourdieu has it: "The conditions which make linguistic misunderstanding possible and tol-erable are inscribed in the very [educational] institution; quite apart from the fact that ill-known or unknown words always appear in stereotyped configu-rations capable of inducing a sense of familiarity, magisterial language derives its full significance from the situation in which the relation of pedagogic com-munication is accomplished, with its social space, its ritual, its temporal rhythms; in short, the whole system of visible or invisible constraints which constitute pedagogic action as the action of imposing and inculcating a legiti-mate culture" (*Reproduction*, 108). Or as an old Etonian, Lord Plumer, put it rather more bluntly, "We are often told that they taught us nothing at Eton. It may be so, but I think they taught it very well."[7]

Allied to the disciplinary work of religion, of the chapel and the Doctor's sermons, were the linked systems of prefecting and fagging. In some ways, these two systems superseded the discipline of religious instruction in organizing and constraining the everyday life of the boys at Rugby and in imprinting upon them, in a far more continuous and sustained fashion than that of the sermon, the normalizing and authorizing signature of a middle-class, Arnoldian conception of Englishness. All of the students in the lower forms of the school were required to fag for, or act as the servants of, the boys enrolled in their final year of instruction; from this oldest group of sixth-form students, Arnold selected an elect number as prefects or praepostors. When Arnold arrived at Rugby, there was a system in place whereby the sixth-form boys were charged with keeping order in the classes. He seized upon this model and shaped it to his purposes, making of the prefects a governing body for all of the affairs of the school. Lytton Strachey, in his wonderfully ironic biographical essay on Arnold, has detected in the Doctor's use of the prefects an attempt to reproduce in the institutional space of the school a Miltonic vision of social hierarchy: "This was the means by which Dr. Arnold hoped to turn Rugby into 'a place of really Christian education.' The boys were to work out their own salvation, like the human race. He himself, involved in awful grandeur, ruled remotely, through his chosen instruments, from an inaccessible heaven. Remotely and yet with omnipresent force. As the Israelite of old knew that his almighty Lawgiver might at any moment thunder to him from the whirlwind, or appear before his very eyes, the visible embodiment of power and wrath, so the Rugby schoolboy walked in a holy dread of some sudden manifestation of the sweeping gown, the majestic tone, the piercing glance, of Dr. Arnold."[8] Strachey has, I believe, read Arnold's intentions largely correctly. The prefects did in fact enable Arnold to reproduce an almost puritan model of social order. But the point that Strachey seems at once to have grasped and missed is that they did so by allowing Arnold to render himself, and the power he represented, invisible.

The prefects existed not as a curtain that Arnold periodically drew aside in order to heighten the dramatic energy of his intermittent appearances, but as a blind with which he masked the socially instituted power that ordered the boys' lives. The prefects' exercise of power enabled the boys to misrecognize, or visually displace, the arbitrary but complete power of the headmaster—until those scattered moments in which Arnold chose to show himself and the power of the class that had appointed him as its representative among these embryonic Englishmen, and then to withdraw. The prefects also served another function. They acted as a mechanism allowing the boys to internalize a disciplinary code that, if it had been invested only in the person of the headmaster, would have remained resolutely external to themselves. The prefects represented the ability of Arnold's construction of Englishness, of morality, of normalized cultural identity, to become an autodisciplinary measure. Both in the praepostors' inspection of themselves and in the younger boys' vision of them, the prefects became a mirror showing the students the image of a mature and "manly" Englishness—inscribed now on their own bodies. As Arnold himself puts it, "*they look upon themselves*," and by looking upon themselves, they looked away from the source of the power that disciplined them and wrote itself upon them.[9]

The prefects performed one final function. Through the system of fagging, they regulated the passages of young bodies across the floor of a highly intimate space, a space that, as Arnold repetitively lamented, constantly threatened to lapse into lawlessness or anarchy. In defending the linked systems of prefecting and fagging, Arnold returned again and again to the need for such systems in an institution grounded on physical intimacy: "I have said that fagging is necessary for a multitude of boys when *living together* . . . by day and by night, they are members of one and the same society, and in closer local neighbourhood with one another than is the case with the ordinary society of grown men" (*On Education*, 128, emphasis original). It is clear from Arnold's repeated returns to this subject that it caused him no little anxiety. And it was to control the close physical proximity of the boys to one another that he appointed his prefects. "Their business is to keep order amongst the boys; to put a stop to improprieties of conduct, especially to prevent that oppression and ill-usage of the weaker boys by the stronger which is so often ignorantly confounded with a system of fagging" (*On Education*, 129–30). Though Arnold proposes fagging as a means of controlling and checking those illegitimate performances of the schoolboys so nervously referred to here as "improprieties" and "ill-usages," the defensiveness of this passage indicates that if he thought that there was an evil afoot in the schools, he was aware that fagging could be read not only as its cure but as the disease itself.

If, in Homi Bhabha's terms, fagging represented the pedagogical inculcation of normalized, masculine, English identity, then, Arnold's language suggests, it might also represent a performative resistance to that regime. For the performative, as Bhabha reminds us, exists not outside the pedagogical, or in simple opposition to it, but within. It appears as an internal disturbance. The performative is culture in the midst of its own invention, a fluctuating movement.[10] In Raymond Williams's terms, it is the emergent. In terms of the Victorian public school discourse of Englishness, one movement of the performative may be located in the system of fagging. But it is located in such a way as to be both an act of resistance to the pedagogical and, at once, available to pedagogical discipline. In this regard, the performative emerges as less resolutely resistant to pedagogy than Bhabha tends to think. For the performative can be captured, frozen, and incorporated into the disciplinary work of pedagogy. As

James's *Beyond a Boundary* reveals, and as I shall discuss in concluding this chapter, the opposite is also true: the pedagogical, in its turn, may be unfrozen, mobilized, and set spinning into the destabilizing work of the performative.

Arnold intended the system of fagging to control the "improper" conduct of the students, and particularly to curb "direct sensual wickedness, such as drunkenness and other things forbidden together with drunkenness in the Scriptures" (*On Education*, 87). Arnold never refers explicitly to homoerotic relationships among the students, but it is difficult to imagine that this was not on his mind, or to imagine that it was not on the mind of Robert Benson, the headmaster of Wellington, who in 1858 made the following note in his journal: "Young boys to retire a certain time earlier than the older ones. While they are undressing, steward and matron to walk up and down in the middle of the dormitories to report any boy who goes out of his own dormitory to another, and by the time that the candles are to be put out the prefects are to come up to bed, and preserve the same order of silence. The danger is in an evening. . . . A vigilant inspection sufficient to prevent evils of a gross nature is next to impossible, and much evil would be the result of such inspection. The best inspection will be the introspection of leading boys of high tone and character."[11] Benson clearly believed not only that any number of the boys might form homoerotic relations in the intimate physical spaces of the public school, but also that it was virtually impossible for the headmaster and his staff to prevent such relations from developing. The only policing of intimacy available to the headmasters was the policing by the older boys themselves. But, and this is the problem of Arnold, Benson, and all their fellows, it was precisely these older boys who were likely not only to become involved in but to initiate such relations. It was often precisely those boys—boys who ran a system of fagging constructed as a means of interdicting the homoerotic—who turned fagging into an opportunity to pursue homosexual relationships.

John Addington Symonds was a student at Harrow in the 1850s. He was a prefect and the head of his school house. His posthumously published memoir shocked his fellow old boys by shattering a public school code of silence. Symonds begins the fifth chapter of his *Memoirs* with this stark, and rather condemnatory, account: "One thing at Harrow very soon arrested my attention. It was the moral state of the school. Every boy of good looks had a female name, and was recognized either as a public prostitute or as some bigger fellow's 'bitch'. Bitch was the word in common usage to indicate a boy who yielded his person to a lover. The talk in the dormitories and the studies was incredibly obscene. Here and there one could not avoid seeing scenes of onanism, mutual masturbation, the sports of naked boys in bed together."[12] Though in this passage, and in the pages that immediately follow, Symonds expresses an open distaste for the homoerotic encounters of the other students, by the end of the chapter he has fully reconciled himself to them, ac-

knowledged his own homosexuality, and initiated his first homosexual relationship. From within the intimacy of this relationship, his attitude toward an
institution he had previously hated begins to shift, and he comes to sympa-
thize with "the comely aspects of the place, the swiftness of young cricketers,
the bodies of divers curving for their plunge, the mirth of laughing boys, the
rich empurpled distance of the champaign when the sun sank over those im-
measurable fields." Symonds alters his relationship to the school in more than
these matters of aesthetic appreciation. Within his homosexuality, he avers, he
has liberated himself from the constraints of the school, from its system of
discipline and its official code of morality: "My mental and moral evolution
proceeded now upon a path which had no contact with the prescribed systems of education. I lived in and for myself. Masters and schools and methods
of acquiring knowledge lay outside me, to be used or neglected as I judged
best. I passed my last term at Harrow, between that April and the ensuing
August, in supreme indifference" (107). That last term, one might say,
Symonds passed into the space of the performative, not only into the space of
erotic performance, but into a space at once within the public school and
beyond the boundary of its cultural pedagogy, a space of resistance to the cult
of manly Englishness, a space not only available to him during that final term
but reentered and re-presented in the subversive performance of his writing.
His movement into the homoerotic, not unlike the movement of Matthew
Bondman's bat, represents the oscillating movement of the "fag" across the
pedagogical into the performative, from the disciplinary space of the public
school into the destabilizing spaces of Englishness.

But the "fag," like the bat, can also move back. Much as E. M. Forster
represents Fielding and Aziz's homoerotic encounter as constantly shifting
from the promise of intimacy to the inevitability of a misunderstanding contingent upon the relentless logic of colonial orderings of power, so Symonds
shifts his position from the destabilizing and resistant space of the homoerotic
to the disciplinary spaces of prefecting and fagging. For though he contends
that he remained untouched by the school in his final term, and though his
explorations of the homoerotic profoundly trouble the Victorian cult of manly
Englishness, he also remained in his position as a prefect, an arbiter of the
school's code of morality and discipline. "I maintained discipline," he allows,
"and on one occasion I remember caning two big hulking fellows" (87). The
issue is not that this maintenance of discipline represents some damning betrayal of the freedom which Symonds found in his homosexuality, but rather
that the exercise of institutional discipline figured in the system of fagging
could contain the intimacy of the homoerotic; that fagging was often at once
an exercise of pedagogical authority and a homoerotic performance; that
when an older boy took a younger as a lover, the homoerotic relation could be
used to inscribe the institution's very structures of authority. I am not suggest-

ing that this was precisely the case with Symonds (his lover did not, in fact, attend Harrow), or that such relationships were necessarily disciplinary (although, in Symonds's description, they often were), but rather that the pedagogical work of fagging could be, and often was, enacted through a homoerotic relationship, through precisely that action which can also be described as a performative destabilization of the work of pedagogy.

THE ENGLISH FIELD OF PLAY

Arnold died in 1842, and within twenty years of his death the public schools incorporated another form of performance into the pedagogical work of inscribing an idea of Englishness onto the public school boy. I am speaking, of course, of cricket. Arnold had not been a great believer in the moral efficacy of games, and the triumph of cricket and other athletic pursuits represents somewhat of a refiguration of his system. Arnold had privileged the chapel as *the* space in which to confront the boys with the claims made on behalf of a moral and manly idea of Englishness, and the sermon as *the* discourse with which to imprint on the boys' minds his version of cultural identity. His successors privileged cricket as the means of writing legitimate culture on the boys' bodies. James is adamant upon this point:

> What actually happened is one of the most fantastic transformations in the history of education and of culture. The English ruling classes accepted Arnold's aims and accepted also his methods in general. But with an unerring instinct they separated from it the cultivation of the intellect and substituted for it organized games, with cricket at the head of the curriculum. . . . What really interested them was Arnold's moral excellence and character training. His intellectual passion they had no use for. They found ample scope for character training and the inculcation of moral excellence in the two games, football and cricket, and of one of them, cricket, they made the basis of what can only be called a national culture. "A straight bat" and "It isn't cricket" became the watchwords of manners and virtue and the guardians of freedom and power. (*Beyond a Boundary*, 162–63)

This transformation of Arnold's system, this substitution of cricket for the chapel and the cultivation of intellect, occurred, James suggests, within two decades of Arnold's death. It was signaled by two events: the publication of Hughes's novel, and the arrival on the scene of public life of W. G. Grace.

Tom Brown's Schooldays was a wildly popular text, going through five editions within seven months of its initial publication. It is a fairly straightforward narrative in which Hughes documents the life of Tom Brown, an allegorical figure of middle-class English boyhood, from his birth through his graduation from Rugby. By far the greatest part of the text describes Tom's years at the public school. He is seen passing through a period of early rebellion against the school's code of conduct, the system of fagging, and his masters' and Doctor Arnold's tutelage, into a final wholehearted acceptance of the Rugby way of life. His internal transformation results from his gradual recognition of the wisdom of the Doctor's system and a friendship that the headmaster forces on him. After several years in which Tom has constantly flirted with expulsion from the school, the Doctor assigns as his new roommate a sickly but resolutely pious and intellectual young fellow named Arthur. This boy, a frailer version of Arnold's own person, gradually influences Tom as the older boy is obliged to protect him from the school's bullies. Arthur rescues Tom from his growing religious indifference, reconverting him to the habit of nightly prayer and daily scriptural study, and frees him from intellectual torpor, convincing him to throw away the various cribs by means of which he has managed to plow his way through his studies. If Arthur, however, represents the Doctor's triumph over Tom and functions, in some respects, as the stylus with which Arnold writes his signature onto Tom's character, then Tom's rescue of the painfully shy Arthur from the school's bullies represents the triumph of cricket and athleticism over Arnold's system. For it is by fighting for Arthur and, eventually, by placing him on the varsity cricket team (which Tom captains) that Tom removes the mark of effeminacy which has attached itself to Arthur's name, and incorporates him into the society of the school's elect. Without Tom and the cricketing skills that Tom teaches him, Arthur would have been damned by his fellows as surely as Tom, without Arthur, would have been damned, so Hughes suggests, by God.

In the penultimate chapter of the book, a description of Tom and Arthur's last days at the school, Arnold has withdrawn from the scene and the game of cricket has appeared to fill the space that he has voided. The chapter is entitled simply "Tom Brown's Last Match," and it describes the final match of the year, played by Rugby's first eleven against a team of London professionals. Tom and Arthur have grown into vigorous manhood, and their best friend, East, has graduated to make a career as an officer of the British Empire. The two students are left alone to stand at the side of the field, watching their teams play, discussing the game with a young master.

> "Come, none of your irony, Brown," answers the master. "I'm beginning to understand the game scientifically. What a noble game it is, too!"
>
> "Isn't it? But its more than a game. It's an institution," said Tom.
>
> "Yes," said Arthur, "the birthright of British boys old and young, as habeas corpus and trial by jury are of British men." (303–4)

They are, of course, exactly right. It was an institution, and it is not an accident that Arthur, in attempting to define its nature, compares it to the juridical institutions of the law and the courts, to another discourse and another space in which identity is constrained and disciplined. Again, James echoes this point: "If it [cricket] could so rapidly be elevated to the status of a moral discipline it was because it had been born and grew in an atmosphere and in circumstances untainted by any serious corruption. The Victorians made it compulsory for their children, and all the evidence points to the fact that they valued competence in it and respect for what it came to signify more than they did intellectual accomplishment of any kind. The only word that I know for this is culture" (164).

The fact that team sports, cricket foremost among them, replaced scholarship, and, to a great extent, the pulpit, as the primary device used by the post-Arnoldian guardians of England's public schools to write a cultural code upon their youthful charges is a virtual commonplace among the historians of Victorian education.[13] In the final, and robustly imperial, decades of the nineteenth century, as J. A. Mangan has demonstrated, this meant not only that the cricket field was the place where boys were taught the virtues of loyalty, obedience, discipline, and conformity which were held to be the characteristic virtues of the English "gentlemen," but that in acquiring these virtues they were also quite consciously being outfitted for the responsibilities of imperial rule: "The chosen medium for the fostering of these virtues was team games. . . . They were the pre-eminent instrument for the training of a boy's character. It was for this reason that the so-called 'games ethic' held pride of place in the pedagogical priorities of the period public school. And by means of this ethic the public schoolboy supposedly learned *inter alia* the basic tools of imperial command: courage, endurance, assertion, control and self-control . . . there was a further and important dimension to the later concept of 'manliness': its relevance to both dominance *and* deference. . . . At one and the same time it helped create the confidence to lead and the compulsion to follow" (*Athleticism*, 18, emphasis original). Or, as Charles Byles, a noted cricket enthusiast and master at the Uppingham school, stated the case for cricket and empire in one of the poems he wrote for his students,

> Hark the Empire calls, and what we answer give?
> How to prove us worthy of the splendid trust?
> Lo! we serve the Empire by the lives we live;
> True in all our dealings, honest, brave, and just,
> Training mind and body for the Empire's need.
>
> (Byles, in *Athleticism*, 137)

Disciplined in mind and body by the refashioning of their identities on the field of play, the boys were also, Byles confidently asserts, being trained to discipline the imperial subordinates whom it was, apparently, their civic fate to govern.

But as much as the late-Victorian public schools enlisted cricket in a disciplinary discourse, they also located it in a discourse of English remembrance.

And "locate," here, is the exact word. For if cricket implies a set of rules, a series of games played according to those rules, and a body of players submitting themselves to those rules, it is also defines a relation to a specific ordering of public space. Celebrating its orderliness, cricket also celebrates its ability to house the nation's past in its ordered spaces. If John Ruskin dreamed of a Gothic cathedral that could unify and inspire the nation, and Thomas Arnold yearned for a place where the character of the nation's youth could be normalized, England's sporting enthusiasts suggested that it was in the laying of the nation's cricket grounds that both these wishes were granted.

Chief among these fields are England's test match grounds—Lord's, the Oval, Trent Bridge, Old Trafford, Edgbaston, and Headingly—sites that, as James Kilburn declares in an adoring essay on these fields, are more than mere expanses of manicured grass: "In the chill and emptiness of winter a first sight of Lord's would be impressive. On a summer's morning, the seating filled and the field prepared for play, the picture checks the breath and clutches at the heart. There are few days from May to September without a match at Lord's and there is no day in the year there without the feel of cricket. Lord's is history modelled in turf and building. . . . Built to be impressive and to last . . . built as cathedrals are built, to dominate and to inspire and with unquestioning faith."[14] Francis Thompson's "At Lord's," the most famous of all cricket poems, also catches its breath before the sight of the time-heavy grounds. "For the field is full of shades as I near the shadowy coast, / And a ghostly batsman plays to the bowling of a ghost, / And I look through my tears at a soundless-clapping host. . . ."[15]

Significantly, though Thompson's poem names Lord's as its ground of memory, the poem recollects an 1878 match played not at Lord's but at Old Trafford, a difference that is worth noting precisely because the poem can so easily elide it. The poem can do so because, despite the fact that each cricket field has some unique characteristics as a playing ground, as spaces of memory England's fields of play are both individual and interchangeable: individual in the particular records of performance they enshrine but interchangeable as essential and generic locations of memory. Metonymic in their relation to one another, Old Trafford and Lord's name both themselves and one another, and all the other test, school, county, and village grounds scattered about the island, and, so long as the logic of metonymy holds, all the cricket grounds strewn across the empire. Metonyms of one another, not only does each of these itemized sites invoke every other item in the series, but, by the added logic of synecdoche, each and all of them name England, or, more accurately, Englishness—which, in its turn, is tautologically defined as a replicable and unchanging seriality, as an essential sameness across history and geography.

Two additional cricketing lyrics collected by J. A. Mangan, the first from the 1914 edition of the *Boys' Own Annual* and the second penned for the 1887

Annual Dinner of the Uppingham Rovers Cricket Club, endorse this appre-
hension of the cricket field as the English territory of the interchangeable and
the same.

> The playing fields of England
> All up and down the land,
> Where English boys play English games,
> How bright and fair they stand!
> 'Tis there in friendly rivalry
> School meets with neighbouring school
> And English boys all "play the game"
> And learn to keep the rule.
> There each one plays for side, not self,
> And strength and skill employs,
> On the playing-fields of England,
> The Pride of English Boys.
>
> (Unattributed, in *Athleticism*, 201)

> The same old game
> The same old game
> To forget or forgo it were a shame.
> When we are past and gone
> The young ones coming on
> Will carry on the same old game.
>
> (Unattributed, in *Athleticism*, 186)

Between them, these two snippets of verse identify what cricket promises to
accomplish for England: it will train the nation's and the empire's governing
class to submit themselves to a deindividuating principle of rule, will define
Englishness as a principle of sameness, and will clear a space of common
belonging in which England can see itself repeated, unaltered, across time and
space. On these grounds memory is thus not only disciplinary but reflective,
for what the nation remembers does not differ from its remembering self but
is a mirror image of the remembering self and a promise of that self's reappearance in another, future, time, or another, distant, place. As England comes to
its cricket fields to recollect itself, it confronts an essentially featureless image
of itself, or an image in which every distinctive feature of the island's and the
empire's countless British subjects has been subordinated to an English image
of "the same . . . the same."

While the cricket field thus emerges as the cathedral ground of an English
cult of memory whose central rite is the obligatory forgetting of difference, the
field offers England another way of remembering itself that is dependent on
the nation's ability to forget precisely what it pretends to be remembering. If

the featureless ghosts haunting Thompson's poem are avatars of an English populace destined to meet and imitate itself in a condition of spectral seriality, then the field across which those specters flit and gaze promises to return to this timelessly identical populace an image of a lost rural past, to return these wandering Englishmen, wherever they may find themselves, to a village England in which an authentic England dwells—but whose salient features they are immediately enjoined to forget.

The association of the cricket field with rural England begins, in the lore of the sport, with the name of the game itself: "cricket" as the editors of *The World of Cricket* attest, is a corruption of "crooked" or "crook," as in the crooks of "the shepherds of the Sussex Downs" who "invented" the game and "handed [it] down from father to son" (655). Blessed with such an unimpugnable patrimony—identified, in fact, with the fact of English patrimony itself, with the transmission of culture across the generations—cricket came by the late nineteenth century to be intimately identified with rural life, and the cricket field with the survival of the rural in the most metropolitan or foreign of spaces. As Mike Marqusee indicates in *Anyone but England*, "This is the myth at cricket's heart, the myth of an enduring and natural hierarchy, the myth of the village green" (29). Gazing on the green grasses of the "field," gathered about this transportable fragment of the English countryside, this everywhere-available "spot of time," the spectator, Geoffrey Moorhouse suggests, can indulge "a romantic illusion about the rustic way of life[;] it suggests a tranquil and unchanging order in an age of bewildering flux" (Moorhouse, in *Anyone but England*, 30).

A rural icon, cricket was nevertheless, or perhaps predictably, a sport that most fully claimed the nation's attention during the final decades of the industrial revolution. Between 1840 and 1860 the number of county clubs almost doubled; between 1836 and 1863 the number of county games tripled and then, in the next thirty years, tripled again; between 1869 and 1896 the Marylebone Cricket Club, *the* club of English cricket, quadrupled its match load.[16] Given this explosion of popularity during the years in which the industrial revolution was depopulating the English countryside and drawing ever more laborers into the nation's cities, while at the same time the final rounds of the enclosure movement were sealing off access to the commons, it seems possible to suggest that the game's burgeoning popularity among the public school and non–public school classes alike was directly related to the vanishing of that idyllic village England it claimed to re-present, that the cricket field, in a very real sense, compensated for a lost space of common belonging. Deprived of the land itself, England's laboring classes, one might say, were offered the cricket field as a substitute common.

The enclosure movement, or at least the ethic that inspired it, may, however, have impinged upon this common space in a more immediate fashion. Before 1870, as Marqusee notes, the rules of the game contained no provision for the field to be bounded; after that year, the fields, like the commons them-selves, were boundaried. While the causal link between the delimiting of the field and the enclosure of the commons is debatable, the structural parallel between the two events is not. For the fact that the dimensions of each village field, like the possession of each village green, could be submitted to a na-tional law, reflects, in each case, the apparent triumph of metropolitan order over rural variousness. The history of cricket may in this sense, like much of the history of England or the history of the English language, be said to be a history of internal colonization, a history of rural vernaculars confronting na-tional standards legislated from the city. Prior to 1744 cricket had no rules, or laws, as they are called, except those decided on in each individual place the game was played. In that year, facing a situation in which each local club arrived at each contest with their own understanding of the way the game was to be played, the London Club drew up a standard code of play. Thereafter the game developed between the poles of vernacularization and standardization: local clubs would introduce innovations and variations uncovered by the na-tional law, the variations would swell to unmanageable proportions and, even-tually, a new ever stricter standard would be produced. From the nineteenth century on, all these standards were legislated by one London club, the Mary-lebone Cricket Club (MCC), which, for almost two centuries, ruled over the cricket world in much the fashion that Whitehall ruled over the empire.

The details of the changing laws of cricket are not, however, the issue here. Rather what must be noted is that however much the grasses of the cricket field have allowed England's cricket audiences to run their eyes across an image of the rural green, and, in doing so, to unify themselves as a community of nostalgics, this ability to read an image of rural England off the surface of the cricket field has, for two centuries, depended on the readers' willingness to forget the local variousness of rural life, to side with a national authority in dismissing the performative instabilities of the game, to see, once more, in the very boundaried fact of the field, the unalterable and disciplinary image of the same.

Within England that image was made available not only to the nation's spectators, not only to those able to attend matches at one of the public schools, county clubs, or test grounds, but to the nation's readers. Indeed, cricket could come to signify what it did, a pedagogical institution, a space in which Englishness was played out and written on the bodies of its players and its audience, not only because it was a sport that could be performed and observed, but also because it was something that could be encountered on the page. It was not only the game but the reproduction of the game in print which made it something that could signify Englishness in a post-Arnoldian England.

But if cricket triumphed on the page, if, in particular, it triumphed on pages such as those of Thomas Hughes's novel—to which young readers, in the

Andersonian anonymity of their reading spaces, could turn to find represented the fetish of their national culture—it could do so, there, only for a limited number of readers. It could do so only for those who were likely to read Hughes's text. And these readers were largely those middle- and upper-middle-class individuals who either were attending, were to attend, or had attended a public school. This was the book's intended audience. Which is not to say that others did not read it, but rather that the institutions and the cricket fields Hughes represents were inaccessible to them. If cricket was to become the moral discipline of Victorian Englishness and one of the nation's disciplinary *lieux de memoire* for any other than the middle and upper classes, if it was to inscribe cultural identity on the working classes and England's colonial subjects also, it would require more heroes than Tom Brown, more fields on which to be played, and more pages on which to be represented. All existed. The heroes were many, but chief among them was W. G. Grace. The fields were scattered across England and the empire. The pages were in the metropolitan newspapers and magazines.

W. G. Grace was not only the preeminent cricketer of his time. He was, most commentators agree, cricket for his time. "Through W. G. Grace," says James in *Beyond a Boundary*, "cricket, the most complete expression of popular life in pre-industrial England, was incorporated into the life of the nation. As far as any social activity can be the life of one man, he did it. . . . He did not merely bring over what he inherited. Directly and indirectly he took what he found and re-created it. It is not certain that the game would so easily and quickly have gained and held its place without the technical transformation and the reclaim he gave to it. This total success might have come in a different way. It came his way, at the perfect historical moment, and it came completely" (169). Throughout his long career as the finest batsman and one of the finest bowlers in the country, Grace sustained immense national popularity. He was a hero of the Victorian age, a hero almost of the sort that Carlyle had suggested the age craved; but he was a hero of all classes. Upon his "bearded image," which Keith Sandiford insists in *Cricket and the Victorians* "was easily the most recognizable and popular among nineteenth-century Englishmen" (4), converged the socially and physically dispersed gazes of the community.

Captured in that gaze, "sustained and lifted higher than ever before by what has been and always will be the most potent of all forces in our universe—the spontaneous, unqualified, disinterested enthusiasm and goodwill of a whole community" (*Beyond a Boundary*, 182), Grace was transformed, precisely, into an "image," a spectacular object that concentrated and made visible the imagined unity, homogeneity, and serial unalterability of a national community moving anonymously through time, moving in pace with his amazing performances. Ronald Mason's comments on Grace emphasize this point. Like the fields he played on, Mason argues, Grace could represent Englishness because, in studying him, his spectators were once again willing to convert indi-viduality into a principle of interchangeability, to transform uniqueness into an image of themselves, to discover in Grace an idealized image of the same.

> The cricket-loving public found itself a symbol in the 1860's in the person of W. G. Grace. . . . a national figure as well known to everyone in the island by name and appearance as Queen Victoria herself. The Victorians, worshiping mas-culine authority and success, accorded the father figure an Olympic adoration. The magnificent physique, proud dominating beard and rich presumptuous char-acter of this astonishing cricketer were as effective in capturing his enormous public as his specialized skill. I would suggest that, wonderful as that skill was, it could never have invested him with the potent mystique that still attaches to his name had it not been for his unusual capacity to represent in his own presence and personality the ideals to which the age itself aspired.[17]

That this biographical sketch for a cricket encyclopedia so swiftly reproduces the mass adoration it seeks to describe, and that the image of Grace chosen by the editors of the encylopedia to accompany Mason's article is a "characteristic photograph" (547) showing Grace striding off an unnamed field on an unspecified date, only testify to Grace's enduring ability to deindividuate even as he is deindividuated, to transform his beholder into an English everyone whom Grace both inspires and is.

If Grace's image could unite the nation, so could his performances, though these too as both unique and reproduced events. Grace was the first player ever to score one hundred centuries. He was the first, that is, to score one hundred runs in a single match on a hundred separate occasions. And on the day in May of 1895 when he reached this mark, citizens all over England celebrated. "On what other occasion," asks James in *Beyond a Boundary*, "sport-ing or non-sporting, was there ever such enthusiasm, such an unforced sense of community, of the universal merged in the individual? At the end of a war? A victorious election? With its fears, its hatreds, its violent passions? Scrutinize the list of popular celebrations, the unofficial ones; that is to say the ones not organized from above. I have heard of no other that approached the celebra-tion of W. G.'s hundredth century. If this is not social history what is?" (182–83). Or, as Antonio Gramsci might ask, if this is not hegemony, what is?

Whatever it was, the celebration of Grace's accomplishment was not a con-sequence solely of the man's performances. It was enabled not only by the actions of this "hero" but by the swarming of institutionalized cricket over the surface of England's and the empire's terrain, and over the pages of the metro-politan magazines and newspapers. For surely if England, and perhaps even some corners of the empire, celebrated Grace's hundredth century, it could not have been because all the men and women of England and the empire had seen Grace score his runs, but because many had read that he had done so. As important as W. G. Grace was, it was the mid-Victorian expansion of the popular press (an expansion that, as Raymond Williams details, was fueled by the rapid increase of sports journalism),[18] which made cricket a visible spectacle of Englishness.[19] The mass celebrations which greeted the news of Grace's accomplishment indicate that it was through the swarming of cricket across the printed page, in conjunction with the sprawl of cricket fields across the surface of England and the empire, that the game, and the disciplinary discourse of cultural identity which it represented, could extended its reach beyond the spheres inhabited by the privileged fathers and sons of the middle class into the quarters occupied by the working classes and the agents and subjects of colonialism.

One of those colonial subjects, and one of the most eminent of all Victorian cricketers, K. S. Ranjitsinhji, bore witness to the fruitful marriage of cricket and print in an essay he wrote for one of the most famous of all cricket texts, *The Jubilee Book of Cricket*, a work commissioned for the Queen's Diamond Jubilee: "Cricket is the best athletic food for the public. . . . Neither time nor money has tarnished it. There are very few newspaper readers who do not turn to the cricket column first when the morning journal comes; who do not buy a halfpenny evening paper to find out how many runs W. G. or Bobby Abel has made."[20] Ranjitsinhji's essay seems, in fact, to testify not only to the services that the newspapers and cricket provided for one another but to the power of cricket, whether played, observed, or read about, to achieve its disciplinary ends among the English middle and working classes and the colonized alike. Ranjitsinhji revels in the fact that at a cricket match tens of thousands of spectators, unknown to one another and drawn from every conceivable social class and occupation, behave themselves with an essentially refined orderliness. "Something," he exults, "which keeps 25,000 people in order without external direction or suppression must be very real" (444–45). "It seems," he continues, "to have an extraordinarily good influence both upon those who take part in it and upon those who are merely spectators . . . games are beneficial to the nation as a whole" (449).

This benefit, Ranjitsinhji suggests, derives from the fact that during the Victorian era cricket became "spectacular." What he means is not that the game became excellent, though he believes this too, but that it became a spectacle, that the cricket field and the textual representation of cricket in the popular press created spaces to which the nation and the empire could come, and in which both could see England's essential nature performed and reflected. In so coming and so seeing, the body of spectators would, Ranjitsinhji suggests, submit themselves to a sympathetic affiliation with the idea of Englishness that the game represented. Cricket, not unlike the bureaucratic pilgrimage, print capitalism, or any of the other phenomena of modernity that Benedict Anderson has suggested are at the origin of the imaginary community of nationalism, could succeed in defining a common space of English identity because, as Ranjitsinhji so pithily says, whether it is encountered on the field or on the page, it "puts many very different people on a common ground" (445).

AN ENGLISH PERFORMANCE

In tracing a Victorian idea of Englishness that emerged first from the public schools over which Thomas Arnold exerted his sovereignty and then, in the years following Arnold's death, from the playing fields that surrounded those schools, I have attempted to illustrate how that essentially featureless idea— or, more accurately, that defeaturing idea—depended on a pedagogical discipline invested with the task of inscribing on a body of middle- and working-class Britons and on the empire's colonial subjects a constraining, deindividuating, and normalizing idea of cultural identity. In considering the Arnoldian application of that idea—in which identity becomes its mode of reproduction—I have also indicated that that pedagogical work may be troubled by a performative resistance articulated as an intimate space of homoerotic instability within the "manly" and "moral" institution of the public school. In concluding this chapter I wish to inquire, to put it most simply, whether cricket "succeeded" where Arnold "failed," whether the field, as Arnold's successors so fervently believed, was indeed mightier than the pulpit. Ranjitsinhji's essay certainly implies that it did and was. Gathered on, or around, the "common ground" of the cricket field, the "many different people" of the empire, he indicates, exchange their difference for sameness, their distinctiveness for an Englishness that exists to repeat and reproduce itself.

The many Victorian and Edwardian public school headmasters who made Cricket the first C in a revised trivium of Cricket, Classics, and Christianity also believed so. As, if J. A. Mangan's impressive research is anything to go by, did the masters of the squadrons of imperial schools who modeled their institutions on Rugby, Harrow, and Eton and fed their colonial charges a daily diet of cricket. Chester Macnaghten, who in 1870 became headmaster of Rajkumar College in Kathiawar, India, a school for the sons of the subcontinent's princely class, clearly believed in the irresistible "moral" and identity-reforming "advantages of cricket." Not content to lay a pitch for his students and to force them onto it to play, he regularly read them the cricketing passages from *Tom Brown's Schooldays* in lieu of a morning sermon.[21] Ford Madox Ford, who, as we have seen, saw in the cricketing excellence of a West African youth educated at a public school sure evidence that Englishness was communicable, was similarly convinced of the identity-transforming power of the game; as are Mangan, and many of his fellow historians, who see in the games ethic of empire evidence for a diffusionist theory of imperial history (the subtitle of Mangan's influential study of the imperial games ethic is, not insignificantly, *Aspects of the Diffusion of an Ideal*). Mangan, to be sure, does not blithely celebrate the power of the empire to Anglicize its subjects. But, like many of his colleagues, he does tend to suggest that on the empire's cricket fields Indian, African, and Caribbean boys were ineluctably transformed into English "gentlemen." Whether, in the process, these boys also altered what it means to be English is as little Mangan's subject as it is the worry of the triumphalist Chester Macnaghten. Once enrolled in one of the empire's mock-Etons or set to play on one of its cricket fields, the empire's subjects, Ranjitsinhji, Ford, Macnaghten, and Mangan indicate, are drawn across the boundary that divides Englishness from everything else. Within that bounded space, it seems, there is no resistance to the pedagogical discipline of Englishness, no performance that can avoid writing a pedagogical code ever more deeply on its performer.

It is against such assumptions that James's *Beyond a Boundary* is, in many ways, written. By describing itself as occupying a space "beyond" the boundary, James's text resists the suggestion that the pedagogical institutions of empire irresistibly write a fixed code of English identity on the subjects drawn within their disciplinary spaces. For what James suggests is that there is, in fact, no imperial space which can be safely identified as within, at, or external to the boundary of Englishness—because the boundary does not exist. James's text is, thus, beyond a boundary not in the sense that it maps a region of culture external to the forcible imposition of Englishness, but because it represents an idea of culture that has dispensed with the boundary altogether. His text represents a collapsing together of the "within" and the "without" of national and imperial culture, an erasure of the inclusive and exclusive space of the border. *Beyond a Boundary* does more than this. It further represents a collapsing of the opposition of the pedagogical and the performative. In looking at John Addington Symonds's memoir of his time at Harrow, I indicated that the pedagogical may incorporate the performative into its disciplinary work. James suggests, more radically, that the pedagogical and the performative cannot be definitively distinguished from one another; that, as much as performance may unsettle pedagogy, or pedagogy incorporate performance, the performative may animate the pedagogical and may make of Englishness its own destabilizing performance. These two aspects of James's work, his erasure of the idea of a cultural limit and of the opposition of the pedagogical and the performative, are not separate from one another. They are, in fact, linked manifestations of the same impulse, the impulse to locate his writing and his cultural identity in a space that is, in the full sense of the word, beyond a boundary.

Beyond a Boundary is a hybrid text: part journalism, part autobiography, part history, part cultural criticism. Its narrative structure moves from James's early childhood and his years as a student in a colonial boarding school, through his time in England as a cricket correspondent and political activist, to his return to Trinidad as a man in his fifties. On the way through this autobiographical recounting, James pauses to sketch the life of his mother, father, and grandparents, to give a history of West Indian cricket, to provide portraits of the great West Indian cricketers, to analyze Victorian culture and the lives and works of Thomas Arnold, Thomas Hughes, and W. G. Grace, and to attempt a definition of art. Throughout it all, however, his constant theme is cricket and the influence the game has had on his character, his intellect, and on English and West Indian culture.

In his essay "Englishness and Blackness: Cricket as Discourse on Colonialism," Manthia Diawara suggests that James's text represents a colonial contestation of the idea and the cultural authority of Englishness.[22] Diawara argues that in the text, the cricket field locates the space of this contest. Cricket, he maintains, represented for the colonists the idea of Englishness by reproducing or embodying at least three of the constitutive features of that idea: first, that England, in relation to the reproduction of culture, occupied the position of the original which the colonized, even in their playing of the game, were condemned to copy; second, that the virtues, manners, and moral discipline of Victorian England were inscribed by and located in the game of cricket; and third, that in providing a common ground of cultural identification for the various classes of English society, cricket contributed to the production of England as a modern nation. Diawara's argument, to this point, is very much in line with what I have been suggesting. But his reading of James's response to the colonial construction of cricket as a disciplinary mechanism of English cultural identity is not. Diawara sees James as engaging with cricket, and the idea of Englishness that it represented, in order to construct an opposite and opposing idea of Caribbeanness or blackness: "When we consider the formal field of cricket in *Beyond a Boundary* it becomes clear that it is the terrain of contestation between the monolithic discourse of Englishness and the emergence of Caribbeanness" (835). Diawara associates this Caribbeanness with the performances of the all-black Shannon Cricket Club which James describes in the text, and suggests that the performances of these players and the black and mulatto spectators' approval of these performances "constitute what I will call a black structure of feeling" (843)—a structure of feeling positioned in profound opposition to the colonists' chauvinistic and oppressive discourse of Englishness.

In constructing an essentialist and pedagogical Englishness and an essentialist and performative blackness locked in opposition to one another, Diawara seems to have ignored James's insistence that the cricket field profoundly complicates these oppositions by functioning as a radically ambivalent ground for the construction of cultural identity. Diawara erases from *Beyond a Boundary* James's own professed ability to oscillate across the spaces of blackness and Englishness, to occupy either space, or both, or both at once; to situate himself, as a student, a writer, and a player, within the overlapping spheres of influence of the pedagogical and the performative. Diawara's read-

ing, in fact, constructs the very conception of culture that, I believe, James's
text collapses—a conception of culture in which Englishness is indissociably
linked with pedagogy, in which resistance, or blackness, is allied with performance, and in which cricket is merely the boundary point at which these
meet. Throughout his text, James resists such stark dichotomizations. He consistently erases the boundary between Englishness and blackness, and, by implication, the distinction between pedagogy and performance, not in order to
suggest that neither set of terms exists, but in order to suggest that they exist
in a condition of constant oscillation across one another's spaces. James manages this—he refuses fixed binary oppostions—by persistently crossing terms,
by reading Englishness as an unbounded and unpossessed space available to
reinscription and reinvention by the Caribbean, and by animating pedagogy
as a performance.

In *The Practice of Everyday Life*, Michel de Certeau suggests that there are
ways of operating by which subordinate groups productively consume "legitimate" culture, making of "the rituals, representations, and laws imposed on
them something quite different from what their conquerors had in mind . . .
using them with respect to ends and references foreign to the system they had
no choice but to accept," and thus escape the hegemonic "without leaving
it."[23] In much the same way, James makes of Englishness something other
than what it represented itself to be, not by inventing an opposing and equally
essentialist discourse, but by subverting colonial discourse from within, by
putting it to his own use. That use is, in fact, more radical than de Certeau's
theories suggest it might be. For whereas de Certeau maintains a conception
of the pregiven and self-contained identity of an imposed system of culture,
James's writing suggests that Englishness is never self-contained, imposed,
and merely troubled from within, but that the discourse of Englishness is fully
available to his writing and reinvention. His writing reveals what I maintain is
always being revealed, that Englishness has no pregiven authenticity or place
of origin, but is always, in the hands of Thomas Arnold, Matthew Bondman,
or C.L.R. James, in the midst of its disciplinary or subversive invention.

In the service of explaining exactly what I mean by this, however, de
Certeau's comments are again useful, especially as they relate to the idea of
social and cultural space. In a chapter titled "Spatial Stories" in *The Practice of
Everyday Life* de Certeau draws a distinction between the idea of place and the
idea of space. Place, he suggests, is a mere expanse, a distributed area, a fixed
order of positioning. Space, by contrast, is defined by motion, by movement
across an expanse. Space is a practiced, or performed, place (117). In de
Certeau's terms, James reveals that Englishness, or even culture, has no
place—it has no static and fixed order of positioning. Culture and Englishness
have only space. They exist, pedagogical protests notwithstanding, only in
their performances; and every performance alters the nature of that space,
further separates it from a mythical, original and prearranged place.

Beyond a Boundary reveals this with an elegant simplicity. James represents the fetishized places and objects of English culture—the public school, the game of cricket, English literature—and reveals not only how these have been invented and transacted by the guardians of English culture, by English public school boys, the British peasantry and working classes, a bear of a man named W. G. Grace, and an Indian prince named Ranjitsinhji, but also how he, his family, friends, and acquaintances have perfomed them, altered them, reinvented them, and made them their own. The portrait of Matthew Bondman is only the first representation of a Caribbean spatialization of the "place" of Englishness. There is no need for James to invent an oppositional idea of Caribbeanness to confront and oppose the idea of Englishness. In sketches of innumerable cricketers, remembrances of his mother's personalized Anglicanism, idiosyncratic readings of Thackeray, and animated depictions of Arnold, Hughes, and Grace, as well as Bondman, Learie Constantine, his parents, and his grandfather Josh, James shows that the Caribbean has multiply entered and performed the space of Englishness, and in thus entering and performing it has revealed that the North Atlantic English neither bound nor possessed that space. Cricket is as Caribbean as Matthew Bondman's bat slashing through the covers, as English as W. G. Grace's hundredth century, as Indian as Ranjitsinhji's writings. There are no boundaries separating these three, or their representations in James's text.

James not only collapses the cultural boundary between "Englishness" and what has been variously identified as external to it. He also reveals that the idea of Englishness can as easily assume a performative as a pedagogical character, and he does so, once again, by analyzing and representing cricket. Before exploring the performative possibilities of cricket, James does, however, examine its pedagogical deployment; and one must, crucially, realize that James does not dispute—nor do I in this reading of his text—the very obvious fact that Englishness, and cricket as a privileged element in the discourse of Englishness, have assumed the repressive and constraining character of a nationalist cultural pedagogy. Rather, James's text suggests the possibility that one might resist the pedagogical not by a simple act of refusal but by incorporating it into the subversive and fluctuating movement of cultural performance. James realizes, however, that the beginning of such an act lies in the recognition of an imperial devotion to the pedagogical inscriptions of licit cultural identity. He can recognize this because he sees the text of a public school narrative of English identity inscribed on himself:

> As soon as we stepped on the cricket or football field, more particularly the cricket field, all was changed. We were a motley crew. The children of some white officials and white business men, middle-class blacks and mulattos, Chinese boys, some of whose parents still spoke broken English, Indian boys, some of whose parents could speak no English at all, and some poor black boys. . . . Yet rapidly

we learnt to obey the umpire's decision without question, however irrational it was. We learned to play with the team, which meant subordinating your personal inclinations, and even interests, to the good of the whole. We kept a stiff upper lip in that we did not complain of ill-fortune. We did not denounce failures, but "Well tried" or "Hard luck" came easily on our lips. We were generous to opponents and congratulated them on victories, even when they did not deserve it. . . . On the playing field we did what ought to be done. Every individual did not observe the rule. But the majority of the boys did. The best and most-respected boys were precisely the ones who always kept them. When a boy broke them he knew what he had done and, with the cruelty and intolerance of youth, from all sides our denunciations poured in on him. Eton or Harrow had nothing on us. (34–35)

It is perhaps remarkable that in the succeeding pages, and in the years which followed this time in his life, James did not attempt to erase this code of Victorian Englishness that had been so thoroughly written over his body. That he did not attempt to simply erase this inscription but chose instead to translate its writing in subtle and powerful ways is a reflection of his profound cultural insight.

For James recognized that if this code of Englishness which cricket had written over him and over his community could not be erased, it could be translated and turned to purposes other than those which the Victorians had envisaged. It could be thus translated for two reasons: because of the nature of the sport itself, and because of what Ranjitsinhji had identified as its spectacular character. In a chapter titled "What Is Art," James considers the aesthetic character of the game and fixes, as the peculiar quality of the game's beauty, on the idea of movement. It is the constant though purposive and directed movement of the cricketer's body, he suggests, that elevates the sport, renders it aesthetically pleasing, and complicates its relation to a discourse of cultural discipline. For in identifying movement as the central aesthetic principle of cricket, James again makes it possible for us to read cricket as a species of the performative that at once disrupts and courts the pedagogical, that, finally, makes it impossible to dissociate the one from the other because both are present within the game's "perfect flow of motion" (206) and the spectator's vision of, and response to, that flow.

Indeed, it is in the spectator's paradigmatic word of response to the movements of the game, in that "long, low 'Ah!'" with which James's text begins, that the game reveals its—and, for James, culture's—quixotic double nature. For the "Ah" with which the spectator greets Matthew Bondman's stroke may be an "Ah" of either recognition or surprise, or both. As an utterance of surprise, the "Ah" welcomes a movement that is, at first glance, entirely performative; a movement that in de Certeau's terms "spatializes" the disciplinary "place" of the field, that reveals a new way of enacting its givenness, articulating its grammar. Viewed in this way, the movements of the game represent an endless set of opportunities to render actual the manifold, but as-yet-unrevealed, strokes, or gestures, or tactics, or routes—call them what you will—otherwise only latent or virtual in the field. As James has it, "the greatness of the great batsman is not so much in his own skill as that he sets in motion all the immense possibilities that are contained in the game as structurally organized" (198). As a performative event, the stroke is thus an affective event, an interruption of the new *within* a settled order of practices.

But, and on this point James is unequivocal, the startling performance that marks a moment of newness, that elicits an "Ah" of surprise from the spectator, can provoke this response, can convince the spectator that what he or she has witnessed is both new *and* significant, only because it takes place within a pedagogical context. It is, he avows, "the relation between event (or, if you prefer, contingency) and design, episode and continuity" (197) that confers meaning upon the event. Absent that relation the event could not signify: "The glorious uncertainty of the game is not anarchy. It would not be glorious if it were not so firmly anchored in the certainties which must attend all successful drama. . . . It is only within the rigid structural frame that the individuality so characteristic of cricket can flourish" (197–98). No partisan of rigid structures or firm certainties, James yet understands that the uncertain possesses an affect that is not autonomous but allusive, that newness is not radically inimical to the continuous but emerges in reference to it. It is for this reason that "Caribbeanness," in this text, is not radically opposed to "Englishness," or the postcolonial present utterly divorced from the colonial past. The commitment to performativity that is so widely acknowledged a characteristic of postcolonial cultural ensembles can meaningfully confront the violent and disciplinary dispensations of imperial history, James's text suggests, only to the extent that the performative retains its willingness to also be translative. The performative, to put it differently, is for James neither antimnemonic nor antigenealogical, as is clear from his comments on T. S. Eliot's suggestion that "the use of memory / Is for liberation . . . / . . . liberation / From the future as well as the past" ("Little Gidding"): "This is exactly what I do not think about these memories [of the colonial past]. They do not liberate me in any sense except that once you have written down something your mind is ready to go further. I do not want to be liberated from them. I would consider liberation from them a grievous loss, irreparable. . . . I do not wish to be liberated from that past, and above all I do not wish to be liberated from its future" (59).

If the performative thus constantly alludes to an antecedent pedagogical tradition that it ceaselessly interrogates and renovates, it also gestures toward its future as an agent of pedagogy. The stroke, which on its first appearance is the cutting movement of the new, a vehicle of surprise, tends toward its reconstruction as an object of recognition: the memorable image. "Every few years," James attests fairly early in the text, "one sees a stroke that remains in the mind" (105). "The image," he explains some hundred pages later, returning to his theme as that theme, like the memorable image itself, suddenly recaptures his attention, "can be a single stroke, made on a certain day, which has been seen and never forgotten. There are some of these the writer has carried in his consciousness for over forty years, some in fact longer, as is described in the first pages of this book" (205). Captured in the spectator's memory, the stroke, reapprehended as an image, gestures toward its reappearance. It returns to the spectator not simply as the remembered but as the anticipation of a repeat performance. Played once, it becomes one of those movements that henceforth define the way in which the game should be played. Indeed, whether or not the stroke is in fact ever played again on a cricket field, it will be replayed in the viewer's mind and, courtesy of James, on the pages of *Beyond a Boundary*, a text that is littered with narrative snapshots of just such strokes-become-images.

But just as surprise is giving way to recognition, the performative to the pedagogical, the innovative to the exemplary, just as James appears to be turning into the Eliot of "Tradition and the Individual Talent" as his text converts the essentially filmic movements of the game into a series of West Indian stills that are then shuffled into the cricketing archives of Englishness, he reverses the process once again, insisting that the stroke cannot, in fact, be captured by the image, that the performance, while memorable, exceeds or eludes its pedagogical recuperation. "What is to be emphasized," he emphatically notes, "is that whereas in the fine arts the image of tactile values and movement, however effective, however magnificent, is permanent, fixed, in cricket the spectator sees the image constantly *re-created*" (205, emphasis added). Troubling over the hyphen in re-create (as carefully as Ruskin troubled over the hyphen in "Re-form"), James stresses that to repeat is not necessarily to coincide, that however valuable the image of the innovative is—whether to teach us how discursive structures are endlessly susceptible to Foucauldian "events," or to teach us how to innovate—there are no models for the re-creation of culture. Or perhaps that the only model is the model of re-creation—which emulates and annuls what it has re-created, which in its turn has emulated and annulled . . . ad infinitum. In suggesting this, in withdrawing the pedagogic authority he has just accorded to those performative actions which exist to re-create their antecedent pedagogical authorities, James is, of course, refusing his own exemplarity, refusing his readers permission to treat his discursive performance as an authoritative lesson on how to resist the pedagogical by re-creating it—while at the same time telling us that if we find his gestures memorable, we should feel free to re-create them, or reward their reappearance with our own long, low "Ah!" of recognition and delight.

With this self-abrogating "lesson" in mind we can return our gazes to the fields of empire, to those innumerable cricket grounds, Gothic train stations, English clubs, and schools like St. Xavier's that dotted the global map of empire. Looking now at those many locations of Englishness that existed, individually, to name one another and, collectively, to re-present England, we can observe that within them the logics of metonymy and synecdoche do, partially, hold; that, in some respects, each of these places does reveal the same thing about Englishness. But now each of these is "the same" only to the extent that in each of them Englishness is never the same thing that it represents itself to be, that in each of them Englishness is continuously discontinuous with what it was a moment ago and what it is about to become. For in each of these locations the same old game is being played, but this is a game whose incessant movements perpetually disclose new possibilities, new gestures, new meanings. Which of course means that these locations of culture are also not the same at all, that in each of the places in which new ways of being English and Indian and Caribbean and black and white emerge alongside and in opposition to and in concert with one another and with all the old ways of being one or many of those things, the only common law is the law of the vernacular, the only standard grammar the local grammar of that everywhere recognizable and everywhere different word: "Ah!"

Chapter Five

AMONG THE RUINS: TOPOGRAPHIES OF
POSTIMPERIAL MELANCHOLY

I lived with the idea of decay. (I had always lived with this
idea. It was like my curse: the idea, which I had had even as
a child in Trinidad, that I had come into a world past its
peak). . . . I grew to feel that the grandeur belonged to the
past; that I had come to England at the wrong time; that I
had come too late to find the England, the heart of empire,
which (like a provincial, from a far corner of the empire)
I had created in my fantasy.
—V. S. Naipaul, *The Enigma of Arrival*

Reminds me of a man who lives by exhibiting to travellers
his grandmother's corpse.
—James Joyce, Letter to Stanislaus Joyce

Sighs of Pleasure, and Regret

The long, low "Ah!" that greets Matthew Bondman's cricketing genius is a
paradoxical utterance, a word given to that strange moment when we recognize the new as something familiar. For C.L.R. James this moment elicits a
moan of pleasure, a release of breath in which, as sound becomes language, he
and his fellow spectators voice delight in Bondman's play and in his vital way
of being. James could thrill to that sight because he understood Englishness as
something always undergoing an imperial revision. But if Bondman's body can
thus elicit joy, it can also offend. His Caribbean translation of cricket's gestures
does not precisely refuse the authority of an English determination of imperial
identity, but it does mark his claim to share that authority. In adopting the
game and altering it, Bondman identifies himself as one of England's cultural
guardians and artisans. But he does more than this. He reveals that the plot-
tings of English identity are never complete, that Englishness has no fixed
shape, that English culture continuously mutates. While this may seem obvious, and while this is a knowledge in which James can take great pleasure, this
knowledge of Englishness can also provoke great sorrow. It can be, and has
been, elaborately refused. In turning from C.L.R James, I wish to consider the

ways in which the lesson in cultural translation implicit in Bondman's body
has provoked not joy but anguish, not affirmation but refusal, not delight but
melancholy. Matthew Bondman, to be sure, is not solely, or even primarily,
responsible for that discourse of postimperial melancholy which I will trace.
Rather, casting their eyes on a contemporary England, a current generation of
dour Britons has discovered in the mutations of England's noble architecture
a cause for lamentation and an opportunity to covertly mourn the losses of
empire. It is with one of the more public expressions of such melancholy
regret that I wish to begin this chapter.

A Sense of Wrongness

On the evening of the 28th of October, 1988, Prince Charles appeared on
BBC's *Omnibus* program to share his vision of Britain. "Sometime during this
century," the prince informed his audience, "something went wrong. For various complicated reasons we allowed a terrible damage to be inflicted on parts
of this country's unique landscape and townscape."[1] In the minutes of the
program that followed, and on the pages of the book published as a companion piece to his film, the prince exhibited a catalog of those architectural horrors visited upon the people of England sometime during this century—the
fifties and sixties, he subsequently avers, were the guilty decades—and conducted his viewers and readers on a tour of that noble architecture of the
English past which had managed, somehow, to survive the devastations of the
present age. What emerges from this catalog and tour is quite evident: a recoil-
ing before the wounded surface of postwar England's architectural page and a
yearning for the nobly built but crumbling spaces of the island kingdom's
past. Though the prince, in his book and film, represents himself as something
of a voice crying in the wilderness, the longing that he expresses for a lost or
vanishing country-house England is not unique to his vision of Britain. Indeed, such agonistic yearnings subtend any number of recent English cultural
productions, a cursory list of which might include the television serialization
of Evelyn Waugh's *Brideshead Revisited*, the Merchant-Ivory productions of
Forster's *Howards End* and *A Room with a View*, and the National Gallery's
massive 1986 exhibition, *The Treasure Houses of Britain*. In all of these productions the country house, and that moment in England's cultural history which
it synecdochically locates, has been rediscovered and fetishized.[2]

For a fetish it has become: a cultural artifact, a spectacular arrangement of
built space, valued less for itself than for the absence or lack that it at once
covers and names. Neither the identity of that desired object nor the reasons
for its disappearance are immediately evident in either the prince's mournful
catalog and tour or in the narratives of these other works. But, clearly, these
cultural works are animated by what, in a related context, V. S. Naipaul has
called a "feeling of wrongness" in postwar British culture.[3] What that "some-

thing" is for which Prince Charles and so many Britons have apparently been
yearning as they reverentially inspect the architecture of an age before things
went wrong might become clear if we consider the emergence, contemporane-
ous to the appearance of this nostalgia boomlet, of what Salman Rushdie has
called a Raj Revival. In his essay "Outside the Whale," published a few years
before the Prince of Wales appeared before his television audience, Rushdie
examines the belated and ghostly twitchings of what, with ghoulish wit, he
calls the "amputated limbs" of empire. He discerns, in the television and filmic
productions of *The Far Pavilions*, *The Jewel in the Crown*, *Gandhi*, and *A Passage
to India*, a fantasy of return to the pleasures of the imperial past, a nostalgic
turning of English men's and women's eyes to "the lost hour of their
precedence."[4]

This imaginative return to the glories of imperial dominance and the
mournful wanderings through the lapsing architectures of the English past are
not unrelated cultural acts. Edward Said, in *Culture and Imperialism*, has examined the relations that obtain between country-house England and the political and cultural economies of empire. In a reading of Jane Austen's *Mansfield
Park*, he discovers a spatial reasoning at work: a reasoning that not only connects the financing of the country house and its structures of life to the capital
extracted from England's sugar estates in the Caribbean but also relates the
ordered moral economy which the country house represents to the apt administration of colonial property.[5] The country house, in Said's reading, ramifies
beyond its own domestic space; it is resonant with more than merely local
significance. It signifies both Englishness and empire, the manifestation in
England's built space of colonial capital and colonial discipline. It represents
an authorized and elite—but increasingly hegemonic—order of English belonging that not only is financed by the acts of colonial possession but finds
in the disciplinary protocols of colonial administration a model for its own
procedures of identity formation and reformation. "More clearly than any-
where else in her fiction, Austen here synchronizes domestic with international authority, making it plain that the values associated with such higher
things as ordination, law, and propriety must be grounded firmly in actual
rule over and possession of territory. She sees clearly that to hold Mansfield
Park is to hold and rule an imperial state in close, not to say inevitable association with it. What assures the domestic tranquility of one is the productivity
and regulated discipline of the other" (87). The country house, in this reading,
cannot be inspected without our becoming aware of its dependence on those
distant, all but invisible, spaces of empire to which it is connected through a
perpetual passing of bodies, capital, and commodities, and from which it derives its principles of order, stability, and rule. This is so for at least two reasons. First, because in the ideology of imperialism, the noble architectures of
eighteenth-, nineteenth-, and twentieth-century England connect the island to
the spaces of imperial rule through an imaginative relation of contiguity or

adjacency. And second, because the country house is the privileged institution of a discourse of cultural discipline, an institution that simultaneously is funded by colonialism, manners its procedures after those proven in the colonies, and, in fully circular fashion, extends to the English citizenry the techniques of subject production that have enabled the perpetuation of imperial sovereignty.

In his essay on Austen, Said cites John Stuart Mill's discussion of colonial space in *Principles of Political Economy*, a discussion in which, as Mill compares England's trade with the West Indies to the "traffic between town and country," he presents a vision of the empire as an expanded locale, as a series of adjacent or contiguous territories brought under the homogenizing dominion of a metropolitan seat of finance and government (*Principles of Political Economy*, 3:693). Mill's argument depends upon a metonymic order of reasoning in which the contiguous items in a series (town, country, empire) do not merely refer, or defer, to one another but virtually become one another. In this act of imperial revisioning, in which Mill sees the colony as little more than a suburb or outlying piece of countryside, to look upon the colonial territory is to look upon England, and to look upon England is to see the colonies (a homogenizing optics of imperialism which, because it assumes that what happens in the colonies is, in effect, happening in England also, is quite in agreement with Mill's desire to prosecute Governor Eyre for crimes which, in Mill's view, must be viewed not only as crimes against several thousand black Jamaicans but as crimes against Englishness).[6]

Mill's vision, and that of many of his contemporaries and inheritors, is a vision of empire without interruptions, a vision of empire without boundaries, or breaks, or, quite frankly, oceans. It describes an imperial semiotics of pure, uninterrupted flow—or, to be more precise, of pure, uninterrupted float. For what renders this vision of empire possible are of course the ships perpetually crossing and recrossing Mill's unnamed oceans, the vehicles of that traffic which renders Trinidad, Barbados, India, Nigeria, and all the other colonial territories mere subordinate counties to London's governing city. Again, however, it is not precisely the ships that allow for this expansive vision of the country and the city, but what the ships carry. The commodities and capital cargoed in England's restless marcantile fleets are the true objects of that traffic between the island's cities and the imperial countryside.[7]

Eric Williams, in his important study *Capitalism and Slavery*, examines the history of that traffic and the social and political consequences of its centuries-long flow.[8] As he demonstrates, the triangular trade linking England, Africa, and the Caribbean provided the foundation for much of the house of modern British capitalism. It was not only the slave, sugar, and rum trades that depended on the health of this triangular circulation of bodies, commodities, and capital; the banking, shipbuilding, cotton, textile, and armaments industries relied on it as well. The trade also, as Mill notes, spilled vast amounts of capital into England for the "benefit of its [colonial] proprietors there" (*Principles of Political Economy*, 3:693). The benefit to those English proprietors of colonial property was indeed great. The returned West Indian planters, and their cousins the East Indian nabobs, converted their colonial capital into the luxurious stuff of social and political life. They purchased not only jewels, paintings, and furniture but political office. In an age of rotten boroughs, the planters could easily outbid their domestic rivals for parliamentary seats. In the 1830 elections, as Eric Williams notes, "a West Indian planter successfully spent 18,000 [pounds] getting himself elected in Bristol" (93).[9] He was not alone. William Beckford, of the renowned planter family, was an M.P. for Shaftesbury for two decades in the middle of the eighteenth century. His brother was M.P. for Bristol, while yet another brother represented Salisbury. John Gladstone, who made his fortune off his plantations in British Guiana and Jamaica, was M.P. for Woodstock and Lancaster, and in 1833 colonial capital purchased his not-yet-famous son William the seat for Newark. The lists go on. Not content with the instruments of power, however, the planters also bought power's trappings. They added noble titles to their names. And they built houses.

Bromley Hill Place in Kent, a house celebrated in England for its architecture and gardens, was built with West Indian capital, as was Fonthill Abbey (a structure whose erection required so many laborers that a village was built to house them), as was the house of the aforementioned William Beckford, M.P. for Shaftesbury.

> It was a handsome, uniform edifice, consisting of a centre of four stories, and two wings of two stories, connected by corridors, built of fine stone, and adorned with a bold portico, resting on a rustic basement, with two sweeping flights of steps: its apartments were numerous and splendidly furnished. . . . Whilst its walls were adorned with the most costly works of art, its sideboards and cabinets presented a gorgeous combination of gold, silver, precious metals, and precious stones, arranged and worked by the most tasteful artists and artisans. Added to these splendours, these dazzling objects, apparently augmented and multiplied by large costly mirrors, was a vast, choice, and valuable library.[10]

A note of discomfort lurks beneath the breathless surface of this early-nineteenth-century description of the planter's country manor. There is a hint of doubt, an unease before a display of wealth so self-insistent that it is not content with a display of splendor but pauses to double and redouble the dazzling object, to reproduce empire's bounty in the gilded mirror's multiplying eye. This unease, which casts the lightest ripple across the surface of the writer's adoring prose, was not entirely uncommon. As Richard Cumberland's popular 1771 play *The West Indian* reveals, not a few eighteenth- and nineteenth-century Britons caught themselves stumbling on the colonial landowners' tripping-stones of wealth.

Cumberland's play opens with the ladies and gentlemen of London society treating Mr. Belcour—a recently repatriated and free-spending West Indian planter—with the ginger shock of incomprehension. Their hesitancy is not ethical, nor does it attach to doubts concerning slavery or empire (indeed, Belcour first wins society's approval by personally funding a military expedition to the west coast of Africa); rather it is a sort of horror of inflation. The very excesses of Belcour's wealth threaten to price London's indigenes out of the social, aesthetic, and matrimonial markets. Finally, however, Belcour and his wealth prove not to be factors that will disrupt the carefully regulated dealings of London's social and political economies, but, quite the contrary, factors that restore balance to the dealings which the locals have allowed to fall out of order. The young West Indian converts the signs of his excessive wealth into symbols of English vitality. Through various modestly heroic acts, he sets an interrupted order of inheritance to rights, finances a British expedition to West Africa, and arranges for the daughter of the lord mayor of London to be suitably married. Dressed in the costume of imperial wealth, Belcour embodies a principle of vigor and moral order similar, indeed virtually identical, to that which Said sees Sir Thomas embodying at Mansfield Park. Returned from the colonies, these men showed themselves to be equipped not only with the capital to build England's noble edifices but with the energy and administrative experience to set those houses in order. Retired to the English countryside, they built and ruled opulent houses that were at once signs of the nation's and the empire's moral well-being and granite signatures of the city's dominance over the country, and of England's dominion over the empire's more distant but imaginatively adjacent countryside.

Raymond Williams has commented on the conversion of the capital extracted from England's "countrysides" into these architectures of power, order, and rule:

> It is fashionable to admire these extraordinarily numerous houses: the extended manors, the neo-classical mansions that lie so close in rural Britain. People still pass from village to village, guidebook in hand, to see the next and yet the next example, to look at the stones and the furniture. But stand at any point and look at that land. . . . Think it through as labour and see how long and systematic the exploitation and seizure must have been, to rear that many houses, on that scale. . . . What these "great" houses do is to break the scale, by an act of will corresponding to their real and systematic exploitation of others. For look at the sites, the facades, the defining avenues and walls, the great iron gates and the guardian lodges. These were chosen for more than the effect from the inside out; where so many admirers, too many of them writers, have stood and shared the view, finding its prospect delightful. They were chosen also, you now see, for the other effect, from the outside looking in: a visible stamping of power, of displayed wealth and command: a social disproportion which was meant to impress and

overawe . . . a mutually competitive but still uniform exposition, at every turn, of an established and commanding class power.[11]

The fine sense of moral outrage that Williams exhibits in this passage depends on the visual economies of the uncanny. By insisting on an optics of cultural remembrance that in looking on these architectures sees not only the glorious granite and marble of their walls but also the role these sites have played in a social theater of cultural discipline, he recalls to our attention a repressed England that the guidebooks would rather not memorialize. He manages also, however, to forget another. For the order that these "great" houses at once assert and represent depends not only on the capital exploitation of the surrounding English countryside but also on the empire's sovereignty over the expanded locale of John Stuart Mill's "England."[12] Williams is of course right to insist on our seeing the national relations of domination and dispossession that these country houses so self-consciously represent. But, as Said has demonstrated, it is also necessary to consider their locations within a vaster imperial cartography of culture and discipline.

Jean Rhys examines the role played by the country house in an imperial drama of cultural discipline in her novel *Wide Sargasso Sea*, a text that returns to Charlotte Brontë's *Jane Eyre* to write the biography of Rochester's mad wife. As a narrative of the containment of colonial excess, Rhys's novel is also, in some respects, a rewriting of *The West Indian*. However, where Cumberland's play stages the conversion of the fiscal surplus of empire into the symbols of English order, Rhys's novel treats the English attempts to discipline colonialism's less manageable, and less mentionable, figures of excess. These excesses—of sexuality, memory, language, and desire—reside in the person of Antoinette Cosway, Rochester's West Indian wife, whom Rochester will eventually imprison in his country house.

Rochester incarcerates Antoinette in a desperate attempt to normalize her identity, to contain those signs of erotic and mnemonic excess which he has attempted to refuse from the first day of their marriage. The disturbance that Antoinette brings to the marriage bed of empire and Englishness is, as Gayatri Spivak has argued, the disturbance of sexuality, but it is also the disturbing articulation of imperial memory.[13] Antoinette has seen too much, remembered too much, and spoken too much of what Robert Young calls the forbidden narrative of "colonial desire."[14] She has lived through the dissolutions of the West Indian slave-owning era, the debauches of her father with slave women, and the coquetry, preening, and drunkenness of her mother. She has survived the collapse of plantation culture that attended the end of that slaveholding age. She has seen the family plantation, no longer supported by coerced labor, lapsing into ruin, witnessed a riotous workers' rebellion, and observed her mother's dalliance with a black man. Most significant, she has failed to forget or to keep silent. She torments Rochester, who is newly arrived from England, with these memories of empire, carrying them with her to their bed, refusing his constant injunctions to forget or be still. "'We won't talk about it now,'" Rochester informs her on one of the nights when she is re-hearsing these memories, "'not tonight,' [Rochester] said again. 'Some other time.'"[15] "Not now . . . Not yet" (75), he reflects on another occasion, in a forbidding echoing of E. M. Forster's words. But the memories cannot be postponed, and Rochester begins to read Antoinette's remembrances as tainted with that same illicit mark with which he brands his wife's overurgent sexual desires. Finally, he comes to classify memory and desire as interchange-able signs of a colonial wildness and excess, and interprets these signs as evi-dences of madness. Rochester finds himself, in a measure, relieved by this diagnosis. For madness, at least, bears the marks of familiarity and absolves him, and the English sensibility he brings to his reading of Antoinette's condi-tion, from any responsibility for the state of a wife who, confronted with her husband's repugnance, has grown increasingly hysterical.

The origins of Antoinette's madness, along with the very question of whether she is in fact mad, lie at the center of Rhys's text. Rochester conve-niently ascribes her condition to genetics—her mother, and brother, he has been told, were mad—and to her dabblings with obeah, the indigenes' sympa-thetic, homeopathic magic. In doing so, he locates madness within the myster-ies of biology and religion and removes the question of its production from the realm of history. More particularly, he separates the fabrication of insanity from the operations of empire. The text suggests an alternative knowledge of madness and its origins, a knowledge that, after the writings of Michel Fou-cault, is not entirely unfamiliar. If Antoinette is mad, this text suggests, it is not because of how she behaves, but because of how she is described. She is mad because Rochester has control of the power of naming—significantly, he not only describes her as insane but changes her name, calling her Bertha (a con-traction of her "mad" mother's name) rather than employing her given name—and uses that power to name as insanity the limits of memory and desire which Antoinette has trespassed. As Rhys reveals these things to her reader, she identifies madness not as a pathology but as a category in an imperial system of classification. And, she indicates, if madness is that which the En-glish husbands and administrators of empire take upon themselves to disci-pline, or contain, it is also that which they produce. For it is the history of empire that has produced the memories which Rochester finds so profoundly threatening, as it is the tautological epistemology of empire that provides that straitjacketing code which, in classifying Antoinette's memories as madness, guarantees that she is indeed insane.

It is also, and perhaps most cruelly, the economy of empire to which Rochester has wed himself in marrying Antoinette that provides the fiscal sur-plus which Rochester spends to ensure that he can safely and discretely contain Antoinette's excesses. While he and his bride are still on their honeymoon, Rochester sits brooding over his predicament, pondering the difficulties of hiding his wife away in Jamaica, and, half-unconsciously, stumbles on a solution to the problem of Antoinette's madness. "However much I paid Jamaican servants I would never buy discretion. I'd be gossiped about, sung about (but they make up songs about everything, everybody. You should hear the one about the Governor's wife). Wherever I went I would be talked about. I drank some more rum and, drinking, I drew a house surrounded by trees. A large house. I divided the third floor into rooms and in one room I drew a standing woman—a child's scribble, a dot for a head, a larger one for the body, a triangle for a skirt, slanting lines for arms and feet . . . it was an English house" (134–35). Despite its apparent simplicity, this is a complex, if almost ludicrously cartoonish, moment of drunken insight. It is a moment in which Rochester realizes that he is a prisoner of that same power of description which he has relied upon to liberate him from his responsibilities to his wife; a moment in which, to his horror, he recognizes that his ability to describe Antoinette as mad derives not from himself but from an imperial system of discourse which circumscribes him also. It is a moment of absentminded revelation that depends on the alchemies of empire's intoxicant, a moment in which imperial drunkenness emerges as the condition of imperial insight, but also a moment in which Rochester realizes that the rum he drinks has more than an intoxicating and vatic use. He can put that rum, and the sugarcane from which it is pressed, to other purposes. He can use the proceeds from its sale to build an "English" country house in which to imprison Antoinette, in which to contain the imperial excesses she embodies. That mansion will be a sort of memory house. But its function will be not to preserve memory but to imprison it. This, finally, is where the text leaves us—with Antoinette, in the prison house of memory. As readers of Brontë's novel, we know what will happen to that house. As readers of the great-house guidebooks, or Prince Charles's nostalgia treatise, we could not have known what such a house had been, or what its ruin represents. It is within the strategic silences of such texts, silences for which Rochester would have been grateful, that Rhys writes her novel. Her text enables us to locate and to read those silences, to read the country house as more than an arrangement of entrance halls, gilded banisters, and central wings. It allows us to read it also as a carceral space, as a reformatory of English identity, as a monument to the cultivated remembrances and willed amnesias of empire.

It is this country-house England—this ordered and disciplinary England that at once is financed by the economies of empire and marks, in dazzling expanses of Italian marble and filigreed iron, the dominion of the metropolis over domestic and colonial countrysides—for which a current generation of English nostalgics yearns. As such an object of remembrance and mourning, the country house is more than a mere arrangement of built space. If it were that, it could not be mourned, for across the surface of the English countryside the great houses survive. What *is* mourned is what has failed to survive, and what those houses, though so vast, can now only fragmentarily represent: the ordered, and hegemonic, moral economy of England's privileged classes; the heyday of British capital; the national and imperial project of identity formation; the Pax Britannica. It is in its invocation of these (though, finally, they never existed as they are remembered or imagined) that the country house is mournfully named, that it is fetishized. It is as such that it must be read, not as the desired thing but as the surviving fragment of the lost object of desire.

Prince Charles's *Vision of Britain* at once whispers, and struggles to avoid naming, this desire. His Royal Highness pretends not to know what he mourns, what precisely was good and true before that moment—sometime in the 1950s and 1960s, the decades, perhaps not uncoincidentally, of the empire's collapse, the years that immediately followed the loss of the Indian jewel in the imperial crown and encompassed the first rounds of African independence—when something went wrong. But though the prince attempts to prevaricate, his text cannot finally conceal the object of its melancholic yearnings. In the center of the text, there is a full-page color reproduction of a 1904 painting by N. M. Lund, a work which Prince Charles describes as "a painting that says everything about the harmony and scale of a City of London where the Lord Mayor's Mansion House and the houses of God were given appropriate prominence—all finding their place comfortably in the landscape" (69).

Lund's canvas depicts a London scene, painted in the soft rosy hues of the urban picturesque. In the foreground, a square opens before the mansion house of the lord mayor of London. In the middle distance, as the apex of a triangle anchored by the corners of the square, the domed spire of St. Paul's rises into the cloudy heavens. In the distance the Thames can be made out, busy with ships, spanned here and there by bridges and railway aqueducts. The painting is called *Heart of Empire*, and it represents a scene of instruction that dwells at the heart of the narratives of imperial dominion, bringing together in its balanced, idyllic spaces images of the two icons of empire: vibrant commerce and orderly rule. The square before the lord mayor's mansion, and the streets around the square, are filled with goods-laden carts, merchants, consumers. Its market space defines the center of a global system of circulation in which capital, commodities, and bodies flow to and from the imperial metropolis, depositing persons and objects before the lord mayor's house, channeling them into side streets, spilling them into the cargo holds of the Thames's many ships, shunting them along the railroad tracks spanning the great river, carrying them to and from the distant, invisible, but ever-present, just-adjacent spaces of rural England and the colonial territories. Presiding over this relentless capital flow are the architectures of sacral and secular order: the cathedral of the Church of England and the mansion house of the lord mayor of London, which look down upon, regulate, and ordain the marketplace of empire. This is the "harmonious landscape" that has been lost; that the country house, in its more sedate idiom, represents; and that the prince and nostalgic multitudes of his fellow Britons mourn, fetishize, yearn for.

The prince's decision to include Lund's painting in his book was by no means gratuitous. For in the years before and after he appeared on television to share his architectural theories, the canvas, as he well knew, had served as more than a representative emblem of the picturesque imperial past the Prince of Wales was mourning. Hanging on the rear wall of the Corporation of London's Public Inquiry Room during those years, Lund's painting had provided a quite specific backdrop for the "longest running planning battle in London's history"[16]—a battle provoked by the attempts of English conservationists to defend the past the canvas aspired to represent.

That planning battle, as Jane Jacobs details, centered on the development efforts of Peter Palumbo, the London real estate speculator who, starting in the early 1960s, had purchased the triangular block of buildings that appear in the middle center of Lund's canvas and form the apex of Bank Junction, the interchange that serves as the heart of *The Heart of Empire*. Palumbo proposed to demolish these structures and replace them with an office tower, a plan that was finally approved thirty years after it was first submitted, but which, for three decades, inspired the wrath and the uncompromising resistance of the Corporation of London and diverse English conservationists, whose most famous, and quite active, spokesperson was the Prince of Wales. In justifying their resistance to the development plan, in hearings held in the very room in which Lund's canvas hung, Palumbo's opponents advanced an argument that equated the values of the imperial, the local, and the picturesque, an argument that, in effect, equated the shape and meaning of these buildings with the shape and meaning Lund had given them in his canvas. As one of the conservationists attested in a 1988 hearing, the "view" of the buildings available from Cornhill, which is precisely the view given by Lund's painting "is not just a view of St. Paul's from afar. It is the relationship between Bank Junction, Mansion House and the Mappin and Webb triangle and the Metropolis and Empire. . . . [This] viewpoint is ideal to give a sense of London as the economic centre of the Empire as well as the spiritual and other-worldly sense of the Empire" (unattributed, in *Edge of Empire*, 51).

This appeal to the value of relationships—both the relationship of one object to another and the relationship of the group of objects to a sensible idea—is embedded, as Jacobs argues, in the ideology of "townscape" planning, a theory of urban design derived from Hubert de Cronin Hastings's writings in the *Architectural Review* which argues that urban space should be laid out around picturesque ensembles much as eighteenth-century English landscape paintings (and Lund's urban canvas) are framed around orderly ensembles. The object of urban planning, de Cronin Hastings and his followers on the Corporation of London and in the conservationist movement argued, should be to recapture in built space the distinctively English aesthetic of the rural locale, to enshrine in painterly architectural arrays the "*genius loci* of place, the intrinsic, indigenous qualities of the local" (*Edge of Empire*, 48). When manifest in the city of London—particularly when manifest in groups of buildings such as those which composed the orderly setting of Bank Junction—the argument concluded, the urban picturesque could thus signify not only the metropolitan survival of the rural English locale but the relationship of that locale to the imperial territory which it regulated and which sustained it. With Lund's canvas hanging over the room in which these arguments were advanced, the conservationists' claim could not have been clearer: to demolish Bank Junction would be to demolish the order of relationships its buildings made visible and ordained; it would be to betray those picturesque English places which managed to signify and order both Englishness and empire; it would be to turn one's back on a London in which there were still one or two locales that could identify the city as the heart of Englishness and empire.

In 1993 the British Law Lords, in one of those decisions that, like the 1981 Nationality Act, has chiseled away the foundations of a localist discourse of English identity, overruled the Corporation of London's objections to Palumbo's scheme and permitted him to demolish the buildings at Bank Junction. While Prince Charles may not have been able to prevent the physical destruction of this location of Englishness, the reproduction of Lund's canvas published in his text does permit him, and those who, like him, mourn the vanishing of such spaces, belatedly to run an eye over the image of this England, to indulge the pleasures of what Rob Nixon calls the "postimperial picturesque."[17] If, that is, such images can afford pleasure. For Prince Charles, whatever his devotion to them, they clearly cannot. His nostalgia is far too melancholy. But in being a melancholy spectator of the English past, the prince is far from alone, among either his contemporaries or his predecessors.

The modern English literature of nostalgia is vast. Melancholy and loss are among the most privileged tropes of a romantic and postromantic canon of English letters, as is the image of the backward-glancing English man or woman, domestic avatar of Walter Benjamin's Angel of History, turning a resentful back on the present and a teary eye toward the image of a dying England, whose death it has been the frequently self-appointed fate of generations of English writers to contemplate. To note only a very few instances, in the period under consideration in this book England's dying has been hyperbolically mourned by Ruskin, Cobbett, and Carlyle; imagined by Joseph Conrad in the closing pages of *The Nigger of the Narcissus*; elegiacally marked in the "Time Passes" section of Virginia Woolf's *To the Lighthouse*; hinted at in the closing pages of E. M. Forster's *Howards End*; and, as I shall discuss in the remainder of this chapter, suffered once more by V. S. Naipaul. The very constancy of this gesture across time suggests that in some strange way to be English is, often, to be a member of a cult of the dead, or, at the very least, a member of a cult of ruin. Let me be quite clear in saying that I am not suggesting that this is the only way to be English. Yet, with astonishing frequency, England's writers have insisted on this form of belonging, asserting that if the nation is an imagined community, then the English nation is a community in mourning.

This melancholic tendency has not been confined to literature. Much English social criticism, both radical and conservative, has been couched in the infinitely rich dialects of nostalgia. Raymond Williams, in *The Country and the City*, suggests that English writing over the past three hundred years has been obsessively concerned with the attempts to compose an image of English identity through a negotiation of the melancholy discourses of nostalgia. In this reading, England is always already lost, wounded, or vanishing, and the act of writing or the function of criticism is repetitively represented in the banal locutions of the "struggle of memory against forgetting." That struggle, as the title of Williams's text suggests, and as I have argued in the first chapter of this book, consistently invokes itself as a struggle of the country against the city, or, analogically, of the past against the present. In that conflict the nation emerges as an accomplished but displaced achievement, and nostalgia emerges not as a sentimental attitude but as an injunctive politics of return, as an allegorical historiography of loss and redemption.

As many contemporary Britons have added to this ash-and-sackcloth tradition by meditating the traumas of the end of empire, images of England's lost past such as those provided by Lund's painting emerge as sources of both pleasure and anguish, as fetishes of the lost past and reminders of that past's pastness. The postimperial picturesque may offer a moment's solace, but it also wounds. And it is with the melancholy mixture of refuge and torment experienced by one of the great masters of the postimperial picturesque in the presence of a country-house England that manages to signify both England's local genius and its imperial majesty—and the loss of both these things—that I wish to conclude this chapter.

Cults of Ruin

V. S. Naipaul's *The Enigma of Arrival* is a strange, compelling, and difficult work. It is an autobiographical text occasionally disguised as a novel, which renders an account of the author's coming to England at the age of eighteen and of his later residence in a cottage on the grounds of an English country house. The narrative of this dwelling constitutes the bulk of the text and stages Naipaul's cautious, slow, and deliberate approach to the enigma of his place in the imbricated discourses of empire and Englishness. The great, if crumbling, house provides the link between those discourses. As an erstwhile subject of empire, and a meticulously self-fashioned Englishman, Naipaul treats the house and his residence on its grounds as objects of unwavering fascination. He recognizes in the vast and beautiful structure a sort of grandeur and finds in that grandeur a little of that long history of dominion which Raymond Williams reads in the facade of the great house. In this opulent architecture, Naipaul discovers a domestic imprint of an empire that "explained my birth in the New World, the language I used, the vocation and ambition I had . . ." (187); an empire that "in the end explained my presence there in the valley, in the cottage, in the grounds of the manor" (191). But although, in these passages, Naipaul identifies the country house and the empire as interchangeable terms which define the terminus and source of a voyage into the heart of Englishness, he ultimately determines that these landmarks of his destination and origin are not the simple interpretive keys to his life. For Naipaul sees more than grandeur. He sees fabrication, and ruin.

Wandering the grounds of the house and the agricultural lands attached to those grounds, Naipaul confronts the inventedness of the England that he believes he has inherited and to which he wishes to belong. Everywhere he looks, he finds signs of the carefully constructed fictions of English identity. At first, Naipaul can admit only parenthetically that he has registered the existence of these signs. Again and again, he qualifies the image of an unchanging and natural England with literally parenthetical admissions of that England's careful and deliberate manufacture. As his knowledge of the house, grounds, and surrounding countryside increases, however, Naipaul abandons his attempts to contain his recognition of this England's inventedness within the defensive bracketing of parentheses. He admires an old stone-and-flint farmhouse on the manor grounds, "preserved for its beauty and as something from the past," but discovers that it is in fact a squash court, recently erected, "built in this 'picturesque' way to suit the setting" (49). He realizes that a Gothic church, which he had taken to be medieval, is an equally recent construction, a plagiarization of the past, "as artificial as the farmhouse" (49). In the village nearby, he finds a cottage in which he takes particular pleasure. "With its privet and rose hedge (hundreds of small pink roses), the pink cottage had looked the very pattern of a country cottage" (33). But when the retired couple who own the cottage leave and a young couple from the city move in, the illusion of the cottage's organic perfection vanishes. "It was only now, with the departure of the old couple, that I understood that the country-cottage effect of their house, and especially the hedge and gardens, had been their work, their taste, the result of their constant attentions. Very soon now, within months, the garden became ragged. The privet hedge kept its tightness, but the rose hedge, unpruned and untrained, became wild and straggly" (33).

A great and understated sadness attends Naipaul's recognition of these apparently slight things, a sadness that issues from his profound investment in an idea of Englishness given to him as a child and young man by the imperial custodians of English identity. To admit to the artifice in the landscape, to the constructedness of this England, is to admit to the inventedness of his own identity. For Naipaul is one of those strange creatures that the British Empire seemed so adept at producing: a colonial subject more rigorously English than the English; a Trinidadian who, by the age of eighteen, was profoundly nostalgic for an England he had never seen. To discover, as a middle-aged man, that that England had never been, or had existed only as a counterfeit of itself, is, to put it mildly, a difficult thing. But Naipaul does not refuse this difficult knowledge, or, as in this passage, he does not seem to: "So much that looked traditional, natural, emanations of the landscape . . . now turned out not to have been traditional or instinctive after all" (147). Eventually, however, Naipaul subtly but firmly represses this newly acquired knowledge of the fictive character of an England that has been so crucial to the construction of his identity.

In a revealing moment, somewhat later in the text, Naipaul returns to consider the erasure of his childhood image of England but now apprehends the fact of that erasure rather differently: "So I grew to feel that the grandeur belonged to the past; that I had come to England at the wrong time; that I had come too late to find the England, the heart of empire, which (like a provincial, from a far corner of the empire) I had created in my fantasy" (130). While Naipaul still acknowledges fantasy, still recognizes that the England of imperial longing exists at once as an invention and as an invention to which he is party, his emphasis has altered. He is now oppressed not by the sense that the England for which he yearns is no more than an invention—while in the same breath admitting that it is an invention—but by the sense that that England has existed but is lost. He has replaced his feeling of anxiety and resentment before the recognition of fraud with a feeling of sorrow in the realization of his belatedness. Between the recognition of himself as a man who has been defrauded and the identification of himself as a latecomer, a crucial change has taken place: Naipaul has admitted his need to believe in the imperial fictions of Englishness, even while acknowledging the fantastic quality of those fictions, and has discovered a means of doing so. In the place of an England that survives as its own counterfeit, he will locate an England that fails to exist, not because it never was but because it has been lost. He will find that England in the very fact of his belatedness and in the resonant stones of ruin.

The pages of Naipaul's text constitute a virtual catalog of ruin. Everywhere he turns he sees, superimposed on the visions of counterfeit, images of decay. He sees not only the slow decline of the manor house but everywhere around it a creeping text of ruin. He observes hayricks, rotting in the damp, moldering before his startled eye. He discovers "not far from the decaying rick . . . the remains of a true house . . . a simple house, its walls perhaps without foundation, it was now quite exposed. Ruined walls, roofless, around bare earth" (12). He warily treads the bridges that once spanned the water-meadows but which are now crumbling beneath his feet. He observes ancient elms, swallowed in ivy, dragged relentlessly to the ground. He studies the tracks of cattle, now disappeared from once flourishing farms. Naipaul's idiom in this catalog is one of compulsive reiteration. He visits and revisits his ruins, displaying them again and again to the reader, worrying fussily over them. In a lengthy sequence near the close of the first section of the text, he conducts a whirlwind tour of every wreck he has previously, and repeatedly, described, and concludes this tour by noting, "And these were set among older ruins," which he then proceeds to display. He is, in this, a little like Joyce's twentieth-century Roman, "a man who lives by exhibiting to travellers his grandmother's corpse."[18]

Joyce's joke, at postimperial Rome's expense, is more than slightly apposite to Naipaul and his English contemporaries. For in exhibiting the corpse of England to his readers, Naipaul does more than make a living—though he does that also. More important, he offers the grandmotherly corpse as proof in an argument of inheritance, genealogy, and history. The counterfeit artifacts disposed all about him throw into question the authenticity of the England that Naipaul at once inhabits, remembers, and invents. The ruins he tirelessly catalogs are the clauses of a counterargument, the fossil proofs that he offers, like the grandmother's corpse or the relics of a saint, of that England's onetime existence. Naipaul advances the ruin as an assurance of the remembered England's past reality. However, he does not do so with an entire lack of ambiguity. He understands the duality of his vision. He admits that in celebrating visions of ruin, he attempts to render invisible images of counterfeit equally visible to him. "I could find a special kind of past in what I saw," Naipaul notes, while simultaneously confessing that "with a part of my mind I could admit fantasy" (18). Gradually, however, Naipaul mutes the admission of fantasy and permits only the image of the special past to survive.

Naipaul celebrates the ruin because of the role that it plays in testifying to the actuality of that special past. It is that past's souvenir, the enduring fragment of its glory. But if Naipaul figures the ruin as a fetish, as that which invokes the presence and the certainty of an uncertain and absent England, then this is a fetish of an unusual order. For the logic of the fetish is essentially the logic of metonymy in which the named thing is valued not for itself but for what it gestures toward. It is a logic of displacement. Though, at times, Naipaul values the ruin as such a ramifying artifact and prizes it for the special past toward which it gestures, more often he reads it not as a fragment but as a self-nominating artifact, as a pure presence, perfection. If the ruin is a fetish, then, again and again in Naipaul's text, it is a fetish of itself. If he celebrates Englishness as architecture and ruin, it is not because the ruin signifies the architecture's fragmentary survival but because architecture gestures toward the ruin it will become. Ruin, in this text, does not finally invoke the desired habitus; the habitus invokes the desired ruin, and the ruin invokes itself. But this requires explanation, and the place to begin is perhaps not with such gnomic contractions but with Naipaul's inspection of decay.

What does Naipaul see when he gazes on the artifacts of England's crumbling? He sees many things, but primarily he observes revenants of England's past and an image of perfection. These are not, finally, the same, but together they compose the enigma of Naipaul's arrival. Naipaul's vision of the past invariably begins with a moment of disappointment in which he recognizes the illusory nature of the England in which he had learned to believe. I have already mentioned Naipaul's resentful discovery of the simulacra of rural Englishness. The text contains a metropolitan equivalent to this moment, an urban discovery that not only the English country but the English city is not what it has been advertised to be.

When he was a child in Trinidad, Naipaul recollects, the Penguin paperbacks that he read contained "advertisements for certain British things—chocolates, shoes, shaving cream—that had never been available in Trinidad. . . . These advertisements—for things doubly and trebly removed from possibility—never struck me as odd; they came to me as an aspect of the romance of the world I was working towards, a promise within the promise, and intensely romantic" (131). When he arrives in London, however, he discovers that these British things, though still advertised in Trinidad, no longer exist, or exist only as advertisements: "In the underground station there were still old-fashioned, heavy vending machines with raised letters. No sweets, no chocolates came from them now. But for ten years or so no one had bothered to take them away. . . . Two doors away from my boardinghouse in Earl's Court there was a bomb site, a gap in the road. . . . Such sites were all over the city. I saw them in the beginning; then I stopped seeing them. Paternoster Row, at the side of St Paul's Cathedral, hardly existed; but the name still appeared on the title page of books as the London address of many publishers" (131–32). The England in which Naipaul had believed does not collapse in his perception of the absence of these things, but it does begin, in his first days in London, the long process of betraying itself. In the absent but advertised commodity and in the obliterated but published address commences the revelation of England's survival as an imperfect imitation of itself, a revelation that will complete itself thirty years later on the grounds of a country house.

Naipaul's response to the appearance of this urban counterfeit is identical to his response to its rural manifestations: disappointment, which he then represses in a turn to the past. As Naipaul indicates, "I was ready to imagine that the world in which I found myself in London was something less than the perfect world I had striven towards. As a child in Trinidad I had put this world at a far distance, in London perhaps. In London now I was able to put this world at another time, an earlier time" (131). By displacing the "perfect world," by locating it in the past, Naipaul saves England from its own false advertising. He does so by altering his reading of the advertisement itself, by reading it not as a sign for which there is no signified object, but as a sign whose object is lost. He now reads the advertisement and address not as symbols of a fictitious England but of an England that was. This act of translation requires an erasure of the present from the processes of reading, an insistence that reference is only to the past, not to the contemporary. In this invocation

of an archaeological epistemology of reading, Naipaul reclassifies the advertisement and the address, like the work of architecture, as fragments, allegories, ruins.

This transformation of the offending object from that which signifies fraud-
ulence to that which signifies loss is crucial to Naipaul's discovery of the past.
For as ruins, both advertisement and architecture hold out the promise of
restoration and redemption. In them, the past endures. In them, Naipaul can
read not falsity or abandonment but "an idea of one's own redemption and
glory . . . the idea of being successors and inheritors" (51). As artifacts of ruin,
they possess a temporality that is diachronic, not synchronic; they place
Naipaul in a relation to the glorious past, not the disappointing present. More
than this, they offer to redeem the present by spilling into it the aura of the
past. The economy of redemption that the ruin signifies is the easy economy
of inheritance. It is an economy that allows Naipaul to exchange the anxiety
of belatedness for a promise of succession. Thus, in inspecting England's ruins
and in writing a chorography of ruin, Naipaul not only permits himself to gaze
upon the beloved English past but announces himself as the successor and
inheritor to an ancient and distinguished family of English writers. (Naipaul
names, or alludes to, many writers whose inheritor he sees himself to be. Most
prominent among them are Wordsworth, Ruskin, Cobbett, Hardy, Gray, and
Goldsmith.)

But if this were all that England's ruin signified to Naipaul, then it would
signify little more than what the surviving fragments of a Victorian and Edwardian past represent to the Prince of Wales. The ruin would then exist within
a familiar discourse of nostalgia as a simple touchstone of the redeeming past.
There are many moments in which the ruins that Naipaul catalogs function in
precisely this way. But Naipaul also has other, subtler responses to the decay
of farm and field and manor house, responses that he signals in passing, contradictory sequences. Here are two such sequences, the first on decay, the
second, which includes his reflections on his plans to restore a cottage, on the
relationship of architecture and ruin:

> I lived with the idea of decay. (I had always lived with this idea. It was like my
> curse: the idea which I had had even as a child in Trinidad, that I had come into
> a world past its peak.) . . . Decay implied an ideal, a perfection in the past. . . . I
> liked the decay . . . while it lasted it was perfection. . . . I lived not with the idea
> of decay. (23, 52, 210)

> To see the possibility, the certainty of ruin, even at the moment of creation: it was
> my temperament. . . . Now I, an outsider, was altering the appearance of the land
> a little, doing what I was aware of others doing, creating a potential ruin. (52, 89)

These passages signal an evident confusion regarding the relations of decay
and perfection, and a reformulation of Naipaul's understanding of the logic of

structure and ruin. In the latter series of statements, Naipaul tends toward a valorization of ruin over structure. He reverses his optics of inspection. Rather than seeing the ruin as the surviving fragment of an architecture of Englishness, he sees that architecture's completion and perfection in the moment of ruin. This inversion is of an order with that expressed in the first series of statements. For in these comments, he first recognizes decay as a sign of belatedness, as the emblem of a decline from a past perfection, then denies this recognition, and finally reconfirms the coincidence of ruin and perfection. Now, however, he finds the ruin's perfection in itself, not in a past that it gestures toward.

From these series of comments the suggestion emerges that it is ruin that Naipaul deems perfect, decay for which he yearns, and collapse, not that which is collapsed, that he desires. If there is an order of nostalgia operative here, it is a proleptic nostalgia that does not see wholeness in the ruin but the promise of ruin in the whole; or, in Raymond Williams's terms, it is a nostalgia that does not see the hegemonic in the residual but imagines the residue latent in hegemony. Again, if there is an order of fetishism operative here, it is one in which the displacing operations of synecdoche are reversed, in which the part does not gesture toward the whole, but in which the whole invokes the part, and one in which the part, as ruin, invokes itself. In less general terms, Naipaul's vision of a decaying, diminished, postimperial England has shifted. Where, at times, he has seen the grandeur of an imperial England surviving in the auratic monuments of its collapse, he now sees that imperial past tending inevitably toward its diminishment and ruin and sees perfection in that moment of ruin, in that moment of postimperial arrival. Having begun with the very conventional gesture of inspecting the artifacts of the nation's decay, and mourning and calling the past which those artifacts represent, he has invented a new form of desire.[19] He has fallen in love with decay itself and has written the love song of the empire's ruin.

This is not at all the same thing as condemning British imperialism. Naipaul does not claim that task. His work is to celebrate the empire in the moment of its closure: the moment of his arrival. His labor is to immortalize the empire's wondrous, awe-full ruins, among which he is counted. If this is not immediately clear to the reader, it is perhaps because Naipaul himself often does not understand—or often obscures—what he is doing. Naipaul says, more than once, that he is not in love with decay, that his text is not an anatomy or an autobiography of ruin. Instead, he asserts, his text is a narrative of change: "One of my early lessons in the valley [was] in the idea of change, of things declining from perfection" (239). "I had lived with the idea of change, had seen it as a constant, had seen a world in flux" (335). In these passages, Naipaul attempts to indicate that he has been able to refuse the seductions of a moment of cultural stasis, of perfect accomplishment. He suggests that he can live without the idea of perfection, and that he can resist the idea that culture has an authentic moment, a time of pure immanence. He is, he avers, reconciled to fluctuance, to uncertainty, to an image of culture caught always within the shifting moments of its own invention. He insists that he is able to read England as an unbound, unfinished text rather than as a narrative of closure and loss.

If this were Naipaul's position, however, he would be quite a different writer from who he is. For this is not an opinion that he can hold. The very frequency with which he repeats this formula to himself—"Not ruin, not poignant perfection: change, flux!"—betrays the efforts of a man trying desperately to convince himself of something that he knows he should believe but knows he cannot. At the exact moment that he denies the image of perfection, he cannot detach his thinking from it. He can define change and flux only as a moving away from the perfect, and it is to perfection that he returns as, finally, he recognizes that his labor is not to deny perfection but to discover its time. "I had trained myself to the idea of change," he indicates late in the text; "I had lived with the idea of change, had seen it as a constant, had seen a world in flux, had seen human life as a series of cycles that sometimes ran together. But philosophy failed me" (335). In recognizing the failure of that personal philosophy, he announces that there is perfection, and that its time is now, within the present temporality of ruin. Ruin, he insists, is perfection, and perfection, death. "And as at a death," he concludes, "everything that had been a source of pleasure and surprise, everything that had welcomed and healed me, became a cause of pain" (335–36).

In this moment of recognition toward which, in many ways, the entire text has been leading, Naipaul subjects his key terms to a rapid process of translation and retranslation; and if he is to be understood, the process must be slowed a little. The crucial movement is from ruin to perfection, from perfection to death, and from death to arrival. Naipaul's sense of ruin is, as I have been suggesting, extremely complex. But he comes to a fairly clear definition in these final pages of his narrative. Ruin is now not a simple allusion to the nation's imperial past. It accommodates that past but accommodates it by signaling that past's terminus, by marking, in fallen stones, its boundary. It is because the ruin of country-house England marks the closure of a narrative of British imperialism that the ruin, as the final page of a national epic, signifies perfection. It closes the book. It is the final utterance in an imperial discourse of cultural belonging. The rest is silence. For a long, long time, Naipaul can contemplate that perfect, completed narrative with pleasure. But not forever. For if that perfect, accomplished narrative of Englishness encompasses the past and the present, it has no place for the future. Because Naipaul understands it to be perfect, because he perceives it as complete, because he registers its refusal of futuricity, he cannot but read it as a form of death. In that death, Naipaul sees himself implicated. The death of that England in which, as a child, he had been taught to believe, coincides with his coming. Its death is, indeed, announced by the fact of his coming. "In that perfection, occurring at a time of empire," in that perfection, whose span is the time of empire, and whose limit and final accomplishment are the stones of England's ruin, in that perfection which is the object of his life's desire, in that perfect England, Naipaul wryly notes, there is "no room for me" (52). His coming betokens its death. This, apparently, is the melancholy enigma of his arrival.

GESTURES OF REFUSAL

In an essay published in 1917, Sigmund Freud addressed the subject of melancholy. The essay, entitled "Mourning and Melancholia," is primarily significant, as Freud's editor James Strachey notes, as a preliminary discussion of the existence of that critical agency which in later years Freud would label the superego.[20] Of greater pertinence here, however, is Freud's consideration of the libidinal economy of melancholy. That economy, he suggests, is like that of mourning in that it is, essentially, an economy of loss. But it is one in which the work of compensation that attends the subject's apperception of loss fails. Unlike the mourner, Freud suggests, the melancholic cannot abandon the lost object of his or her desire and discover a new object of libidinal investment and attachment. Melancholy, then, is distinguished from mourning by an inability to surrender the lost object, by a brooding refusal of the new, by what Freud calls an "exclusive devotion to mourning . . . [in which] the existence of the lost object is psychically prolonged" (14:244–45).

In completing his essay, Freud discusses the reasons for this and its consequences. The history of the melancholic's relation to the desired object prior to that object's loss is characterized by two stages. In the primary stage of attachment, for reasons that Freud cannot explain, the subject does not simply desire the object but identifies with it narcissistically, wills to incorporate the object into himself or herself, and "wants to do so by devouring it" (14:250). Subsequent to this act of cannibalization, there is an experience of loss. Owing to what Freud demurely calls a "real slight or disappointment" issuing from the loved and ingested object, "the object-relationship is shattered" (14:249). The loss experienced here derives, then, not from the death of the desired thing, but from its degradation, from the subject's reevaluation of it as diminished or tarnished. But because this devaluation of the desired object succeeds its psychic ingestion, the object cannot be abandoned, and the "shadow" of degradation that it throws is thrown over the subject, whose image of self is then drastically diminished. The wounded subject, finally, is imprisoned within the brooding cell of melancholy, where, unable to abandon the lost object of desire, unable to return to it, and unable to erase the marks of its degradation from his own person, "he reproaches himself, vilifies himself and expects to be cast out and punished . . . he describes himself as petty, egoistic, dishonest, lacking in independence, one whose sole aim has been to hide the weaknesses of his own nature" (14:246).

Apart from whatever value it might have as an investigation of psychic disorder, Freud's discussion of melancholy is of interest as a reading of the imbrication of the tropes of attachment, loss, disappointment, cannibalization, and chastisement: figures that are familiar to readers of Naipaul, and of the Prince of Wales. The coincidence of these tropes to Freud's reading of melancholy and to Naipaul's and Prince Charles's writings reveals less about the clinical condition of either writer than about the libidinal economy of a postimperial English nationalism. For the erotics of the nation, like that of the melancholic, is curiously narcissistic. The hortatory rhetoric of nationalism demands that the citizen not only adore the nation but identify with it, insists on the coincidence of a narrative of national belonging and the citizen's autobiography, requires that the citizen manifest the nation's mystic geography in his or her own flesh. So that wherever the subject is, the nation is also. So that to be English is at once to belong to an imaginary community and to locate, in one's own person, the address of that community. The erotics of the nation, to return to Freud's tropology, is an erotics of ingestion, of absorption, of cannibalization.

If the nation's erotics of attachment is cannibalistic, then the plot of desire to which the nation is committed is almost inevitably a narrative of melancholy. For the nation, thus imagined, always disappoints. Or, to be more precise, the nation always disappoints if it is imagined as perfect. That image of perfection may survive as a commissioned portrait of the past, but it cannot survive the fluctuance of the everyday; it cannot survive the present's art of perpetual invention. In changing, in denying the dream of changelessness announced in Ernest Renan's dictum ("We are what you were, we will be what you are"), the nation disappoints precisely because it refuses to play dead, or to rest in peace. It is degraded, tarnished, diminished. Confronted with the nation's degradation, a degradation written also on his or her own person, the citizen laments. Unable to mourn (because the nation is not dead—better it were dead—only diminished), unable to abandon this object of desire, unable to return to the nation's lost time of accomplishment, the citizen can only brood. Turning longingly to the past, the citizen sees the portrait of lost perfection; turning resentfully to the present, he or she sees diminishment. Melancholy follows, with its vilifications of the present, and a yearning for death: if not the nation's, then the citizen's; if not the citizen's, then the present's, that one might be reborn into the past.

This is allegory. But it describes an allegorical plot remarkably similar to the melancholy plots of Naipaul's text and the Prince of Wales's *Vision*. At the heart of Naipaul's narrative there is, in fact, an allegory from which he draws the title of his text and that, he indicates, offers the interpretive key to the work. In that allegory, suggested to him by Giorgio de Chirico's painting *The Enigma of Arrival*, Naipaul imagines a traveler who arrives on the quay of a foreign city, is drawn into the city's intrigues, but gradually is overwhelmed by a sense of purposelessness, by a feeling of helplessness, by an awareness of betrayal and danger. Naipaul imagines the tale ending so: "He would lose his sense of mission; he would begin to know only that he was lost. His feeling of adventure would give way to panic. He would want to escape, to get back to the quayside and his ship. But he wouldn't know how. . . . At the moment of crisis he would come upon a door, open it, and find himself back on the quayside of arrival. He has been saved; the world is as he remembered it. Only one thing is missing now. Above the cut-out walls and buildings there is no mast, no sail. The antique ship has gone. The traveler has lived out his life" (98–99). In the surreal landscape of this allegory, to which he sometimes refers as a vision of his own death, Naipaul discerns a primal scene of instruction. A voyage to an adopted culture has become a nightmare of loss and betrayal from which the traveler hopes to escape through an act of remembrance, through the better dream of return, only to discover that return is impossible. The traveler is trapped. Life is over.

This tale aptly depicts Naipaul's voyage to an England that is not as he remembered or imagined. It is this England, an England pervaded with a sense of "wrongness," from which not only Naipaul, but the Prince of Wales, a host of Raj revivalists, and a generation of country-house nostalgics wish to flee, from which they wish to escape to a remembered world, from which they wish to launch a voyage of return. But Naipaul has realized what his fellows have not: return is impossible; there is no route back from the difficulties and the enigmas of England's postimperial arrival. He responds to this knowledge, however, with a gesture of refusal. If the present is unbearable, and the past impossible, the future, one might think, would hold some promise or hope. But Naipaul refuses the future: life, he unambiguously insists, is over. And it is this gesture of refusal, finally, that characterizes the English discourse of postimperial melancholy.

But what aspect of the future does Naipaul so categorically shun? In generic terms, Naipaul refuses narrative—not narrative per se, but its continuance. Naipaul denies the possibility that England's plot of belonging survives the end of empire; he dismisses his awareness that England has not had the good taste to time its death with the "ending" of its empire. In specific terms, this dismissal entails the rejection of the contemporary city. For it is in the island's metropolises that the inscriptions of a postimperial plot of English belonging are most evident. Prince Charles's text and film are animated throughout by an almost hysterical refusal of the image of the postwar city. The prince does not overtly connect that image with the postwar arrival of significant numbers of West Indian, Pakistani, and Indian immigrants. But the historical moment in which the city becomes unbearable to him, the moment in which "something went wrong," coincides rather exactly with the moment of imperial collapse and the moment of a large-scale migration of ex-colonial subjects to the cities of England. It is the urban presence of those immigrants which gnaws at the melancholy heart of a Thatcherite politics of denial and Enoch Powell's politics of return. And it is the city, transformed by the presence of these ex-colonial migrants, that Naipaul refuses.

Naipaul only fleetingly registers London in his text, and when he does acknowledge the city, it is as a scene of disappointment. "I had come to London," Naipaul says, "as to a place I knew very well. I found a city that was strange and unknown. . . . The disturbance in me, faced with this strangeness, was very great" (134). His disturbance is not only a response to what he does not find in London—the city's obliterated addresses and those "British things" to which he had imagined the great city was home—but to what he does find there. He discovers not the metropolitan seat of that imaginary England in which he had come to believe but a city of migrants, a city filled with people such as himself. "In 1950 in London I was at the beginning of that great movement of peoples that was to take place in the second half of the twentieth century. . . . This was a movement between all the continents. . . . Cities like London were to change. They were to cease being more or less national cities; they were to become cities of the world. . . . But I noted nothing down. I asked no questions" (141–42). This city, Naipaul allows, might have become his theme. The emergence, in cities like London, of a postwar narrative of English habitation and belonging might have sustained his invention of himself as an English writer. But, with admirable honesty, he admits that this is not what he wanted. "I noted nothing down. I asked no questions." Migrancy was not to be his theme. He rejects the image of a city of migrants, where, even after the end of empire, the imbricated narratives of imperialism and Englishness continue to be written. From this rejection follows that complex turning to the authentic past which I have been discussing. What follows is not only a melancholy turn to the past but a yearning for perfection and closure, and a dalliance with death.

"I'M NOT DEAD YET"

Naipaul is not a popular writer among many postcolonial critics. He is a writer whom many critics are tempted to damn: for celebrating Englishness, for dragging the ruined remains of a rhetoric of authenticity over into a moment in which many of his readers (at least his professional academic readers) have had more than enough of the authentic. Like a bad party guest who insists on showing off images of his dead ancestors, Naipaul tends to spoil the unanimity of conversation at the postcolonial dinner party. But as many critics in the field, like many guests at a dinner party, would agree, it is also rather convenient to have someone like Naipaul around, someone to mock when his or her back is turned. The two photographs that illustrate a recent article on Naipaul in the journal *Transition* are eloquent in this regard. The first, a reproduction of a conventional book-jacket head shot, shows the aging writer peering contemplatively into the eye of the camera and is captioned "V. S. Naipaul, marmoreal mandarin and travel writer . . ." The second, which depicts the writer scribbling in a handheld notebook, a handkerchief knotted around his head, completes the ellipses, ". . . Or itinerant handkerchief head?"[21]

Let me be honest. It is hard not to laugh at these photographs. Particularly if one is convinced of the dangers of that discourse of authenticity which Naipaul, in *The Enigma of Arrival*, so forcibly, if broodingly, defends. But disagreement, even ardent disagreement, need not express itself as ridicule. Perhaps the willingness to derogate Naipaul for offering himself as the spokesman of a lost, authentic, Englishness, rather than to disagree and to argue with him, simply indicates that postcolonial critique is, finally, human, all too human. But it also seems to indicate that Naipaul, possibly more than any other writer, can unnerve the participants in a critical discourse that is rapidly becoming self-congratulatorily unanimous in its convictions. And perhaps this is because, as he hauls out his cache of snapshots, Naipaul reminds us that the rumors of the death of the authentic have, in fact, been greatly exaggerated.

If we are to come to terms with the unwillingness of that shade to play dead (whether in the Balkans, Great Britain, Central Africa, or the United States), snickering laughter will not do. For what Naipaul seems to understand is that no matter how carefully we demonstrate the constructedness and the artificiality of the authentic—as he has demonstrated these things to himself—the patent inventedness of a phenomenon does not prevent it from having a very real affective appeal, from seducing, from convincing its beholder to forget that it is a piece of counterfeit, or to worship it regardless. Naipaul knows that England was never the ideal he wishes it to be. But he also knows how much pleasure that ideal has afforded so many people: an anguished, melancholy pleasure, to be sure; but pleasure nonetheless. And, most crucially, he understands that pleasure defines its own ways of knowing, that it is canny, haughty, willfully dismissive of inconvenient counterfactuals, untroubled by its own inconsistencies, tenaciously devoted to its object. One may disagree with Naipaul, but until we understand that we cannot dismiss the siren call of the authentic either with insults or with proofs of its fictitiousness, we certainly have something to learn from him.

Michael Gorra has suggested that while Salman Rushdie, for whom identity is always already splendidly inauthentic, provides "a model of the way things should be," Naipaul offers "an account of the way things are."[22] I take Gorra to mean not that the language of origins, essences, and authenticity is the true language of the world, but that it is the language most people enjoy speaking, the language that seduces people's affections, while Rushdie's hybridizing discourse, however theoretically convincing, is a weaker suitor of our everyday affections; weaker because it demands too much of us, because it exhausts us, because it insists that we allow our identities always, always to be in play. Whereas, like Naipaul, what we frequently want to do is to rest, to delude ourselves, to put aside the knowledge that we, and the cultures we inhabit, are, as Rushdie has it, always "two, or three, or fifteen," and to pretend for a while that we are "one, one, one."[23] Not everyone feels that way, of course. But those who do not can learn from Naipaul that in expressing disagreement to those who do, a critical practice that aspires to convince those who do not already share its presuppositions will need to argue with more than laughter and with more than proofs that we are always contingent, uncertain, multiple. It will need to reveal why even Naipaul or the Prince of Wales should desire to be that way. It will need to show why things *should be* as it, in fact, believes they *are*. And that, to disagree with Gorra, and to anticipate the argument of the ensuing chapter, is precisely what I understand to be the accomplishment of *The Satanic Verses*, an infinitely seductive piece of writing which responds to Naipaul's and the Prince of Wales's postimperial melancholy by offering its readers the pleasures of knowing that what we should be *is* what we are, and what we are is what we should *want* to be: two, three, fifteen, splendidly inauthentic.

Chapter Six

THE RIOT OF ENGLISHNESS: MIGRANCY, NOMADISM, AND THE REDEMPTION OF THE NATION

How does newness enter the world? Of what fusions,
translations, conjoinings is it made?
—Salman Rushdie, *The Satanic Verses*

In its afterlife—which could not be called that if it were
not a transformation and a renewal of something
living—the original undergoes a change.
—Walter Benjamin, *Illuminations*

THE VIEW FROM THE MILK TIN

In the days of his childhood in Trinidad, V. S. Naipaul informs the reader of *The Enigma of Arrival*, the labels on the cans of condensed milk in his kitchen were illustrated with an image of beautiful black-and-white English cows chewing the green grasses of an English down. In the closing pages of the text, Naipaul indicates that wandering the grounds of the country house where he has come to live, he discovers the "original" of that gentle, pastoral image. "Always on a sunny day on this walk, and especially if at the top of the slope some of the cattle stood against the sky, there was a corner of my fantasy in which I felt that some minute, remote yearning—as remote as a flitting, all but forgotten cinema memory from early childhood—had been satisfied, and I was in the original of that condensed-milk label drawing" (331). Settled into the splendid grasses of his pastoral retreat, Naipaul finds that he can turn away from the English present, from the confusions of England's postcoloniality, and, above all, from England's cities. In those cities, he knows that he can discover countless men and women similar to himself, ex-colonial migrants who have come to England to make a new home. He refuses the city because he believes that though so many of its inhabitants share an experience of displacement very much like his own, many do not share his vision of England. Crucially, he discerns that many of his fellow immigrants and their children refuse to join him in mourning England's death and instead insist on marking the nation's urban expanses as places in which the narratives of empire and Englishness continue to be written. Naipaul does not fail to know that England survives the formal endings of empire. He simply refuses to countenance his knowledge of the nation's continuing transformation. Rejecting an England that dares to outlive imperialism, he codes his refusal as a denial of the metropolis and invents the English countryside as the landscape of the past, and the past as the landscape of rest. While Naipaul's attitude is comprehensible, it demands that he blind himself. His rigorous refusals of the city prevent him from recognizing that while England's cities are certainly places in which the nation's cultural identity continues to be refashioned, this does not mean that the inhabitants of the metropolis have betrayed England. As it is the object of this chapter to indicate, the labors of cultural translation by which the nation's urban migrants, among others, have written the text of England's newness can also be read as labors devoted to England's redemption. But in order to understand how the narratives of postcolonial migrancy can generate a reading of England's contemporaneity that identifies the migrant not as England's vandal but as its redeemer, we must turn from the scene of Naipaul's self-imposed exile to those city streets he has declined to gaze upon and to a moment in which Naipaul would assuredly discover England's immigrants, and their children, announcing themselves as the enemies of Englishness.

Scenes of Violence

On the 12th of April, 1981, the Sunday edition of the London *Times* greeted its morning readers with front-page photographs of a bleeding police inspector and a smoke-filled London street littered with bricks and the glass of shattered windows. Above and below these photographs ran banner headlines: "The Bloody Battle of Brixton . . . 114 Police Hurt; Area Sealed Off."[1] By the time London's newspaper readers had unfolded their papers, gazed upon these images, and absorbed the grim statistics of this outbreak of urban violence, the news that the *Times* trumpeted was, however, no longer new. From the evening of Friday, April 10, onward, British television had carried live broadcasts of the riotous spectacle the *Times* was belatedly reporting. Into countless English homes these broadcasts poured the "news" that hundreds, if not thousands, of "youths" had taken to the streets in one of the city's "immigrant" neighborhoods and were "rioting." The publication of volumes of writing would follow these television broadcasts, as diverse scholars, activists, and politicians tried to decide if this was, in fact, what had happened, and labored to determine what it all meant. Unwilling to be left out of this process in which the riot, first reproduced as video, was now produced once again as text, Parliament established a committee to investigate the "disorders." And it is with the report of that committee that I wish to begin my reading of the location of riot in a contemporary discourse of English identity.

In the first sentence of the report that he submitted to Parliament, Lord Scarman, chair of the committee charged with the task of investigating the disorders, indicated that the riot itself was perhaps less significant than the fact that the riot had "happened" on television. "During the weekend of 10–12 April (Friday, Saturday and Sunday)," Lord Scarman noted, "the British people watched with horror and incredulity an instant audio-visual presentation on their television sets of scenes of violence and disorder in their capital city, the like of which had not previously been seen in this century in Britain."[2] Scarman's language is arresting. For it is unclear from his phrasing whether he wishes to suggest that the violence of the riot was unprecedented, or is convinced that this April weekend was epochal because it had gathered the nation in an inspection of televised violence. Whatever he was trying to say, it is clear that in Lord Scarman's mind the horror and incredulity of the "British people" extended not only to what was happening in Brixton but to what was literally taking place in their own homes, on the glass surfaces of their television screens.

If Lord Scarman's nervous obsession with the appearance of the riot on television allegorizes the terror of shattered windows invoked by the photographs on the front page of the *Sunday Times*, and, in thus technologizing the window dividing the watchers from the watched, registers the profound fragility of that glass boundary separating the "British people" from the riotous mob on the street, then his report admits another fear. Turning from the immediate nature of the events in Brixton, Scarman pauses to contemplate a future in which "disorder will become a disease endemic in our society" (2). This identification of riot as a species of contagion invokes a time-honored understanding of the crowd as a social form that reproduces itself through an act of contaminated touching.[3] As his report unfolds, it becomes apparent that Scarman's initial nervousness about the televising of the riot connects not only to the possibility that the television may be a window through which the architectures of Englishness are opened to the crowd's performative disorders, but also to his suspicion that the television screen locates the point of the "British people"'s contact with the contaminations of the rioters. Disorder, he fears, will become endemic precisely because television, rather than acting as a glassy prophylactic against riot, will act as the technological organ of the riot's communication. His fear is not only that certain viewers, watching the violence, will leave their homes to join the rioting. Scarman fears a comprehensive infection of the general populace in which future viewers, impelled by whatever reasons, will abandon their homes, take to the streets, and shatter the image with which he began: the "British people" at home, distinctly separate from the plague in the street. Though he never indicates what might prompt this general, self-cultivated infection, Scarman cannot avoid betraying the suspicion that the "British people" might choose to reproduce themselves as the crowd they have seen because riot carries not only a threat of violence but a promise of pleasure.

But what sort of pleasure does rioting elicit?

Scarman's report indicates that if rioting does produce pleasure, its more dangerous delights are those of observation, not participation; that what is at stake in a reading of the televisual reproductions of rioting are not the immediate gratifications of crowd disturbance but the *affective* delights which attach to the visual consumption of the riotous event. In a recent essay, Brian Massumi (the American translator of Deleuze and Guattari's *A Thousand Plateaus*) has suggested that affect is something like what Paul Fry calls the "ostensive" moment.[4] Affect, he argues, defines a certain vacation from, and of, significance; as an experience of "intensity" it occupies a bewilderingly "happy" moment in which we become aware of the suspension of the structuring economies of meaning:

> Intensity is qualifiable as an emotional state, and that state is static—temporal and narrative noise. It is a state of suspense, potentially of disruption. . . . It is not exactly passivity, because it is filled with motion, vibratory motion, resonation. . . . Much could be gained by integrating the dimension of intensity into cultural theory. *The stakes are the new.* For structure is the place where nothing ever happens, that explanatory heaven in which all eventual permutations are prefigured in a self-consistent set of invariant generative rules. Nothing is prefigured in the event. It is the collapse of structured distinction into intensity, or rules into paradox. . . . *Could it be that it is through the expectant suspension of that suspense that the new emerges?*[5]

I will not dwell on the ease with which Massumi's description of the affective—as a space of vibratory motion, noise, disruption, and dis-ordering—can be translated into a journalistic description of riot. Instead, I want to address the construction of newness that Massumi derives from this reading of affect, a construction of the new which is implicit in Lord Scarman's description of the Brixton disturbances. For these understandings of affect and rioting ignore an alternative account of how newness enters the world, an account that permits us to read riot not as the space of the asignificant but as the site of a certain uncertainty, as the expression not merely of a nomadic but of a migrant politics, as the space not only of disruption but also, potentially, of redemption.

In Massumi's account, newness names not only a break from the prison house of meaning but a flight from that economy of expectation which houses events within structures. Because the new is not merely the emergence of the unexpected, but that which we cannot expect to reemerge, it gestures neither to the future nor to the past. A profoundly untimely form of rupture, it neither differs nor defers; it neither translates nor renders itself translatable. A pure performance, a pure uncertainty, a purely areferential newness, affect, Massumi insists, "is the system of the inexplicable: emergence, into and against (re)generation . . . unqualified. As such, it is not ownable or recognizable, and is thus resistant to critique" (87–88). And it is precisely because of this auton-

omous and haughty indifference that Massumi associates affect and newness
with pleasure. A perfect amphetamine, the affect-event offers to trip its consumer into the narcotic spaces of a radically deterritorialized newness, to liberate us into the intensity of meaninglessness, to send us on a vacation to the isle
of the lotus-eaters. As an affective catalyst of the new, rioting, in such a reading, manifests itself as the nomadic par excellence, as a perfect performance of
the deterritorializing war machine.

As a special 1981 issue of the journal *Race and Class* testifies, it would be
quite possible to read the Brixton uprisings in such terms. In the concluding
essay of the issue, which was published in response to the April events, Paul
Gilroy draws attention to those British laws of suspicion—commonly referred
to as Sus laws—to which the uprising was in many ways a response. Operating
under these laws—which permitted the police to arrest individuals not only
for crimes that had been committed but for crimes that the police believed the
"suspect" was about to commit, and which further allowed the police to identify large areas of a city as "criminal" and hence to arrest any person found
within these contaminated spaces—the Brixton police launched a street cam-
paign on the 7th of April, 1981. By the end of the week, the police had
stopped and questioned over a thousand people and had arrested over one
hundred. On the evening of Friday, April 10, a group of approximately one
hundred black youths surrounded a car in which the police were holding a
young man, and released him. The officers in the car radioed for help, sixty
policemen, with dogs and riot gear arrived, and a fight ensued. For the next
three days Brixton was engulfed in riot. In its April 12 edition, the *Sunday
Telegraph* published a comment by a young black man that offered to decode
the riot's economy of violence: "It's not against the white community," the
man said, "It's against the police. They have treated us like dirt."[6] A reader
content with Massumi's Deleuzian theory need read no further. One could
conclude with an interpretation of the riot as an event in a nomadic politics
that articulates itself as a waging of war upon the state and the state's policing
of movement, and with a reading of the rioter as nomad, as one who exists to
deterritorialize, to manifest that deliriously vacant new space of which Massumi dreams.

And undoubtedly this is, in some respects, what the uprising signified—or,
in Massumi's terms, deliriously failed to signify. But it is worth considering the
ways in which these events open themselves to an additional understanding of
newness, and, in so doing, permit us to read the moment of urban rioting not
as a "black hole" in the time of the imperial afterward, but as a moment in
which the affect-event—understood now as a principle of allusive repetition,
as a *certain* uncertainty—takes place within a disciplinary structure whose
orders and arrangements of meaning the riot re-collects and re-creates (in
much the same fashion as the flowing game of cricket visible to C.L.R. James
re-creates the disciplinary structures of Englishness). To read it thus is by no

means to ignore the comments of the man cited in the *Sunday Telegraph*, but to offer an alternative account of what his words might mean: to insist, first of all, that his words do, in fact, have some meaning, that a battle against the police is a "significant" event, and, second, that a fight *against* something is also, in this context, a fight *for* something. It is to argue that the urban riot manages not merely to vandalize but to reorganize England's spaces of belonging, to introduce newness to the world not simply as a schizophrenic epiphany but, as Rushdie puts it in *The Satanic Verses*, as a process of "fusions, translations, conjoinings" (8). To supplement a nomadological hermeneutic of rioting with such a reading is to reveal that the riot zone is not simply an affect-event but—like the country house, the cricket field, and the Victoria Terminus—one of England's contested spaces of memory, an English *lieu de memoire* refashioned, in this case, by the cultural politics of postcolonial migrancy.

We can begin this alternative reading by noting that the Sus laws were not the only English laws which had a bearing upon the Brixton uprising. During the week of the Brixton riots, Parliament was debating Margaret Thatcher's British Nationality Act, a piece of legislation that, in the succinct words of the *Sunday Times*, "for the first time seeks to define British Citizenship and those who 'belong to Britain' . . . [and] to abolish the historic right of common British citizenship enjoyed by the colonial peoples."[7] As discussed in the introduction to this book, the Nationality Act defined the nation's community of belonging according to the principle of "patriality." To be British, it mandated, one had to trace a line of descent to an ancestor born on the island. In effect, the law thus drew the lines of the nation rather snugly around the boundaries of race and erased the present as a space available for new engenderings of national identity. If the nation must express a relation to its past, the act suggested, then that past is the past of biology, not of history.

The Nationality Act provoked widespread dissent. Labour M.P.'s attacked it relentlessly; Indira Ghandi, whom the prime minister was visiting during the week of the riot, denounced it; and multitudes of Britain's inhabitants protested it in the press, through their elected representatives, and on the street. The Brixton riots, which were in many ways a riot against the police, must also be read in the context of this collective outrage. But in that moment in which riotous protest is directed against a police force whose government has proposed to pass a law that threatens to contract the boundaries of the community of national belonging, the cultural politics of riot shifts from the extranational domain of nomadism to the intranational domain of migrancy. Or, to state the argument rather differently, if riot can be represented as a vehicle of a nomadic politics whose object is to locate the individual outside of the nation-state's space of operation, then it can also be read as the expression of a migrant politics whose object is to *reposition* the individual within a national community of belonging. And, in assembling as a crowd to articulate their grievances as *citizens*, the Brixton rioters were acting not only in the name of the nation but in the most English of ways.

In one of his more important essays, E. P. Thompson, drawing on the work of his fellow historian George Rude, has insisted that historians read the English crowd not according to tropes of randomness, madness, treason, or disarray, but within the metaphors of an ordering disorderliness. The English crowd, Thompson suggests, acts to protect a customary body of rights that its members believe to be threatened, customary rights that, crucially, typically enshrine local ways of being, local traditions of organizing the social, the political, and the economic.[8] The particular series of customary rights that the riotous crowd perceives to be threatened and acts to defend is, in some respects, less significant than the crowd's defense of the principle of the local *and* the relation which the crowd establishes between its present time and the time of the nation's past. The English crowd, Thompson argues, appeals to the past, or invents the past, in order to address or erase the depredations of the present, and it does so not that it might vandalize the nation, but in the name of restoring the nation to itself, in the name of re-creating England as a diverse assortment of local communities, local knowledges, and local polities.

And this, according to Paul Gilroy, is precisely the labor of those rioting crowds which, in the summers of 1981 and 1985, took to the streets of Brixton and Handsworth. Stressing that the behavior of these urban crowds was not, as media reports suggested, "anomic [or] irritational" but entirely "purposive" (*"There Ain't No Black in the Union Jack"*, 239), Gilroy argues that the purpose of these rioters was to defend the right of a local community to define its own "particular set of values and norms in everyday life" (234). The riots, in his reading, were a fight *against* the police and *for* a sense of "community" that assumed as its first principle "the strong association of identity and territory" (243). Local knowledges, values, and norms are, on this account, precisely knowledges that derive from the locale; the defense of the one was, Gilroy indicates, the defense of the other. And it was for this reason that in these neighborhoods the flow of riotous protest became a very *spatial* competition, a "competition between the police and the mob for control of the riot-torn area," a competition in which, for Gilroy, the major question to be resolved was whether "local people might gain control over their own neighborhood" (241).

That Gilroy, like most commentators, recollects the Brixton and Handsworth riots precisely as Brixton and Handsworth events, rather than London or Manchester happenings, does not mean that they were not also English events. Rather they can be understood as recent interventions in a very long struggle to define what England is: a unitary, homogeneous, nation ("one, one, one"), or a variegated array of local communities, local dialects, local ways of playing the game ("always two, or three, or fifteen"). Gilroy is clearly no great fan of E. P. Thompson, largely because in some of his political writings,

Thompson seems willing to assume the givenness of the category of the nation and to forget, as Gilroy is prompt to remind him, that many Britons "recognize and define themselves primarily in terms of *regional* or *local* tradition" (*"There Ain't No Black in the Union Jack"*, 55, emphasis original), but there is a profound similarity between Gilroy's account of the communitarian politics of the rioters and Thompson's reading of the "moral economy" of the "English" crowd. Gilroy's rioters are not, therefore, the designated "inheritors" of the ideological convictions of Thompson's eighteenth- and nineteenth-century crowds (discursive genealogies rarely produce such simple lines of descent). But in defending the right of the nation's subjects to define themselves as citizens whose primary loyalty is nevertheless to a "regional or local tradition," they re-create one of the country's traditional ways of being English.

This historical irony provides the keynote of Salman Rushdie's response to the Nationality Act in an essay entitled "The New Empire within Britain." Imagining himself to be addressing a primarily white audience, Rushdie informs his readers that, whether they realize it or not, in assaulting the nation's communities of immigrants, the bill has simultaneously assaulted the nation's past.

> This already notorious piece of legislation, expressly designed to deprive black and Asian Britons of their citizenship rights, went through in spite of some, mainly non-white, protests. And because it didn't really affect the position of the whites, you probably didn't realize that one of your most ancient rights, a right you had possessed for nine hundred years, was being stolen from you. This was the right to citizenship by virtue of birth, the *ius soli*, or right of the soil. For nine centuries any child born on British soil was British. Automatically. By right. Not by permission of the state. The nationality act abolished the *ius soli*. From now on citizenship is the gift of government. You were blind, because you believed the Act was aimed at the blacks; and so you sat back and did nothing as Mrs Thatcher stole the birthright of every one of us, black and white, and of our children and grandchildren for ever.[9]

Rushdie is clearly outraged. He is almost as obviously unoriginal in the phrasing of his argument. But if his arguments are a trifle familiar, they are productively so. For Rushdie is here mimicking the outraged voices of England's eighteenth- and early-nineteenth-century crowds, crowds whom, as George Rude argues, most commonly conceived of themselves as defenders of the rights of the "freeborn" Englishman. Their discourse, like Rushdie's here, was the discourse of the *ius soli*; their outrage the outrage of those to whom the rights of the soil had been denied. This echo is not, however, the only chord of repetition that Rushdie strikes. He returns also to that moment in the English past to which generations of English crowds were most willing to return, to an imaginary and ideal past associated with a pre-Norman England. The rights of the soil, Rushdie asserts, are nine centuries old. They are the rights, that is, of an England that predates the invasion of 1066, an England toward which the conservatively utopic crowd was incessantly willing to turn a mournful and nostalgic eye. "One of the most remarkably persistent beliefs of all," Rude notes, "was that perfect 'liberties' had existed under the Saxon Kings and that these had been filched, together with their lands, by the invading Norman knights."[10] Rude traces the persistence of this belief to the Chartist constructions of an English past, to which the radical ideologues of the Charter claimed they were returning the nation. Rushdie's essay marks the strategic survival of that belief into the late twentieth century. More significant, the essay marks the availability of a mythologized English past to a migrant's protest against England's present betrayals of itself.

It is in assuming this role of the defender of the English past that Rushdie, in this essay, is most interesting. By constructing his audience as a body of white Britons, he positions his voice quite carefully. His, apparently, is a voice of protest, a voice of a black and Asian Britain. As the self-announced voice of this community, however, his delight is to surprise his imagined reader by raising his protest both on behalf of his fellow migrants and on behalf of the nation, the national past, and the nation's future. In fastening on the *ius soli*, Rushdie quite carefully repeats one of the basic gestures of English social criticism, the gesture not simply of measuring the present against the past but of calling on the present to submit itself to the past. But he does so in order to reveal that the national past has become the possession not only of the state but of the nation's communities of postcolonial migrants. He does so in order to reveal that England's history is also his, and that the politics of remembrance may as often be oppositional as reactionary.

Homi Bhabha, in a seminal essay on England's postcoloniality, crowd disturbance, and the temporality of the nation, offers some partially consonant insights. In an attempt to understand riot as an element of that "contemporary within culture" with which the custodians of the state are so uncomfortable, Bhabha refers to two memorable images in *Handsworth Songs*, a documentary film shot during the "black uprising" in Handsworth in 1985. "Two memories repeat incessantly to translate the living perplexity of history into the time of migration: the arrival of the ship laden with immigrants from the ex-colonies, just stepping off the boat, always just emerging . . . [the other] image is of the perplexity and power of an emergent peoples, caught in the shot of a dreadlocked rastaman cutting a swathe through a posse of policemen. It is a memory that flashes incessantly through the film."[11] Bhabha's concern in calling our attention to these images is to name the tropes of the performative in the cultural discourse of the nation. The performative is Bhabha's collective name for the contemporary, the emergent, and the time of migration; it is also his word for what Frantz Fanon, in his celebrated essay on national consciousness, called that space of anticolonial struggle, that "zone of occult instability

... [that] fluctuating movement which the people are just giving shape to" (*The Wretched of the Earth*, 227). This area of fluctuance is the space of cultural self-fashioning out of which, Fanon suggests, the postcolonial nation emerges as an uncertain and perpetual invention. Bhabha glosses this occult performativity as "the prodigious, living principle of the people . . . [the] continual process by which national life is redeemed and signified as a repeating and reproductive process" (297), and then collapses all of this—the performative, the emergent, the time of migration, the redemptive, repetitive, living principle of the people—onto that memorable image of urban riot in which a rastaman is seen "cutting a swathe through a posse of police."

The invocation of this catalog of mutually defined tropes by the image of a dreadlocked man battling with the police suggests that we have moved quite a distance from that reading of riot rendered available by Massumi and Deleuze. At the moment in which the rastaman and the police appear in Bhabha's essay, they are linked, Bhabha's argument suggests, not by the rioter's war on the English state, but by his attempts to redeem England from the depredations of its juridical and regulatory institutions. The rioter appears here not as the nation's enemy but as its savior. This move, which is emblematic of the movement that I am attempting to trace from the placement of riot in the nomadic war machine to its location in the cultural politics of migrancy, is enabled by Bhabha's willingness to graft a Benjaminian branch onto Frantz Fanon's discursive tree. Benjamin's Messianic labor of redemption finds articulation, Bhabha suggests, not strictly in an act of remembrance in which the nation is obliged to conform its present to the available memories of the past, but through a difficult Fanonian performance by which the contemporary reveals the nation not as the prisoner of the past but as its liberator. In the image of the redemptive rioter, it is not the past that redeems and disciplines the unruly present, but the riotous present that perpetually gives birth to itself by redeeming the past.

But if we are to follow Bhabha, and to say that the problem of reading the Handsworth or Brixton riots is at least in part the problem of determining what such events remember, then we must ask what past, or pasts, the Brixton riots recollect and performatively redeem. Bhabha, unfortunately, is of limited help here. For, with the makers of the documentary on Handsworth, he can find "no stories in the riots, only the ghosts of other riots" (307). At this moment, as Bhabha identifies uprising as the antirepresentational, as a performative newness that gestures to nothing but itself or manages to invoke itself only as a figure of repetition which never exceeds the specificity of a list of other, earlier, uprisings, his reading of riot approaches Massumi's reading of affect. If there are no stories in the riots, then there are only serial intensities that not only are resistant to critique but offer no commentary on England's postcoloniality.

Bhabha's reading of riot thus places him in only partial agreement with Rude's and E. P. Thompson's readings of the moral economy of the English crowd. The three writers converge on the figure of the crowd as the nation's self-announced redeemer. But redemption is a trope both of salvation and of repetition. And on the issue of what the crowd manages—or purports—to repeat, Bhabha's reading diverges from that of the historians. Rude and Thompson indicate that the desire of previous generations of rioters was not to announce England as mass disorder, or to mark their Englishness by repeating the disorderly behavior of their ancestors, but to disorder the distortions of their contemporaneity, to return England to its imaginary self, to mark their Englishness as a threatened England's "true" citizens, guardians, and redeemers. Bhabha's argument suggests that the rioters work to allow England to repeat itself as a riotous affect-event.

The question that arises, then, is whether the contemporary generation of rioters with which Bhabha and Gilroy are most concerned redeem the nation *as* rioters or *through* rioting, whether they announce that England is most itself in its repetitive moments of asignifying disorder, or re-create England through an act of disorderly protest. Do the rioters, in the words that Bhabha borrows from *Handsworth Songs*, recall earlier riots in which there are "no stories"? Or do they, as Gilroy's arguments suggest, remind England of earlier crowds gathered to perform the "story" of their recollective possession of England, and to redeem their local space in the nation's corporate community of belonging? My inclination is clearly toward Gilroy, but it is an inclination that is accompanied by several questions. If the recollective work of riot is referential, must not the Brixton and Handsworth risings refer to something more than the history of English working-class protest? Must they not recollect an additional body of local knowledges, an additional set of "values and norms," an additional series, indeed a *global* series, of cultural vernaculars? Moreover, whatever local knowledges the riots defend, how does this defense of the local, and the locale, differ from the nostalgic celebrations of the local, and the locale, that I have suggested are central to the culture of British imperialism? How can the zone of riot be both a *lieu de memoire* and a space of newness? And finally, to return to the question with which I concluded the previous chapter, if the zone of riot is a space of newness, how can such riotous newness be rendered desirable? How can it seduce its participants *and* its beholders away from a longing for the fixed, the essential, the unitary?

PERMANENCE AND UNSETTLEMENT

Answers to all of these questions are contained in the riddle of postcolonial migrancy, and in Rushdie's posing of that riddle in *The Satanic Verses*. But as often as Rushdie, in this text, represents migrancy as a condition of remembering an "English" *and* an-other history, of discovering the nostalgic as the breeding ground of the new, and of learning to surrender the pleasures of the unitary for the love of the multiple, he also indicates that migrancy can entail a rejection of other histories, a denial of newness, and a refusal of multiplicity. He indicates that to understand how migrancy can encompass the former, essentially affirmative gestures, one must investigate, rather than merely dismissing, the latter acts of refusal. He suggests that we must begin at the end, with the migrant's refusal of multiplicity, if we are at last to arrive at the beginning, to reencounter those other histories, those other locations of identity, those other local knowledges which the migrant is willing to defend—in an act of riot if necessary—and through the defense of which the migrant redeems the nation as a corporate but locally differentiated space of belonging.

If *The Satanic Verses* is, among other things, an anatomy of the condition of postcolonial migrancy, then the condition of being *among other things* is not only a description of the place of a narrative of migrancy in a text that has not one but many, even too many, stories to tell. It is also, in Rushdie's reading, the ineradicable fact of migrancy itself. Migrancy, he suggests, is the living among other, and other's, things; the inhabiting of not one but many places; the condition of belonging to, or being implicated by, not a single but a multitude of narratives. It is, as Rushdie has it late in the text, a "moving through many stories at once" (457). As Aijaz Ahmad has noted, however, to belong to so many places and so many narratives is to surrender to such an excess of determinations that the migrant ultimately risks belonging nowhere, precisely because he or she "belongs to too many places."[12] Rushdie is quite aware of this, and if he generally renders migrancy visible as the delirium of the multiple, he also represents it as the refusal of multiplicity, as the desire for unity, the longing to inhabit a known and bounded space and to be possessed by a sole and unitary narrative.

It is partially—though only partially—for this reason that Islam assumes such importance in this text. For Islam's governing metaphors, in Rushdie's reading, are metaphors of the one: belonging to the one, confessing the one, and residing in the one. Rushdie understands the promise of Islamic residence that Mahound makes to the people of Jahilia—the promise of inhabiting a settled and unitary space that is as much a historical locale as it is a space in the sacred imaginary—to be a promise in which the postcolonial migrant, whether Muslim or not, wishes to believe.

> The city of Jahilia is built entirely of sand, its structures formed of the desert whence it rises. It is a sight to wonder at: walled, four-gated, the whole of it a miracle worked by its citizens, who have learned the trick of transforming the fine white dune-sand of those forsaken parts—the very stuff of inconstancy,—the quintessence of unsettlement, shifting, treachery, lack-of-form,—and have turned it, by alchemy, into the fabric of their newly invented permanence. These people are a mere three or four generations removed from their nomadic past, when they

were as rootless as the dunes, or rather rooted in the knowledge that the journey-
ing itself was home.

   Whereas the migrant can do without the journey altogether; it's no more than
a necessary evil; the point is to arrive. (94)

For Rushdie, nomadism is the condition of living in a displacement so radical
that it ceases to exist. Nomadism is the name for the inhabitation of the journey. If the nomad has a home, it is a home whose rooms are walled by the
dislocations of travel. Within the dispersed spaces of the nomadic habitus, the
nomad need never leave and never arrives. According to Rushdie, however,
for the migrant the point is to arrive. Most specifically, the desire of the migrant is to succeed where the citizens of Jahilia have succeeded, to transform
the quintessence of unsettlement into an invented permanence. This yearning
for permanence becomes, in fact, less a longing to arrive than a desire to have
arrived. It is a wish to be done with the endless business of arriving, a tedium
before the infinity of ports to pass through, languages to learn, schools to
enter, papers to file, and laws to satisfy. It is a desire to rest, to belong. The
politics of migrancy, therefore, may not necessarily be a nationalist politics,
but migrancy certainly encompasses a politics of emplacement. This means
that for the migrant, as for any other subject, cultural identity can be the
product as much of what is forgotten as of what is remembered, that arrival
might entail a willed forgetting of unsettlement, a refusal of multiple loyalties,
a submission to the seductions of the one.

   In *The Satanic Verses*, Rushdie connects this longing to have arrived to the
acts of forgetfulness and the labors of redemption. In brief, Saladin Chamcha
enacts his longing to arrive as a deliberate, if selective, forgetting of himself in
the interest of redeeming himself as English and unitary. Gibreel Farishta,
alternatively, marks his arrival through a re-creation, a multiplication of the
place to which he has come, in the name of redeeming that place for the
English and the erstwhile subjects of empire. The distance between Chamcha
and Farishta is in many ways a product of this profound difference of opinion
regarding the objects of redemption. For Chamcha, it is the migrant who must
be redeemed in order that he, or she, might be reconciled to England. For
Farishta, it is England that requires redemption in order that the nation might
be reconciled to its migrants.[13] But to say this is to offer a contraction rather
than a reading, and in order to understand Rushdie and to trace a return from
Chamcha and Farishta to the location of riot in the contemporary narratives of
Englishness, one must read the novel.

   Saladin Chamcha is, in the fullest sense of Stephen Greenblatt's words, a
self-fashioned man. An Indian actor residing in London, he is the product of
a meticulous and relentless labor of self-erasure and self-fabrication. Even his
name is an invention, or, rather, a censored translation of a given original.
Born Salahuddin Chamchawala, he has contracted himself, torn the difficult

syllables from his name and offered himself to his English brethren as a word that can be easily pronounced. He is, as the narrator of *The Satanic Verses* describes him, "a creature of *selected* dis-continuities, a *willing* reinvention; his preferred revolt against history being what makes him, in our chosen idiom, 'false'" (427). Chamcha codes his revolt against history as a revolt against India and a revolt against his past. He survives through an act of willed amnesia, a forgetting of his origins, a denial of his dislocatedness. Gayatri Spivak, in an essay on *The Satanic Verses*, has suggested that migrancy is a condition of "turned-awayness."[14] By this she seems to mean that the migrant turns away from the space that he or she now inhabits to remember the abandoned space of "origin," to dwell in remembrance and desire in the cultural landscapes from whence he or she has departed. There are characters in *The Satanic Verses* who live this way. Hind Sufyan, Chamcha's unwilling hostess at the Shandaar B and B and Café, lives in London but turns from it to inhabit the Bangladesh from which her husband has taken her. Surrounded by the subcontinental foods that she cooks and the Hindi and Bengali movies she rents, she dwells in the absence from which she has migrated. Saladin Chamcha, however, has turned the other way. He has turned away from India, away from the land-scapes of the past in which he has lived, to a nation that he has adopted and in whose image he longs to reproduce himself.

If, however, as the narrator of the text fleetingly suggests, this marks Chamcha as false, then his falsity is a product not only of what he no longer pretends, even partially, to belong to, but of the falsity of that England which he claims to inhabit and by which he wishes to believe himself redeemed. For Chamcha's England, the England that he imaginatively occupies, is a museum. "Him and his Royal Family," his weary English wife declaims, "you wouldn't believe. Cricket. The Houses of Parliament, the Queen. The place never stopped being a picture postcard to him" (175). Chamcha is punished for his pretense. The England he discovers is a place that refuses to conform to the picturesque renderings of itself. The English actors with whom he works seem intent on betraying their cultural heritage: they guzzle cheap American cham-pagne, dress in Donald Duck T-shirts, and, most horrifically, tart themselves up in Indian garb. This is all thoroughly intolerable to Chamcha, who has made his pilgrimage to England not to discover ersatz versions of the sub-contintent or America but to be saved from the accident of his Indian birth by the glories of the English past. "For a man like Saladin Chamcha," the narrator almost pityingly observes, "the debasing of Englishness by the English was a thing too painful to contemplate" (75). Chamcha responds to this debasement as he has responded to India: he turns away, refuses to contemplate what is before him, and surrounds himself with a postcard picture of England. But he is not permitted to continue in this devotional act. Punished once by an En-gland that insists on displaying its hybrid tawdriness, he is punished again by a narrator who deems it time for him to see a little more of the nation he has

come to inhabit, explodes the plane in which he is flying, transforms him into
a goat-horned devil, and deposits him in an attic room of Muhammad and
Hind Sufyan's Shandaar Café.

The Shandaar Café is a multiply inhabited space. It is not only an eatery but
a hostel of sorts, a run-down bed-and-breakfast housing recent immigrants to
England. Above the ground-floor café, the Sufyans rent out rooms to new
arrivals, some of whom have entered the country legally, many of whom have
not, and all of whom find that they are not yet done with the wearying business of arriving. Among them these diverse inhabitants define a catalog of
migrancy. Six immigrant families, who have qualified for borough-funded
temporary housing but have not yet secured the right to permanent residence
in England, are, at best, a sort of footnote to that catalog. They are a community in hiding, lodged five to a room, who live less in the Shandaar Café than
in the gaps of the Home Office's memory. They live in deferral, not sure
whether they wish the government to remember or to forget them, as they
await the resolution of their status. These families are, in truth—or at least
before the law—not yet migrants. For them the Shandaar Café is not a terminus; it is limbo. They live in anticipation of a moment in which their legal
identities will catch up with their bodies, a moment in which their waiting will
end and they will have arrived. Ghostly presences in the café, glimpsed only
behind the crack of a rapidly shutting door, they are, Rushdie mournfully
reflects, "temporary human beings, with little hope of being declared permanent" (264). Trapped in an uncompleted journey between the homes they
have left and the new home to which they would come, these thirty wanderers
are the frustrated specters of the migrant uncanny. They are the empire's repressed, patiently awaiting permission to return.

Their landlords, however, *have* arrived. Muhammad and Hind Sufyan, and
their daughters Mishal and Anahita, have been in England more than a dozen
years and have passed through loss and waiting to the accomplishment of licit
habitation. The family's response to the permanence of their arrival is not,
however, unitary. Edouard Glissant has suggested that there are a variety of
cultural strategies available to a transplanted people as they struggle to survive
the shock of their displacement. These strategies tend to be organized around
the migrant's willingness, or unwillingness, to be changed "into something
new, into a new set of possibilities."[15] A desire to resist the new, which is also
an investment in "maintaining the old order of values in a new locale," manifests itself in what Glissant terms the impulse toward "reversion." "Reversion
is the obsession with a single origin: one must not alter the absolute state of
being. To revert is to consecrate permanence, to negate contact. Reversion will
be recommended by those who favor single origins" (16). Hind Sufyan is an
apostle of reversion. She is, as Glissant's argument suggests, devoted to permanence, but not to the permanence she is offered in England. To have arrived
and settled in London is, for Hind, to be a prisoner of loss, and she responds

to the cultural amputation she has suffered by clutching the subcontinent to herself with the eager palm of a phantom limb. As Chamcha lives by his voice, so Hind lives by her hands. But where Chamcha's voice sighs to the cadences of the King's English, Hind's hands shape and cook the delicacies of Bangladesh. In her kitchen, she turns away from England and returns to the pantries of her past. When she is not in her Proustian kitchen, she is before her television, bathing in the video waters of "an endless supply of Bengali and Hindi movies on VCR through which. . . . [she can] stay in touch with events in the 'real' world" (250–51). When she is not in her kitchen or watching television, she is nowhere. She does not go out. We never see her leave the Shandaar Café, her little Bangladesh in England.

Her teenage daughters, though they live in her house, inhabit another world. They survive, to follow Glissant a little further, not in reversion but in assimilation. They are English, and aggressively so, though not as Chamcha is English. Theirs, rather, is the debased England of his fellow actors and of his manager. They wear scandalously formfitting clothing emblazoned with images of "the new Madonna"; cut and dye their hair in late-punk styles; abominate their mother's cooking; yearn for bangers and mash; trip the "radical," "crucial," and "Fucking A" syllables of a Bethnal Green patois off their saucily London tongues; and think nothing of the nation in which they were born. "Bangladesh in't nothing to me," Mishal informs Chamcha, who is horrified to discover that the girls understand themselves to be, like him, English, "Just some place Dad and Mum keep banging on about . . . Bungleditch . . . What I call it, anyhow" (259).

Mishal and Anahita force the terrible realization on Chamcha that he and the girls are the only people in the café who consider themselves "English," and further require him to recognize that though their respective Englands are radically dissimilar, they are nevertheless alike in their flirtations with Englishness and their rejections of the suit of a subcontinental past. Yet the thoroughness with which the girls reject "Bungleditch" also reveals that the girls are less unlike their mother than they might wish. Anahita and Mishal's denial of Bangladesh and their wholesale adoption of a working-class London order of Englishness is not profoundly different from their mother's commitment to the landscape of her youth and her refusal to make contact with the city in which she finds her body, if not her self. Both mother and daughters, to return to Glissant's language, are hostages to an obsessive belief in single origins. Both, like Chamcha in his turn, are resolutely turned away. To survive the shock of their translations, each of these migrants, in their various ways, worships culture as a locale and deifies one genius loci by forgetting another. Spivak maintains that within such "turned-awayness," "Rushdie implants the migrant's other desire, the search for roots as far down as they'll go. The name for this radical rootedness is, most often, religion" (*Outside in the Teaching Machine*, 223). The various obsessions of Anahita, Mishal, Hind, and

Chamcha imply that if, as Spivak argues, migrancy entails a structure of sacral belief, then the gods of such a polytheist religion might as often be localities—whether imaginary, experienced, or remembered—as extraterrestrial divinities. Spivak's comment further suggests that the commitment to locality, by which the migrant defines a self through the manipulations of a sentimental economy of refusal and avowal, is a commitment also to the common sacral fantasy of redemption.

An essential sadness, however, attaches to Hind's, Mishal's, Anahita's, and Chamcha's strategies of survival. In a text repeatedly constructed as a narrative of mourning, Rushdie does not hesitate to pour the bitter sorrow of his prose over these four figures. This common sadness suggests that even as the "strategies" of reversion and assimilation are united in their pursuit of a single locality of belonging, they are unified also as failed epistemologies of redemption. Glissant, who is less willing than he should be to recognize the similarity of these modes of living in displacement, is quite clear on this point. Both reversion and assimilation fail to save the migrant from the terrors and difficulties of living a life in translation, he argues, because both strategies begin and end with an act of deliberate misrecognition. Rushdie renders this misrecognition manifest as the syllabus of English persons and English things that Hind and Chamcha decline to gaze upon. For Chamcha, the contents of that syllabus of refusal are quite fixed: he will refuse to recognize the existence of anything outside the frame of his postcard England. Or, as he announces to his hosts at the Shandaar Café, "You're not my people. I've spent half my life trying to get away from you" (253). For Hind, the list of the not-seen is rather less certain. It begins, however, not in aesthetic repugnance but in fear: "They had come into a demon city in which anything could happen, your windows shattered in the middle of the night without any cause, you were knocked over in the street by invisible hands, in the shops you heard such abuse you felt like your ears would drop off but when you turned in the direction of the words you saw only empty air and smiling faces, and every day you heard about this boy, that girl, beaten up by ghosts . . . best thing was to stay home, not go out for so much as to post a letter, stay in, lock the door, say your prayers, and the goblins would (maybe) stay away" (250). But of course neither Hind's goblins nor Chamcha's "people" will stay away. However much they are refused, however resolutely they are turned away from, they reappear. To deny them is to enter a closeted life whose door can at any moment be suddenly, and rudely, opened. To misrecognize the unruly intrusions of the English present or the subcontinental past is not to be redeemed; it is to deny the trauma of a wound.

Within such a denial there is an investment in the redemptive—or at least the preservative—capacities of an act of cultural blasphemy. If it has been the fate of Rushdie's text to be read as an exorbitantly blasphemous artifact, then there is a failure of reading in such understandings of *The Satanic Verses* that extends beyond the tragedies of misreading attaching to the "*Satanic Verses* affair." For while the text expresses more than a little interest in the blasphe-mous, its primary interest is in suggesting that an act of *cultural* blasphemy is impossible, that cultural codes of belonging can be denied or refashioned but not recanted. This exposure of the impossibilities of blasphemy derives not from the text's demonstration of that familiar dynamic in which blasphemy cannot be spoken of outside a context of belief, or even of that operation in which those artifacts of the sacred that a commodity-centered culture renders merely decorative are resacralized precisely at that shocking moment in which they are dipped in the curiously sanctifying brine of an artist's urine. Rather, they are exposed through Rushdie's manipulation of the economies of mem-ory and forgetting. Rushdie represents cultural blasphemy as a desire to forget and reveals its impossibility at those moments in which his characters, to their horror, learn that if they can fail to remember, they cannot choose to forget.

The yearning to forget is an expression of that form of melancholy which desires to erase the not-wanted, which invokes itself as a naming of the not-wanted, and which, in this act of naming, guarantees that the not-wanted cannot be forgotten. It is a cognitive loop sequence: a commitment to brood-ing, tantalization, frustration, and failure. In Rushdie's novel, Saladin Chamcha is the most desperate to blaspheme, India is that which he most frequently longs to forget, and India is that which he cannot fail to remember. There is a lesson here for those custodians, fabricators, and readers of national identity who wish to posit the nation as a pure present, to forget its founding violences, or to resist the disciplinary submissions of the nation to a reified anteriority by counseling us to learn how to forget. To believe that the nation, or the subject, can be redeemed through an act of willed forgetting is to deny the difficulties and persistencies of memory in the vain hope that the struggles to belong can be completed without reference to the looming anteriorities of history. It is to commit to the bankrupt areferentiality of a purely perfomative invention of the present. Ultimately, it means failing to recognize that while blasphemy may be desirable, it is not possible. It is also, Rushdie insistently suggests, to misapprehend the labor of redemption, to believe, with Chamcha, that it is the migrant, or the migrant's procedures of cognition, which must suffer a reinvention, rather than the migrant habitus which must be redeemed.

There is, however, one inmate of the Shandaar Café committed to the re-demption of the English habitus through a translative rewriting of England's spaces and discourses of belonging. Jumpy Joshi, who attended an English university with Chamcha but did not besot himself with the liquors of Olde England, is the minor hero of Rushdie's text. Alone among the inhabitants of the Shandaar Café, he refuses to submit to the terrorism of the categorical imperatives of Englishness or Indianness.[16] Alone among the café's commu-nity of migrants, Jumpy Joshi insists that to define the migrant subject as that which requires re-formation or redemption under the reified signs of a unitary locality of belonging is to embrace life as a victim of place. Joshi agrees that the migrant is a victim of his or her dislocative emplacements, but argues that to choose to manufacture a life as the emblem of a fetishized place, as Hind, Chamcha, Mishal, and Anahita in their various ways have done, is to *court* the twinned statuses of victim and caricature. It is to make oneself, Rushdie suggests through the voice of Joshi, a prisoner of description, to define the self as an allegory of the described and worshiped place. In the moment of Chamcha's goaty apotheosis, Joshi discovers the inevitable end of a project of migrant desire that begins and ends with the decision to re-form the self. For while Chamcha longs to represent himself as a mannequin of Englishness, the police who discover his postwreck body envision him as an immigrant Satan. And, as Chamcha belatedly discovers, it is the police and not the migrant who add to the powers of description the sanctions of law.

Joshi responds to the plight of his fellows by turning their attention from the costuming of the self to the labor of reconstructing the English habitus. Glissant's word for this is diversion, a trickster strategy that defines itself not as a refusal to see, or as a flight from the horrors of the seen, but as an intentionally skewed way of seeing. To divert England is to devour even the most barbed of English fare, to stew England in the migrant's gastric juices, and to return England to itself as markedly, perhaps aromatically, different. Joshi's politics are less olfactory. He sets out to reform England by rewriting its most exclusionary narratives of belonging. He returns to Enoch Powell's infamous "Rivers of Blood" speech to offer a poetic misreading of the politician's dream of ruin. "Reclaim the metaphor, Jumpy Joshi had told himself. Turn it; make it a thing we can use" (186). Adopting but estranging Powell's metaphor, he revels in the effervescence of blood, tropes the street as capillary effluence, and offers the migrant as England's life-sustaining transfusion. Joshi's tragedy is that while he has an acute understanding of the productive values of an act of cultural misprision, he is a weak poet. When a friend discovers and reads his poetry, he recoils from the banal locutions of his own language and hides his verses. Thereafter they are never read again. They disappear from Rushdie's text, as the Satanic Verses disappear from the Koran. In a fashion, however, Joshi's poetry may be said to reappear in the novel, and to resound on the same tongue that speaks the Koran's censored verses. Gibreel Farishta, who as the Angel Gibreel articulates the Koranic repressed, gives a new voice to Joshi's hidden verses. In his speaking, however, the river of blood is not only a word on the page. It is, as Powell feared, an event in the street, an act of riot.

TROPICALIZATION

Gibreel Farishta, like Chamcha, identifies the experience of migrancy as a labor of redemption. In his reading, however, it is not the migrant who must be redeemed by the spaces that he or she inhabits. Rather, like Jumpy Joshi, Farishta suggests that it is the space of cultural inhabitation which must be redeemed, and the migrant who will act as England's cultural redeemer. If Farishta and Chamcha disagree on this issue, then they differ also in their definitions of who, or rather what, the migrant is, or should be. For Chamcha, the migrant is a multiple personality yearning for perfection and rest in the integrity of the one. For Farishta, who as an actor in India has become famous as the filmic incarnation of a pantheon of gods, identity is polyphony, excess, a moving through many stories at once. More significant, while Chamcha unswervingly believes that for the migrant to "arrive" in England he or she must strip away those signs of cultural alterity which it was the object of the English empire to repress, Farishta delightedly discovers the migrant's arrival in England as a riotous return of the repressed and desires to save England, as the English crowd had so often offered to save the nation, by returning England to the blinked-away landspaces of its elsewhere and its past.

Farishta enters London armed with a text of the city. The text is an atlas, *London A to Z*, a map that Gibreel proposes to use to plot the route of a passage in which he, as the most angelic of wanderers, will mark his transforming presence on the streets and walls of the city. "The atlas in his pocket was his master plan. He would redeem the city square by square. . . . He would redeem this city, Geographer's London, all the way from A to Z" (326). However, in plotting his redemptive approach to the city as an ordered march, square by square, through the gridded spaces of Geographer's London, Gibreel confronts one of those paradoxes that are Rushdie's signature. Gibreel wishes to save the city for multiplicity, for the abundance and superfluity of the thousand and one narratives that are the substance of England's migrant history. He intends to reveal that England is not unitary, that England's spaces of inhabitation are not interrupted or vandalized by the returns of the postcolonial migrant, but that Englishness, as John Ruskin briefly dared to believe, is constituted as an imperfect and perpetually incomplete construction. Through Gibreel's incursive visitation to the city of London, Rushdie labors to free England from the "confining myth of authenticity" to which Saladin Chamcha has submitted, and to redeem England for "eclecticism," uncertainty, mutability (52). But in choosing to plan his redemptive march through the city on the basis of his guidebook's knowledge of the city, Gibreel assumes that the city has awaited his coming. He labors under the conviction that London is, as the Geographer indicates, a fixed and gridded space, a disciplined territory. As he attempts to plot his route through the city, however, he discovers what Ruskin had discovered a century before: that the city itself is migrant, that its streets and squares and alleys have refused to submit to discipline, that it exceeds and frustrates the best intentions of cartography. "The city in its corruption," he learns, "refused to submit to the dominion of the cartographers, changing shape at will and without warning, making it impossible for Gibreel to approach his quest in the systematic manner he would have preferred" (327). To his surprise, Gibreel learns that the city has anticipated his arrival, that it has already begun to divert itself, that it is its own redeeming angel.

This recognition raises a question: if London contains within itself the principle of its own transmutation and redemption, what need is there for Gibreel to proceed? A partial answer to that question lies in the pocket of Gibreel's coat. The simple and confident existence of the map dwelling in that pocket suggests that although London is uncontainably various, it is not officially known as such. Gibreel's labor, then, assumes a familiarly angelic function. His work is not to act but to announce; not to redeem but to broadcast redemption's accomplishment. But this is an incomplete answer and one with which Rushdie is ultimately dissatisfied. For Rushdie's interest, finally, is not in mutability and the eclectic as pure forms, but in what he refers to in *The Satanic Verses* as a "historically validated eclecticism" (52). The problem with the city, as Gibreel discovers it, is that it reveals a passion for the various without regard to variety's content. Rushdie may be a prophet of cultural uncertainty, but he is not a priest of that postmodern cult in which the uncertain emerges as an unnamed god. In this he differs from a critic such as Homi Bhabha who, in wedding the postcolonial to the postmodern, can discover in such events as the Brixton riots no stories, only the ghosts of unspoken earlier stories, in the performative no local significance, only the asignificances of the affect-event.

Rushdie aspires not simply to demonstrate that the narratives of Englishness are narratives of the multiple, but to name at least a fraction of what such multiplicity encompasses. In this regard his response to *Handsworth Songs* is revealing. It is in this film that Bhabha discovers that raging rastaman whom, together with the film's makers, he manages to read as embodying no story— only the ghost of some other story. Rushdie, in reviewing the film, has no patience with such narrative evacuations. The film fails, he suggests, because it gestures toward the "other stories" of the migrant inhabitation of England but refuses to tell them. Indeed, Rushdie argues, the film manages to plot the thousand and one narratives of postcolonial migrancy solely as a unitary narrative of rage and, in doing so, manages to erase the other stories of a contemporary England that a place like Handsworth locates: "It's important, I believe, to tell such stories; to say, this is England. Look at the bright illuminations and fireworks during the Hindu Festival of Lights, Divali. Listen to the Muslim call to prayer, 'Allahu Akbar,' wafting down from the minaret of a Birmingham mosque. Visit the Ethiopian World Federation, which helps Handsworth Rastas 'return' to the land of Ras Tafari. These are English scenes now. English songs."[17] Rushdie's stress is on the Englishness of the scenes he is describing, but it is a stress heightened by his sense of the need to give the multiple ways of being English a local habitation and a name. He appeals to his reader not to look upon the "performative" but to gaze upon the particular and diverse ways in which English identity is rehearsed. He asks that we see the rastaman not simply as the embodiment of a principle of cultural fluctuance but as the carrier of one of those stories—one suggesting that Haile Selassie is now as English as the Festival of Lights or the Book of Common Prayer.

If Rushdie desires to elicit the stories of England's hybridity, then Gibreel Farishta is the servant of that desire. As much as he is an angelic wanderer, Gibreel is a roaming repository of England's narratives. All who come in contact with him surrender to an impulse to reveal themselves, to divulge their tales, to pour their voices into the portals of his semidivine ear. As he wanders through the city of London, he finds himself wandering through a collection of stories whose only connection to one another is that, for all their dissimilarities, they are English. Gibreel influences more than the people he meets: his passing affects the city also. And it is in forcing the city to disclose itself, not simply as multiform, but as a hybrid whose various branches have been grafted from cuts of an imperial tree, that he most fully accomplishes his redemptive work.

Confronted with a metropolis that frustrates his desire for multiplicity not by being singular but by exhibiting itself as generically and blankly mutable, Gibreel resolves to "tropicalize" the city and indulges himself in a contemplation of the consequences of his act. "Gibreel enumerated the benefits of the proposed metamorphosis of London into a tropical city: increased moral definition, institution of a national siesta, development of vivid and expansive patterns of behaviour among the populace, higher quality music . . . better cricketers; higher emphasis on ball control among professional footballers. . . . Religious fervour, political ferment, renewal of interest in the intelligentsia. . . . Spicier food; the use of water as well as paper in English toilets . . ." (354–55). Gibreel's musings on the consequences of his transformation of the English weather indicate that there is more involved in his act of tropicalization than a simple fiddling with meteorological phenomena. In the trope of tropicalization, and in Gibreel's unpacking of that trope, Rushdie finds a way to render the uncanny as the redemptive and to discover a riotous merging of the discourses of migrancy and Englishness. In enumerating his list of "benefits," Gibreel constructs a catalog of cultural difference consonant with Saladin Chamcha's catalog of the refused and the unseen. Spicy food, religious fervor, expansive behavior, and all the other items on this burlesque list are entries in Chamcha's encyclopedia of the Not-English. But they are Not-English in a particular way, for they are the eclectic fragments of the cultures that the English empire collected. They are the metonyms of the Not-England that England occupied, reluctantly abandoned, and now wishes to forget. In Gibreel's tropicalizing proclamation, however, it becomes impossible for England to forget this catalog of alterity—not because Gibreel will magically require spicy foods, religious fervor, and expansive behavior to manifest themselves in London, but because, as always, he will render visible what is already there. Gibreel's real magic is not to rain this catalog of difference upon England but to erase the difference of difference. To tropicalize London is not to make the metropolis a foreign city but to deny the foreignness of these differences to the city, to announce that London is a conurbation of such differences, to reveal that when he speaks of siestas, better cricketers, and the use of water as well as paper in toilets, he speaks of "English scenes."

In tropicalizing London, Gibreel rewrites the cultural cartography of the city. He erases its boundaries and collapses the distinction between the here and the elsewhere. He opens London's gates to that most spectacular return of the repressed, in which the willfully forgotten double appears not as an image of the *unheimlich* but as a coinhabitor of the home. In doing so, in allowing the elsewhere of English history to become coincident with an English locale, Gibreel manages also to answer a question around which much of Rushdie's narrative has been organized. "How does newness come into the world?" the narrator asks in the opening pages of the book; "How is it born? Of what fusions, translations, conjoinings is it made?" (8). The latter questions, which appear simply to clarify the opening query, contain, in fact, the clues to the answer that Gibreel will provide. Newness, it appears, enters the world not as an utter beginning or the manifestation of some pure element never seen before, but as a novel conjoining of what already exists, as transfusion, as the hybridization of the here and the elsewhere, the now and the then. The paradox of newness in this text is that the new is not the negation or opposite of the old or the past but the conjunction of diverse pasts, the overlapping of the histories of the English here and the imperial elsewhere in London's present. This moment of newness, in which the new emerges as the marriage, in the present, of various "English" pasts, is more than similar to that moment of redemption embedded in Benjamin's Messianic time in which the past is collapsed onto and revealed within the now. Newness and redemption are, in Rushdie's text, identical—and both are manifest in Gibreel's act of tropicalization. In returning England's elsewhere to its here, and in collapsing the multiple landscapes of its imperial past onto the metropolitan expanse of its postimperial present, Gibreel has succeeded in redeeming the city. He has brought newness into the world. He has revealed a new way of being English.

And this, of course, is also an old way of being English, and a riotous way of being English. Gibreel boisterously returns England to its pasts and its elsewheres not in order to vandalize the nation but to save England for itself. And this, as I have discussed earlier in this chapter, is the historic work of the rioting English crowd. The crowd's labor, to finally reconcile Bhabha to E. P. Thompson and George Rude, is the labor of a determinate indeterminacy. In its act of riot, the crowd raises its disruptive voice not in the name of disruption but in order to disorder what it perceives to be the distortions of the contemporary; it does so by wedding the present and the here to the—perhaps imaginary—particularities of a displaced past or elsewhere. This suggests that if riot is to be read as a meaningful cultural event, rather than according to tropes of randomness and disarray, then the performative occasion of riot must be seen as writing a *certain* uncertainty onto the spaces of cultural inhabitation. In the eighteenth century, this certain uncertainty can be seen in the moral economy of crowd behavior that led rioting English laborers to spill through the market squares of the island's cities in order to restore the market to a "customary," preindustrial way of operating. In the twentieth century, this ordered disorder can be detected in the riotous demands of a Brixton crowd to reclaim those citizenship privileges of the *ius soli* filched by the 1981 Nationality Bill. Either instance suggests that the crowd, in its moments of "newness," is often the most historically minded of cultural performers—and this is assuredly true of that exuberantly crowdlike actor Gibreel Farishta, whose yearnings for the overseas and displaced spaces of English history manifest themselves in his tropicalizing riot of the English habitus.

Of course, should the crowd's, or Gibreel's, desire become merely a yearning to return to the apparent perfections of the past, then we would be confronting something that is not at all "new." We would then be addressing a discourse or a cultural performative committed yet again to purity, the authentic, and the erasure of the present rather than its productive corruption and hybridization. Since, finally, this is not what I believe is figured in Gibreel's riotous performances, we must, however briefly, turn from his tropicalization of the city to the text's most recognizable scene of crowd disturbance. Toward the end of the novel a riot breaks out in the urban neighborhoods around the Shandaar Café when Uhuru Simba, a black political activist, dies in police custody. The terms by which this riot can be read are apparently familiar. The collective outrage at the death of Simba bespeaks not only anger before an act of police violence but a desire of those black Britons who take to the street to protest his death that he and they be recognized before the law as legitimate inhabitants of the national community, that they be invested with the juridical protections attaching to English civic identity, that their bodies be granted the rights of inviolability which are the privileges of the English body when in the custody of the English state. The riot, in this reading, emerges as an expression of a migrant politics of emplacement, as an insistence that black Britons must be recognized to occupy spaces within the island's towns and cities *and* a legitimate place within the geography of citizenship. Asked what he thought of English civilization, Mahatma Gandhi reportedly once suggested that he thought it would be a good idea. The riot on the streets around the Shandaar Café can be read as an extended gloss on that pithy wisdom, as a demand not that England disband itself, but that it be faithful to its own good idea.

That, of course, is not the only available reading of this event, and Rushdie signals his awareness of the riot's hermeneutic indeterminacy by staging it—as Lord Scarman staged the Brixton disorders—as an event on television. Rushdie represents the riot not from its bewildering ground level but from

above, from the recording eye of a helicopter-mounted television camera.
Gazing down on the scene, and broadcasting the digitized images of what it
observes to the living rooms of an aghast nation, the camera sees this scene: "A
man lit by a sun-gun speaks rapidly into a microphone. Behind him there is
a disorderment of shadows. But between the reporter and the disordered
shadow-lands there stands a wall: men in riot helmets, carrying shields. The
reporter speaks gravely; petrolbombs plasticbullets policeinjuries water-can-
non looting . . . But the camera sees what he does not say. A camera is a thing
easily broken or purloined; its fragility makes it fastidious. A camera requires
law, order, the thin blue line. Seeking to preserve itself it remains behind the
shielding wall, observing the shadow-lands from afar, and of course from
above" (454–55). In surrendering the narrative voice of his text to the recording machinery of the camera, Rushdie reveals the camera's capacity not only
to record events but to produce them. More significant, he demonstrates that
the camera's electronic eye does not simply observe territory but manufactures
a symbolic geography. What the camera sees, and visually disseminates, is not
a riot but a bordered space, a realm of order and a terra incognita beyond. It
fabricates a cartography of the recognized and the unknown, of the sunlit and
the shadowland, of the grave and the disordered. Locating itself exactly at the
space of the thin blue line, the camera defines its glassy lens as the limit of
civility and vandalism. Standing in for the screens of the viewing audience, the
lens of the camera defines the border of the culturally licit. Separating the
watchers from the watched, the camera serves also to separate the English
viewing public from the denizens of the shadowland beyond.

   This reading of the riot is also familiar. As are the failures of the television
to separate the watchers from the watched; its simultaneous closing and opening of the houses of the viewing public to the spaces of riot; its tendency at
once to render the rioter untouchable and to invite him or her to slip through
a video-window into the "nation's" living room. There is, however, at least one
more reading of the riot available to us, a reading that attends both to the riot's
location in the discourses of migrant emplacement and nomadic deterritorial-
ization, and to its position within the recollective moral economies of the
English crowd and the narrative constructions of English "newness." Prior to
his death, Uhuru Simba addresses the court in which he is being arraigned in
the following words: "Make no mistake . . . we are here to change things. I
concede that we ourselves shall be changed; African, Caribbean, Indian, Pakistani, Bangladeshi, Cypriot, Chinese, we are other than we would have been
if we had not crossed the oceans, if our mothers and fathers had not crossed
the skies in search of work and dignity and a better life for their children. We
have been made again: but I say that we will also be the ones to remake this
society, to shape it from the bottom to the top. We shall be the hewers of the
dead wood and the gardeners of the new" (414). In this unabashedly polemi-
cal outburst, Rushdie, through the ventriloquized voice of Simba, comes as

close as he will allow himself to a manifesto. Within that manifesto he seeds a trope that is crucial to his project as a novelist and a cultural critic.

In turning to the metaphors of "crossing over," Simba alludes to the metaphors of translation that have become central to attempts to read the postcolonial condition. To be translated is, as Rushdie informs us in *Midnight's Children*, to be borne across. It is also to have been begun again, or, less passively, to begin again. Translation is a belated writing, an act of repetition. But it is also, as Walter Benjamin has taught us, an act of enunciation in which the copy brings into question the authoritative status of the original. It is a moment of cultural production divested of the compulsion to originate, a moment in which beginning is posterior to the begun, in which newness emerges as a reinscription, a cross-inscription, a writing over. Migrancy, Rushdie's narratives repetitively announce, is an act of translation. It is a bearing across of bodies, of narratives, and, as Virgil and Hind Sufyan would instruct us, of household gods. In being borne across, however, the migrant is obligated neither to forget the departed nor to eradicate the arrived at but to transfuse, to conjoin, to translate the one into the other—in the hope of realizing the hyphenated difficulty of the one-another.[18]

This is what Rushdie marks in the tropicalization of London. This is the translative newness toward which so much of the narrative of *The Satanic Verses* tends, and of which Uhuru Simba speaks. But, the troubling question remains, is this what is achieved not in the metaphoric and meteorological riot of tropicalization but in the bloody event of riot on London's streets? The answer must be both yes and no. As the riot flames to its most intense heat and fire consumes the Shandaar Café and claims the lives of Hind and Muhammad Sufyan, Gibreel Farishta stumbles into the pitchy, smoldering mass of the boardinghouse to discover Saladin Chamcha, his bitter adversary, trapped and choking beneath the weight of a fallen timber. As Gibreel contemplates Saladin in this moment of crisis, Rushdie's narrative swings close to the narrative of Forster's *A Passage to India*. Here again, a plot of revenge is offered the counterplot of redemption. And here, once again, a path to redemption, a path from war to friendship, is chosen. In words that are among the most poignant and sentimental of this too frequently mournful text, Rushdie directs his dark angelic instrument: "Gibreel Farishta steps quickly forward, bearing Saladin along the path of forgiveness in the hot night air; so that on a night when the city is at war, a night heavy with enmity and rage, there is this small redeeming victory for love" (468).

Rushdie's invocation of love at this moment serves to remind us that if love is capable of the labors of redemption, then it is also frequently prone to violence. It would be too easy, and ethically too cavalier, to attempt to derive from this imbrication of the discourses of love, violence, and redemption a model of reading that would present the act of riot, whether in the pages of Rushdie's text or on the streets of Brixton, as a simple labor of love. But in allying these three discourses, Rushdie's text's reminds us that it would be equally naive not to see the passions of riot as, in some measure, animated by that outrage which is love. Rushdie's language at this moment not only turns us to the capacities of the loving and the redemptive to commune with the violent but returns us, once more, to the trope of translation. For in this moment in which love and redemption emerge so fully into the open, their accomplishment is guaranteed by an act of bearing across. As Gibreel carries Saladin out of the flames, the two men return to that sky-tumbling moment in which, intertwined in the indeterminacies of being "Gibreelsaladin Farishta Chamcha," they are marked not by their divergencies but by "a fluidity, an indistinctness, at the edges of them" (8). Locked in this moment of embrace, of fusion, of translation into the spaces of one another's arms, the two men join one another as a metonymic miniature of cultural hybridity. If England is ever to be realized as a good idea, it is, Rushdie suggests, in such an utterly hybridized moment of riotous newness and redemption that is "of fusions, translations, conjoinings" made.

But, inevitably, the sentimentality of this moment cannot survive the crisis of its performance. Like Forster's offer of intimacy this moment cannot endure the shock of embrace to dwell in the banalities of the everyday. This is the problem with a reading of riot that attends to its redemptive grounds of possibility. Riot is an exceptional event whose slender victories may never counterpoise its violence. But even could its violence be discounted, and it cannot, the sheer exceptionality of riot limits its translative and redemptive capacities. As long as newness is figured as a performative event that exists only in the brevity of crisis, it can be invoked but not depended on. Rushdie's challenge, finally, is not to render riot synonymous with the redemptions of the new but to find a temporality of the new that is not catastrophic, to discover a time for newness, for translation, for the one-another, which can survive the boredoms of the everyday. He discovers this in the trope of tropicalization. For it is finally weather, and not riot, that visits us each day; weather that washes over us, marks us, and translates our corporeal and cultural physiognomies. It is the English weather that Rushdie will translate into the riotous precipitant of the new.

THE METEORICS OF REDEMPTION

In order to read Gibreel's tropicalization of London as an act of riot in which the nation is redeemed by recalling its present to a past and an elsewhere, we must return to one of the questions with which this book and this chapter began. We must, that is, examine the ways in which the occasion of riot is also a moment of remembrance. For remembrance, as I began this study by suggesting, and as I have argued throughout this book, is often intimate with forgetting. The experience of remembrance as a simultaneous commitment to

forgetting animates the brooding passions of V. S. Naipaul's postimperial melancholy. It governs the "village green" nostalgia of cricketing discourse, disciplines the practices of imperial tourism, and blinds the visitor to the Victoria
Terminus to those "marks of difference" written on that edifice. John Ruskin's
calls for national remembrance are invigorated by a similar courting of amnesia. For Ruskin's desire was not simply to redeem England from the depredations of modernity by subordinating the present to the past, but to recall the
past in order to erase the present. In either case, he demands that the nation
forget its contemporaneity—and particularly its urban contemporaneity—in
order that England might be recollectively redeemed. In appealing to the
memory of his readers, Rushdie risks marking his tropicalized discourse as a
discourse of repetition that yet again refuses the present. But Gibreel's act of
riot does not thus obliterate the urban present. For London survives its tropicalization. It survives, however, as something that is both old and new, both
here and there. It survives as that which globalizes the locale and localizes the
global. In the moment of riot, which is in this sense a less imaginatively violent
moment than that for which Ruskin longed, Rushdie tropes the present not as
a table of erasure but as an overwritten text.

Yet in the figure of writing over, Rushdie does return to a moment in
Ruskin's work, though this is a moment that the Victorian critic, symptomatically, proved himself too willing to forget. In the final pages of his essay on the
"Lamp of Memory," Ruskin pauses to consider those flaws and fissures with
which time marks the surfaces of the work of architecture. In these wandering
superinscriptions traced onto the mnemonic locations of English identity by
"the passing waves of humanity" (*Works*, 8:234), Ruskin discovers a "parasitical or engrafted sublimity" (*Works*, 8:238). The sublimity of these "rents" and
"fractures" is the sublimity of a meandering, migrant, English history capable
of marking the score of its passing onto the stones of the nation's habitus. It is
the sublimity of the historical text that is rendered apparent not as a univocal
document but as a polytropic artifact. It is the sublimity of a community of
belonging that is revealed not as unified and complete but as perpetually in
progress. In attending to the marks of history continuously written over, or
"engrafted" onto, the space of English belonging, Ruskin fleetingly recognizes
that the locations of Englishness are resolutely and repetitively hybridized by
the survival of the English past into the moments of its present. Perhaps more
significant, Ruskin acknowledges that in order to read England, to trace its
character and identity on the surfaces of its built space, one must attend both
to the shape of the nation's design and to those "golden stain[s] of time"
(*Works*, 8:234) which, in being written over the designed space, render England visible as a space, in Salman Rushdie's words, "of fusions, translations,
conjoinings."

But what are those "golden stains of time"? Ruskin equivocates, indicating
at one moment that they are the signatures of the "passing waves of humanity,"

and, at another, that they are the "lines which rain and sun [have] wrought" (*Works*, 8:243). They are, of course, both: the imprints of an English weather that manifests itself at once in fogs, mists, and winds, *and* in the squalls and storms of human lives washing through the island's towns and cities. Most specifically, for my purposes here, these marks of time and weather are the cuts of that tropicalized meteorics which engraft onto the surface of the English metropolis the stains of empire. Spicy foods, better cricketers, the Festival of Lights, and cries of "Allahu Akbar" are the stone-altering dew of England's postwar atmospherics. In coming to England, the migrants from the island kingdom's ex-imperial territories brought not only their bodies but their "weather patterns" and a capacity to weather England's spaces of belonging. In the "tropicalizing" riot that Gibreel Farishta invokes, England's migrants emerge as the sublime principle ensuring that the laid stones of the English habitus continue to live as they re-create and redeem the nation by recalling it to that which it has attempted to displace. With all the island's other subjects, these tellers and makers of English stories flow through the nation's streets, schools, cricket clubs, train stations, houses, and cathedrals not as a shattering of windows but as a weathering storm, cutting their thousand and one inscriptions into the nation's spaces of belonging, marking England's newness, returning overseas histories to the island locale, revealing the nation as a space of "fusions, translations, conjoining."

SOMETHING RICH AND STRANGE

> Full fathom five thy father lies;
> Of his bones are coral made;
> Those are pearls that were his eyes;
> Nothing of him that doth fade
> But doth suffer a sea change
> Into something rich and strange.
> —William Shakespeare, *The Tempest*

> We thereby live, we have the good fortune of living, this
> shared process of cultural mutation, this convergence that
> frees us from uniformity.
> —Edouard Glissant, *Caribbean Discourses*

SUFFERING A SEA CHANGE

In his remarkable study, *The Transparent Society*, the Italian philosopher Gianni Vattimo offers a reading of the emancipatory potential of what he, with so many others, calls the postmodern. "Emancipation, here," Vattimo argues, "consists in *disorientation*, which is at the same time also the liberation of differences, of local elements, of what could generally be called dialect."[1] In lauding disorientation, and in linking the promises of cultural bewilderment to the vernacular and the local, Vattimo seems to identify emancipation as something akin to what I have called tropicalization. Like Rushdie, Vattimo sees hope in the disorganization of cultural coordinates, in the collapse of fixed cartographies of identity and belonging, and in the emergence of an epistemology of the local. Though he is unusually eloquent in his formulations and interrogations of the postmodern, Vattimo's central analysis of our contemporaneity is not unique. The tendency to identify postmodernity with the experiences, or at least the metaphors, of spatial confusion and to venerate the emergence of a body of "local rationalities" has become a critical gesture if not ubiquitous then at least numbingly predictable. It might even be said that much of contemporary criticism relies on a willingness to replace a Leavisite and New Critical valorization of complexity and irony with a celebration of dislocation and, somewhat paradoxically, the local. As this book has approached the rhetorics not precisely of emancipation but of redemption, and as it has attended to the idioms of displacement and location, the question arises as to whether this work amounts to a covert apology for postmodernism. More important, the ease with which Vattimo's "disorientation" and Rushdie's "tropicalization" seem to suggest one another demands that we ask whether these two zones of confusion are in fact interchangeable, and whether they, together with the other terrains I have been plotting, are in some sense "emancipatory."

In charting a course from John Ruskin to Salman Rushdie and back to Ruskin again, I have tried to show that the loss of cultural certainty, the disorienting "shock" that Vattimo and many other readers of the postmodern have isolated as the defining characteristic of our time, is by no means something new. To be more exact, I have indicated that England has been suffering the confusions attendant on what Vattimo calls the disappearance of "a solid, unitary, stable and 'authoritative' reality" for at least 150 years (8). Over those years, the nation has experienced this loss of a unitary "reality" as the loss of an authoritative and stable definition of what it means to be English. But loss is, perhaps, not the best word, both because it betokens a singular moment of abandonment at odds with the serial collapses of authentic identity I have examined, and because England has endured less the *vanishing* of Englishness than the *dispersal* of its locations of identity.

While this scattering might be attributed to any number of factors, I have found it to become most visible when the nation literally displaces itself onto an overseas empire. Since the middle of the nineteenth century, if not before, the nation's cultural guardians have associated Englishness with certain privileged spaces, with uniquely resonant locales. Ruskin so intensely correlates Englishness with location that he comes to posit identity *as* locale. In this, he is not alone. As I have suggested, the history of English imperialism and of the imperial determinations of English identity can be read as a history of contested spaces, of locations in which the English colonists at once attempted to manifest their cultural identities and to discipline the identities of their subordinates. But as England dispersed its Gothic cathedrals, cricket fields, imperial maps, costumed bodies, and country houses across the surface of the globe, it found that these spaces, and the narratives of identity they physically embodied, were altered by the colonial subjects who came into contact with them. Each of the chapters of this work, whether attending to the decay written into the Gothic habitus, the Caribbean "spatializations" of English "place," or the riotous hybridizations of the postimperial metropolis, has traced the destabilizations and re-creations of England's disciplinary narratives of belonging. Together, they indicate that if, as Ruskin and his romantic precursors indicated, identity is location, then imperialism has made the geography of Englishness a geography of displacement. Crucially, however, these readings reveal that the lapsings and dispersals of England's "authoritative" cultural locales are neither exclusively postmodern occurrences nor uniquely postimperial events. The topographies of Englishness, as I have attempted to demonstrate through the very variety of the spaces and moments I have examined, are always sprawling, mutating, solidifying, and collapsing once again.

If these serial dispersals of the "authentic" spaces of English identity and belonging indicate that the experience of cultural "dizziness" is not a singularly postmodern experience, then the manner in which I have described the imperial displacements of English identity reveals a crucial difference between what I have alternately called bewilderment, translation, and tropicalization, and what Vattimo calls disorientation. Most simply, the difference between the two sets of terms is the difference between excess and absence. Whereas readings of the postmodern repeatedly imply a cartographic vacation, an experience of spatial confusion that originates in loss, the cultural estrangements I have plotted return again and again to the scandal of excess. Kim does not annul Englishness; he hybridizes it. Forster does not erase the untouchable body of the colonist; he fleetingly engrafts it onto the body of the friend. Rushdie does not obliterate London; he opens its spaces and charts its fluid here-and-there, now-and-then cartography. Like Gibreel Farishta, the England I have mapped experiences the bewilderments of the past century and a half as the act of moving through too many stories at once.

It is not enough, however, simply to indicate that in cultivating an empire, England has made itself host to a thousand and one narratives of belonging. As Rushdie has so passionately argued, those stories must be told. The metaphor of multiplicity, which Vattimo and critics such as Homi Bhabha invoke, is not enough. I have paused at length over the intensely particular vernacularizations of English identity because the differential inscriptions of English identity must be given a local habitation and a name, so that the dialectic estrangements of Englishness may become more than a banal metaphor for "diversity," so that we may *read* rather than merely *celebrate* difference.

The imperative of the local provides, finally, the central organizing principle of this work, not only because I find myself in agreement with Rushdie's demand but, more important, because notions of location have been so consistently vital to the diverse constructions of English identity I have discussed. But while the mid-Victorian reifications of locality once again indicate that we are dealing with something not entirely "new," the varying ways in which the writers whom I have examined have read the imbricated discourses of location and identity also reveal that the turn to the local does not necessarily imply a turn to the emancipatory. As he closes the introduction to his text, Vattimo pauses to acknowledge that "individually and collectively, we still have a deep-seated nostalgia for the reassuring, yet menacing, closure of horizons" (11). At the opposite ends of this work, John Ruskin and Saladin Chamcha attest to the truth of Vattimo's mournful comment. Both the Victorian critic and the "imitator of non-existing men" indicate that the worship of the local does not necessarily entail the refusal of nostalgia but sometimes demands the embrace of closed horizons.

Throughout this work, I have labored to read the ambiguities of England's cultural locales, to identify the spaces of imperial Englishness as simultaneously carceral and unbound. The Victoria Terminus in Bombay is the most obviously schizophrenic architecture I have examined. Finally, however, it stands as an allegory of each of those bewildering locations in which colonized and colonizer meet, as at once a factory of Englishness and a monument to England's re-creation, as both a museum and a bazaar. In some respects, the emancipatory potential of the local emerges as a product of its mnemonic function. As spaces of belonging devoted to obedient acts of memorialization and hence to the subordination of the present to the past, the Gothic cathedral, the cricket field, and the country house are tabernacles of nostalgia. As spaces open to inventive, even disobedient, acts of remembrance, as sites to be inhabited and marked by the "passing waves of humanity," these same spaces are the marketplace of England's reinvention, its continuing vibrancy, its ongoing sea change.

With the idea of a sea change, I return to a concept subliminally central to this work: a notion of cultural estrangement and mutation that has quietly but insistently haunted my thinking. I wish to close with the metaphor of sea change not only because Ariel's song so eloquently defines my sense of the nature of England's imperial transformations, but because the idea of briny metamorphosis gestures both toward the violence of imperialism so often noted in discourses on the colonial and postcolonial conditions *and* toward the hopes and possibilities too frequently excluded from such readings. Edouard Glissant has expressed his understanding of the brutalities and promises of an oceanic mutation in his comments on a fellow historian's suggestion that the Caribbean possesses a "submarine" unity:

> To my mind, this expression can only evoke all those Africans weighed down with ball and chain and thrown overboard whenever a slave ship was pursued by enemy vessels and felt too weak to put up a fight. *They sowed in the depths the seeds of an invisible presence.* And so transversality, and not the universal transcendence of the sublime, has come to light. It took us a long time to learn this. We are the roots of a cross-cultural relationship.
>
> Submarine roots: that is floating free, not fixed in some primordial spot, but extending in all directions in our world through its network of branches.
>
> We, thereby, live, we have the good fortune of living, this shared process of cultural mutation, this convergence that frees us from uniformity.[2]

Unwilling to abandon the horrors of a submarine world that graved so many shackled women and men, Glissant also shows himself discontent with a simple declaration of outrage. In the waters of the Caribbean, he discovers not the mute testimony of corpses but an enduring, mutated, and mutating presence, an archive of coral-becoming bones that render the seas of the triangular trade at once a cemetery and a continuing liquid principle of cultural change and exchange. Derek Walcott represents the imperial ocean as a similarly haunting place, an expanse that contains both "the nameless bones of all . . . drowned in the crossing" and "some white memory of a midshipman . . . a white turning body."[3] Like Glissant, Walcott first responds to this appearance of the drowned with abhorrence but then recognizes that he cannot refuse this terrifying space of memory. As he admits this, acknowledges the ocean couplings of the English and the African dead, and tropes these as an "inheritance," Walcott identifies the submarine as a space of productive translations and mergings. He discovers it as a container of memories that may not only torment but fructify our contemporary moment, and names it as a site out of which an imperial past and a Caribbean and English present can emerge as something floatingly intertwined, rich, and strange. It is to the sorrow, the horror, and the strange promise of that sea change that this book has responded.

NOTES

1. Salman Rushdie, *The Satanic Verses* (Dover: The Consortium, 1992), 343. All further references are to this edition and will be indicated parenthetically in the text.

2. See Edward Said, *Culture and Imperialism* (New York: Alfred A. Knopf, 1993) and *Orientalism* (New York Vintage Books, 1979); Gayatri Chakravorty Spivak, *In Other Worlds: Essays in Cultural Politics* (New York: Methuen, 1987), *The Post-Colonial Critic: Interviews, Strategies, Dialogues*, ed. Sarah Horasym (New York: Routledge, 1990), and *Outside in the Teaching Machine* (New York: Routledge, 1993); and Homi Bhabha, ed., *Nation and Narration* (London: Routledge, 1990) and *The Location of Culture* (London: Routledge, 1994).

3. Bhabha's reading of Fanon is in his essay "DissemiNation: Time, Narrative, and the Margins of the Modern Nation," in *Nation and Narration*, 291–322. Fanon uncovers that "zone of occult instability" which is at once the space of contact between colonizer and colonist and the space out of which the postcolonial nation is formed, in his essay "On National Culture," in *The Wretched of the Earth*, trans. Constance Farrington (New York: Grove Press, 1963), 227.

4. See Benedict Anderson, *Imagined Communities: Reflections on the Origin and Spread of Nationalism*, rev. ed. (London: Verso, 1992).

5. See Pierre Nora, "Between Memory and History: *Les Lieux de Memoire*," trans. Marc Roudebush, *Representations* 26 (Spring 1989): 7–25. I discuss Nora's concept of *lieux de memoire* at some length later in this introduction.

6. On cultural "contact zones," see Mary Louise Pratt, *Imperial Eyes: Travel Writing and Transculturation* (New York: Routledge, 1992), especially 1–15.

7. Simon Gikandi also argues that Englishness has been repeatedly defined through "acts of [imperial] inclusion and exclusion," in his excellent study *Maps of Englishness: Writing Identity in the Culture of Colonialism* (New York: Columbia University Press, 1996), 6. Gikandi suggests that this is both generally true and particularly true of the 1960s, 1970s and 1980s, decades in which Enoch Powell championed a "view of empire as simultaneously desirable (the source of the greatness of Britain) and threatening (the 'natural' home of the black immigrants)," and Margaret Thatcher "vowed to restore the 'Great' to Britain even as she raised the spectre of the empire's black subjects as an 'alien swamp'" (71).

8. Linda Colley, *Britons: Forging the Nation, 1707–1837* (New Haven: Yale University Press, 1992), 6.

9. For a discussion of the *ius soli* and medieval conceptions of subjecthood, see Ann Dummett and Andrew Nicol, *Subjects, Citizens, Aliens and Others: Nationality and Immigration Law* (London: Weidenfeld and Nicolson, 1990), 21–38. For another lucid study of British nationality law, see Vaughan Bevan, *The Development of British Immigration Law* (London: Croom Helm, 1986).

10. F. Pollock and F. Maitland, *History of English Law*, 2d ed. (Cambridge: Cambridge University Press, 1952), 1:458. Cited in Dummet and Nicol, *Subjects, Citizens, Aliens and Others*, 25.

11. Edmund Burke, in *The Works of the Right Honorable Edmund Burke* (Boston: Little, Brown and Co., 1865–67), 7:94.

12. See Dummett and Nicol, *Subjects, Citizens, Aliens and Others*, 60–63.

13. The "Englishness" of this deference to custom depends, of course, on the debatable acknowledgment of a Burkean conception of Englishness as the canonical conception.

14. Benedict Anderson, "Nationalism, Identity, and the World-in-Motion: On the Logics of Seriality" (paper presented at the Whitney Humanities Center, Yale University, New Haven, Conn., Spring 1997).

15. Dummett and Nicol, *Subjects, Citizens, Aliens and Others*, 120.

16. Arjun Appadurai, "Sovereignty without Territoriality: Notes for a Postnational Geography, " in *The Geography of Identity*, ed. Patricia Yaeger (Ann Arbor: University of Michigan Press, 1996), 47.

17. For a particularly cogent critique of the act's racist implications, see Paul Gilroy, *"There Ain't No Black in the Union Jack": The Cultural Politics of Race and Nation* (Chicago: University of Chicago Press, 1987), 44–51.

18. Granada Television program, "World in Action," January 30, 1978.

19. Spivak, *Outside in the Teaching Machine*, 226.

20. For readings of the tendency of "Britishness" to imply an Englishness that overwhelms and erases the particularity of Scots, Welsh, and other regional cultures, see Keith Robbins, *Nineteenth-Century Britain: Integration and Diversity* (Oxford: Oxford University Press, 1988); and Michael Hechter, *Internal Colonialism: The Celtic Fringe in British National Development, 1536–1966* (Berkeley and Los Angeles: University of California Press, 1975). For an account of the reassertion of such identities against a homogenizing Britishness, see Thomas Nairn, *The Break-up of Britain: Crisis and Neo-Nationalism* (London: NLB, 1981).

21. Enoch Powell, "To the Annual General Meeting of the West Midlands Area Conservative Political Centre," in *Reflections of a Statesman: The Writings and Speeches of Enoch Powell*, ed. Rex Collings (London: Bellew Publishing, 1991), 378.

22. For an excellent reading of Powell's speech, and of Powellite discourse in general, see Gikandi, *Maps of Englishness*, 69–83.

23. In Anne McClintock's terms, Englishness is thus, for Powell, entirely a fetish figure: a hallucinatory and always just ungraspable ideal born of a disavowal that does not quite manage to hold off the abject object it defined itself by abjecting. For McClintock's original rereading of fetishism and abjection, see her *Imperial Leather: Race, Gender and Sexuality in the Colonial Contest* (New York: Routledge, 1995), throughout but especially 181–85.

24. Powell's racially based defenses of Englishness are also not without their immediate governmental precursors. In the 1950s Conservative M.P.'s such as Norman Pannell and Sir Cyril Osborne attempted to persuade their party to explicitly tie immigration law to issues of race; in 1955 Osborne unsuccessfully attempted to introduce a bill controlling immigration by nonwhites (Dummett and Nicol, *Subjects, Citizens, Aliens and Others*, 180). In 1944 a Royal Commission created to study population trends insisted on the need to find ways to protect England's "good human stock," and a

confidential 1948 Population and Planning Report noted that "To permit large-scale immigration of superior stocks while refusing selective immigration is to invite a lowering of the quality of the British people . . . [absorbing] large numbers of non-white immigrants would be extremely difficult" (cited in Dummett and Nicol, *Subjects, Citizens, Aliens and Others*, 174).

25. Paul Peppis, "Thinking Race in the *Avant Guerre*: Typological Negotiations in Ford and Stein," *Yale Journal of Criticism* 10, no. 2 (Fall 1997): 371–95. See also Hugh A. MacDougall, *Racial Myth in English History: Trojans, Teutons, and Anglo-Saxons* (Hanover, N.H.: University Press of New England, 1982).

26. Edward A. Freeman, *The Growth of the English Constitution* (London: Macmillan and Co., 1876), 22–23. Cited in Peppis, "Thinking Race in the *Avant Guerre*."

27. Daniel Defoe, *The True-Born Englishman*, in *The Novels and Miscellaneous Works of Daniel Defoe* (London: George Bell and Sons, 1896), 441–42.

28. David Simpson, "Literary Criticism, Localism, and Local Knowledge," *Raritan: A Quarterly Review* 14, no. 1 (Summer 1994): 70–88.

29. Ford Maddox Ford, *The Spirit of the People: An Analysis of the English Mind* (London: Alston Rivers, 1907), 44. Peppis provides an excellent discussion of this text in "Thinking Race in the *Avant Guerre*."

30. Benedict Anderson and Simon Gikandi, in terms fairly similar to Ford's, have commented on the strange place that William the Conqueror occupies as an "originary" figure in English historiography. See Anderson, *Imagined Communities*, 199–203, and Gikandi, *Maps of Englishness*, 24–26. For yet another rereading of the relationship of the William the Conqueror myth to the discourses of Englishness and empire, see the "Rosa Diamond" section of Salman Rushdie's *The Satanic Verses*.

31. John Ruskin, *The Complete Works of John Ruskin*, ed. E. T. Cook and Alexander Wedderburn, 39 vols. (London: George Allen, 1903–12), 8:246. All subsequent references are to this edition—abbreviated as *Works* in the text—unless otherwise indicated.

32. Thomas Babington Macaulay, in *Selected Writings*, ed. John Clive (Chicago: University of Chicago Press, 1972), 249.

33. Powell's sense of the absolute failure of English place to guarantee the Englishness of England's inhabitants is yet more starkly marked in the earlier speech in which the "once respectable street" on which the "harassed" landlady lives is utterly unable to domesticate the immigrants, or to prevent them from turning it—and, synecdochically, England—into "a place of noise and confusion."

34. David Cannadine, *The Pleasures of the Past* (New York and London: W. W. Norton and Co., 1989), 258. See also Patrick Wright, *On Living in an Old Country: The National Past in Contemporary Britain* (London: Verso, 1985).

35. For an excellent analysis of the fiscal and cultural linkages between the English country house and colonialism, see Said, *Culture and Imperialism*, 62–96. I address this issue more fully in chapter 5.

36. Ernest Renan, "Qu'est-ce qu'une nation?" trans. Martin Thom, in Bhabha, *Nation and Narration*, 19. Renan says that this refrain from a Spartan song "is, in its abridged simplicity, the hymn of every patrie."

37. Powell does believe that that body is *extrinsically* menaced, that violence may be done to it, but he does not imagine that its *intrinsic* integrity can be challenged; his nightmares are not the nightmares of miscegenation.

38. See Enoch Powell, *Biography of a Nation: A Short History of Britain* (London: John

Baker, 1970). Powell unambiguously asserts that English culture was fundamentally uninfluenced by the British Empire: "There was this deep, this providential difference between our empire and those others, that the nationhood of the mother country remained unaltered through it all, almost unconscious of the strange fantastic structure built around her—in modern parlance, 'uninvolved.' . . . So the continuity of her existence was unbroken when the looser connections which had linked her with distant continents and strange races fell away" (*Biography of a Nation*, 254); cited in Gikandi, *Maps of Englishness*, 78.

39. A serious caution is necessary here. While Powell, and Thatcher, regularly represented the black presence in Britain as something original to the second half of the twentieth century, that view is simply innacurate. As Peter Fryer and Gretchen Gerzina have shown, there has been a significant black presence in England, Scotland, and Wales since at least the sixteenth century. The number of black individuals residing in the United Kingdom did increase significantly after the Second World War, and it is this demographic trend, which from the 1950s onward made it impossible for anyone to pretend that the United Kingdom did not have a black population, that triggers the frontier anxiety I mention. See Fryer's *Staying Power: The History of Black People in Britain* (London: Pluto Press, 1984) and Gerzina's *Black London: Life before Emancipation* (New Brunswick: Rutgers University Press, 1995).

40. Samuel Daniel, *The Complete Works in Verse and Prose of Samuel Daniel*, ed. Rev. Alexander B. Grosart (Blackburn, 1885), 239.

41. Richard Helgerson, "Language Lessons: Linguistic Colonialism, Linguistic Postcolonialism, and the Early Modern English Nation," forthcoming in *Yale Journal of Criticism*.

42. Among the many such efforts chronicled by Helgerson are the decision by Edward VI in 1550 to adopt an English liturgy, Richard Mulcaster's publication in 1582 of an English grammar designed to liberate the English language from its "thralldom and bondage" to Latin, and Parliament's 1650 decision to use English rather than French in courts of law.

43. This formulation is preserved, but exactly reversed, in much post-1950s British discourse, where England is understood, once again, to exist after empire, though now as the nation that once conquered the world, and before it, as the nation about to be invaded by immigrants from the ex-colonial territories.

44. Samuel Johnson, *The Works of Samuel Johnson, LL.D.* (Oxford: Oxford University Press, 1825), 5:21. For analyses of the *Plan* and the dictionary itself, see Allen Reddick, *The Making of Johnson's Dictionary: 1746–1773* (Cambridge: Cambridge University Press, 1990); and Elizabeth Hedrick, "Fixing the Language: Johnson, Chesterfield, and *The Plan of a Dictionary*," *ELH* 55, no. 2 (Summer 1988): 421–42. For a reading very much in line with my own, see Martin Wechselblatt, "The Pathos of Example: Professionalism and Colonialization in Johnson's 'Preface' to the Dictionary," *Yale Journal of Criticism* 9, no. 2 (Fall 1996): 381–403.

45. The opening chapters of Ford's *The Spirit of the People* can be read as an extended development of this trope as Ford gets at the business of defining Englishness by gazing at England from the shifting point of view of the island's many conquerors. In *Heart of Darkness*, a work that James Clifford has convincingly argued represents Joseph Conrad's attempt to define Englishness and claim it for himself, Conrad repeats Ford's, Johnson's, and Daniel's gesture: "'And this also,' said Marlow suddenly, 'has been one

of the dark places on the earth. . . . I was thinking of very old times, when the Romans first came here. . . . Imagine him here—the very end of the world, a sea the color of lead, a sky the color of smoke, a kind of ship as rigid as a concertina—and going up this river . . . cold, fog, tempests, disease, exile, and death—death skulking in the air, in the water, in the bush. . . . He has to live in the midst of the incomprehensible, which is also detestable. And it has a fascination, too, that goes to work upon him. The fascination of the abomination—you know, imagine the growing regrets, the longing to escape, the powerless disgust, the surrender, the hate.'" Joseph Conrad, *Heart of Darkness* (London: Penguin Books, 1983), 29–31.

46. Samuel Johnson, "Preface" to *A Dictionary of the English Language*, 3d ed. (London: Thomas Ewing, 1763), i.

47. This sentiment, Colley argues, is demonstrated by Sir David Wilkie's 1822 painting *Chelsea Pensioners Reading the Gazette of the Battle of Waterloo*, a canvas that depicts Welsh, Scots, English, and Irish troops, and a black soldier, gathering together to celebrate the news of their common, British, victory over the French. See *Britons*, 364–68. Discussing the same canvas, Simon Gikandi argues that it indicates that the "modern British nation cannot be imagined outside the realm of empire . . . [that] imperialism becomes the raison d'être of Britishness itself" (*Maps of Englishness*, 31).

48. Robert Bridges, "The Society's Work," tract no. 21 (n.p.: Society for Pure English, 1925), 5. Cited in Michael North, *The Dialect of Modernism: Race, Language, and Twentieth-Century Literature* (New York and Oxford: Oxford University Press, 1994), 16.

49. See, among others, J.G.A. Pocock, "Burke and the Ancient Constitutions: A Problem in the History of Ideas," in *Politics, Language and Time* (New York: Atheneum, 1973); David Bromwich, "Burke, Wordsworth and the Defense of History," in *A Choice of Inheritance: Self and Community from Edmund Burke to Robert Frost* (Cambridge: Harvard University Press, 1989); and David Simpson, *Romanticism, Nationalism, and the Revolt against Theory* (Chicago: University of Chicago Press, 1993).

50. David Simpson, *The Academic Postmodern and the Rule of Literature: A Report on Half-Knowledge* (Chicago: University of Chicago Press, 1993), 138–39, emphasis original. See also Alan Liu, "Local Transcendence: Cultural Criticism, Postmodernism, and the Romanticism of Detail," *Representations* 32 (1990): 75–113.

51. James Chandler, *Wordsworth's Second Nature: A Study of the Poetry and Politics* (Chicago: University of Chicago Press, 1984).

52. In *The Poetical Works of William Wordsworth*, ed. Ernest de Selincourt and Helen Darbishire, 5 vols. (Oxford: Clarendon Press, 1940–49).

53. Edmund Burke, *Reflections on the Revolution in France*, in *Works of Edmund Burke*, 3:359. Cited in Chandler, *Wordsworth's Second Nature*, 44. As Chandler notes here, Wordsworth echoes this phrase both in his tract *The Convention of Cintra* ("There is a spiritual community binding together the living and the dead; the good, the brave, and the wise of all ages") and in book 10 of *The Prelude* ("There is / One great society alone on earth: / The noble living and the noble dead"). Ruskin's conviction that architecture "connects forgotten and following ages" also reveals the influences of this rhetorical tradition.

54. Simpson, *Romanticism, Nationalism, and the Revolt against Theory*, 153. Simpson, unlike Chandler, does not, however, see Wordsworth as entirely Burkean. There is also, he argues, a touch of Paine's democratic aspirations in Wordsworth's valorizations of rural communities. See 152–59.

55. William Wordsworth, the "Reconciling Addendum" to "The Ruined Cottage," in *The Poetical Works of William Wordsworth*, ed. Ernest de Selincourt and Helen Darbishire (Oxford: Clarendon Press, 1940–49), 5:400. Cited in Chandler, *Wordsworth's Second Nature*, 125.

56. Cited in Judy Edgerton, *Making and Meaning: Turner, The Fighting Temeraire* (London: National Gallery Publications, 1995), 10. The catalog of a 1995 National Gallery exhibition devoted to the ship, this publication indicates that the tradition of memorializing the *Temeraire* as a fetish of a triumphant, but lost, England continues to endure: the exhibition included a room devoted to the display of the ship's surviving timbers and furnishings.

57. George Sims, *How the Poor Live and Horrible London* (London: Chatto and Windus, 1889), 1.

CHAPTER ONE
THE HOUSE OF MEMORY

1. There are a number of histories of the Morant Bay uprising of 1865, and the subsequent controversy that surrounded Governor Eyre, some of which are useful, some of which are hysterical, one of which is excellent. In the first category, Gad J. Heuman's *Between Black and White: Race, Politics, and the Free Coloreds in Jamaica, 1792–1865* (Westport, Conn.: Greenwood Press, 1981) is representative; in the second, Geoffrey Dutton's *In Search of Edward John Eyre* (Melbourne: The Macmillan Company of Australia, 1988), while admirably researched, too rarely resists casting itself as a belated, and frequently venomous, diatribe against the governor's detractors. The finest, most balanced work is Bernard Semmel's *The Governor Eyre Controversy* (London: MacGibbon and Kee, 1968), on which I have largely drawn for the following synopsis of events. For an excellent discussion of the vagaries of British West Indian historiography, see Eric Williams, *British Historians and the West Indies* (Port of Spain: P.N.M. Publishing Company, 1964). As my concern here is less with what took place in Jamaica than with how events in Jamaica were represented in England, I have chosen to avoid altogether any attempt to determine whether what occurred in Jamaica in October 1865 constituted a brief local disturbance or a meaningful revolt against colonial rule. I leave that determination to the competent historian.

2. *London Times*, August 23, 1866.

3. For a particularly fine discussion of the imaginary solidarity that the British working classes formed with the black citizens of Jamaica during this period, see Semmel's chapter: " 'Reform,' Southampton and Charles Kingsley," in *The Governor Eyre Controversy*, 81–101. It is perhaps this fleeting display of solidarity, however limited or hypothetical, which most justifies Paul Gilroy's repeated suggestion that the Morant Bay uprising, and the response to that uprising, are understudied events in the history of the English discourses of nation, class, and race. For Gilroy's arguments on this point, to which my own decision to consider these events is indebted, and his penetrating discussions of the contemporary collapsings and occasional achievements of working-class and black solidarities in Great Britain, see Paul Gilroy, "Cultural Studies and Ethnic Absolutism," in *Cultural Studies*, ed. Lawrence Grossberg, Cary Nelson, and Paula Treichler (New York: Routledge, 1992), 187–99.

4. *London Times*, August 24, 1866.

5. These figures are drawn from Bernard Semmel's research. See *The Governor Eyre Controversy*, 116–19.

6. Needless to say, not everyone acceded to this demand. Carlyle, in particular, insisted on referring to a hypothetical black Jamaican subject as "Quashee." Crucially, however, despite the more than pejorative implications of this term, even Carlyle considered this "Quashee"'s actions to have direct bearing on the condition of England. See Thomas Carlyle, "Shooting Niagara: And After?" in *Thomas Carlyle: Critical and Miscellaneous Essays* (London. Chapman and Hall, 1895), 5:1 49. All future references to Carlyle's writings are to this edition unless otherwise indicated.

7. John Stuart Mill, *Principles of Political Economy*, ed. J. M. Robson (Toronto: University of Toronto Press, 1965), 3:693.

8. For a superb reading of the ceremonial anointing of Queen Victoria as empress of India, see Bernard S. Cohn's essay "Representing Authority in Victorian India," in *The Invention of Tradition*, ed. Eric Hobsbawm and Terence Ranger (Cambridge: Cambridge University Press, 1983), 165–209.

9. Charles Buxton, cited in Semmel, *The Governor Eyre Controversy*, 74.

10. A reading of the repeated appearances of this vanishing England may be found in Raymond Williams, *The Country and the City* (New York: Oxford University Press, 1973). See especially 1–13.

11. In this substitution of wounding empire for fatal city, Buxton's rhetoric anticipates a postimperial discourse of English decline that identifies the island's miseries with the metropolitan arrival of the imperial migrant. For discussions of the narratives of postimperial decline, see Wright's *On Living in an Old Country* and Nairn, *The Breakup of Britain*. I consider the issue at some length in chapter 6.

12. Thomas Carlyle to Hamilton Hume, August 23, 1866. Cited in Semmel, *The Governor Eyre Controversy*, 107.

13. Carlyle, "Shooting Niagara," in *Thomas Carlyle: Critical and Miscellaneous Essays*, 5:21–22.

14. I am indebted for this reference to Derrick Leon's *Ruskin: The Great Victorian* (London: Routledge and Kegan Paul, 1949), 27. Other than Leon's superb biography I have found John D. Rosenberg's *The Darkening Glass* (New York: Columbia University Press, 1961) to be the finest general guide to Ruskin's writing.

15. I am deeply indebted for my understanding of the functionings of a rhetoric of proleptic nostalgia to Sara Suleri, who in conversations, in lectures, and in her writings has prompted and encouraged my interest in this matter.

16. Paul Sawyer, in his reading of this passage, which is among the most famous in all Ruskin's writing, locates an expression of Ruskin's belief in not only the nationally constitutive but the nationally redemptive capacities of the architectural edifice that is very much in line with what I am suggesting. See Paul Sawyer, *Ruskin's Poetic Argument: The Design of the Major Works* (Ithaca: Cornell University Press, 1985), 77–89.

17. Renan, "Qu'est-ce qu'une nation?" in Bhabha, *Nation and Narration*, 11.

18. Walter Benjamin, *Illuminations*, trans. Harry Zohn (New York: Schocken Books, 1969), 254.

19. To be entirely fair to Anderson, it must be noted that in the revised edition of *Imagined Communities*, he too now recognizes a yearning toward such agreement between past and present as foundational to the construction of a narrative of national genealogy.

20. For an intriguing reading of Ruskin's refusals of the present not only as a moment in history but as a time of perception and a tense in writing, see Jay Fellows, *The Failing Distance: The Autobiographical Impulse in John Ruskin* (Baltimore: Johns Hopkins University Press, 1975), particularly 73–82.

21. "The Great Invasion," in *Household Words*, vol. 5 (n.p., 1852).

22. "The Greatness of London," in *Working Man's Friend*, vol. 1 (n.p., 1852).

23. Matthew Arnold, *The Complete Prose Works of Matthew Arnold*, ed. R. H. Super (Ann Arbor: University of Michigan Press, 1960–77), 1:20.

24. These figures are drawn from H. J. Dyos and D. H. Aldcroft's study *British Transport: An Economic Survey from the Seventeenth Century to the Twentieth* (Leicester: Leicester University Press, 1969).

25. Nicholas Taylor, "The Awful Sublimity of the Victorian City," in *The Victorian City: Images and Realities*, ed. H. J. Dyos (London: Routledge and Kegan Paul, 1973), 2:431–48.

26. Williams, *The Country and the City*, 163–64.

27. Ruskin directly invokes such language in his essay in his references to the metropolitan worship of the "divinity of decomposition." See Ruskin, *Works*, 3:270.

28. Henry Mayhew, *London Labour and the London Poor* (London: Charles Griffin and Company, 1851), xv.

29. Sims, *How the Poor Live*.

30. The discovery of this space of imperial darkness in the very center of London will, of course, find its culminating expression in Joseph Conrad's *Heart of Darkness*.

31. See Catherine Gallagher, *The Industrial Reformation of English Fiction: Social Discourse and Narrative Form 1832–1867* (Chicago: University of Chicago Press, 1985), particularly 3–36.

32. The very literal quality of this dream of return, and its connection to Ruskin's excoriation of a society that worshiped the railroad aesthetics of movement and speed, is reflected in a passage in *The Seven Lamps of Architecture* in which Ruskin suggests that the 150 million pounds which had recently been spent on the construction of a railroad might better have been spent on the building of churches or beautiful houses. "Suppose, on the other hand, that we had employed the same sums in building beautiful houses and churches. We should have maintained the same number of men, not in driving wheelbarrows, but in a distinctly technical, if not intellectual employment; and those who were more intelligent among them would have been especially happy in that employment, as having room in it for the development of their fancy, and being directed by it to that observation of beauty which, associated with the pursuit of natural science, at present forms the enjoyment of many of the more intelligent manufacturing operatives. . . . Meanwhile we should ourselves have been made happier and wiser by the interest we should have taken in the work with which we were personally concerned; and when all was done, instead of the very doubtful advantage of the power of going fast from place to place, we should have the certain advantage of increased pleasure in stopping at home" (Ruskin, *Works*, 8:263–64).

33. Robert Hewison has offered a fine reading of Ruskin's devotions to the imperfect in his study *John Ruskin: The Argument of the Eye* (Princeton: Princeton University Press, 1976), especially 119–47.

34. Stephen Greenblatt, "Resonance and Wonder," in *Exhibiting Cultures: The Poetics and Politics of Museum Display*, ed. Ivan Karp and Steven D. Lavine (Washington, D.C.: Smithsonian Institution Press, 1991), 42–56.

35. Gary Wihl has offered a fine reading of the affront that the Crystal Palace offered to Ruskin's architectural philosophy. See Gary Wihl, *Ruskin and the Rhetoric of Infallibility* (New Haven: Yale University Press, 1985), 168–83.

36. Ruskin concludes the essay as follows: "Lastly, *Read* the sculpture. Prepatory to reading it, you will have to discover whether it is legible (and, if legible, it is nearly certain to be worth reading). On a good building, the sculpture is *always* so set, and on such a scale, that at the ordinary distance from which the edifice is seen, the sculpture shall be thoroughly intelligible and interesting. In order to accomplish this, the uppermost statues will be ten or twelve feet high, and the upper ornamentation will be colossal, increasing in fineness as it descends, till on the foundation it will often be wrought as if for a precious cabinet in a king's chamber; but the spectator will not notice that the upper sculptures are colossal. He will merely feel that he can see them plainly, and make them all out at his ease. And having ascertained this, let him set himself to read them. Thenceforward the criticism of the building is to be conducted precisely on the same principles as that of a book; and it must depend on the knowledge, feeling, and not a little of the industry and perseverance of the reader, whether, even in the case of the best works, he either perceives them to be great or entertaining" (Ruskin, *Works*, 10:269).

37. Renan, "Qu'est-ce qu'une nation?" in Bhabha, *Nation and Narration*, 19.

38. See "Of Mimicry and Man: The Ambivalence of Colonial Discourse" and "Signs Taken for Wonders: Questions of Ambivalence and Authority under a Tree outside Delhi, May, 1817," in *The Location of Culture*.

39. T. Roger Smith, "Architectural Art in India," *Journal of the Royal Society of Arts* 21 (1873): 286–87.

40. On Victorian representations of the Irish as black, see Vincent J. Cheng, *Joyce, Race, and Empire* (Cambridge: Cambridge University Press, 1995), 15–57; and Robert J. C. Young, *Colonial Desire* (New York: Routledge, 1995), 55–90.

41. For a reading of Ruskin's elaborations of Gothic as a literally utopic cultural habitus, see Jeffrey L. Spear, *Dreams of an English Eden: Ruskin and His Tradition in Social Criticism* (New York: Columbia University Press, 1984).

CHAPTER TWO
"BRITISH TO THE BACKBONE"

1. Thomas R. Metcalf has discussed the logic that allows Ruskin at once to praise and damn Indian art, and to see in the apparently antinaturalistic idiom of a subcontinental aesthetic a manifestation of that same distortion of personality which articulated itself in the Mutiny. Metcalf's discussion of this issue is in his essay "Arts, Crafts, and Empire," in *An Imperial Vision: Indian Architecture and Britain's Raj* (Berkeley and Los Angeles: University of California Press, 1989), which is one of the finer recent studies of imperial architecture.

2. Matthew Arnold, "Culture and Anarchy," in *Poetry and Criticism of Matthew Arnold*, ed. A. Dwight Culler (Boston: Houghton Mifflin Company, 1961), 430.

3. A term that I, of course, borrow from Pierre Bourdieu. See his "Postface," in E. Panofsky, *Architecture gothique et pensée scolastique*, trans. P. Bourdieu, 2d rev. ed. (Paris: Minuit, 1970), 133–67.

4. For useful histories of this period of English architecture, see Roger Dixon and Stefan Muthesius, *Victorian Architecture* (London: Thames and Hudson, 1978); and Peter Ferriday, ed., *Victorian Architecture* (New York: J. B. Lippincott Co., 1963).

5. Philip Davies, *Splendours of the Raj: British Architecture in India, 1660–1947* (London: J. Murray, 1985), 156–57.

6. For a superb reading of the emplacement of English literature in the imperial projects of subject-fashioning, see Gauri Viswanathan's *Masks of Conquest: Literary Study and British Rule in India* (New York: Columbia University Press, 1989). The identification of Gothic as England's "national" architecture invites a certain incredulity. As the Anglo-Indian architect T. Roger Smith admitted in his address on imperial architecture, Gothic is at best a "naturalized" style, a sort of resident alien. To preserve English identity by disposing about the island and the empire the walls of this immigrant architecture demands either a highly cultivated sense of irony or an equally fastidious capacity to forget. See Smith, "Architectural Art in India."

7. Smith, "Architectural Art in India," 282.

8. Conrad, *Heart of Darkness*, 71. In Conrad's text, the resonant artifact is a manual on seamanship that Marlow discovers shortly before he stumbles into Kurtz's camp. This book, and the elaborately suited body of a colonial accountant who, by refusing to surrender his European dress even in the sweltering heat of the tropics, wins Marlow's lasting respect, serve as ramifying allegories of a distant Europe that might yet save Marlow from the "general demoralization" of empire.

9. Anonymous, "Imperialism and Architecture," *Builder*, September 27, 1912, 346.

10. See 1 John 3:2. This allusion to holy writ is more than conveniently apposite. The decision of the Camden Society (the organization devoted to disseminating A. W. Pugin's Gothic principles) to entitle their magazine the *Ecclesiologist* is but one indication of the overlap between Victorian discourses on architecture and the rhetorics of redemption.

11. See Cohn, "Representing Authority in Victorian India."

12. The phrase is one sometimes used by translators and seems particularly apposite in the description of what is, in essence, an imperial labor of dual translation in which the English habitus is, quite literally, translated onto the Indian terrain, and the Indian subject is rewritten as culturally English—or at least so Macaulay and his disciples imagined. The earliest use of the phrase that I have seen is, appropriately enough, by John Pory, the translator of Leo Africanus's *History and Description of Africa*, one of the oldest documents in England's imperial archive. The full title of Pory's translation is *The History and Description of Africa, and of the notable things therein contained, written by al-Hassan ibn-Mohammed al-Wezaz al-Fasi, a Moor, baptised as Giovanni Leon, but better known as Leo Africanus. Done into English in the year 1600, by John Pory.*

13. The exchange between Smith and Emerson, as Thomas Metcalf has noted, reproduces an Anglo-Indian battle of styles in miniature. The choice before the empire's architects was less between Gothic and another idiomatically "English" form of construction than between an "Anglicist" and "Orientalist" form, and to this extent replicated that earlier pedagogical contest between the exponents of an English and an Indian curriculum of literary study which Gauri Viswanathan has studied in *Masks of Conquest.*

14. Emerson himself was in fact less interested in purely Indian forms than in the realization of the architectural hybrid, as his remarks on his design for the Muir College in Allahabad make evident: "The beautiful lines of the Taj Mahal influenced me in my dome over the hall, and the Indian four centered arch suggested itself as convenient for my purpose, as well as working well with the general Gothic feeling. The details show

how the Gothic tracery is blended with the Cairean Moucharabyeh wood-work; Gothic shafts and caps are united with Indian arches; and the domes stand on Gothicised Mohammedan pendentives and semi-circular arches. . . . Indeed are not many of the most lovely flowers and plants hybrids, and has not the intermingling of different families of the human race produced some of the noblest types of men?" (cited in Davies, *Splendours of the Raj*, 187–88).

15. Homi Bhabha, "Of Mimicry and Man," in *The Location of Culture*, 86.

16. For a fine discussion of the Arts and Crafts movement in India, see Metcalf, "Arts, Crafts, and Empire," in *An Imperial Vision*, 141–75.

17. Sara Suleri, *The Rhetoric of English India* (Chicago: University of Chicago Press, 1992), 76.

18. Edmund Wilson, *The Wound and the Bow: Seven Studies in Literature* (New York: Oxford University Press, 1947), 123–24.

19. This is Annan's comment in full: "No doubt this is what a courageous liberal writing at a time when Ghandi and Congress were struggling for Indian independence did expect. No doubt the future life of a young agent would have entailed confounding Indian resistance to the British, but this is an *ex post facto* judgment, and in the novel such a career is depicted as the maintenance of that minimum of order such as is necessary to prevent foreign intrigue, frontier invasions, and injustices by native princes and to permit the joyous, noisy, pollulating mess of Indian life on the Great Trunk Road to continue." Noel Annan, cited in Irving Howe, "The Pleasures of *Kim*," in *Art, Politics, and Will: Essays in Honor of Lionel Trilling*, ed. Quentin Anderson, Stephen Donadio, and Steven Marcus (New York: Basic Books, 1977).

20. Rudyard Kipling, *Kim* (London: Penguin Books, 1989), 60. All subsequent references are to this edition.

21. Edward Said, introduction to *Kim*, 26.

22. Thomas Richards, *The Imperial Archive: Knowledge and the Fantasy of Empire* (New York: Verso, 1993), 23–24. Despite several reservations regarding Richards's reading, which I treat in the following paragraphs, I have learned much from his discussions of the nomadic and cartographic economies of Kipling's text.

23. Spivak, *Outside in the Teaching Machine*, 226.

24. For information on the Survey of India, I have relied on Mary Lynette Larsgaard's *Topographic Mapping of Africa, Antartica, and Eurasia* (Provo, Utah: Western Association of Map Libraries, 1993) and John Noble Wilford's *The Mapmakers* (New York: Alfred A. Knopf, 1981), 161–73.

25. Patrick Brantlinger also uses the expression "imperial Gothic" in his *Rule of Darkness: British Literature and Imperialism, 1830–1914* (Ithaca: Cornell University Press, 1988); see especially 227–54. Brantlinger, however, uses the term to refer to an imperial manifestation, and refabrication, of the literary genre, whereas I am using it more in the sense of a Bourdieuvian habitus.

26. For Kipling—who, from that moment in which he so warily introduced Kim, has been struggling to return "English" to the catalog of colonial identity-positions—this is all thoroughly intolerable. In the remaining chapters of the novel, he conspires to free Kim from Creighton's clutches, stages an overdetermined scene in which Kim abandons the implements of cartography, and, finally, as if to punish Creighton by exorbitantly de-Englishizing Kim, hands Kim over to the lama and accords to the holy man the right to give the little friend of all the world an adult name. For a reading of

how the lama's naming of Kim as "beloved" can be construed as yet another act of incarceration, see Suleri, *The Rhetoric of English India*, 111–31.

CHAPTER THREE
THE PATH FROM WAR TO FRIENDSHIP

1. In *Imperial Eyes* Mary Louise Pratt defines the "contact zone" "as an attempt to invoke the spatial and temporal copresence of subjects previously separated by geographic and historical disjunctures, and whose trajectories now intersect. By using the term 'contact,' I aim to foreground the interactive, improvisational dimensions of colonial encounters so easily ignored by diffusionist accounts of conquest and domination" (7).

2. E. M. Forster, *A Passage to India* (London: Harcourt, Brace, 1984), 182. All future references are to this edition.

3. See Homi Bhabha, "Day by Day . . . with Frantz Fanon," in *The Fact of Blackness: Frantz Fanon and Visual Representation* (London: Institute of Contemporary Arts; Seattle: Bay Press, 1996), 195. "Anxiety," in Bhabha's reading, is a structure of dread experienced from within a condition of settlement or arrival that is nevertheless haunted by memories of a prior condition of cultural dissolution, and which experiences that haunting memory through the anticipation of a future return to this past time. As such, as I argue in this chapter, Anglo-Indian memories of the 1857 Insurrection, memories which surface as a conviction that the Mutiny will repeat itself, are precisely "anxious."

4. Fanon, *The Wretched of the Earth*, 38–39. For a particularly insightful reading of Fanon's highlighting of the spatial dynamics of empire, see Otu Sekyi-Otu, *Fanon's Dialectic of Experience* (Cambridge: Harvard University Press, 1996), 72–99.

5. See Jenny Sharpe, *Allegories of Empire: The Figure of Woman in the Colonial Text* (Minneapolis: University of Minnesota Press, 1993), particularly 113–36. Sharpe's excellent reading of Forster's text suggests, as I do, that *A Passage to India* represents a critical response to English recollections of the 1857 uprising. Where Sharpe's primary concern is to read the ways in which Forster interrogates the central narrative patterning these memories—the narrative of rebellion as rape—I am most concerned with the way in which Forster returns to the Insurrection in order to find within it a lost counter-narrative of intimacy and friendship.

6. For readings of these textual monuments to the Insurrection, see Brantlinger, *Rule of Darkness*, 199–226; and Suleri, *The Rhetoric of English India*, 75–110.

7. Frederick Roberts, *Letters Written during the Indian Mutiny* (London: Macmillan and Co., 1924), viii.

8. Edward Thompson, *The Other Side of the Medal* (London: Hogarth Press, 1925), 117–18.

9. The queen's proclamation announced the formal annexation of India to the Crown in the following terms: "Now, therefore, we do by these present notify and declare that, by the advice and consent aforesaid, we have taken upon ourselves the said government; and we hereby call upon all our subjects within the said territories to be faithful, and to bear true allegiance to us, our heirs and successors, and to submit themselves to the authority of those whom we may hereafter, from time to time, see fit to appoint to administer the government of said territories, in our name and on our

behalf." Cited in Vincent A. Smith, *The Oxford History of India: From the Earliest Times to the End of 1911* (Oxford: Clarendon Press, 1923), 728.

10. Cohn, "Representing Authority in Victorian India," 179.

11. John Murray, *A Handbook for Travellers in India, Burma, and Ceylon* (London: The Firm of John Murray, 1924), xxiii.

12. Conrad, *Heart of Darkness*, 46.

13. Carl von Clausewitz, *On War* (Princeton: Princeton University Press, 1976), 214.

14. See Paul Virilio, *Speed and Politics: An Essay on Dromology*, trans. Mark Polizzotti (New York: Semiotext(e), 1986).

15. Rupert Brooke, "Peace," in *The Collected Poems of Rupert Brooke* (New York: Dodd, Mead and Company, 1931), 111.

16. It is unfortunate that in appointing himself the task of righting the historical record, Thompson is more than susceptible to charges of Orientalism. He proceeds from the conviction that "Indians are not historians; . . . they rarely show any critical ability. . . . They are not able to arrange their knowledge so as to gain the first essential towards a historical judgment, a hearing" (*The Other Side of the Medal*, 27–28). This willingness to deny the capacity of the subcontinent's natives to narrate their own history casts a pall over Thompson's work and reveals a certain ignorance regarding the politics of "historical judgment." The ability to secure "a hearing" is, finally, related more to the policing of the spaces of articulation than to scholarly or critical competence. There were Indian histories of the Insurrection extant at the time of Thompson's writing, texts such as Veer Savarkar's *War of Indian Independence of 1857*, which failed to secure a hearing in England not because it was not written, but because it was banned. Despite these problems, Thompson's work as a revisionist historian is important, precisely because he could secure a hearing, and in that section of his book in which he turns his attention to the distorted record of the Insurrection, he proves himself an able and damningly witty writer.

17. Sir Henry Cotton, *Indian and Home Memories* (London: T. F. Unwin, 1911), cited in *The Other Side of the Medal*, 92.

18. Cooper was a district commissioner who in 1857 systematically executed 282 prisoners; Cowan is the official of Maler Kotla fame.

19. The suggestion is William Kerrigan's in an eponymous chapter in *The Sacred Complex: On the Psychogenesis of Paradise Lost* (Cambridge: Harvard University Press, 1983), 126–92.

20. Lionel Trilling, *E. M. Forster: A Study by Lionel Trilling* (New York: Hogarth Press, 1951), 7.

21. While *The Hill of Devi* was first published in 1953, I have chosen to refer, throughout, to the 1983 edition (*The Hill of Devi and other Indian writings* [London: Edward Arnold, 1983]) because that edition includes an appendix entitled "Kanaya" unpublished in the first edition. I consider the "Kanaya" manuscript later in this chapter.

22. Susan Stewart, *On Longing: Narratives of the Miniature, the Gigantic, the Souvenir, the Collection* (Baltimore: Johns Hopkins University Press, 1984), 135, 139.

23. The connection between dress and cultural loyalty was to become a matter of some import in India, most notably in Ghandi's campaigns, and is unwittingly touched

on by Forster in the 1912 journal. On the 24th of January, he met a man named Mazharul Haque, a lawyer and founder of the Muslim League. Mazharul Haque appears in the journal as a fleeting presence, visible only as a costumed mannequin who "resembles an English dandy, [and] is said to be charmed with me" (*The Hill of Devi*, 184). By 1920 he was to cut a rather different figure, appearing on the political stage in indigenous dress. In this incarnation, however, he appears in Forster's journal only from the subtextual position of a footnote. Citing Sachidananda Sinha, editor of the *Hindustan Review*, Forster's editor reports on Mazharul Haque's transformation: "Until he became a non-cooperator, in 1920, Haque was one of the best-dressed Indians. . . . But once he accepted the Mahatma's lead, Haque suddenly became a changed man. He locked up his fastidiously well-tailored suits, metamorphosed himself from a clean-shaven man into literally a bearded pard" (*Hill of Devi*, 185n). Haque was subsequently imprisoned.

24. E. M. Forster, *Abinger Harvest* (New York: Harcourt, Brace, and World, 1936), 310–11.

25. For Williams's discussion of the place of the "residual" and the "emergent" within a theory of cultural hegemony, see *Problems in Materialism and Culture* (London: Verso, 1980), 37–42.

26. This movement from strictly private to deliberately public writing, in which the censorship of vision is complicit with the production of India as a space of tourism, can be traced in Forster's multiple accounts of his visit to Jodhpur. In his journal, he finds the city rather indifferent, laments the sights of police drilling, and on visiting the fort comments on the prominent visibility of public toilets. In a letter to his aunt he cleans Jodhpur up, neglecting, as he notes wryly to himself, to "mention view of W.C.s from parapet: nor indeed of city generally . . . all foreshortened." He does, however, manage to tell her that "Jodhpur is—after Agra—the finest place I have been to yet. Please tell this only to the very nice, or the very feeble, for it is undiscovered so far by the tourist, and all the inhabitants, English and Indian, tremble in fear of this irruption" (*Hill of Devi*, 209). On his return to England, Forster published an essay on Jodhpur in which, freed once again from the menacing specter of its public toilets, the city emerges as virtually perfect, and as a sure destination for those tourists from whom, only a year before, Forster had thought to guard it.

27. It is ironic that in attending to the suggestion with which he brought his journal to a close (the idea that the problem of English India could be resolved through the cultivation of friendship), Forster ignores that suggestion's accompanying wisdom: that friendship proceeds from a surmounting of forgetting. In compiling this selection of his letters as a micronarrative of his friendship with H.H., Forster, somewhat paradoxically, obliged himself to forget any of his correspondence that failed to touch upon this theme.

28. I am indebted to Sara Suleri for my understanding of the place of invitation in Forster's text.

29. This passage is from the manuscript entitled "Kanaya" not printed in the 1953 edition of *The Hill of Devi* but included as an appendix to the 1983 edition published following Forster's death. Elizabeth Heine, Forster's editor, suggests that the typed manuscript of "Kanaya" was prepared by Joe Ackerley from Forster's handwritten original, and that Forster wrote the text for reading at the Bloomsbury Memoir Club. *Hill of Devi* (1983), 314–15.

30. Rustom Bharucha, "Forster's Friends," *Raritan: A Quarterly Review* 5, no. 4 (Spring 1986): 114.

31. Sara Suleri, "The Geography of *A Passage to India*," in *E. M. Forster's A Passage to India*, ed. Harold Bloom (New York: Chelsea House, 1987), 112.

32. Lionel Trilling, "A Passage to India," in *E. M. Forster's A Passage to India*, 20.

33. Said, *Orientalism*, 244.

34. Bharucha, "Forster's Friends," 118.

35. E. M. Forster, diary entry of March 25, 1923, cited in P. N. Furbank, *E. M. Forster: A Life* (New York: Harcourt Brace Jovanovich, 1977), 2:115.

36. Suleri, *The Rhetoric of English India*, 139.

CHAPTER FOUR
PUT A LITTLE ENGLISH ON IT

1. C.L.R. James, *Beyond a Boundary* (New York: Pantheon Books, 1963), 14.

2. Raymond Williams, *The Long Revolution* (New York: Columbia University Press, 1961), 125–55.

3. David Newsome, *Godliness and Good Learning: Four Studies on a Victorian Ideal* (London: William Clowes and Sons, 1961), 35. The 1864 Clarendon Commission on the public schools reflected much the same position and, in the report that it submitted to the government, implied a link between the public schools and the administration of empire. "It is not easy to estimate the degree to which the English people are indebted to these schools for the qualities on which they pique themselves most—for their capacity to govern others and control themselves, their aptitude for combining freedom with order, their vigor and manliness of character, their strong but not slavish respect for public opinion, their love of healthy sport and exercise. These schools have been the chief nurseries of our statesmen; in them and in schools modeled after them, men of all the various classes that make up English society, destined for every professsion and career, have been brought up on a footing of social equality, and have contracted the most enduring friendships, and some of the ruling habits of their lives; and they have had perhaps the largest share in the moulding of the character of the 'English Gentleman.'" Cited in *The Victorian Public School: Studies in the Development of an Educational Institution*, ed. Brian Simon and Ian Bradley (Dublin: Gill and MacMillan, 1975), 153.

4. Thomas Arnold, *Introductory Lectures on Modern History* (London, 1874), 16–17.

5. Pierre Bourdieu, *Reproduction in Education, Society and Culture* (London: Sage Publications, 1977), 108.

6. Thomas Hughes, *Tom Brown's Schooldays* (London: Sidgwick and Jackson, 1913), 122–23.

7. Cited in Simon and Bradley, *The Victorian Public School*, 23.

8. Lytton Strachey, *Eminent Victorians* (New York: Capricorn Books, 1963), 204.

9. Arnold's full sentence runs, "They look upon themselves as answerable for the character of the school, and by the natural effect of their position acquire a manliness of mind and habits of conduct infinitely superior, generally speaking, to those of young men of the same age who have not enjoyed the same advantages." Cited in *Thomas Arnold on Education*, ed. T. W. Bamford (Cambridge: Cambridge University Press, 1970), 130.

10. Bhabha, *The Location of Culture*, 148.

11. Robert Benson, cited in Newsome, *Godliness and Good Learning*, 44–45.

12. John Addington Symonds, *Memoirs* (New York: Random House, 1984), 94.

13. J. A. Mangan is the most distinguished of these historians. See his *The Games Ethic and Imperialism: Aspects of the Diffusion of an Ideal* (Harmondsworth, Middlesex: Viking, 1986) and *Athleticism in the Victorian and Edwardian School* (Cambridge: Cambridge University Press, 1981). See also Keith A. P. Sandiford, *Cricket and the Victorians* (Aldershot: Scolar Press, 1994); and Mike Marqusee, *Anyone but England: Cricket and the National Malaise* (London: Verso, 1994).

14. J. M. Kilburn, in *The World of Cricket*, ed. E. W. Swanton (London: Michael Joseph, 1966), 1017–18. Kilburn was a county cricketer, a longtime cricket correspondent and Holgate Grammar old boy.

15. Francis Thompson, "At Lords," in Swanton, *The World of Cricket*, 139.

16. These figures are drawn from Sandiford's *Cricket and the Victorians*, 53.

17. Ronald Mason, "W. G. Grace and His Times: 1865–1899," in Swanton, *The World of Cricket*, 543–44.

18. In *The Long Revolution*, Raymond Williams documents the growth of the English popular press, an institution controlled, from the mid–eighteenth century, by the capitalized middle class, but which in the period from 1855 onward massively expanded its working-class readership. This expansion followed the 1853 lifting of the advertising tax and the 1855 lifting of the Stamp Act, measures that drastically reduced both costs of production and the prices demanded for newspapers. This enlargement of a working-class readership derived also from improvements in technology, which allowed more pages to be printed at a cheaper rate each hour; improvements in methods of distribution, particularly through reforms of the postal service, which allowed the metropolitan and regional papers to disseminate their products more widely and more efficiently; the rise of collective purchasing by circulating clubs, workshops, and public houses; and the rapid growth of Sunday weeklies and evening editions, which carved out a vast readership by emphasizing sensationalist journalism and by reporting on football and cricket, publishing the results of each day's play. See *The Long Revolution*, 173–213.

19. On the influence the metropolitan newspapers had in defining a corporate national identity in the eighteenth and nineteenth centuries, see Colley, *Britons*, especially 220–21.

20. K. S. Ranjitsinhji, *The Jubilee Book of Cricket* (London: William Blackwood and Sons, 1897), 458.

21. See Mangan, *The Games Ethic*, 135.

22. Manthia Diawara, "Englishness and Blackness: Cricket as Discourse on Colonialism," *Callalloo* 13, no. 4 (Fall 1990): 830–44.

23. Michel de Certeau, *The Practice of Everyday Life*, trans. Steven Rendall (Berkeley and Los Angeles: University of California Press, 1984), xiii.

CHAPTER FIVE
AMONG THE RUINS

1. His Royal Highness the Prince of Wales, *A Vision of Britain: A Personal View of Architecture* (London: Doubleday, 1989), 21.

2. David Cannadine has discussed the capitalization on this phenomenon in his essay "Nostalgia," in *The Pleasures of the Past*, 256–71.

3. V. S. Naipaul, *The Enigma of Arrival* (New York: Random House, 1988), 130. All further references are to this edition.

4. Salman Rushdie, "Outside the Whale," in *Imaginary Homelands: Essays and Criticism 1981–1991* (London: Granta Books, 1991), 92.

5. See Said, *Culture and Imperialism*, 80–97.

6. To the extent that this seems to open a space for a hybridization of vision, for an optics of cultural inspection which allows for the visibility of the one-another in the one, this act of re-visioning seems analogous to the moment of translative, tropicalized inspection that, as I shall discuss in the final chapter of this work, emerges in Salman Rushdie's *The Satanic Verses*. There is, however, a crucial difference between Mill's and Rushdie's visions of the globe. In Mill, the colonies are marked through and through with the signatures of English presence, but England is not written as a hybrid text; in Rushdie, quite the contrary, both England and the erstwhile spaces of empire are multiply cross-written by one another.

7. For an intriguing discussion of the Caribbean within the traffic of this transoceanic machine, see Antonio Benitez Rojo, *The Repeating Island: The Caribbean and the Postmodern Perspective* (Durham: Duke University Press, 1992).

8. Eric Williams, *Capitalism and Slavery* (Chapel Hill: University of North Carolina Press, 1944), 51–84. See also Lwell Joseph Ragatz, *The Fall of the Planter Class in the British Caribbean, 1763–1833: A Study in Social and Economic History* (1928; reprint, New York: Octagon, 1963).

9. The ensuing information is drawn from Eric Williams's research.

10. J. Britton, *Graphical and Literary Illustrations of Fonthill Abbey, Wiltshire, with Heraldical and Genealogical Notices of the Beckford Family* (London, 1823), 25–26.

11. Williams, *The Country and the City*, 105–6.

12. For discussions of Raymond Williams's failure to consider the relations between the inventions and re-presentations of English culture and the projects of British imperialism, see Gauri Viswanathan, "Raymond Williams and British Colonialism," *Yale Journal of Criticism* 4, no. 3 (Spring 1991): 47–66; Gilroy, *"There Ain't No Black in the Union Jack"*, 44–50; and Said, *Culture and Imperialism*, 82–84.

13. Spivak, "Three Women's Texts and a Critique of Imperialism," in *Race, Writing, and "Difference"*, ed. Henry Louis Gates (Chicago: University of Chicago Press, 1988), 262–80.

14. See Robert Young, *Colonial Desire: Hybridity in Theory, Culture and Race* (London and New York: Routledge, 1995), especially 159–82.

15. Jean Rhys, *Wide Sargasso Sea* (London: Penguin Books, 1993), 106. All future references are to this edition.

16. Jane M. Jacobs, *Edge of Empire: Postcolonialism and the City* (London: Routledge, 1996), 43.

17. See Rob Nixon, *London Calling: V. S. Naipaul, Postcolonial Mandarin* (New York: Oxford University Press, 1992).

18. James Joyce to Stanislaus Joyce, September 25, 1906, in Richard Ellman, *James Joyce*, rev. ed. (Oxford: Oxford University Press, 1982), 225.

19. Williams's discussion in *The Country and the City* of what he describes as the "Green Language" sketches the lineaments of the convention Naipaul is revising: "A way

of seeing has been connected with a lost phase of living, and the association of child-hood and happiness has been developed into a whole convention, in which not only innocence and security but peace and plenty have been imprinted, indelibly, first on a particular landscape, and then, in a powerful extension, on a particular period of the rural past, which is now connected with a lost identity, lost relations and lost certain-ties" (138–39). For discussions of the inventedness and internal complexities of this rural past, see *The English Rural Community: Image and Analysis*, ed. Brian Short (Cam-bridge: Cambridge University Press, 1992).

20. See editor's note on the essay, "Mourning and Melancholia," in *The Standard Edition of the Complete Psychological Works of Sigmund Freud*, ed. James Strachey (Lon-don: Hogarth Press, 1966), 14:239–42.

21. The photographs accompany Rob Nixon's essay "V. S. Naipaul, Postcolonial Mandarin," in *Transition* 52 (1991): 101.

22. Michael Gorra, *After Empire: Scott, Naipaul, Rushdie* (Chicago: University of Chi-cago Press, 1997), 172.

23. Rushdie, *The Satanic Verses*, 102.

CHAPTER SIX
THE RIOT OF ENGLISHNESS

1. *Times* (London), April 12, 1981, 1.

2. The Rt. Hon. Lord Scarman, O.B.E., *The Brixton Disorders: 10–12 April 1981, Report of an Inquiry* (London: Her Majesty's Stationery Office, 1981), 1.

3. See Gustav Le Bon, *The Crowd* (New York: Penguin Books, 1960).

4. See Paul Fry, *A Defense of Poetry: Reflections on the Occasion of Writing* (Stanford: Stanford University Press, 1995).

5. Brian Massumi, "The Autonomy of Affect," *Cultural Critique* 31 (Fall 1985): 86–87 (emphasis added). Massumi derives the notion that the asignificances of the affective elicit pleasure, or happiness, from a series of experiments in cognitive psychology in which a group of children frustrated a team of researchers by identifying the "saddest" and least coherent of a series of cartoons as the most pleasant. For a full reading of these experiments, see Hertha Sturm, *Emotional Effects of Media: The Work of Hertha Sturm*, ed. Gertrude Joch Robinson (Montreal: McGill University Graduate Program in Com-munications, 1987), 25–37; and Massumi's comments in "The Autonomy of Affect," 83–85.

6. *Sunday Telegraph* (London), April 12, 1981. Cited in Frances Webber, "Notes and Documents," *Race and Class*, nos. 2/3 (Autumn 1981): 225.

7. *Sunday Times* (London), April, 19, 1981.

8. E. P. Thompson, "The Moral Economy of the English Crowd in the Eighteenth Century," in *Customs in Common* (London: Merlin Press, 1991), 185–258.

9. Salman Rushdie, "The New Empire within Britain," in *Imaginary Homelands*, 136.

10. George Rude, *The Crowd in History, 1730–1848* (New York: John Wiley and Sons, 1964), 230.

11. Homi Bhabha, "DissemiNation, Time, Narrative, and the Margins of the Modern Nation," in *Nation and Narration*, 306.

12. Aijaz Ahmad, *In Theory: Classes, Nations, Literatures* (London: Verso, 1992), 127.

13. It could be argued that Farishta's desire is to redeem England in order to recon-

cile the nation to Islam. If, however, his language is attended to at that moment in which—acting as the vengeful angel of history—he redeems London in riot and fire, it becomes apparent that it is his desire to remake England not in the image of Islam but in the cartoon image of the ex-imperial tropical cultures from which so many of the nation's migrants have come: "Gibreel enumerated the benefits of the proposed metamorphosis of London into a tropical city: increased moral definition, institution of a national siesta, development of vivid and expansive patterns of behaviour among the populace, higher-quality popular music. . . . better cricketers; higher emphasis on ball-control among professional footballers, the traditional and soulless English commitment to 'high work-rate' having been rendered obsolete by the heat. . ." (*The Satanic Verses*, 335). This is only a fragment of Gibreel's catalog, to which I will return later in this chapter.

14. Spivak, "Reading the Satanic Verses," in *Outside in the Teaching Machine*, 223.

15. Edouard Glissant, *Caribbean Discourse: Selected Essays*, trans. J. Michael Dash (Charlottesville: University of Virginia Press, 1989), 14.

16. I borrow this translation of Kantian rhetoric from Gayatri Spivak. See her "Three Women's Texts and a Critique of Imperialism," especially 267–68.

17. Salman Rushdie, "Handsworth Songs," in *Imaginary Homelands*, 117. Rushdie's criticism of the film provoked a round of animated responses that ranged from Stuart Hall's condemnation of the author's "lofty, disdainful," and complacent attitude to Darcus Howe's defense of Rushdie's insistence on intimate and particular acts of narrativization. See *Guardian* (London), January 12, 15, 19, 1987.

18. Or, as Walter Benjamin has it, of discovering that "afterlife" moment in which "the original undergoes a change." See "The Task of the Translator," in *Illuminations*, 73.

Afterword
Something Rich and Strange

1. Gianni Vattimo, *The Transparent Society*, trans. David Webb (Baltimore: Johns Hopkins University Press, 1992), 8 (emphasis original).

2. Glissant, *Caribbean Discourses*, 66–67 (emphasis original).

3. Derek Walcott, *Omeros* (New York: Farrar, Straus and Giroux, 1990), chapter 24, section 2, 33–34, 57–58.

INDEX